EDUCATION AND CAREER

EDUCATION AND CAREER

S.K. YADAW

ISHA BOOKS
DELHI-110009

Education and Career

ISBN : 978-81-8205-515-5

Published in 2010 in India by
ISHA Books
B-63, 1st Floor
New Gupta Colony,
Near DDA Market,
Delhi - 110009

Lasse Type Setting by: Rudra Computer Graphics, Delhi
Printed at : Gian Ridhi Offset Printer, Delhi

Contents

Foreword 9

Preface 13

1. **Accounting and Auditing** 19
(a) Accountants (b) Auditors (c) Assessors (d) Chartered Accountancy (e) Cost Management Accountancy (f) Economists (g) Film and Video Editors (h) Financial Services (i) International CFA (j) Tax Examiners, Collection and Revenue Agents.

2. **Administrative Services** 35
(a) Acturial Science (b) Actuaries (c) Administrative Service Managers (d) Cost Estimators (e) Credit Analyst (f) Disaster Management (g) Environmentalists (h) Entrepreneur (i) Event Manager (j) Forest (k) Hospitality Industry (l) Hotel Management (m) Logistics and Supplychain Management (n) Management Analyst (o) Project Management (p) Property, Real Estate and Community Association Managers (q) Wedding Management

3. **Architect** 72
(a) Architecture

4. **Art** 77
(a) Acting (b) Dance (c) Magic (d) Music (e) Museology (f) Theatre and Visual Arts

5. **Army** 94
(a) Armed Forces (b) Army Officers (c) Defence Services (d) Merchant Navy (e) Navy

6. **Aviation** 107
(a) Air Hostess and Flight Steward (b) Astronaut (c) Aviation (d) Pilot

7. **Clerical Profession** 119
(a) Adjustment Clerk (b) Meeting and Convention planners (c) Precision Printing Workers (d) Purchasing Managers (e) Receiptionists and Information Clerk (f) Tellers

8. **Educational Courses** 126
(a) Economics (b) Fashion Business Education (c) Film Direction (d) International Business (e) Journalism (f) Mass Communication (g) Medical Engineering (h) Packaging (i) PhD (j) Photojournalism (k) Physical Education & Sports (l) Sociology (m) Some Useful Courses after passing 10+2 Exam.

9. **Engineering Courses & Profession** 159
(a) Agricultural Engineering (b) Boarder Road Organization (c) CAD/CAM (d) Chip Designing (e) Fire Technology (f) Food Technology (g) Gemmology (h) Industrial Engineering (i) Information Technology (j) Lighting (k) Plastic Processing (l) Retailing (m) Tool and Die Making

10. **Farming** 198
(a) Agriculture (b) Agri-Business (c) Agriclinics (d) Floriculture (e) Horticulture (f) Organic Farming (g) Seed Industry

11. **Insurance** 221
(a) Insurance (b) Insurance Policy Processing Clerks

12. **Legal View** 226
(a) Law (b) Legal Secretaries

13. **Library** 231
(a) Information Science (b) Library and Information Science

14. **Linguistic View** 239
(a) Foreign Language (b) Linguistics

15. **Medical Courses and Profession** 245
(a) Aromatherapy (b) Ayurveda (c) Dentistry (d) Health Sanitary Inspector (e) Health Educators (f) Health Care (g) Homeopathy (h) Medical Profession (i) Medical

Transcription (j) Microbiology (k) Pharmacognosy (l) Pharmaceutical Sector (m) Physiotherapy (n) Prosthetic and Orthotics (o) Speech Language Pathology and Audiology (p) Unani system of Medicine

16. **Operating** **282**
(a) Call Centres (b) Camera Operators (c) Computer Operator (d) Duplicating Machine Operators

17. **Publishing** **288**
(a) Desk-top Publishers (b) Electronic Media (c) E-publishing (d) Hand compositors and typesetters (e) Word Processors & Typists

18. **Secretarial Profession** **293**
(a) Company Secretary (b) Secretarial Work (c) Secretaries except Legal, Medical and Executive (d) Medical Secretaries

19. **Scientific View** **303**
(a) Aquaculture and Marine Biotechnology (b) Biotechnology (c) Dairy Technology (d) Djing (e) Environmental Science (f) Forensic Science (g) Life Sciences (h) Oceanography (i) Psychology (j) Trichology (k) Veterinary Sciences

20. **Teaching** **341**
(a) Montessori Teaching (b) Teaching (c) Teacher Assistant

21. **Technician** **349**
(a) Cartoonists (b) Dental Laboratory Technician (c) Dieticians & Nutrition (d)Film Laboratory Technician (e) Medical Records & Health Information Technician (f) Pharmacy Technicians

22. **Self employment Opportunities** **356**
(a) Service Institutes and Programmes

Index **363**

[illegible]

[illegible]

[illegible]

18. [illegible]

19. [illegible]

[illegible]

21. [illegible]

22. [illegible]

Foreword

Entering high school is perhaps the most crucial phase in the life of a teenager. This is the time when one has to make concrete plans about one's future. This in turn determines the course of the rest of one's life.

The moment a student enters XI standard, one should make a judicious choice of subjects. An ideal thing to do is to consult academicians, relatives and guardians. Moreover, one must give due considerations to the circumstances, social status, priorities of one's family, a person's physical attributes, his own limitations and capabilities and so forth.

Few examples are being submitted in the career prospects for all the upcoming young generations to consider the right direction of future planning. If a young boy of average health but are rather short, the Armed forces or the Police services are out for him, as these require cadets above a certain height. On the other hand if a one is very tall, burly, well built possessing a good physique, then certainly these jobs are for him as are merchant navy, coastguards, detective services and so on. Those young girls who are tall, possess slim figure can try for being a model, classical dancer or even an airhostess et al.

The career choice is determined by the interests, temperament, physical strength, energy level etc. If persons are indolent instead of active, then go in for some sedate job. There are plenty of them going around. These include library science, school teaching, lectureship, medical transcription, dietician, psychiatrist/ clinical psychologist, all sorts of computer related jobs etc. wherein the *Author of the Book Shri Sudesh Kumar Yadaw* has tried to enlighten some important career and education topics preparing for young generations for their life style very enjoyful and wonderful. On the other hand, if any boys/girls are an extremely creative in nature, then why not try their hand in journalism, copywriting and advertising, TV production, multimedia, fashion or even jewellery designing?

Very important that if a young boy happens to hail from a well to do family that has been successfully running more than one business ventures, then it would natural on the part of the parents/ elders to expect that he join in the family business. The desire of any boys/girls to become a doctor or engineer or a professional singer or actor would hardly be appreciated. In that case, they are suggested to change their mindset and opt for MBA, CA etc.

Then of course, psychological and emotional factors too play their part. If a young boy happens to be the only child, then parents of the family would prefer to see him settled in a suitable profession, where he can be in proximity with them. If this happens in the case of any enthusiastic boy, then he might find it difficult to opt for any branch of the Defence forces, Paramilitary services, Intelligence services, Sales & marketing, Travel & tourism- jobs which are likely to take him away from their home and family for longer.

Coming to proficiency in subjects, if any boys/girls are strong in sciences, mathematics etc., then architecture, medicine, engineering, biotechnology, biochemistry, molecular biology, microbiology, genetics are surely going to be good for them.

Apart from the conventional education that leads to formal degrees, there are vocational courses as well. As an individual make up your mind as to what you really want to do and what your capabilities are. For instance if any boys/girls are adept in cutting, tailoring and stitching jobs, go in for a vocational course, rather than a formal BA or MA degree. Similarly, if they are deeply interested in becoming a beautician or hair stylist, join one or more of these vocational courses after finishing the high school.

Always bear in mind that if anything the persons have got to fight their own battle and the onus of convincing their parents lies entirely on them. They are likely to face stiff resistance no doubt, but he/she must put up a brave face and take everything in their stride. However, ultimately you are the one who has to take the final decisions about your career.

In the preceding paragraphs, very good idea and tactics about the **"CAREER"** has been elaborated in good spirit. After that, some basic facts on the **"EDUCATION"** which has been summarized & reproduced for the knowledge of new generations. It is a settled fact that the Constitution (42nd Amendment) Act, 1976, shifted Education, in general, from the "State List" to the "Concurrent List", thus giving both Central and State Governments jurisdiction over it, concurrently. The concept of concurrency was fleshed out in para 3.13 ("A Meaningful Partnership") of the ***NATIONAL POLICY ON EDUCATION***, 1986, which reads as follows—

"The Constitutional Amendment of 1976, which includes Education in the Concurrent List, was a far-reaching step whose implications—substantive, financial and administrative—require a new sharing of responsibility between the Union Government and the States in respect of this vital area of national life. While the role and responsibility of the States in regard to education will remain essentially unchanged, the Union Government would accept a larger responsibility to reinforce the national and integrative character of education, to maintain quality and standards(including those of the teaching profession at all levels), to study monitor the educational requirements of the country as a whole in regard manpower for development, to cater to the needs of research and advanced study, to look after the international aspects of education, culture Human Resource Development and, in general, to promote excellence levels of the educational pyramid throughout the country. Concurrency signifies a partnership, which is at once meaningful and challenging; National Policy will be oriented towards giving effect to it in letter and spirit".

The Indian Government has expressed a strong commitment towards education for all, however, India still has one of the lowest female literacy rates in Asia. In 1991, less than 40% of the 330 million women aged 7 and over were literate which means today there are over 200 million illiterate women in India. This low level of literacy not only has a negative impact on women's lives but also on their families' lives and on their country's economic development. Numerous studies show that illiterate women have high levels of fertility and mortality, poor nutritional status, low earning potential and little autonomy within the household. A women's lack of education also has a negative impact on the health and well being of her children. For instance, a recent survey in India found that infant mortality was inversely related to mother's educational level. Additionally, the lack of an educated population can be an impediment to the country's economic development.

The Indian government's commitment to education is stated in its constitution with an article promising *"FREE & COMPULSORY EDUCATION FOR ALL CHILDREN UNTIL THEY COMPLETE THE AGE OF 14"* (The World Bank, 1997b). The National Policy on education which was updated in 1992, and the 1992 Program of Action both reaffirmed the government's commitment to improving literacy levels, by providing special attention to girl's and children from scheduled castes and scheduled tribes.

Although literacy levels are low, there has been progress in improving educational attainment for both sexes in India over the last several decades. In 1971, only 22% of women and 46% of men were literate (Registrar General & Census Commissioner(RGCC), 1977). By 1991, 39% of women and 64% of men were literate (RGCC, 1993). Thus, there has been a large increase in the proportion of women who are literate in just 20 years. Despite the improvements in literacy, there continues to be a large gap between the literacy level of men and of women. For India as a whole, the gender gap in literacy has been decreasing since 1981, in some States, however, the disparity in literacy between the sexes has been growing.

There are several reasons for the low levels of literacy in India, not the list of which is the high level of poverty. Over one third of the population is estimated to be living below the poverty line (The World Bank, 1997 a). Both school attendance is free, the costs of books, uniforms and transportation to school can be too much for poor families. Poor families are also more likely to keep girls at home to care for younger siblings or to work in family enterprises. If a family has to choose between educating a son or a daughter because of financial restrictions, typically the son will be chosen.

The above on "Education & Career" are submitted in the right spirit on the request of Author & good knowledge for all the school/ college going children who can better judge about the future prospects. The better & useful collection of the Education & Career material is not only beneficial for the upcoming generations but also it will improve the illiteracy situation of the country knowing about the good education & career by the coming generations. I really thank Mr.Sudesh Kumar Yadaw who has done great collection from the eminent & valuable resources to make in the shape of this book. I think that Mr.Sudesh Kumar Yadaw has done enormous task in respect of school/college going children & I am sure, people of great India alongwith people of outside country will take benefit & directions from the wonderful book.

Sd/-
(A.R.Pathak)
DIRECTOR
State Institute of Science Education
(M.P.) JABALPUR

Preface

The golden word of Smt.Indira Gandhi that "Education is a liberating force, and in our age it is also a democratizing force, cutting across the barriers of caste and class, smoothing out inequalities imposed by birth and other circumstances". The thinking of Late Smt.Indira Gandhi, former Prime Minister of Great India is more energetic message for the people of India to enhance the value of education & thought. Keeping this message in mind that our country is full of villages and undeveloped rural areas in comparison to metropolitan cities and other modern cities, the graph of the villages are very high where the condition of education is very poor. People of villages are, still, not aware about the elements of proper education criteria for which their next hierarchy/ward are unable to get proper guide and education. Needless to mention that poor status & unawareness about good education & career, they are unable to develop due to their struggle for existence in daily life cycle. Surprising to note that till date by village personalities, unaware of the meaning and status of the bureaucrats and nobody knows what is the higher position like Indian Administrative Service (IAS), Indian Foreign Service(IFS),Indian Forest Service (IFS), Indian Police Service (IPS), Indian Telecommunication Service (ITS), Indian Ordnance Factory Services(IOFS), State Administrative Service (SAS) except some positions like Engineer,Sub Divisional Officer, Time Keeper,Clerk,Doctor, Nurse, Collector,SDM,Tehsildar, Block Development Officer,Revenue Inspector, Patwari, Inspector, Police Constable, Teacher, Postman, Forest Guard, Watchman, Peon. Simple higher degrees like MA, M.Com, M.Sc. which have not been solved the unemployment problem of our country, where making like this book, for the some extent, it is tried to make the people more aware about the good

EDUCATION AND CAREER through job oriented courses *which can reach upto the remote rural undeveloped areas and villages of the country.*

EDUCATION

The word "Education" is derived from two Latin words. One is "Educere" and the other "Educare". The first one means "to train" and the latter to "nourish". In total, education means to train and to nourish with knowledge. In fine, the life of the person who goes for education should be transformed in the general outlook and commitment. As a matter of fact, what are the aims of education? In a nutshell, it can be narrated as the promotion of autonomy to give the individual a cultural background, and for the individual, he or she, should have the ability to take part in society through a profession. But what are the social needs? Economic development to retain the society's culture and to produce good citizens. In the present day situation "Discipline", which is the kernel of education, is lacking. Therefore, those who are in the field of education should try to practice discipline among student community. It is an undeniable fact that our education should produce good leaders.

Education gives empowerment. The citizens of a country should know his rights and privileges and he should contribute to the development of the society. For this, he has to be trained as a potential contributor to the needs of the society. He should also be aware of the developments that are taking place beyond his national borders. Also, education should give skill to those who need. Just as a rough stone becomes an invaluable sculpture of artistic beauty when it is in the hands of a sculpture, education should reveal the inherent personality of a man.

"Education Eradicates Illiteracy"

"Education is the Mirror of a Society"

"Education is the pace-setter of Modern Economy"

From the above sayings, it is quite evident that education permeates in the overall development of a society.

According to Dr.S.Radhakrishnan, "A good teacher must know how to arouse the interest of the pupil in the field of study for which he is responsible, he must himself be a master in the field and be in touch with the latest developments in his subject, he must himself be a fellow traveler in the exciting pursuit of knowledge".

Hon'ble President A.P.J.Abdul Kalam once said that when he was in school, his teacher taught the students about the flying of birds. Later in the evening, the teacher assembled the students near the sea-shore and practically shown how the sea-gulls fly and the students were inspired by the teacher. No wonder that aroused the curiosity of young mind of his student who later went on to become a scientist interested in the field of aeronautics.

CAREER

The word "career" essentially means a full time job or profession-especially one with opportunities for progress or promotion. A career offers immense scope to an individual for putting into use his lifetime's education, training and other skills. How satisfying or fulfilling a career is, depends a good deal on the monetary angle, i.e. the emoluments which a person gets, that enables him to make out a decent if not too comfortable a living.

The basic idea of a career option springs from a student's like or dislike of a particular subject, his/her aptitude, proficiency and fundamental knowledge, etc. Well, the best thing for one is to judge him/her self. Decide which is your strongest subject or combination of subjects; pick the ones in which you have had consistent high marks. The next step would be to consult the subject teacher who can be able to teach you in this matter. Next you could look around in your social circle. A doctor aunt, a botanist uncle or perhaps an MBA brother in law would be too glad to help you. You could rely on their personal experiences in their respective fields and then make up your mind. What is more, you could even ask them to judge you in specific subjects as to whether you are brilliant, average or dull. Their verdict need not dishearten you. Remember it is far better not to take up an unsuitable career rather than adopt a wrong one and regret ever after.

Presently, there is unlimited accessibility to all types of information, touching each and every aspect of our lives. And education, (career oriented education, to be more specific) is no exception.

All national as well as regional dallies carry prolific information on prominent schools, colleges, universities and institutions; the various academic disciplines, what course is available and where, the common admission tests conducted countrywide(for the purposes of admissions or recruitment or both), the paraphernalia of rules and regulations, eligibility conditions etc.; results of the foresaid examinations, scholarships/ fellowships and grants available to the crème de la crème students for the pursuit of higher studies and research, within the country or abroad and so forth.... The list is virtually endless. Then there are numerous career related magazines, scientific and medical journals that disseminate wealth of information to career aspirants, attempting to put them on the right track.

Keeping this situations in mind, the humble attempts in this direction to form a such book should be in public interest, based on new idea and direction of **Education and Career** in easy language for upcoming generations. The Author especially thanks to the Editor of the Employment News who has, time and again, published many tactics & ideas about career counseling and it is the greatest achievement for the Author to compile the suggestions & ideas for the readers in the shape of book. The author is also received the views from Internet & some esteemed News Magazines like Readers Digest, India Today, The Hitwad, Times of India, Hindustan Times etc. & Career Consultants from reputed Institutions to present his own opinions to the country.

Author also grateful to **wife Sudha Yadav**, **Son Chandrakant Yadav** and **daughter, Ku. Bhawna Yadav**, who have given full moral and family support during preparation of such Book. Author really grateful to all the colleagues who rendered full cooperation and support with enhancement of moral support alongwith Dr.Neeru Singh, Officer Incharge, Regional Medical Research Centre for Tribals, Jabalpur, staffs and Officers from which this book become more useful, knowledgeable and future education with career guide for all. Author also acknowledges with thanks to well wisher colleagues and good friends Dr. S.C. Dixit, Ex-RO of RMRCT,Jabalpur, my best friend Mr.S.N.Singh and Shri Vijay Gadge & family, Dr. K.B. Saha, Dr. Neelima Mishra, Dr. Dashrathi Das, Shri Gyanchand Jain, Dr.Rajiv Yadav, Dr.Jyoti Bhatt, Smt.Prem Bai Mandavi,Member,National Commission for Scheduled Tribes, Govt. of India, New Delhi, Shri P.K. Sukhdeve, Gen. Secretary of All India NTPC SC/ST Employees Association,Bilaspur (CG),Shri Prabhat Mishra,Social Worker,New Delhi, Dr. Devendra Ture, Civil Surgeon, Kanker, Shri P.S. Yadav, DGM, Raipur (CG), Shri Prem Magendra, Journalist, Shri Sudhir Kasar, Journalist,Dr.Narendra Tripathi,Journalist, Shri Sudhir Gupta,Journalist,Shri Sunder Yadav,Social Worker, Shri Ramesh Yadu,Social Worker and Shri Rameshchander, Asstt. Director General (Admn.), Shri Joginder Pal, Sr. Administrative Officer, Shri Bharat Bhusan, PS, Shri Vinod Bhatt, PA, Shri Raj Kumar Sharma, PA of Indian Council of Medical Research, Ansari Nagar, New Delhi who all have, time and again, enhanced my morale status resulting such unique book has come for the worldwide people.

Author especially grateful to Shri A.R. Pathak, Director, State Institute of Science Education, (M.P.) Jabalpur for giving special **FOREWARD** through this Book to upcoming generations for better understanding on "Education and Career".

Author of the book feels that on the successful publication of such book, if interesting by all the people of our great nation, it will be a great honour and respect to the People of INDIA which will be presumed ***as MANDAMUS OF ALMIGHTY TO MAKE SUCH TYPE OF EDUCATION BOOK IN PUBLIC INTEREST.***

Last but not the least, during preparation of such book, all the prons and cons have been adjudged, but if any mistakes, Readers/

Viewers are humbly requested to feel free to advise to the Author with good suggestion to include the new ideas, tactics without any hesitation as ***TO ERROR IS HUMAN BUT FORGIVE THE DIVINE***.

With Love !!!

Respect to Mother, Father and Great Mother Land,

Sudesh Kumar Yadaw

> My Grandfather once told me that there are two kinds of people: those who work and those who take the credit. He told me to try to be in the first group; there was less competition there.
>
> Smt. Indira Gandhi

1

Accounting and Auditing

(a) ACCOUNTANTS

Description

Analyze financial information and prepare financial reports to determine or maintain record of assets, liabilities, profit and loss, tax liability, or other financial activities within an organization.

Experience

A minimum of two to four years of work-related skill, knowledge, or experience is needed for these occupations. For example, an accountant must complete three years of college and work for several years in accounting to be considered qualified.

Education

Most of these occupations require a bachelor's degree.

Training

Employees in these occupations usually need several years of work-related experience, on-the-job training, and/or vocational training.

Tasks

1. Analyzes operations, trends, costs, revenues, financial commitments, and obligations incurred, to project future revenues and expenses, using computer.
2. Predicts revenues and expenditures and submits reports to management..
3. Surveys establishment operations to ascertain accounting needs.
4. Computes taxes owed, ensures compliance with tax payment, reporting, and other tax requirements, and represents establishment before taxing authority.
5. Directs activities of workers performing accounting and bookkeeping tasks.
6. Adapts accounting and record-keeping functions to current technology of computerized accounting systems.

7. Appraises, evaluates, and inventories real property and equipment and records description, value, location, and other information.
8. Prepares forms and manuals for workers performing accounting and bookkeeping tasks.
9. Audits contracts and prepares reports to substantiate transactions prior to settlement.
10. Establishes table of accounts and assigns entries to proper accounts.
11. Develops, implements, modifies, and documents budgeting, cost, general, property, and tax accounting systems.
12. Develops, maintains, and analyzes budgets and prepares periodic reports comparing budgeted costs to actual costs.
13. Analyzes records of financial transactions to determine accuracy and completeness of entries, using computer.
14. Reports finances of establishment to management and advises management about resource utilization, tax strategies, and assumptions underlying budget forecasts.
15. Prepares balance sheet, profit and loss statement, amortization and depreciation schedules, and other financial reports, using calculator or computer

(b) AUDITORS

Description

Examine and analyze accounting records to determine financial status of establishment and prepare financial reports concerning operating procedures.

Experience

A minimum of two to four years of work-related skill, knowledge, or experience is needed for these occupations.

Education

Most of these occupations require a bachelor's degree.

Training

Employees in these occupations usually need several years of work-related experience, on-the-job training, and/or vocational training.

Tasks

1. Reviews data about material assets, net worth, liabilities, capital stock, surplus, income, and expenditures.
2. Reports to management about asset utilization and audit results and recommends changes in operations and financial activities.
3. Analyzes data for deficient controls, duplicated effort, extravagance, fraud, or noncompliance with laws, regulations, and management policies.

4. Examines payroll and personnel records to determine worker's compensation coverage.
5. Verifies journal and ledger entries by examining inventory.
6. Examines records, tax returns, and related documents pertaining to settlement of decedent's estate
7. Directs activities of personnel engaged in filing, recording, compiling, and transmitting financial records.
8. Supervises auditing of establishments and determines scope of investigation required.
9. Examines records and interviews workers to ensure recording of transactions and compliance with laws and regulations.
10. Evaluates taxpayer finances to determine tax liability, using knowledge of interest and discount, annuities, valuation of stocks and bonds, and amortization valuation of depletable assets.
11. Confers with company officials about financial and regulatory matters.
12. Audits records to determine unemployment insurance premiums, liabilities, and compliance with tax laws.
13. Reviews taxpayer accounts and conducts audits on-site, by correspondence, or by summoning taxpayer to office.
14. Inspects cash on hand, notes receivable and payable, negotiable securities, and canceled checks.
15. Analyzes annual reports, financial statements, and other records, using accepted accounting and statistical procedures, to determine financial condition.
16 Inspects account books and system for efficiency, effectiveness, and use of accepted accounting procedures to record transactions.

(C) ASSESSORS

Description

Appraise real and personal property to determine its fair value. May assess taxes in accordance with prescribed schedules.

Experience

A minimum of two to four years of work-related skill, knowledge, or experience is needed for these occupations.

Education

Most of these occupations require a bachelor's degree, but some do not.

Training

Employees in these occupations usually need several years of work-related experience, on-the-job training, and/or vocational training.

Tasks

1. Appraises real and personal property, such as aircraft, marine craft, buildings, and land, to determine fair value.
2. Inspects property, considering factors such as market value, location, and building or replacement costs, to determine appraisal value.
3. Writes and submits appraisal and tax reports for public record.
4. Interprets property laws, formulates operational policies, and directs assessment office activities.
5. Assesses and computes taxes according to prescribed tax tables and schedules.

(d) CHARTERED ACCOUNTANCY

CPA, to explain simply, is an equivalent of Indian CA degree in United States of America. It can help one to undertake the similar job there or in the global companies outsourcing same work in other locations, like India and China.

The new computer based test, scheduled to commence April 2004, will incorporate the assessment of critical skills, such as research and communication, and will include increased emphasis on information technology, general business knowledge, as well as broadening the scope of the examination in the audit and at test area.

The CBT CPA exam. is administered during two of every three months in a calendar year quarter in USA. For instance, in 2005, the exam is offered in January and February, March is a non testing month. April/May are testing months; June is a non testing month.

The four parts are Auditing and Attestation. Financial Accounting and Business Environment and Concepts.

Auditing and Attestation covers knowledge of auditing procedures, generally accepted auditing standards and other standards related to attest engagements, and the skills needed to apply that knowledge.

Financial Accounting and Reporting covers generally accepted accounting principles for business enterprises and accounting and reporting for governmental entities and not-for-profit organizations.

Regulation combines federal taxation, ethics, professional and legal responsibilities and business law topics.

Business Environment and Concepts covers knowledge of general business environment and business concepts including business structures; economic concepts essential to obtaining an understanding of an entity's operations, business and industry; information technology and planning and measurement (cost accounting).

The eligibility for these courses is 15 years of education. Indians holding a degree like B.Com, M.Com, CA, ICWAI, CS, MBA and Engineers are eligible for this exam. CPA and CMA qualification can be acquired within just eight months after graduation and without any article ship or practical training.

There is a common myth about the Chartered Accountancy (CA) examination that it is difficult to pass, and that, passing percentage is very low. This misconception can be traced practically everywhere in India.

In CA course, there is no restriction at entry level, no minimum marks requirement, unlike in Medical and Engineering courses where only students with very high percentage marks are admitted. Hence, percentage of passing is bound to be low. Because admission is easy to get, many students do not take the exams seriously and treat it just like any other graduation exam.

CA exams are like any other professional examination, which requires thorough study, dedication and hard work. An average student who possesses these qualities can pass the CA exams. Of course, under the guidance from professionally qualified teachers.

Most students are unable to complete it even after struggling for years. This is a professional course, where the knowledge of students in the relevant professional subjects is tested via exam. Hence, those students who simply believe that study is nothing but memorising, miserably fail. In today's education system, there is no correlation between percentage of marks scored and the knowledge acquired.

It is not surprising to find that students coming in merit in Commerce do not succeed in the CA exams because of poor knowledge background. A professional examination requires conceptual and not just learning by rote.

A student who has mastered the concepts well and prepares in a planned manner will pass the CA exams.

Even 12th rank holders are not able to pass exams in 1st attempt.

Sometimes XIIth Commerce rank holders (even toppers) have failed at CA Foundation (PE-I) level itself, forget about Intermediate (PE-II) and Final level. But nobody tries to search the reasons for it.

If any XIIth Commerce rank holders is not performing satisfactorily in CA exams, the reason is that his approach of study in XIth and XIIth has been absolutely faulty and he continued to follow the same for CA exams as well. His approach of education has been learning devoid of knowledge and memorising without understanding. Even in practical papers like Accounts, which is the base/ foundation of CA curriculum, his approach is mechanical.

The Right approach for the CA exams.

The following tips are quite relevant in your march to success in CA exams.

(i) **Have a positive attitude**

Get rid of the fear of failure. You must have the confidence that you are capable of succeeding and you will succeed.

(ii) Professional guidance

Take guidance/ coaching from only those who themselves are professionally qualified. Trust such professional teachers and work on their advice.

(iii) Correct approach to studies

Have correct approach of study (procedures and practices) i.e. give more importance to understanding rather than memorising, specially, practical papers like Accounts, Financial Management, Costing, Taxation, Auditing etc. which are the backbone of this profession. Remember, a professional ought to be an expert in the areas of his profession.

(iv) Learning has many facets and their importance in the order of preference (from highest to lowest) is as follows:

(a) Listening to the expert teachers with rapt attention.

(b) Reading good quality books, notes and materials with analytical mind.

(c) Working practical problems, case studies etc. in class as well as at home but always, with a view to understand.

Therefore, listening, reading and writing, all must be coupled with critical and comparative thinking, searching answers for why and how. Be flexible and adaptive. Remember, you are studying all subjects in the context of a business and commercial organisation, which are dynamic, developing and changing according to the environment. Hence, these are not rigid, so you also learn them with open mind and understand that same issues may be dealt with differently under different conditions.

To enjoy good health, to bring true happiness to one's family, to bring peace to all one must first discipline and control one's own mind. If a man can control his mind he can find the way to enlightenment, and all wisdom and virtue will naturally come to him.

We are formed and molded by our thoughts. Those whose minds are shaped by selfless thoughts give joy when they speak or act. Joy follows them like a shadow that never leaves them.

You can search throughout the entire universe for someone who is more deserving of your love and affection than you are yourself and that person is not to be found anywhere. You yourself, as much as anybody in the entire universe deserve your love and affection.

(e) COST AND MANAGEMENT ACCOUNTANCY

It was during the early years of World War II that the concept of cost as an independent entirely made its beginning in the industrial circles of the world. Due to prohibitive cost of defence operation, the then governments at war found it difficult to ascertain the price of defence purchases and thus evolved the concept of cost plus contracts. This necessitated the contractors to submit the estimates of cost for the works being undertaken by them for the award of the contracts.

Origin of the Profession in India

The Institute of Cost and Works Accountants of India is the only professional body specialized I the field of cost and management accountancy in India. The Institute was first formed as a limited company in 1944 under the then Company Act.,1913. In 1994, the Institute celebrated Golden Jubilee Year of its formation.

But after gaining independence in the year 1947, Government of India accorded statutory recognition to the institute with the parliament passing the Cost and Works Accountants Act, 1959 (23 of 1959) in the year 1959.

The Institute of Cost and Works Accountants of India

The Institute of Cost and Works Accountants of India is a statutory professional body established under the act of parliament. It has its headquarter at Kolkata and four regional offices at Mumbai, Delhi, Kolkata and Chennai representing western, northern, eastern and southern regions respectively. Under the jurisdiction of the respective regional councils there are 92 chapters (branches) located in major cities/ towns all over the country and 6 overseas centres engaged in promoting the profession of cost and management accountancy (for addresses etc. webside can ; be seen).

The Objectives of the Institute

The Institute stands for the following ideals:-

1. Developing the profession of cost and management accountancy.
2. Developing the body of members and properly equip them for functions.
3. To ensure sound professional ethics.
4. To keep abreast of new developments.

Prospectus and Fields forCost and Management Accountants after Passing of India

Statutory Field

As on date over 44 selected industries have been covered under statutory maintenance of cost accounting records under section 209 (i) (d) of the Companies Act, 1956. Further, under section 233-B of the same Act, audit of the cost accounting records by a qualified practising cost accountant (ICWA), have been prescribed.

Non-Statutory Fields

The other fields for Cost Accountants include installation of costing system, techno-economic studies of projects, specific cost studies, pricing optimum utilization of capacity and resources, value analysis/ engineering, cost reduction, efficiency and profitability improvement, profit planning, introduction of standard costing system, services to banks, financial institutions, conducting project appraisal, feasibility studies, project monitoring, project management and control, financial management, project consultancy, design of management, organisation and methods, tax planning, diagnosis and revival of sick units, merchant banking, investment counselling, management and internal audit, training energy audit and environment audit. It is to mention that in last 10 years scope for nonstatutory field have tremendously increased for the cost and management accountants being good result shown by them in the relevant fields.

Apart from the above, ICWAI has been accorded due recognitions by:-

(a) **Universities**- Many Indian Universities have recognised ICWA qualification as sufficient for pursuing the PhD. It was also resolved by Association of Indian Universities to accept Bachelor Degree holder plus ICWA for registration as M.Phill and PhD candidates in the Commerce and allied disciplines. Fellow member of ICWAI has been taken as equivalent qualification of PhD for eligibility of professor by some universities like Indore University.

(b) **State Governments and other organisations**- In addition to cost audit and cost consultancy services, the professional has been recognised by the state governments for conducting Internal Audit in the State PSU's. Several nationalized banks have empanelled cost accounts for conducting the physical verification of inventories declared by their clients for availing working capital assistance. The profession has also been recognised for conducting loss survey for insurance policy.

(c) **Indian Cost Accounts Service (ICAS)**- Government of India has constituted an all India cadre known as Indian Cost Accounts Service (ICAS) at par with other Class-I Service such as IAS, IFS etc. to advise the government in Cost and Pricing and in framing the appropriate fiscal and tax policies.

Here it is mentioned that job opportunities are adequately available in Govt./ PSU's/Private Sector with due consideration comparable with other professional qualifications. Fees and expenses on the courses are quite affordable.

Eligibility for Enrolment

Any person who is above 18 years of age and completed graduation in any discipline is eligible for direct registration for intermediate course. Those who do not have the above qualification but passed 10+2 standard shall pass a foundation course examination before entry as a student for Intermediate Course 'A'. The course fee is quite affordable.

The institute has on its rolls a large number of registered students appearing for intermediate and final examination conducted by the institute. Every student of the institute shall undergo mandatory coaching for a specified period either through a chain of oral coaching centres established all over the country or through postal coaching with the respective Regional Council.

The examinations for foundation course, intermediate and final examinations of the institute are held twice in a year in June and December. The Institute's examinations have been acclaimed as one of very high standards of proficiency. Qualified and experienced Cost and Management Accountants are in continuous demand in the industry as well as other organisation for placements at senior and middle level management positions.

The Institute is a member of the International Federation of Accountants Committee (IFAC), the Confederation of Asian and Pacific Accountants (CAPA) and the South Asian Federation of Accountants (SAFA). The Institute as a leader in the field in the South Asian Region is also imparting training to accountants from overseas countries.

ICWAI is a premier, dynamic and vibrant professional institution actively associating itself in the industrial and economic development of the nation. The profession places itself at the service of the nation, government, industry and the society to realize the objectives of a welfare state resulting in the prosperity and well being of its entire people. Member's of this profession are the driving force in the team of management as a personnel and a key consultant, an effective Cost and Management Auditor and an appropriate advisor in practice.

(f) ECONOMISTS

Description

Conduct research, prepare reports, or formulate plans to aid in solution of economic problems arising from production and distribution of goods and services. May collect and process economic and statistical data using econometric and sampling techniques.

Experience

Extensive skill, knowledge, and experience are needed for these occupations. Many require more than five years of experience.

Education

A bachelor's degree is the minimum formal education required for these occupations. However, many also require graduate school.

Training

Employees may need some on-the-job training, but most of these occupations assume that the person will already have the required skills, knowledge, work-related experience, and/or training.

Tasks

1. Studies economic and statistical data in area of specialization, such as finance, labor, or agriculture.
2. Formulates recommendations, policies, or plans to interpret markets or solve economic problems.

3. Develops economic guidelines and standards and preparing points of view used in forecasting trends and formulating economic policy.
4. Devises methods and procedures for collecting and processing data, using various econometric and sampling techniques.
5. Assigns work to staff.
6. Teaches theories, principles, and methods of economics.
7. Testifies at regulatory or legislative hearings to present recommendations.
8. Provides advice and consultation to business and public and private agencies.
9. Supervises research projects and students' study projects.
10. Compiles data relating to research area, such as employment, productivity, and wages and hours.
11. Reviews and analyzes data to prepare reports, to forecast future marketing trends, and to stay abreast of economic changes.
12. Organizes research data into report format, including graphic illustrations of research findings.

(g) FILM AND VIDEO EDITORS

Description

Edit motion picture soundtracks, film, and video.

Experience

A minimum of two to four years of work-related skill, knowledge, or experience is needed for these occupations.

Education

Most of these occupations require a bachelor's degree, but some do not.

Training

Employees in these occupations usually need several years of work-related experience, on-the-job training, and/or vocational training.

Tasks

1. Edits film and videotape to insert music, dialogue, and sound effects, and to correct errors, using editing equipment.
2. Studies script and confers with producers and directors concerning layout or editing to increase dramatic or entertainment value of production.
3. Supervises and coordinates activities of workers engaged in editing and assembling filmed scenes photographed by others.
4. Evaluates and selects scenes in terms of dramatic and entertainment value and story continuity.
5. Trims film segments to specified lengths and reassembles segments in sequence that presents story with maximum effect.

6. Reviews assembled film or edited videotape on screen or monitor and makes corrections.

(h) FINANCIAL SERVICES

With the advent of economic reforms initiated in 1991 various sectors of the economy have witnessed rapid, structural and dynamic changes, Prior to reforms economy was dominated by agriculture and allied activities followed by manufacturing, trading and other services. At that time agriculture and related sector based constituted about 60% of the GDP and service Sector. Now after fourteen years of reforms it is the service sector which has ample opportunities and scope.

It is apparent from the table 1.1 above that during the last fourteen years the importance of the service sector has significantly improved. In the service sector too financial services has the highest plan priorities and growth rate after communication. In the 10th plan (2002-07) the target growth of financial services is 11.69% while in 9th plan and 8th plan the actual growth rates were 8.93% and 10.21% respectively. Table (1.2)

Tenth plan (2002-07) priority is employment growth in low capital sectors like agriculture, construction, other transport, financial services and other services which is sufficient reason for avenues for employment generation in financial sector.

The following table shows the importance of service sector in recent years:

Table 1.1
Showing contribution of sectors of economy (as a percentage of GDP) (on the basis of new base series 1993-94)

Sector	*1950-51 1970s*	*Decade of*	*1990-91*	*2000-01*	*2003-04*
Primary (agriculture & related)	59.2	42.8	32.2	26.5	22.1
Secondary (industry)	13.3	22.8	27.2	25.0	26.9
Tertiary (service)	27.5	34.5	40.5	48.5	51.0

The market driven and customer controlled economic sector has propagated the need for efficient, alert, skilful and professional people to fight competition and create a niche in the market.

Now the role and priority of government has changed in line with the changes in the policy stance. The stat today is confined only to facilitate the functioning and general supervision of economy. Liberalisation, globalisation and privatisation have put pressure on young professionals to achieve the targets as desired by their employers. Among the service sector : transport, communication, banking, courier, capital markets, consultancy, portfolio management, asset management, brokerage, insurance, financial services have emerged as major employers and service providers in these fields in recent years.

Table 1.2
Sectoral Growth Rate (as a percentage of GDP during plans)

Sl.No.	*Sector*	*8th plan (actual)*	*9th plan (actual)*	*10th plan (target)*
1.	Agriculture & allied	4.69	2.06	3.97
2.	Communication	14.31	17.14	15.00
3.	Financial Services	10.21	8.93	11.69
4.	Other Services	6.22	8.19	9.26

Financial service sector is gaining importance day by day. Insurance, banks, asset management companies, stock market, financial institutions, depositories, depository participants, portfolio managers, financial analysis, financial planners, financial managers, treasury managers, are the positions available for young professionals.

With the inception of WTO, the significance of financial services has increased in recent years to overcome the difficulties arising out of technical and professional nature of skills and jobs required. The areas of broad specialization in financial services include: corporate financial management, tax administration, finance solution with software skills and development, portfolio management, fund and asset management, treasury management, foreign exchange management, corporate risk management, capital market and money market, derivatives, lease and hire purchase, project management, financial planning and control, export-import financing, counselling and consultancy, teaching and research, media etc. As far as employment in these fields is concerned, it can be broadly categorized as follows:-

Career in Corporate Finance

In the first category of corporate finance, there is ample scope and opportunity for finance professionals in services like corporate finance, working capital management, accounting and auditing, tax advisory services etc. In every organization, there exists a department with responsibility and duties of raising, controlling and auditing of professionals who have acumen with desired qualifications in management field for these positions. From inventory management to financial decision making the people from finance background are preferred. The appointments are done either through campus or on the basis of experience. The qualifications are MBA/PGDM with specialization in finance from any recognised university or institute recognised by AIU or equivalent qualifications. There is a misconception that commerce graduates can do better in finance field. The basic requirement of finance executive is an analytical brain with calculative and quantitative aptitude. It is surprising that MBAs having engineering background are doing well in finance. If you enjoy playing with numbers, figures and data interpretation, an excellent career is waiting for your in finance. In fact the career growth is faster in finance than in any other functional area of management. Recent placement trends of select institutes of repute reveal that corporate finance has emerged as the most preferred career option by young MBA degree holders. The reasons are clear: fast growth and lucrative sector. Some universities and institutions are providing MFC (Master of Finance and Control); MBA (Finance), MMS (Master of Management Science with specialization in finance) at post graduate level and BBA, BBM etc. at graduation level. Sometimes MBE (Master of Business Economics) with specialization in finance and M.Com (Business Administration) degrees are suffice to get a job in corporate finance but generally corporates are allured by an MBA/PGDM from good institutes. In the same connection it is to be noted that in case of finance it is the knowledge and skills which matter and not the institutions as in the case of marketing and HRM. From time to time PSUs like IOC, ONGC, SAIL and others conduct tests followed by GD and interview to appoint management trainees in finance through direct entry route instead of going campus recruitment. The purpose is to attract and place deserving candidates from universities and institutions all over India. Hence, no need to worry, every finance PG has equal possibility to get selected.

Career in Banks and Financial Institutions

During the reforms, banking sector witnessed sea changes in the policy of government. After implementation of Narasimhan committee's recommendations in the same, whole banking structure of Indian financial system underwent operational changes which are directed towards bringing competence and transparency. Now banks are no more a government monopoly. More and more private sector banks and financial institutions are coming up in Indian financial sector. The increased pressure and competition has given rise to opening of new bank branches by private and foreign banks. Similar is the case of financial institutions which are now converted into universal banks catering the need of public as well as corporates. Technology and innovation driven banking demands for young professionals in banking business who can design and deliver the products and services to fulfil the needs of customers. Banks are now a days involved in multifarious activities like maintaining current and savings account, providing consumers loans, housing loans, imparting insurance facilities to customers (known as banc assurance), preparing project reports and monitoring projects of entrepreneurs , managing portfolios, credit delivery and its record keeping, educational loan to students and researchers, lease financing and hire purchasing activities, term loans to small and big industries etc. With the advent of innovative products in banking and financial sector, the need of people having technical and professional calibre has arisen in the recent years. Banks are today functioning as agents to safeguard the interest of the public fund and accordingly invest the same in order to give good returns to their customers. For this purpose, people with finance sense are required in bank's services, which can take decisions regarding investments, products, markets and risks associated with them. The desired necessary qualifications are the same as mentioned in the previous paragraphs. Private and foreign banks like ICICI, IDBI, Bank of Punjab, ABN Amro, HSBC, Citi Bank, Bank of America etc. appoint on the basis of campus placement or on experience in various capacities as management trainees in credit, personal loan, project finance, equity segment divisions etc. Public sector banks have started recruiting trainee managers from finance field to serve as advisors, security analysts, risk analysts, project managers, investment advisors and economists. Knowledge with skills in addition to professional degree or diploma are mandatory conditions to get absorbed in these jobs. National Institute of Bank Management, Pune; ICFAI (Institute of Chartered Financial Analysts of India, Hyderabad) offer special programs and PGDM courses for students and working executives interested in banks and financial institutions.

(i) INTERNATIONAL CFA

International CFA is the gateway to the world of financial markets, the symbol of professional excellence in the investment management field, the international passport to a financial career. International CFA can also help you to get closer to your eventual ambitions. International CFA is one of the most rigorous professional credentials of the Investment industry. This exam is administered by the Association for Investment Management and Research (AMIR, HYPERLINK, www.aimr.org, www.aimr.org).

The CFA program curriculum is broken into three "levels", each of which is build upon one another and concludes with an examination. Each of the examinations is offered annually in June, while the Level I exam is offered both in June and December of each year. Candidates who fail in one of the examinations are not permitted to advance to the next level, though they are permitted to repeat the examination.

To register for the CFA program, candidates must have a Bachelor's degree or equivalent OR be a college/ university Senior (final year student) scheduled to receive a Bachelor's degree. Additionally, they must have 4 years of qualified professional work experience OR a combination of 4 years of college/university and professional work experience. This experience need not be investment related, though summer, part-time and internship positions do not qualify.

The Eligibility of these courses is 15 years of education. Indians holding a degree like B.Com, M.Com, CA, ICWAI, CS, MBAs are eligible for this exam.

There are three CFA program levels. Each level culminates in a six-hour examination, administered in two three-hour parts. These examinations are live, proctored exam. and are offered at myriad locations throughout the world including India.

The "Level I" examination is offered twice a year, in June and December. The Levels II and III examinations are offered annually in June. Technically, if a candidate took the December Level I exam., he/she can complete the following June Level II exam, and the ensuing June Level III exam. in approximately 18 months, not including preparation time. The 2005 Level I Exam. is composed completely of multiple-choice questions.

The 2005 Level II Exam. consists of item set questions, which are essentially multiple choice questions based on a common vignette or problem.

The 2005 Level III CFA Exam. includes both essay and item set questions.

For the passing the International CFA exam., candidates have to score 52% for Level I, 54% for Level II, 65% for Level III. Financial analysts are involved in the process of securities analysis, investment and risk management and investment banking.

(j) TAX EXAMINERS, COLLECTORS AND REVENUE AGENTS

Description

Determine tax liability or collect taxes from individuals or business firms according to prescribed laws and regulations.

Experience

A minimum of two to four years of work-related skill, knowledge, or experience is needed for these occupations.

Education

Most of these occupations require a bachelor's degree, but some do not.

Training

Employees in these occupations usually need several years of work-related experience, on-the-job training, and/or vocational training.

Tasks

1. Examines and analyzes tax assets and liabilities to determine resolution of delinquent tax problems.
2. Recommends criminal prosecutions and civil penalties.
3. Serves as member of regional appeals board to reexamine unresolved issues in terms of relevant laws and regulations.
4. Participates in informal appeals hearings on contested cases from other agents.
5. Confers with taxpayer or representative to explain issues involved and applicability of pertinent tax laws and regulations.
6. Directs service of legal documents, such as subpoenas, warrants, notices of assessment, and garnishments.
7. Conducts independent field audits and investigations of federal income tax returns to verify or amend tax liabilities.
8. Examines selected tax returns to determine nature and extent of audits to be performed.
9. Selects appropriate remedy, such as partial-payment agreement, offer of compromise, or seizure and sale of property.
10. Secures taxpayer's agreement to discharge tax assessment or submits contested determination to other administrative or judicial conferees for appeals hearings.
11. Analyzes accounting books and records to determine appropriateness of accounting methods employed and compliance with statutory provisions.
12. Investigates legal instruments, other documents, financial transactions, operation methods, and industry practices to assess inclusiveness of accounting records and tax returns.

2

Administrative Services

(a) ACTUARIAL SCIENCE

Risk, uncertainties, dangers, insecurities are all the dark shades of life. In the modern times, human beings have developed various devices to minimise the harms brought about by risks and uncertainties of life. It's true that certain risk like fear of an early death or an accidental death can not be avoided but the disastrous repercussions associated with that risk, i.e., financial loss to the family of the breadwinner in case of his early death can be minimised to some extent by making some arrangements well in advance. Among such financial arrangements can be mentioned insurance, bank deposits, mutual fund, pension schemes and so on. But these tools require an efficient management system in order to provide long-term monetary benefits to the clients and also to manage the risk and uncertainties of their lives. Here comes the role of an Actuary. The actuaries are considered to be the analytical backbone of a country's financial security programmes.

Actuaries are the professional who, by using the probability theory and mathematical, statistical and financial techniques; analyse the financial consequences of risk to enable businesses to make better informed decisions. They assess the financial impact of uncertain future events by methodically analysing the past, modelling the future and quantifying the likely range of financial outcomes from different future events. Their work involves a combination of strong analytical skills, business knowledge and understanding of human behaviour in order to design and manage the programmes that control risk.

The expanding horizon of the scope of actuarial functionaries

Earlier the, Actuaries were demanded only in the insurance sector. In India, LIC, GIC were the major employers of the Actuaries but certain factors like liberalisation, privatisation and emergence of some new professions in the Indian economy have given rise to the emergence of the need of Actuaries in other fields as well. These new fields include viz. commercial banks, investment banks, retirement funds, employees benefit departments of large corporates and all those businesses that need to manage financial risk. In other words, wherever there is uncertainty, there is scope for Actuarial Science. That is why, a career as an Actuary is better described as a "business" career with a mathematical basis than as a "technical" mathematical career.

Strategic position of the Actuary

Actuaries are the key player in the management team of the financial companies. Their work is directly related to the strategic management decisions. Since their judgement is heavily relied upon; actuaries career path often leads to upper management and executive positions.

Role of Actuaries in Insurance

Insurance, the most powerful tool of managing risks, is almost unthinkable without actuaries. Under insurance, we reduce our risk of financial loss by transferring it to an insurance company that accepts the risk for a price (the insurance premium). Actuaries play a key role to design insurance plans, determine the premium, monitor the profitability of the insurance companies and recommend corrective actions. They also ensure that the companies have set aside enough funds to pay claims.

Pre-requisites for being an Actuary

A strong ability and liking for numbers is a must for the aspirants of Actuarial career. Equally essential is a firm determination towards a prolonged study period, five to seven years on an average. Acquaintance with the business environment, economics, finance and accounts are also needed. Good communication skills, computer knowledge and decision making ability are some other requisites for this career. Actuarial course is considered as a tough course, that's why; the dropout rate is very high. But crossing the barriers of the path successfully would mean reaching out to the soaring heights of name, fame and money.

A highly paid profession

This is a well known fact that Actuaries are the one of the highest paid professionals. In the beginning of the career itself, an

Actuary can earn up to Rs.8 lakhs per annum in India. Stipend for an Actuarial trainee is approximately Rs.25,000 per month. The career opportunity begins as soon as the student completes the first five papers.

Essential Qualifications for doing Actuarial Studies

One can opt for this career, if one has any of the following qualifications:

1. Graduate in Maths/Statistics/Econometrics/ Computer Science with a minimum 55% marks.
2. MBA (Finance) CA/CWA/MCA

The Actuarial Course: In India, a fellow member of the Actuarial Society of India (ASI), Mumbai is referred to as an Actuary. The Actuarial course (offered by ASI) consisting of 16 papers can be completed between 4-5 years depending upon the time devoted by the student for the preparation of the examinations.

The examinations are divided into four parts- 100 series, 200 series, 300 series and 400 series. On passing the 100 series subjects, a student is eligible to get the Certificate in Actuarial Techniques (CAT). On passing all the subjects up to and including 300 series, a student is eligible to be admitted as an Associate member of the Society AASI. After passing the chosen subject from the 400 series, an Associate is awarded Fellowship and can use FASI against his/her name. The examinations are essentially approached through self study. The course material is provided by the society in all subjects excluding the entrance examination. On occasions, the society organises oral classes and group tuitions. Current cost of the entire course including tuition material can work out to Rs.50,000. The examinations are conducted twice a year during the months of May and November. Depending upon the efforts put in, one may get through the examinations in four to six years on an average.

Future: The expansion and privatisation of the Indian economy is a boon for the rise of Actuary as one of the most demanding professions of the country in the days to come. Privatisation of the insurance sector has not only created innumerable employment opportunities for the Actuaries but has also led to the popularity of this profession. Actuarial profession, hitherto not a layperson's cup of tea, is now understood and thought over by the commoners as a challenging but highly paid profession. Apart from lucrative jobs in private insurance companies, the opening up of the insurance sector will give rise to many associated opportunities in underwriting marketing, product design, reinsurance and consulting. These factors are suggesting a bright future of the Actuarial profession.

Potential Employers

1. Insurance Companies (General and Life)
2. Banks
3. Investment Companies
4. Consulting firms
5. Public Accounting firms
6. Big Corporate and business houses
7. Pension department (Govt. and private sectors)

Institutes offering courses in Actuarial Science

(a) Indian

1. Actuarial Society of India, 9, Jeevan Udyog, 3rd Floor, 278, Dr.D.N.Road, Fort, Mumbai-1
2. Bharatidasan University, Palkataipur, Tiruchirapalli-620 024
3. University of Kalyani, PO-Kalyani-741235 Dist.-Nadia W.B.
4. Kurukshetra University, Kurukshetra-132 119
5. University of Mumbai, M.G.Road, Fort, Mumbai-32
6. Goa University, Taleigao Plateau, Goa-403 002

(b) Foreign

1. Institute of Actuaries Staple Inn Hall, High Halborn, London
2. Society of Actuaries, 475, North Martingale Road, Suit 800, Schaumburg, IL 60173-226
3. American Academy of Actuaries 1100-17th Street, NW 7th Floor, Washington DC 20036
4. City University Northampton Square, London EC 1V OHB

(b) ACTUARIES

Description

Analyze statistical data, such as mortality, accident, sickness, disability, and retirement rates and construct probability tables to forecast risk and liability for payment of future benefits. May ascertain premium rates required and cash reserves necessary to ensure payment of future benefits.

Experience

Extensive skill, knowledge, and experience are needed for these occupations. Many require more than five years of experience.

Education

A bachelor's degree is the minimum formal education required for these occupations. However, many also require graduate school.

Training

Employees may need some on-the-job training, but most of these occupations assume that the person will already have the required skills, knowledge, work-related experience, and/or training.

Tasks

1. Determines mortality, accident, sickness, disability, and retirement rates.
2. Constructs probability tables regarding fire, natural disasters, and unemployment based on analysis of statistical data and other pertinent information.
3. Designs or reviews insurance and pension plans and calculates premiums.
4. Ascertains premium rates required and cash reserves and liabilities necessary to ensure payment of future benefits.
5. Determines equitable basis for distributing surplus earnings under participating insurance and annuity contracts in mutual companies.

(c) ADMINISTRATIVE SERVICES MANAGER

Description

Plan, direct, or coordinate supportive services of an organization, such as recordkeeping, mail distribution, telephone operator/receptionist, and other office support services. May oversee facilities planning and maintenance and custodial operations.

Experience

A minimum of two to four years of work-related skill, knowledge, or experience is needed for these occupations.

Education

Most of these occupations require a bachelor's degree, but some do not.

Training

Employees in these occupations usually need several years of work-related experience, on-the-job training, and/or vocational training.

Tasks

1. Coordinates activities of clerical and administrative personnel in establishment or organization.
2. Prepares and reviews operational reports and schedules to ensure accuracy and efficiency.

3. Formulates budgetary reports.
4. Hires and terminates clerical and administrative personnel.
5. Conducts classes to teach procedures to staff.
6. Recommends cost-saving methods, such as supply changes and disposal of records, to improve efficiency of department.
7. Analyzes internal processes and plans or implements procedural and policy changes to improve operations.

(d) COST ESTIMATORS

Description

Prepare cost estimates for product manufacturing, construction projects, or services to aid management in bidding on or determining price of product or service. May specialize according to particular service performed or type of product manufactured.

Experience

A minimum of two to four years of work-related skill, knowledge, or experience is needed for these occupations.

Education

Most of these occupations require a bachelor's degree, but some do not.

Training

Employees in these occupations usually need several years of work-related experience, on-the-job training, and/or vocational training.

Tasks

1. Analyzes blueprints, specifications, proposals, and other documentation to prepare time, cost, and labor estimates.
2. Prepares estimates used for management purposes, such as planning, organizing, and scheduling work.
3. Prepares estimates for selecting vendors or subcontractors and determining cost-effectiveness.
4. Reviews data to determine material and labor requirements and prepares itemized list.
5. Prepares time, cost, and labor estimates for products, projects, or services, applying specialized methodologies, techniques, or processes.
6. Conducts special studies to develop and establish standard hour and related cost data or to effect cost reduction.
7. Computes cost factors used for preparing estimates for management and determining cost-effectiveness.

8. Consults with clients, vendors, or other individuals to discuss and formulate estimates and resolve issues.

(e) CREDIT ANALYSTS

Description

Analyze current credit data and financial statements of individuals or firms to determine the degree of risk involved in extending credit or lending money. Prepare reports with this credit information for use in decision-making.

Experience

A minimum of two to four years of work-related skill, knowledge, or experience is needed for these occupations.

Education

Most of these occupations require a bachelor's degree, but some do not.

Training

Employees in these occupations usually need several years of work-related experience, on-the-job training, and/or vocational training.

Tasks

1. Analyzes credit data and financial statements to determine degree of risk involved in extending credit or lending money.
2. Reviews individual or commercial customer files to identify and select delinquent accounts for collection.
3. Consults with customers to resolve complaints and verify financial and credit transactions and adjust accounts as needed.
4. Confers with credit association and other business representatives to exchange credit information.
5. Generates financial ratios, using computer program, to evaluate customer's financial status.
6. Compares liquidity, profitability, and credit history with similar establishments of same industry and geographic location.
7. Completes loan application, including credit analysis and summary of loan request, and submits to loan committee for approval.
8. Evaluates customer records and recommends payment plan based on earnings, savings data, payment history, and purchase activity.
9. Analyzes financial data, such as income growth, quality of management, and market share, to determine profitability of loan.

(f) DISASTER MANAGEMENT

A disaster is a serious disruption of the functioning of a society, causing widespread human, material or environmental loss which exceed the ability of the affected society to cope using only its own resources. Disasters may be sudden (like an earthquake/tsunami) or slow (like a drought) or they could be natural or man-made.

As India has a large number of vulnerable regions, natural disaster management has emerged as a top priority for the country. India has an integrated administrative machinery for the management of disasters at the National, State, District and Sub-district levels. The basic responsibility of undertaking rescue, relief and rehabilitation measures in the event of natural disasters at present is that of the State Governments concerned with the Central Government supplementing the efforts of the States by providing financial and logistical support.

Response to Disaster Management

The Ministry of Home Affairs is the nodal Ministry for coordinating relief, response and overall natural disaster management, and the Department of Agriculture and Cooperation is the nodal Ministry for drought management. Other Ministries responsible for other categories of disasters are Ministry of Civil Aviation for air accidents, Ministry of Railways for railway accidents, Ministry of Environment and Forests for chemical disasters, Ministry of Health for biological disasters and Department of Atomic Energy for nuclear disasters.

Training and Education

One of the important initiatives of the Government of India, Ministry of Human Resource Development in its Tenth Five Year Plan includes the inclusion of disaster management in the curriculum of schools and professional education.

The Central Board of Secondary Education (CBSE) has introduced the subject on Disaster Management in Social Science for Classes VIII in the year 2003, for Class IX in 2004 and for Class X thereafter. The curriculum, course content, etc. has been developed with support from the Ministry of Home Affairs, Govt. of India and the United Nations Development Programme (UNDP).

- Certificate programme in Disaster Management (CDM)
- P.G.Diploma programme in Disaster Management (PGDDM) Indira Gandhi National Open University, Maidan Garhi, New Delhi-110 068 (www.ignou.ac.in); University of North Bengal, P.O. North Bengal University, Dt.Darjeeling-734 430 (www.nbu.ac.in)
- 1-Year Post Graduate Diploma in Disaster Management International Centre of Madras University, University of Madras, Chepauk, Chennai-600 005

- PG Diploma in Disaster Management Sikkim Manipal University of Health, Medical and Technological Sciences, Tadong, Gangtok, Sikkim (www.sikkimmanipal.net) in association with Indian Institute of Ecology and Environment (A- 15 Paryavaran Complex, Saket, Maidangarhi Marg, New Delhi- 110 030) (www.ecology.edu)

Further Training

Disaster Management Institute (DMI), E-5, Paryavaran Parisar, Arera Colony, Bhopal-462 016 (www.dmibpl.org) established by the MP Government organises training for working managers and government officials in the areas related to the management of natural disasters.

Centre for Disaster Management (CDM)(www.yashada.org) was set up in August, 1996 with support from the Natural Disaster Management Division, Department of Agriculture and Cooperation, Ministry of Agriculture, Government of India. It conducts training programmes and Workshops on various aspects of disaster management for Class I Officers of the Government of Maharashtra, elected representatives/ non- officials and voluntary activists.

The National Civil Defence College, Nagpur (www.ncdcnagpur.nic.in) was founded on 29th April, 1957. This college has also been identified as a premier training establishment in Chemical Disasters by the Ministry of Environment and Forests and has been selected as one of the advanced training center in India on Search and Rescue by the Office of the Federal Disaster Agerncy (OFDA) of USA and Asian Disaster Preparedness Center (ADPC) Bangkok. The college has been recognized as a nodal training institute for Nuclear, Biological and Chemical Emergencies training by the Ministry of Home Affairs in the year 2002.

The United Nations Disaster Management Training Programme (DMTP) (www.undmtp.org) was launched by the UNDP and the Office of the United Nations Disaster Relief Coordinator in cooperation with UN Agencies in 1990. DMTP is a learning platform addressing crises, emergencies and disasters for the UN Member States, the UN System and international and non-governmental organisations.

Disaster Management Center, 432, North Lake Street, Madison, Wisconsin, 53706, USA (www.dmc.engr.wisc.edu) offers a self study course curriculum in international disaster/ emergency management available in English. (Listing is indicative).

Importance of Disaster Management Expertise

Disaster Management personnel are invaluable when disaster strikes. They are trained to manage emergency situations and respond to the needs of the people and areas affected in a quick and efficient manner. They may be responsible for evacuating a town in danger, managing the distribution of food to people in crisis, or overseeing the provision of medical care to injured people. They are needed in large and small emergencies including hurricanes, terrorist attacks and chemical spills.

Career Opportunities

Careers in disaster management are usually government jobs, jobs with emergency services, law enforcement, local authorities, relief agencies, non governmental organisations and international agencies such as the United Nations etc. Private sector careers are also available while fulfilling their corporate social responsibilities. Training and workshops on disaster management are helpful to administrative/ civil servants, civil engineers, police and defence personnel, fire fighters and other protective service workers.

Systems or network administrators, database analysts or administrators, security administration or operations analysis are positioned to participate in an organisation's disaster recovery planning and management in the sphere of information technology. Social workers, engineers, medical health experts, environmental experts, rehabilitation workers, scientists etc. could also have careers in disaster management, disaster mitigation and rehabilitation.

(g) ENVIRONMENTALIST

The subject now labelled as Environmental Sciences has its roots in ecology which is the study of how the living and non living things in nature relate to one another. Ecologists have discovered many basic truths about these relationships. In their research, they often study issues that relate to the effects of human activities upon population and ecosystems. As a consequence, ecological research has identified and characterized many of the most significant problems threatening the future of humanity. They have forged these into principles that serve as a foundation for modern ecology and for Environmental Sciences in general. The basic principles of ecology, therefore, are the starting point of all environmental problems.

Civilization still depends on the natural environment not only for energy and materials but also for vital life-support systems such as air and water cycles. The survival of the human race thus depends on knowledge and intelligent action to preserve and enhance environmental quality by means of harmonious rather than disruptive technology. New inventions and processes have been continuously developed to improve our way of life. But most of the technological advances were made without consideration of the adverse effects they would have on environment. Apart from technology, social and economic causes have also been contributing to environmental degradation and pollution.

Wildlife habitats continue to be threatened. Water contamination, air pollution are critical problems that need immediate attention. Global effort towards an environment that is clean and free of pollution is noticeable. In this scenario, opting for a career as an Environmentalist can prove to be a good decision.

Environmental Science is, 'Applying knowledge from many disciplines to the study and management of the environment. It deals with the analysis of the conditions, circumstances and influences affecting life and how life in turn responds'. (Purdon and Anderson, 1983). This subject encompasses many disciplines each having varied concepts and principles.

THE PERSONAL FACTOR

To take up this rather unusual career-choice seriously, what you need to have, is, not only a passionate concern for the environment, but also a clear idea about what needs to be done towards improving it.

A logical mind, scientific acumen, and a working knowledge of subjects like geography, geology, botany, chemistry and zoology are very necessary. Good communication skills would not be wasted in this career, nor would the ability to put your ideas into words and action. Decision making skills are also a must-have.

THE PROSPECTS

Employment opportunities are in diverse fields. Government agencies, industries, the manufacturing sector, nuclear stations, waste disposal organizations, consultancies, research organizations, NGOs etc. offer opportunity to environmental scientists. You could join an industry as part of an environmental management team. These teams include a diverse set of professionals- lawyers, engineers and post graduates in social work. Stricter pollution control laws and increasing industrial activity are now making environmental professionals indispensable in the manufacturing sector. Government institutes could hire you as an Environment specialist.

STUDY ROUTES

Environmental related education could be pursued through different disciplines.

1. Biologists study the effect of changes in the environment on living thing.
2. Bacteriologists, biochemists, botanists, horticulturists work on developing safer pesticides and herbicides.

3. Microbiologists, mycologists and toxicologists look at the chemical and biological aspects of the environment.
4. Chemists, ecologists, soil scientists, foresters, aqua culturists, may all work in areas related to management.
5. Environmental Scientists are from many disciplines such as botany, zoology, oceanography, ecology, chemistry, economics, engineering, environment studies etc.

ENVIRONMENTAL SCIENTISTS

The tasks

1. *Treatment of waste* - From industries (fertilizer, food processing, electroplating, tannery, textiles etc.) refineries, distilleries, mines etc. Toxic wastes hazardous to the environment have to be detected and treated.
2. *Solid Waste Management* - Chemists, engineers and hydrologists, geologists, radioactive waste experts and industrial waste managers are concerned with cutting down the dangers from solid wastes.
3. *Air Pollution Management* - Acid rain, ozone depletion, green house gases are threats to the environment. Analytical chemists, toxicologists and air quality specialists analyse the effects of various harmful gases, which are emitted as a result of fuel or garbage combustion. They also study the effects of these on human as well as plant life.
4. *Water Quality Management* - Water is a very critical component of environment without which survival of organisms is impossible. Environmental scientists, environmental engineers, people from water shed management are concerned with the preservation and purification/ recycling of water in rivers, lakes, streams and all surface and ground waters.
5. *Land Conservation* - This area of work overlaps that of forestry and wildlife managers and also incorporates planning for better use of land and water. Conservation of perks, outdoor recreation sites, re-greening of urban areas need professions from a background in geology, landscape architecture, wildlife management, forestry etc.
6. *Environmental Modelling* - This is a new area of research and development field, which has a tremendous scope with respect to Environmental planning and Conservation. Here simulation models are built of developed and experimented in nature. Models can be developed for Climate Change, Air Quality, Water Quality, Noise, Rainfall Pattern, Toxicological studies to study the impacts or movement of pesticides and fertilizers in the

environment etc. To pursue a career in this you need to have a basic knowledge of Computer programming.

7. *Remote Sensing(RS) and Geographic Information System(GIS) techniques as Tools for Environmental Scientists* - RS and GIS are the key tools for mapping. It is to be borne in mind that RS and GIS are only Tools and not subjects by themselves. A person who wants to pursue a career in RS should have the knowledge of GIS and GPS. The RS techniques are useful for more or accurate spatial data collection and GIS is useful in processing as well as analysing the data. Both these techniques are widely used to map the natural resources, in forestry studies, impact assessment studies, weather and geological studies, crop inventory, yield prediction models, watershed development programmes.

ENVIRONMENTAL PLANNERS:

The tasks

1. Planning preservation of natural habitats, planning of transport systems, general planning of urban areas.
2. Implementation

ENVIRONMENTAL ENGINEERING:

The tasks

1. Designing, construction, and maintaining systems to control waste streams produced in urban and rural areas or by the industries.
2. Develop strategies for protecting areas under environmental threat.
3. Impose regulations for the protection of the environment.
4. Management of water and land resources.
5. Dealing with public health, terrain and water management.
6. Management of air pollution by dealing with air quality management and other special bodies that deal with emissions.
7. Management of hazardous waste.

ENVIRONMENTAL EDUCATION AND COMMUNICATION

The tasks

1. Teaching in college/school- awareness programmes
2. Coordinating community awareness programmes- rural and specific urban issues.
3. Working as guides for wildlife parks and sanctuaries

4. In public communication- television, radio and other media

ECO-TOURISM

The tasks

1. Development and preservation of flora and fauna in different parts of the country.
2. Education linking tourism and environment protection.
3. Study of tribal cultures, folk art forms, artefacts, temples, forest wealth and preservation of the same.
4. Archaeological restoration

ENVIRONMENT JOURNALISM

Growing public awareness has generated enthusiasm for environmental protection. People's voices are heard and repeated in the media. Reporting environmental issues such as nuclear tests, construction of dams etc. making of documentaries concerning the environment, production of films on environmental issues are areas environmental journalists have been exploring.

JOB DESCRIPTION

To put it simply you will be involved in the study of flora and fauna, pollution of air, water and soil. Today's workplace has environmental scientists and educationists, environment related technologists working in the laboratories and in close collaboration with oceanographers, botanists, zoologists etc. Environmental technologists design, construct and maintain systems for waste control in cities. Environmental scientists handle solid waste management, devising methods for disposing solid waste as well as reducing harmful contents in them.

Below is just a small list of some of the types of careers you can be involved in :-

1. Teacher- Secondary School focusing on outdoor/environmental issues through literature, science, history, politics teacher working at a school with an outdoor programme, educator at an Environmental Centre, Educator at an Outdoor Centre, Management Consultant focusing on corporate challenges and development.
2. Outdoor Trip Leader- Outward Bound, National Outdoor Leadership School, or similar programme, Programme Director/ Manager for outdoor centre, environmental centre, environmental organisation, conservation group.
3. Scientist- University setting, private foundation, environmental organisation, state or federal government. Lobbyist for an environmental organisation, conservation group.

4. Engineer working for an environmental consulting firm, environmental organisation, conservation group, state or federal government. Lawyer working for an environmental consulting firm, environmental organisation, conservation group, state or federal government.
5. Urban Planner/Architect working on a state or local level, Forest Ranger working for state or federal government, Fund Raiser for an environmental organisation, conservation group, Foundation researcher for an environmental organisation, conservation group international development agencies like UNDP, UNEP, Water Management Companies.

PLUS POINTS

1. Growing importance of profession, means professional growth too.
2. Careers available with a variety of employers: international bodies, national governments, corporate houses and NGOs.
3. As a general rule, specialisations where qualified talents are scarce, are usually well paid.
4. Chance to work in some interesting geographical locations.

MINUS POINTS

1. Work could be outdoors in rather unpleasant areas depending on your specialisation.
2. Field work can keep you away from home and family.
3. Possibility of physical danger in say forestry or oceanography related jobs.

A brief list of institutions where Environmental Science related studies can be pursued:-

1. Aligarh Muslim University, Aligarh, Uttar Pradesh-202 002
2. Cochin University of Science and Technology, Lakeside Campus, Cochin-682 016
3. School of Science- Gujarat University, Navrangpura, Ahmedabad-380 009
4. Indian Institute of Forest Management, Nehru Nagar, Bhopal-462 003
5. Indian Institute of Technology, C.E.E., Mumbai-400 076
6. Jadhavpur University, Calcutta-700 032
7. Jawaharlal Nehru University, School of Environmental Sciences, New Delhi- 110 067
8. Nagarjuna University, Deptt. Of Botany, Nagarjunasagar-522 510
9. Pondicherry Central University, Salim Ali School of Ecology, Kalapet, Pondicherry-14

10. Sambalpur University, School of Life Sciences, Jyoti Vihar, Burla-768 019

Quarrel not at all. No man resolved to make the most of himself can spare time for personal contention. Still less can he afford to take all the consequences, including the vitiating of his temper and loss of self control.

(h) ENTREPRENEUR

Career conscious individuals are always on the look out for options which are not only lucrative, but also satisfying. If one tracks the career graph of most of the successful personalities from the world of corporates, it is pretty clear that after a span of time, most of the so-called street smart and self-starting luminaries quit the organisation or the sectors they have served for years together in order to start off a venture of their own, might be in the same industry where they have gathered abundant experience or into any allied sectors or they might start off as consultants.

Examples like Phaneesh Murthy, ex-marketing head of Infosys Technologies starting his own set up, Vivek Paul, the erstwhile high flying head of Wipro Technologies, who has given an altogether new global image to the company and increased its turnover manifold, has joined an altogether new set up to leverage his long experience to do something more fulfilling.

There are also instances where fresh pass-outs kick off their career with their own start ups, more so, if they happen to represent new economy or knowledge sectors like Information Technology, Biotechnology, Pharmaceuticals where the availability of funds or capital investments are comparatively easier to gather through venture capitalists or angel investors, who became a talking folklore during the Information Technology boom.

If one sifts through the developments taking place in this sector of entrepreneurship, one can very well realise that the opportunities prevailing for a start up are tremendous, only the entrant has to get into the environment at the opportune time, with the necessary resources. Owing to extra pressure to sustain in a competitive market and the constant supervision of the boss and the stakeholders, most of the times, executives prefer to walk out of a company only to have flexible timings in the workplace and do things as per his or her own wishes and interests.

The necessary skill sets one has to possess in order to be a successful entrepreneur are as follows:

Self-starter. An entrepreneur has to be self starter. He has to take his own decisions from time to time and most importantly, he should be a self motivator, which enables him to drive the people around him, finally resulting in he realising his dreams. For instance, an engineer, who has worked for years together in the operations and R&D department of a lubricant manufacturing and marketing company, can start off his own venture at the local level after assembling the requisite resources, including the capital expenditure. More than his know-how in manufacturing lubricants, the drive to start off the set up from scratch is an absolute must. Half the aspirants of launching a start up fumble because they are not self starters.

Calculated risk taker: Calculated risk taking ability is an inherent quality of an entrepreneur. Dhirubhai Ambani would not have been a rags to riches story if he would not have possessed the ability of taking the risk of investing his hard-earned dinars in his synthetic rayon venture at Mumbai. The same holds true for Subrata Roy, Chief Managing Worker, Sahara Group, who started off with three colleagues and Rs.3,000/- as initial investment and has never looked back since. There are instances where, even an entrepreneur with little resources, could reach the pinnacle only on the basis of his risk-taking abilities.

An able Manager and Administrator: As an entrepreneur, one has to have managing and administrative qualities, which are the basic skills required to run the show. Managing all resources, starting from manpower, money, materials, minutes, with the required administrative capabilities are the essentials to be a successful entrepreneur. Although MBA has become synonymous with management and business administration, there are instances where, even non matriculates and college dropouts like Dhirubhai Ambani, Azim Premji of Wipro and Bill Gates of Microsoft have created a mark as successful entrepreneurs. But one should not forget the difference between exceptions and rule. The ones mentioned above are in a different league altogether.

So, one has to incorporate all these attributes before taking the plunge as the stakes to survive in this era of cut-throat competition are extremely high. The best way to go about it is to take a formal business management degree in order to supplement the basic degrees and industry experience the aspirant has gathered.

A prospective entrepreneur who has, lets say, worked on the shop floor, needs to understand all the nuances of business management viz.Marketing, Human Resources, Finance, Operations, Systems so as to maneuver an organisation. The all-round skills are the pillars of running the business and a one-dimensional approach won't suffice to be an entrepreneur.

(i) EVENT MANAGER

Event Management is a sunrise sector that is set to gallop in the coming years. Managing mega events is no longer an amateur operation but a full time profession that has thrown open a host of opportunities for dynamic youngsters. Imagine a ramp that creaks like a rickety staircase, arc lights that blink incessantly, smoke bombs that refuse to explode, models who trip on the catwalk, a music system that is an acoustic nightmare and a jury that gets into a mix-up in the run up to the results. It is such fiascos that make us knock on the doors of an event manager, the Mr Fix-it who carries an event from inception to fruition , taking care of all the hiccups.

***For Amateurs no more*:** There was a time when the back room managers were mostly amateurs. However, the boom in the infotainment industry, a plethora of TV channels and the phenomenal growth in the advertising budget of corporate houses have changed all that. In a short span, our homespun backroom boys have beauty pageants, musical fantasies, star studded extravaganzas and even political summits to their credit.

Potent promotion tool: On a mundane plane, event management is all about planning, organising and executing an event, which facilitates brand bonding with the consumer. The event, of course, could take the form of an exhibition, an exposition, a concert, a rock show or a cricket match. Companies have realised that events like sports, musicals and live concerts can work wonders for their brand and corporate image. Likewise, individuals might seek the help of professional planners to organise a theme wedding, a birthday bash, a book release, a film mahurat or a press conference. A team of event managers is, therefore, expected to conceptualise, create, innovate and take care of the logistical and technical details, design and décor and venue management. Conceptualisation means being able to see the event as a brand and tailoring it to suit the needs of the client. Creativity, of course, is the core ingredient, which sets one company apart from the rest. Innovation, a natural spin-off in the creative process, begins at the operational stage.

It's about multi-tasking: A regular event management company has five departments- (a) Client Servicing, which involves interaction with the client, understanding his needs and presentation of alternative solutions; (b) Production, which involves managing back end jobs like stage fabrication, sound and lights, projections etc; (c) creative, which involves visualisation and formulation of the appropriate message and the relevant ambience (d) operations, which involves dealing with vendors and managing the artists and (e) Sales and Marketing, which involves gathering marketing intelligence and making the sales pitch. Initially, youngsters are put into production, sales and client servicing . Technical expertise, experience and flair can take them into visualisation, operations and marketing, though this route is not strictly followed. However, the bottom line is talent which can take one anywhere.

Special Courses help: Earlier, an MBA degree was considered desirable, if one wished to pursue a career in event management. However, the phenomenal growth of the industry has spawned an avalanche of exclusive courses in event management. Professional courses help as they prepare one for the tasks ahead. While working on projects organised by the institute, one can gather a basic idea about different aspects like production and execution of events. To get an admission into a post graduate course, one should be a graduate from any stream; for a Diploma, one should have done at least plus two. Event management institutes provide practical training in the events at national level like Filmfare awards, Femina Miss India contest, Gladrags, Mumbai marathon, MTV music awards and many more.

Pre-requisites for success: While starry-eyed students might enrol for a course hoping to make it big in a few years, success often boils down to individual flair, talent and hands-on experience. To begin with, an aspiring event manager needs to be an organised person. Commitment and enthusiasm often takes precedence over age and experience. The key, therefore, is a right blend of hard work and dynamism.

The success of an event management team also depends upon its capacity to procreate themes that have never been thought of before. Again one should have an in-depth understanding of the product or the brand for which the event is being organised. An ability to comprehend technical details and a flair for design help one turn the presentation into a spectacle.

To sharpen your skills as an even manager, try organising programmes in your housing society. Most important are your networking skills. So, you should be a good public relations and marketing person. You should develop contacts in the corporate sector and be able to rustle up sponsors. Good contacts in the media are also an asset. If you can given value for money to sponsors, nothing can stop you from reaching the top.

The flip side: One the flip side, in event management, you can be propelled into the fast lane at an early age. Owing to tight deadline schedules, one can end up working marathon hours, often without sleep. One needs stamina, energy and a cool head to withstand the pressures.

Future scenario: The future outlook is extremely bright. This growing industry offers you a starting salary of Rs.8,000/- to 12,000/- per month. As it has been rightly pointed out, " Events begin where glamour ends".

(j) FORESTRY

Forestry is an important and interesting field of study. Forests from part of the vital natural resource systems of any country. India occupies approximately 2.5% of the total global geographic area, 1% forest area of the world that is supporting about 16% human population and 18% cattle population. The FSI Report (2001) states that the forest area of India is 76.8 million hectares or 23.38% of the total geographic area of the country, which is managed by the government through the Forest Department. From times immemorial forest resources have been a source of human sustenance providing it with a large number of direct and indirect benefits. It provides for with some of the most amazing herbs, medicinal plants, natural cosmetics etc. apart from the diverse wildlife found in it. It also helps in management of the ecosystem and watersheds, soil and water conservation in maintaining biodiversity and hydrological cycles and most importantly in carbon sequestration. Forest wealth also contributes significantly to the economy of the country as well as provides livelihood support to millions of people who live around forest areas particularly where agriculture is poor and mostly rain fed. Specially trained personnel are therefore required to maintain and regenerate the forest cover, forest wealth and resources.

Forest administration came into existence in India during the later part of the 19th Century. During the initial period, the timber orientation of the British and the German foresters was the theme of forestry management. In the pre-independence era, much of the wood from our forests was used in the development of railways in India and the shipbuilding industry in western countries. In the post-independence era, large-scale artificial plantations were raised on forestlands for improving productivity of forests so that more revenues could be generated. During this period, the forests became the victims of the focus on agriculture by diversion of forestland for agricultural and other uses. Large chunks of forest patches also made way for the large-scale multi-purpose irrigation projects. The Government set up the National Commission on Agriculture in 1976, which suggested the adoption of the *Social Forestry* program. After the introduction of the JFM program in 1990, the aim of forest management gradually changed to address regeneration of degraded forests patch by forest protection with people's participation. It was mainly conservation oriented and primarily meant for meeting the local needs of timber, fuel wood and Non-Timber Forest Products, particularly in rural areas.

Forestry till the 70s was a highly neglected subject. Till then only the Forest Research Institute and its associated institutes were offering forestry related courses. Apart from these courses, the Indian Forest Service was the other important program that held great mass appeal. Following the recommendations of the National Commission on Agriculture in 1976. Indian Institute of Forest Management was established in 1982 and 14 State Agricultural Universities and 5 general Universities initiated B.Sc. forestry courses. This was followed by 5 Universities offering M.Sc. and Ph.D. courses. In 1991, the University Grants Commission, Government of India granted Deemed University Status to Forest Research Institute, Dehra Doon for providing Post Graduate and Doctoral courses in forestry and environment.

FORESTRY- Sectoral Challenges and its importance in the Context of India

Presently, forest constitutes approximately about 20% area of the country i.e. approximately 76 million hectares of the forest area. The 1952 National Forest Policy had proposed to increase this to 33% of the total land area of the country. The total demand wood for paper and pulp industry is 8 million cubic meters while the annual fuel wood requirement for energy purposes is about 210 million tonnes. The total fodder requirement of India is approximately 1462 million tonnes of which nearly 830 tonnes is met from the forest. The quality of the forest is poor with degraded forest areas being the dominant forest type. However, the threat to forests have been ever increasing day by day as the population pressure on them increases. There is, therefore, a need for sustainable forest management of integrated water, biodiversity and forestry product development and development of agro forestry in the agriculture land.

A large number of products like fruits, tubers, roots, flowers and leaves are consumed by the villagers and sold in the market for livelihood support. Apart from these, there are a large number of indirect benefits from forestry like watershed services, soil and water conservation and carbon sequestration. This had lead to the loss of forest cover in all parts of the globe where poverty is high. Therefore, most Government and Non-Government agencies all over the world have started taking steps towards ensuring sustainable management of forests.

The concept of forest management requires sound policy and planning forest management is the practical application of scientific, economics and social principles to the administration of a forest estate for specified objectives. Forest management involves the control of composition and the structure of the growing stock, harvesting and marketing of forest produce/ products and administration of forest property and personnel.

Intensive forestry practices must be used to increase productivity of forests and maintain forest ecosystem. It will help in meeting the demands of industry as well as the local community. Social forestry was initiated in 1980 to meet the demands of the local people. Agro-forestry, a branch of forestry, also encourages to establish a sustainable land management system which could improve the existing system quantitatively and qualitatively, capable of deriving long term benefits, reduce environmental damage practically feasible and socially acceptable to the farmers.

As such, management of forest thereby assumes prime importance. For the sustainable management of forests, trained professional staff is therefore required in large number. Therefore, forestry education assumes prime importance in the context of India.

FORESTRY EDUCATION AND RESEARCH ABROAD

Forestry Education is well known in European countries with Germany occupying the topmost position. However, forestry education is fast taking root in many countries in the context of prevalent forestry situations. The following are a few examples of research organization prevalent in certain reputed forest research institute such as the Oxford Forestry Research Institute (United Kingdom), European Forestry Research Institute (Finland), New Zealand Forest Research Institute and the Forest Research Institute, Malaysia (FRIM). In addition, there are about more than 20 forestry schools and 8 research institutes in the United States and Canada combined, 15 forestry schools and 12 research institutes in the Europe and a few Australia and New Zealand. A number of Universities like University of California at Berkeley, Yale University, Oxford University, University of Reading, Queensland University, University of Toronto have very good forestry education and research programs. Apart from the above public institutions, there are a number of other international forestry organization like Center for International Forestry Research (Indonesia), Regional Community Forestry Training Centre for the Asia and Pacific (Thailand), International Centre for Integrated Mountain Development(Nepal), Overseas Development Institute (United Kingdom) and the World Forestry Institute (USA), Institute of Forestry (Nepal), Pakistan Forest Research Institute, Institute of Forestry (Bangladesh), Chinese Academy of Forestry are doing commendable work in the field of forestry.

A thematic approach to forestry research by bringing together of different disciplines for closer interaction has facilitated to a greater extent multi- or inter-disciplinary research within these organization. Such a structure has also fostered holistic, approaches to problems. Almost all forestry institutes in the western countries have adopted this inter-disciplinary approach.

FORESTRY RESEARCH AND TRAINING INSTITUTES IN INDIA

There are eight research institutes and one advanced centre under the Indian Council for Forestry Research and Education (ICFRE). The eight research institutes and one advanced centre are :-

1. Tropical Forest Research Institute(TFRI), Jabalpur(M.P.)
2. Arid Forest Research Institute(AFRI), Jodhpur(Raj.)
3. Temperate Forest Research Institute(TFRIS), Shimla(HP)
4. Institute of Forest Productivity(IFP),Ranchi(Jharkhand)
5. Institute of Wood Science and Technology (IWST),Bangalore (Kar.)
6. Institute of Forest Genetics & Tree Breeding (IFGTB),Coimbatore
7. Institute of Rain and Moist Deciduous Forest Research (IRMDFR),Jorhat
8. Centre for Social Forestry and Edo-Rehabilitation (CSFER),Allahabad

ELIGIBILITY FOR UNDERTAKING FORESTRY COURSES IN INDIA

Those with Physics, Chemistry and Biology at the intermediate level can go for a B.Sc. Forestry course. The Masters' level offer specialization in subjects like Forest Management, Commercial Forestry, Forest Economics, Wood Science and Technology, Wildlife Science, Tree Improvement, Genetics, Forest product Marketing etc. Those with Bachelors degree in related subjects can appear for Indian Forest Service (IFS) exam conducted every year by Union Public Commission of the Government of India an the State Forest Services (SFS) of the State Public Commission Board of the individual states. After IFS and SFS training they are appointed as Deputy Conservator of Forest/ Divisional Forest Officer and Assistant Conservator of Forest respectively.

CAREER OPTIONS IN THE FIELD OF FORESTRY

But what are the various career options after a degree in forestry? Career options are now as wide as it can get in forestry sectors and the sky is the limit for the go-getters. Based on the type of exposure one wants, one could enter the Non-Government Sector working in the field of forestry in rural areas. One could also join the forest based industry and the much-coveted Indian Forest Services where of course one has to go through the regular recruitment process. Between 1968 and 2001, the IGNFA has trained 2130 IFS Officers for postings in various states and there are bound to be several vacancies in the coming years. One could also take up advance course abroad after their primary degrees in India.

Other than the government and the NGO sectors, one can also chalk out a career in the forestry-based private sector by joining the various paper companies, timber and wood companies, saw mills and plantation companies. A motivated individual might also consider having ones own plantation company or wood products industry. A number of companies took up initiatives to raise raw material their industries like ITC, Bhadrachalam Paper Boards Ltd. WIMCO Ltd, JK Corps Ltd., Ballarpur Industries Ltd., Orient Paper Mills, Century Mills and Andhra Pradesh Paper Mill etc. require professionally qualified forest managers to run their show.

Apart from the professional courses, one could always take up Masters' and Ph.D. programs from one of the several universities and researches institutes in India and abroad and trace the career chart in the lines of education, extension and research in the field of forestry in India or abroad. The total outlay in the forestry sector for the 9th Five Year Plan was Rs.12,601/- crores and is expected to increase still further given its growing importance. There are a large number of areas that need further research in the field of forestry ranging from its technical to its social aspects.

Nowadays, one can also enrol as Chartered Foresters for providing technical assistance to the people willing to take up forestry on their private holdings. Though very common in some advanced countries, this arrangement is a recent development in India despite their being a demand for technical guidance for forestry to people in their private capacity. Under these provisions, any person or group of persons fulfilling certain eligibility criteria, including educational and technical qualification and professional experience may apply for enrolment as Chartered Forester and subsequently provide technical services of forestry to people on demands. Persons with a minimum degree of a B.Sc./ PGDFM in forestry along with a few years of work experience can be a Chartered Forester. The emergence of this institution of Chartered Foresters is a new concept to the private forest legislation in India.

Apart from these traditional lines there are always the international agencies working in the field of forestry. One could also consider joining the international donor organization like the World Bank, International Union for the Conservation of Nature and Natural Resources, World Wide Fund for Nature and Japan Bank for International Cooperation as Consultants, Advisors or Programme Officers for International exposure. Bilateral projects like Swedish International Development Agency, Danish International Development Agency, Canadian International Development Agency and Department for International Development also absorb professionals in forestry and environment/ development field. They are highly paying jobs and candidates with talent, knowledge and a fair amount of grassroots experience could always aspire to land such plum jobs in these agencies and carve a niche for themselves in the international arena.

(k) HOSPITALITY INDUSTRY

Do you love people and understand them? Do you like catering to the needs of others? Do some of these qualities from part of your personality? If communication skills and an outgoing personality is also a part of your persona, then hospitality industry is the perfect career. With the boom in tourism and travel industry, the hospitality industry has grown rapidly in the past decade and is still growing. The demand for manpower in this industry is on the increase. Hospitality industry offers career choices in hotels, restaurants, airlines etc. Here is a list of industries where you can make a career.

- Restaurant Management/ Fast Food Joint Management.
- Club Management/Recreation and Health Centre Management.
- Cruise ship Hotel Management.
- Institutional and Industrial Catering.
- Airline Catering and Cabin Services.
- Hotel and Catering Institutes.
- Hotel and Tourism Associations.
- Catering Departments in banks and Insurance houses.
- Govt. owned catering departments e.g. railway, armed forces, ministerial conventions et c.
- In food, confectionery, beverage production industries.

A degree in Hotel Management is usually the basic requirement to take the first step towards a career in the hospitality industry. Hotel management as a career stream is paying.

Where to Study

The National Council for Hotel Management and Catering Technology (NCHMCT) is a Registered Society under the Ministry of Culture and Tourism, Govt. of India. The Council regulates courses in Hospitality Management through structured courses of studies at 24 Institutes of Hotel Management and 8 Food Craft Institutes located in different parts of the country. The Council offers eleven different Professional Programmes designed for the Hospitality and Service sector.

The eligibility criteria to enter a course in hotel management is 10 + 2. Institutes coming under the National Council offer a 3-4 year diploma course while private institute offer a 4 year Bachelor's Programme. The selection procedure in most of these institutes comprises a test followed by a group discussion and interview. Here is a list of some of the Institutes in India that offer a diploma or degree programme in hotel management:- National Council for Hotel Management, Catering Technology and Applied Nutrition, Delhi;

- Institute of Hotel Management, Aurangabad
- Welcomgroup Graduate School of Hotel Management, Catering and Nutrition, Delhi
- Oberoi School of Learning and Development, Delhi

- International Institute of Hotel Management, Kolkata
- NIPS School of Hotel Management, Kolkata
- Institute of Hotel and Restaurant Management, Kolkata
- Subhas Bose Institute of Hotel Management, Kolkata
- Institute of Hotel and Tourism Management, Ghaziabad
- Canan School of Catering and Hotel Management, Chennai
- Moti Mahal Academy of Hospitality Education, Mangalore
- Shri Shakti College of Hotel Management, Hyderabad
- Institute of Hotel Management, Catering Technology and Applied Nutrition, Meerut

A degree in Hotel Management is however not absolutely essential for working in the hospitality industry. The industry requires trained staff for all these departments:-

Reception: This is the 'front end' of the hotel where candidates with good personality, patience and good grooming will excel.

Customer Relations: The public relations function will receive all the complaints and the occasional praise. They will need to coordinate with the other departments to maximise customer satisfaction. Candidates must have amiable personality and good communication skills.

Accounting and Financial Management: Commerce graduate and accounting professionals can find work here in accounting, cash flow and managing the finances.

The Back Office: The Reservations Officer in the back office must be qualified in ticketing, basic geography, calculating time zones, the international codes used by the hotel and airline industry etc.

Food & Beverage: A degree in nutrition or food technology will help you to get a job in this industry.

Horticulture: The grounds of a hotel or resort are embellished with beautiful gardens and exercise areas.

Communication and IT: Communication Engineers and System Administrators can find openings in this area of hotel management.

Whatever your qualification or the area you choose to specialise in, the pre-requisite for a career in this industry is to be able to handle people, it is about understanding people and their requirements. There is also a requirement for general management skills, which means that hospitality professionals have to continuously update their knowledge base and adopt innovative and out-of-the box thinking as well.

Once you have the requisite qualifications, sky is the limit for your career in this booming industry. Besides, the environment & working conditions are attractive and there is opportunity to meet all types of people.

(I) HOTEL MANAGEMENT

With the world becoming a melting pot of cultures, we seldom find places that do not serve a plethora of cuisines. In such a scenario, hotel management becomes a very lucrative profession. However, you have to dispel the notion of it being an easygoing path.

This profession requires tremendous hard work, dedication and above all, the aptitude to survive to an extremely competent environment.

ELIGIBILITY

The eligibility to enter a course in hotel management is class 12th. Institutes under the National Council a three year diploma while private institutes offer a four year Bachelor's programme. There is a two hour entrance test consisting of English, reasoning, general science and general knowledge, held around April every year. The test is followed by a group discussion and interview. Academic sessions usually start by July/ August. There are options of short-term courses also. One can join a food craft institute after class 10 or 12. Such institutes provide training in catering and food processing.

HOW TO CHOOSE AN INSTITUTE

One critical factor is the choice of the institute. The 19 institutes under the National Council follow a standardized curriculum prescribed by the council. There are the institutes run by hotel chains and finally the private institutes. Some institutes run by private hotels: Oberoi Centre for learning and development in Delhi, Taj Group's, Indian Institute of Hotel Management (IIHM) in Aurangabad, Welcomgroup's Graduate Hotel Management School in Manipal.

One should try to get into the chains of reputed hotels because one can get exposure to a working hotel. Getting into these institutes is very difficult, though.

ABOUT THE COURSE

There are a variety of subjects that are taught extensively during the course. They range from food production, food and beverage services, front office, and accommodation operations to application of computers, hotel engineering and accountancy. The course curriculum is quite interesting and forms an eclectic blend of topics. As you move on through the programme, you will be introduced to technical subjects like research methodology, quantity kitchen, financial management, facility planning etc.

PROSPECTS

With numerous hotels emerging in record numbers to cater to the evergrowing domestic and international traveller, the demand for trained professionals has multiplied in the country. Therefore, a career in the hospitality industry can be quite rewarding and stimulating.

(m) LOGISTICS AND SUPPLY CHAIN MANAGEMENT

After independence Logistics Service in India has grown-up rapidly. All forms of transportation Roads, Railways, Air, Sea and Inland Waterways are now available throughout the country. The industry is in fact an assortment of international shipping lines, worldwide logistics companies, big Indian private business houses, Government owned public sector undertakings, small to medium private companies and individuals – all contributing to its development. Without this spirited and dynamic logistics services, growth of India's foreign trade in the 1990's and beyond would have never been possible. India spends nearly thirteen percent of its GDP on logistics compared to an average of ten percent in other developing countries. This has created a need for a range of Logistics and Supply Chain Management Solutions ranging from logistics, supply chain, transportation and material handling to storage, warehousing, IT, Inventory management etc. that benefit the productivity and efficiency of the entire value chain in the multiple dimensions of customer service, costs, profits and speed. Better supply chain management, worldwide, has reduced logistics costs by nearly one percent in a decade. The Indian industry is looking at this improvement in the supply chain and logistics activities as a means to gain the competitive edge by adopting logistics and SCM concepts and practices.

LOGISTICS:- Council of Logistics Management defines logistics as part of the Supply Chain Management process that plans, implements and controls the efficient, effective forward and reverse flow and storage of goods, services and related information between the point of origin and the point of consumption in order to meet customers' requirements. Logistics Management activities typically include inbound and outbound transportation management, fleet management, warehousing, materials handling, order fulfilment, logistics network design, inventory management of third party logistics services providers. To varying degrees, the logistics function also includes sourcing and procurement, production planning and scheduling, packaging and assembly and customer service. It is involved in all levels of planning and execution—strategic, operational and tactical. Logistics Management is an integrating function, which coordinates and optimises all logistics activities, as well as integrates logistics activities with other functions including marketing, sales manufacturing, finance and information technology.

SUPPLY CHAIN MANAGEMENT-It covers planning and management of all activities involved in sourcing and procurement, conversion and all Logistics Management activities. It also includes coordination and collaboration with channel partners, which can be suppliers, intermediaries, third party service providers and customers. In essence, Supply Chain Management integrates supply and demand management within and across companies. Supply Chain Management is an integrated function with primary responsibility for linking major business functions and business processes within and across companies into a cohesive and high performing business model. It includes all of the Logistics Management activities noted above, as well as manufacturing operations, and it drives coordination of processes and activities with and across marketing, sales, product design, finance and information technology.

ADVANCED CONCEPT OF LOGISTICS

Logistics is comprised of many moving components that repetitively interact, constantly adding substance to an evolving process. The supposition that "logistics" is a chain is being challenged now, and it further rejects the concept that it is comprised of two distinct sides, supply and demand. The chain portrays logistics to be stagnant and linear; it also suggests that supply and demand is two separate chains. Logistics and supply/ demand chain are words that are wrongly used interchangeably and to describe each other. It, therefore, follows that the application and reasoning are circular, so, effective articulation, with resultant success, is impossible. These factors, tied with the belief that logistics is a chain have made the objective of world-class logistics excellence formless.

Most companies all over the world have embraced logistics and its significant in achieving superior customer service, operations and profit improvement. There has been a propagation of logistics software systems, products, tools and services over the last several years. They are obtainable by general developers. 3PL's (Third Party Logistics) and by other companies whose initial development purpose was for internal use. Further, there has been immense deal of dialog within and between companies, addressing the subject specifically for the benefit of those business partners. Additionally, the dialog is occurring in many forms such as, seminars, case studies, white papers, online communities, management presentations, lectures at educational institutions and advertisements. Through this labyrinth, little consensus has been achieved, therefore, diminishing the ability to achieve a higher level of logistics success as well as limiting effective collaboration. It is clear that the logistics discipline and practice needs to advance.

To understand the Logistics and Supply chain management we must discuss its vital aspects like warehousing, distribution, transportation, material handling equipments, storage, tracking systems, bar coding etc. in a systematic way.

The Logistics Services feature solutions & services ranging from third party logistics, warehousing, distribution, transportation, shipping, consulting, inventory management activities etc. that make logistics & supply chain operations of manufacturing, trading & service industry more efficient and competitive. The major components include: Transportation/Fleet Operators, Freight Forwarders, Warehousing & Storage, Shipping Lines, Parts & Terminals, Express Services- Courier, Air Freight Consultancy, Labelling & Packaging Solutions, Project Cargo/ Bulk Cargo/ Multi-modal.

The Logistics Technology provides solutions, ranging from tracking systems, bar coding, ADC, AIT, ERP, Enterprise IT Solutions, SCM collaboration software, e-business and WMS to software and telecom solutions which will give both the users and logistics service providers the competitive edge. In short the technological aspect features:- Tracking Systems, Telematics, Automatic Data Capture (ADC) & Bar coding, Enterprise IT Solutions ERP/CRM/SCM Software & IT Solutions for Logistics and SCM, E-business (e-commerce, e-procurement, e-SCM).

E-Commerce and Supply Chain Management:- Electronic commerce can significantly reduce operating costs, streamline cycle times and increase profitability through linking the marketing , operations, financial and logistics processes of individual firms into a information flow spanning an entire supply chain. Business-to-business relationships have frequently changed as these information flows have permitted 'virtual supply chains' to replace traditional ''bricks and mortar' infrastructure. Implementing IT for commercial operations requires the development of new strategies for using and managing this real-time information, redeploying inventories and building new inter company relationship.

The Module of Logistic Management Courses:- Resource planning, Customer relationship management, Logistics Operation & Services- 3pl, 4lpi, Integrated SCM and logistics- over view. Distribution Management, Multi Model Transportation, International Buying, Buyer, Buyer-Seller Relationship EDI, e-business in SCM, e-commerce, CRM, B2B Initiatives, E-Business and the Internet, Information, Hubs, Electronic Marketplaces, Logistics and E-commerce. Ware House Management, Layout, Material Handling, Inventory Management, Forecasting, Tracking, Quantitative Techniques, Value Chain Strategies, e-enabling supply chain & SQAP, TQM & ISO Standards. Benefits of e-Commerce to Supply Chain Management, Supplier/Buyer Integration, Import/Export Facilitation and Documentation, Steps to

Improve Supply Chain, Management via Internet Technologies, Current Status/ Diagnosis, future.

COURSES AND INSTITUTES

Certain institutions in India offer certificate, Diploma and PG Diploma courses in logistics and supply chain Management. The Confederation of Indian Industries Institute of logistics (CII-IL) offers certificate courses in logistics and distribution management. The Bangalore and Kolkata Centre of Indian Institute of Material Management also offers courses in logistics and supply chain management. Indian Institute of Management, Indore offers PG Dıploma in Logistics and Supply Management. Centre for Logistics and Integrated Materials Systems (C-LAIMS), NISIET (An Organisation of the Ministry of SSI, Govt. of India)Yousufguda, Hyderabad offers diploma in Logistics and SCM. Management Development Institute, Gurgaon has also designed courses on Logistics and Supply Chain Management. The Institutes of excellence overseas include Massachusetts Institute of technology (Sioan), Michigan State University and Stanford University in United States where special courses have been designed or the students of supply chain management.

JOB CATEGORIES

Stores and inventory Managers, Material Procurement Manager, Logistics Managers, Logistics and Supply Chain Executives, Project Managers etc.

WHERE TO FIND A JOB

Transport Companies, Shipping Industry, Cargo Companies, Warehousing and Freight Forwarding Services , loading and unloading services, Port Agencies, Multimode Transport Agencies etc. Firms like OTIS Elevators, GATI Management Services, Maruti Udyog Limited, TELCO, Britania Industry, Bombay Dyeing, DHL, AFL, Container Corporation of India Ltd., Aquamarine logistics, Dynamic Logistics, etc. also offer job opportunity in this field. Some of the leading logistic services providers worldwide include- Menlo Worlwide, 12 Technologies, QAD, Manugistics, American Software, Ligility, Peoplesoft , SAP, TNT and Oracle.

(n) MANAGEMENT ANALYST

Description

Conduct organizational studies and evaluations, design systems and procedures, conduct work simplifications and measurement studies, and prepare operations and procedures manuals to assist management in operating more efficiently and effectively. Includes program analysts and management consultants.

Experience

A minimum of two to four years of work-related skill, knowledge, or experience is needed for these occupations.

Education

Most of these occupations require a bachelor's degree.

Training

Employees in these occupations usually need several years of work-related experience, on-the-job training, and/or vocational training.

Tasks

1. Reviews forms and reports and confers with management and users about format, distribution, and purpose, and to identify problems and improvements.
2. Develops and implements records-management program for filing, protection, and retrieval of records, and assures compliance with program.
3. Prepares manuals and trains workers in use of new forms, reports, procedures, or equipment, according to organizational policy.
4. Recommends purchase of storage equipment and designs area layout to locate equipment in space available.
5. Gathers and organizes information on problems or procedures.
6. Documents findings of study and prepares recommendations for implementation of new systems, procedures, or organizational changes.
7. Analyzes data gathered and develops solutions or alternative methods of proceeding.
8. Confers with personnel concerned to ensure successful functioning of newly implemented systems or procedures.
9. Plans study of work problems and procedures, such as organizational change, communications, information flow, integrated production methods, inventory control, or cost analysis.
10. Designs, evaluates, recommends, and approves changes of forms and reports.
11. Interviews personnel and conducts on-site observation to ascertain unit functions, work performed, and methods, equipment, and personnel used.

(o) PROJECT MANAGEMENT

Did you know that Project Managers are right on top of the list of the 10 best paid contractual jobs in the world? Or that with outsourcing becoming the latest trend, Project Management and cross functional team building are going to be two functions in hot demand with the MNCs? Pick up any newspaper and you will see the record number of new openings for certified Project Managers, across sector.

Earlier, Project Management was thought to be applicable only to the construction sector. And there too, projects were executed more by chance than design, which explains why cost and time over runs have been a norm with most mega-budget projects in the public sector. However, these days, intensified competition does not allow even PSUs the luxury of indulging in such costly trial and error methodology.

Corporate houses everywhere want results and want them fast, delivered to exact specification. This is especially true of the IT sector, where, historically, project success has been extremely dismal - a mere 13 per cent, according to a KPMG survey conducted seven years ago. Worse, despite the growing off-shoring trend, different countries have different norms for rating project success.

To evolve a common system of practice, representatives of 36 countries got together in 1965, to prescribe a Minimum International Competency Baseline in the form of a time-bound, four-level Certification Scheme (QPMP), which is globally recognised and administered by Switzerland based, International Project Management Associates(IPMA).

In India, the certificate (QPMP) is administered by NOIDA – based Project Management Associates(PMA) that has been conducting this test twice a year (in June/July and December) since 2000. Open to graduates from any discipline who have a minimum work experience of three-four years. QPMP comprises an objective and subjective type paper that evaluates the candidate's understanding of complex project environments, cost estimations, earned values, project scheduling, risk and resource management, "Although some of these subjects have been covered under 'Operation Management' in a general MBA programme, students wishing to get specifically into the field of Project Management must try to obtain a formal certification in it ", recommends Ashish Kumar, Associate Professor (Finance) at Amity Business School, NOIDA. "This would definitely fetch them brownie points in the job market", he adds.

Professionals have also found the certification useful. "I enjoyed taking the exam, which answered a lot of may queries while handling mega projects for the Indian government", says Group Captain Sanjay Sharma , an ex-army man who took the QPMP last year.

Experts contend that Project Management (PM) can have tremendous implications for a resource starved country like India. "In China, PM has taken the form of a national movement. They are introducing it as part of the national curriculum in schools and colleges but in India we are all lagging far behind," says P.D.Karan, Executive Director, Project Management Associates, a non profit agency that certifies project managers in India. So far, a majority of the students who took the test were non MBAs with engineering backgrounds but as karan explains it is a useful qualification for anyone who wants to learn some basic fundamentals of project implementation and accountability.

However, Project Management can be best applied to telecom, power, finance and the IT sector, where, statistics indicate that the rate of project failure is still the highest (about 23 per cent). In 2003-2004, this resulted in the cancellation of 23 per cent of the IT projects while 49 per cent were adversely affected by cost and time over runs (Source:Standish Group,USA)

"Another area where Project Management principles are applicable is the NGO sector", says Karan, "where it dramatically improves our response to emergency events and the management of limited resources".

Work experience, however, is essential if you wish to extract the full benefit from the certification, as otherwise, "students are not able to correlate theory to actual work situations", says Ruchira Jain, QPMP Director at PMA. She also says that most of her students come from junior to middle rung management levels, "although lately the programme has begun to attract a few CEOs." The bottomline is that Project Management is not just about writing copious reports or making interesting power point presentations. It also involves better performance, better profits and better accountability. "Companies that don't (or can't) invest too heavily in R&D can stay competitive merely by resorting to project planning," says Karan.

Small wonder then that a number of employers these days (especially from the public sector) are footing the certification cost of their managers. A recent study indicates that certified Project Managers earn 30 to 40 times higher salaries than their counterparts in other divisions. And in more than 50 per cent of the Fortune 500 companies there is a dedicated "Project Management Cell".

(p) PROPERTY, REAL ESTATE AND COMMUNITY ASSOCIATION MANAGERS

Description

Plan, direct, or coordinate selling, buying, leasing, or governance activities of commercial, industrial, or residential real estate properties.

Experience

A minimum of two to four years of work-related skill, knowledge, or experience is needed for these occupations.

Education

Most of these occupations require a bachelor's degree, but some do not.

Training

Employees in these occupations usually need several years of work-related experience, on-the-job training, and/or vocational training.

Tasks

1. Manages and oversees operations, maintenance, and administrative functions for commercial, industrial, or residential properties.
2. Directs collection of monthly assessments, rental fees, and deposits, and payment of insurance premiums, mortgage, taxes, and incurred operating expenses.
3. Meets with clients to negotiate management and service contracts, determine priorities, and discuss financial and operational status of property.
4. Plans, schedules, and coordinates general maintenance, major repairs, and remodeling or construction projects for commercial or residential property.
5. Investigates complaints, disturbances, and violations and resolves problems following management rules and regulations.
6. Recruits, hires, and trains managerial, clerical, and maintenance staff, or contracts with vendors for security, maintenance, extermination, or grounds-keeping personnel.
7. Directs and coordinates the activities of staff and contract personnel and evaluates performance.
8. Maintains records of sales, rental or usage activity, special permits issued, maintenance and operating costs, or property availability.
9. Purchases building and maintenance supplies, equipment, or furniture.
10. Develops and administers annual operating budget.
11. Negotiates for sale, lease, or development of property, and completes or reviews appropriate documents and forms.
12. Inspects facilities and equipment and inventories building contents to document damage and determine repair needs.
13. Assembles and analyzes construction and vendor service contract bids.

14 Confers with legal authority to ensure transactions and terminations of contracts and agreements are in accordance with court orders, laws, and regulations.

15. Maintains contact with insurance carrier, fire and police departments, and other agencies to ensure protection and compliance with codes and regulations.

16. Prepares reports summarizing financial and operational status of property or facility.

Meets with prospective leasers to show property, explain terms of occupancy, and provide information about local area.

(q) WEDDING MANAGEMENT

If marriages are made in heaven, there has to be price to pay. And the swish set- whether based in Delhi or abroad- is quite content to dole out a few lakhs here and there as long as the *Shaadi* is a replica of the wedding sets of Sooraj Barjatya's, Hum Saath Saath Hain. The budget takes care of the venue, food, decoration, dance and music.

And to top it all, you no longer need to approach different people in different fields any more. Hire a wedding manager/ planner and see the extravaganza fall into place.

Says Vikas Gutgutia, Managing Director, Ferns N' Petals Group of Companies, a leading wedding management company, "With the increase in spending potential and growing awareness about lifestyle and image projection, people are ready to spend lavishly on weddings. As a consequence, wedding management is fast becoming a lucrative career option today. A wedding manager is required to coordinate with service providers like caterers, decorators, mehndiwalis, make arrangements for the ladies sangeet and other 'performances' as per the client's budget".

While wedding management was once considered part of event management, today it is fast emerging as a totally independent and promising career option. Says Triptee Chaudhary, Wedding Planner: Shaadionline, "Wedding management means planning, coordinating and executing the entire wedding to the last ritualistic detail, in a systematic fashion. Like all other areas where professional expertise is required, today too, a wedding is looked upon as a project to be handled and executed professionally. It would consist of understanding what a family may want to put together (in terms of budget and taste), sourcing vendors/ agencies who would provide the required services and ensuring the smooth flow of functions and ceremonies".

As far as salaries go, a Designer (Operations) in a wedding management company can get anywhere between Rs.6,000-Rs.20,000, Staffers with Food and Beverage background Rs.6,000/- -

Rs.25,000/- and Florists Rs.3,500 – Rs.15,000/-. A person who runs such a company could net profits worth Rs.12 lakhs per year.

However, not every one is cut out to be a wedding planner, Says Meher Sarid of Wedding Art, Sound of Music, "You have to be aware, organised, have practical architectural knowledge and be able to adhere to deadlines. Since you will be into organising functions/ parties, it is necessary to have a Food and Beverages background to start with".

Adds Gutgutia, "Any graduate can become a wedding planner provided he/she has good communication skills, is pleasant and friendly and has a positive attitude".

"The ability to perceive what the family needs, the sensitivity to understand and handle difficult situations patiently and the confidence to manage any crisis are important pre-requsites, " Says Chaudhary.

The best way to train as a wedding planner is to work for a wedding management company as an intern.

Ferns N' Petals is setting up a Flower Management Institute to fill the lacunae for professional training in this field. "The institute (slated to open by March next year) will run courses in flower arrangement and Event Management (pertaining to weddings)," Says Gutgutia. A note of caution: do not expect instant returns, "Students who want to take up this career need to understand that this is not a glamorous job. It involves a lot of stress, pressures and long working hours. Since you are taking on the client's burden, everything is your responsibility. The success of the wedding is based on options you have put together and suggested to the client" says Chaudhary.

The onus is on you!

3

Architect

(a) ARCHITECTURE

The construction industry in any economy is the mirror of its growth and prosperity. In the last few decades there has been a boom in this industry. Building Complexes, from small roads to national highways, every big and small human pursuit entails building and construction. It is a multifarious industry employing a variety of talents, experts and technologists. The construction industry covers two broad functions - A technical one where in a design is evolved and the other which gives shape to the design.

Architecture deals with design, plan of buildings and structure. This vast field comprises creative, technical and craft aspects. The architect is responsible for the planning, designing and supervising construction works. An architect has to keep in view consideration of stability, utility and beauty while planning and designing all civil works. A client's requirement of appropriate, safe and economical shelter are satisfied through efficient planning, and by devising pleasant interior space and a beautiful exterior. The building is planned in such a way as to impart to beauty, grandeur and interest. Appropriate use of suitable structure techniques and economy in building material are always kept in view. An Architect would design the work by visiting the site to survey the area on which the structure is to be built. He consults clients, plans lay out of structures and prepares sketches of proposed buildings. The final design shows the exact dimensions of every position of the building including the location of electrical outlets, plumbing and air-conditioning etc. An architect should be aware of the local building rules and regulations, climatic conditions, soil etc. He should also be familiar with the construction methods and materials to be used. In designing homes people often stress decorative over functional design. Clients approach architects with the idea as to how their homes should look like. It is for the architect to strike a healthy balance between aesthetics and functionality. Detailed plans are prepared for approval of the client. At times, a number of designs may have to be prepared with different lay-outs to give the client a wider choice. After client's approval, the design is finalised, blue prints are prepared and submitted to the local authority (cantonment boards, municipal corporations, improvement trusts) which sanctions the plan, after satisfying itself, that the plan conforms with the prescribed building rules and bye-laws. Having got the sanction of the local authority, detailed working drawings are prepared, giving complete instructions and information to contractors and engineers. Estimates of materials, equipment, cost and building time are prepared to ensure economy and to facilitate calling of tenders by the client.

There are town and country planners who ensure best utilisation of land at their disposal. A planner designs layout and coordinates, development of towns, cities and colonies taking into consideration various aspects such as financial resources, location of residential areas, industries, schools, parks etc. The town planner presents his plan in the form of a model or a chart of sketching. The design of a building involves far more than its appearance. Building should be safe, economical and suitable to the needs of the people. These all aspects are taken into consideration while designing a building. The architect has to discuss various aspects of the building with the client including estimated budget available. It is the responsibility of the architect to obtain building permission from the local authority, prepare and negotiate contracts with building contractors, civil engineers and surveyors etc. He often visits sites for monitoring the progress as per specifications.

Architects design a wide variety of buildings, offices, schools, factories, temples, churches, hospitals, houses, airport terminals, flyovers, bridges, shopping centres, residential colonies and apartments etc. Advice is also given by the Architect to plan, improve or beauty landscapes, highways, towns, estates, historical buildings etc. Alterations, additions, extensions and adaptation to existing buildings are also planned. Service is also rendered in preparing land surveys and in evaluation of lands and buildings for insurance, sale, mortgage, transfer, taxation and other purposes. The work of an architect is varied, interesting and creative and offers opportunities to both men and women. They have to work with engineers, planners, interior decorators and other professionals.

Personal Characteristics

Should have an aptitude for drawing and sketching. Should possess an amicable temperament as her/she has to deal with people from variety of backgrounds, should possess creativity and imagination. Spatial knowledge is very much required. Mathematical ability for working out estimated costs. Should be able to understand legal language related to the profession. Flexibility and patience are considered an asset. Excellent communication skills, keen sense of observation, appreciation of colours and proportions, hard work and perseverance are considered key words in this profession.

Training Facilities

One needs specialized training for becoming an architect. Various polytechnics offer three year diploma in Architectural Assistantship. This programme is open to matriculates with 60% marks. The diploma may be upgraded to the level of degree by passing the four year course conducted by the Institute of Architects. The requirements for this course is three years diploma with 2 years work experience. The admission to diploma course is based on marks secured in qualifying examination or through an entrance test of objective nature. For admission to 3 years Diploma in Engineering Trades including architecture in polytechnics in Delhi, Common entrance test is conducted by GGSIP University, Delhi.

There are more than 100 institutes which impart training in the field of architecture. The minimum educational qualification for admission to degree course is 10+2 with English, Science and Maths with at least 60% marks. In most of the institutes, the selection is through an entrance exam. The entrance exam. Is of objective type consisting questions pertaining to general awareness, English and general intelligence including aptitude test. Duration of the course is generally 5 years. In some institutes the weightage is given to the marks obtained in qualifying exam also.

Some of the Reputed Institutes are :

1. TVB School of Habitat Studies, Vasant Kunj, New Delhi-110 070
2. Sushant School of Art and Architecture, Gurgaon-122 001
3. College of Architecture, Bandra, Mumbai-400 051
4. Vastu Kala Academy, 9/1, Institutional Area, Aruna Asaf Ali Marg, New Delhi-110 067
5. Govt. College of Arch., Lucknow-226 002
6. Chandigarh College of Arch, Chandigarh-160 012
7. College of Arch, Goa University, Goa-403 001
8. Sri J.J.College of Arch, Dr.D.N.Road, Mumbai-400 001
9. College of Arch.,Shivaji Path, Kolhapur-416 012
10. School of Planning and Arch.,Hyderabad-500 028
11. Centre for Environment and Planning Tech.,Navrangpura, Ahmedabad0380 009
12. Birla Institute of Tech., Mesra Bihar

13. IIT Kharagpur-721 302
14. School of Arch. and Planning, Chennai-600 025
15. School of Architecture, Indore-452 001(Affiliated to Devi Ahilya University, Indore)
16. (Affiliated to Guru Gobind Singh, I.P. University, New Delhi)

School of Planning and Arch.,New Delhi-110 002 offers two courses at undergraduate level (i) 5 years B. Arch (68 Seats) and (ii) 4 years B Planning (20 Seats) through All India Engineering/ Architecture Examination (AIEEE) conducted by CBSE, New Delhi. Only those candidates who have passed 10+2 with Physics and Maths and anyone of the following Chemistry, Computer Science, Biology and Engineering drawing are eligible for admission to B.Arch Course. The exam consists of paper on Maths and an aptitude test. The exam. is held in May at various centres. The cost of the examination bulletin inclusive of examination fee is Rs.300/- for General Category and Rs.150/- for SC/ST candidates. The Institute also offers PG (three semester) degree programmes. There is also facility for research leading to a PhD in all disciplines taught at the Institute. Sushant School of Architecture offers 5 years B.Arch Course for 10+2 (50% with English and Maths) from any discipline not necessarily science students. Selection is through a written test conducted by GGSIP University, New Delhi. IITs (Kharagpur and Roorkee); School of Planning and Arch, Hyderabad, Nagpur University etc. also offer PG Courses in Arch. The educational requirement for admission to PG courses is B.Arch.

Employment Opportunities

Ample employment opportunities are available in Centre/State Govt. Following organizations Deptt. Offer ample employment opportunities to architects.

Departments:- Centre/ State- Public Works Departments; Irrigation Projects; Railways; Defence Services; Flood Control Boards; Central Water & Power Commission, Road Research Institute, Housing Boards, Cooperative Societies and various other construction units and agencies. Ministry of Urban Development is responsible for, construction and maintenance of the Central Govt. buildings, houses for Central Government employees and for management of Central Govt. land and property. It handles a wide range of projects such as housing, educational institutes, sports complexes, hospitals, factories, hostels, airports, roads, bridges, flyovers etc. through its attached and subordinate offices such as CPWD, National Building Organization and Town & Country Planning Organization. Besides these organizations, there are various other undertakings- Housing and Urban Development Corporation, New Delhi; National Building Construction

Corporation Ltd., New Delhi Hindustan Prefab Ltd., New Delhi who offer good job opportunities to architects. Various city development authorities such as DDA, Ghaziabad Development Authority etc. are involved in various types of construction activities. Housing societies also construct residential accommodation to meet the growing need of houses. In big cities due to growth of population at an alarming rate, the existing roads are not able to meet the demand of transport. The flyovers are being constructed to meet the growing demand. In Kolkata and Delhi even metro-rail projects have been taken up. Ministry of Railway, Defence and various public sector undertaking take up lot of construction work. All these activities require the services of architects besides other construction workers. Many architects prefer to set up their own practice. The teaching department of schools of architecture and town planning, engineering colleges, polytechnics also offer good job opportunities.

4

Art

(a) ACTING

Actors work either for stage performances or in films, television and radio. Some actors specialize in one medium.

In brief, the following tasks are performed by an actor:-

- Study scripts in order to understand the part they are playing.
- Rehearse their roles and discuss their character with the Director and other actors they are working with.
- Perform their kroles before a live audience, a microphone, or a camera.
- Use props, costumes, verbal and facial expressions to convey ideas.
- Work with other crew members responsible for lighting, costumes, makeup and props.
- Promote the production through various media.
- In some roles, actors may be required to sing and dance.

Entry to this overcrowded profession is extremely difficult. There are usually no minimum educational qualifications for becoming an actor. However, since acting is involved with so many facets of our society, a college degree helps one to be better prepared for the challenges of the profession.

Admission to premier schools of drama and acting is open only to graduates with very few exceptions.

Training

While formal training is helpful, experience and talent are more critical for success. Degree/Diploma course in acting are conducted at premier training institutions as well as University Departments of Arts/Dramatic Arts/ allied departments.

Some of them are:-

- Dr. B.R. Ambedkar Marath-wada University, Aurangabad-431004 (Bachelors Degree in Drama)
- Madurai Kamraj University, Madurai-625021 (Diploma in Dramatics)
- University of Mysore, Mysore-570005 (Diploma in Film Acting)
- Faculty of Fine Art, Rabindra Bharati University, Kolkata-700050 (BA and MA course in Drama)
- University of Rajasthan, Gandhi Nagar, Jaipur-302004(PG Diploma and BFA in Dramatics)
- Sambalpur University, Jyoti Vihar, Burla, Sambalpur-768019 (BA in Drama)
- Faculty of Performing Arts, M.S. University of Baroda, Vadodara-390002 (BPA and MPA in Acting and Dramatics)
- Pondicherry University, Kalapet, Pondicherry-605014 (BPA)
- University of Hyderabad, Hyderabad-500046 (MPA in Theatre Arts)
- Bhartiya Natya Academy, Lucknow-226010 (Dip. In Acting)
- Punjab University, Patiala (Dip.in Dramatic Art)
- Andhra University, Weltair (Dip. In Acting)
- Satyajit Ray Film and Television Institute, Kolkata-700094
- Film & TV Institute of Tamil Nadu, Chennai-600113
- Image Acting School, Film City, Noida-201301
- Asian Academy of Film & Television, Marwah Studios Complex, FC-14/15,Film City, Sector 16A, Noida-201301
- Film and Television Institute of India, Law College Road, Pune-411004
- Rai University, Mathura Road, New Delhi-110044 (BPA in Acting & Choreography)
- National School of Drama, Bahawalpur House, Bhagwandas Road, New Delhi-110001 (3 year Diploma in Drarmatic Arts)

Eligibility

Graduate, participation in at least 10 productions, working knowledge of Hindi and English. Age 18-30 years. Selection through a preliminary test followed by a workshop in NSD premises.

With the increasing number of new cable TV channels, strong demand for commercials growth of regional theatre and with a steady stream of new films, there will be jobs for the skilled, and talented actors. Despite the growth in opportunities, competition for roles is extremely keen because the glamour associated with this profession attracts large number of individuals. So only the most dedicated and determined will find steady work in this fiercely competitive market.

(b) **Indian Fine Arts - DANCE**

WE ALL choose careers with a lot of contemplation: after all it is going to define our life, our whole existence. The world is abundant with opportunities; we just need to define for ourselves what we really want to do and would love to.

Here very important to introduce an unconventional area of work and career. DANCE......... not many of us venture in this area; but the few who do are sthe stalwarts like...... Birju Maharaj, Padmashri Guru Jay Rama Rao & Vanashri Rao, Radha and Raja Reddy, Mallika Sarabhai, Sudha Chandran just to name a few.

What is dance?

Dance is a visually powerful art form. It uses vivid and eloquent mudras for communication. Dance communicates man's deepest, highest and most truly spiritual thoughts and emotions far better than words, spoken or written. It is used effectively to convey some meaning, emotion and cultural values. Dance is the limitation of our own action, reaction and conviction presented in sophisticated gesticulation, exploiting the body, mind and soul. A dancer dissolves her identity in rhythm and music, and makes her body an instrument for experience of the soul. Martha Grayham has said, "Dance is a song of the body; either of joy or pain".

The expression of Dance in India has seeped into several other realms like poetry, sculpture, architecture, literature, music and theatre. The earliest archaeological evidence is a beautiful statuette of a dancing girl's dated around 6000 B.C. Bharata's Natya Shastra (believed to be penned between second century B.C. and second century A.D.) is the earliest available treatise on dramaturgy. All forms of Indian classical dances owe allegiance to Natya Shastra regarded as the fifth Veda.

Indian dance is a blend of nritta- the rhythmic elements; nritya- the combination of rhythm with expression and natya- the dramatic element.

Nritta is the rhythmic movement of the body in dance, pure dance. It does not express any emotion.

Nritya is usually expressed through the eyes, hands and facial movements.

Nritya combined with nritta makes up the usual dance programmes. Nritya comprises abhinaya, depicting rasa (sentiment) and bhava (mood). To appreciate natya or dance drama, one has to understand and appreciate Indian legends. Most Indian dances take their themes from India's rich mythology and folk legends.

In the study of dance the entire body is divided as Anga, Pratyanga and Upaanga, Anga:Head, Hands, Chest, Waist, Bottom, Legs and Neck.

Pratyanga: Shoulders, Arms, Stomach, thighs, Knees, Wrist, elbow and Ankle.

Upaanga: Sight, Eyebrow, Eye lids, Eye Balls, Cheeks, Nose, Gums, Lower Lip, Teeth, Tongue, Chin and Face.

Classical Dance Forms of India

India offers a number of classical dance forms, each of which can be traced to different parts of the country. Each form represents the culture and ethos of a particular region or a group of people. They are extremely intricate art forms requiring skill, hard work and discipline portraying some expression of life and almost every posture herein has a specific meaning.

Principles of classical dance have their origins in the Vedas which detail the forms of dance and drama Dance is considered to be a form of worship and meditation. Many Indian classical dancers credit Nataraja (the Hindu deity Shiva depicted as lord of the dance) with teaching mankind how to dance. You may be familiar with his image-balanced on his right leg, his left leg lifted across his body and his four arms flared in different positions. While Nataraja has come to personify classical Indian dance, he is more than a depiction of movement. The deity represents myth, symbolism and mysticism everything classical Indian dance embodies.

The Indian classical dance involves body as well as mind. The major dance forms very briefly are :-

Bharatnatyam

The dance form is based on 'Adavu' (Steps) and 'Hasta Mudra' (handgestures). The dancer artistically tells stories and events from the epics through mudras (movements of the hand and feet) and facial expressions. This dance is poetry in motion. Bharatnatyam gives importance to Padartha Abhinaya. The music of Bharathanatyam is based on Carnatic Classical Music.

Mohiniyattam

The theme of Mohiniyattam dance is love and devotion to God. Mohiniyattam gives more imdportance to gestures and facial acting. The expression which is shown to express poetic meaning, is Abhinaya, Navarasas (Nine Moods) comes under the Abhinaya or Expression part in dance. The music used in Mohiniyattam is based on Classical or Semi-Classical compositions.

Kathakali

Kathakali is the classical dance-drama of Kerala. It is a complete art, which constitutes the three fine arts- Abhinaya (acting) and Nritya (dancing) and Geeta(Music). A Kathakali actor enacts his ideas sthrough mudras. Kathakali characters communicate through the language of hand-gestures, body movements and facial expressions. All its themes are selected from the great Indian epics. Kathakali music has developed into a distinctive type of singing known as the sopana style. Only men, originally performed Kathakali with female characters played by men, but in recent years women have also joined the league.

Kathak

The word Kathak, derived from 'Katha', literally means storyteller. In Kathak, more emphasis was laid on nritta, the pure dance aspect and less on abhinaya. Tatkar is the basic footwork of kathak. It is the fundamental footwork from which all other foot sounds and compositions are created. Dancers perform Kathak keeping their bodies straight. Both men and women perform Kathak dances. Kathak is bound with classical Hindustani music and the table d or pakhawaj accompanies the rhythmic nimbleness of the feet.

Kuchipudi

Kuchipudi is originated as a form of dance drama with religious themes. Kuchipudi gives importance to Vakyartha Abhinaya (use of words or dialogues). According to tradition men of the Brahmin community originally perjform this dance. It has a rich repertoire of Kalapas and yakshagnas, dance dramas and solos. Kuchipudi music is based on pure classical ragas and taalas.

Manipuri

The technique of Manipuri dancing is based on an interesting principle of compensatory movement with the objective of achieving rounded movements and avoiding any jerks, sharp edges or straight lines. Manipuri dances are devotional or ritualistic rather than entertainment of the eyes. The Mudra's or hand movements in Manipuri dance are quite different from other classical dance forms. Dhak, Kartal, Mangkang and Sembong are the soul of Manipuri Sankritana music and Classical Manipuri Dance

Odissi

Odissi is a graceful style of classical dance that is inspired thematically by the literature, art and spiritual movements of the Vaishnaya (worshippers of Vishnu). It was performed in the temples of Orissa as a religious rite and offering by the Devadasis known as Maharis. Odissi presents a fine synthesis of lasya (feminity) and Tandava aspects of the Indian Classical Dance. The dance numbers are either in Sanskrit or Orissi and the music is a combination of Hindustani and Carnatic classical styles.

Besides the various category of dances, there are several semi-classical dances that contribute to the plethora of Indian dances. Apart from the classical dances, India is particularly rich in folk idioms. Each area has its own special varieties, be they martial, seasonal, ritual, sacrificial, celebratory, instructional or talismanic. It can vary from village to village, but they all share a common heritage of myths and symbols. Some of the folk forms of India are Chhanu dance of Bihar, Garba of Gujarat and Bhangra of Punjab and Banjara of Andhra Pradesh, to name a few.

Apart from these classical, semi-classical and folk dance forms one can also learn the western dance forms like salsa, living, cha cha cha, tango etc. if one wants to experiment with a new dance form.

Career Options

Career options available in this area are that of performer,teacher and choreographer.

Performing

For individual stage performance one needs to work really hard on the basics of the form. This needs consistent practice to hone up the skills immaculately. One needs to work on the areas like one's appearance, rhythm, expression, interpretation of roles and stage presence. Besides professional training; dedication, talent and the right contacts can only help a performer to become well established. Performing artists can form their own troupes or even work with other troupes. They also have the option of starting schools and devote time for teaching.

Teaching

Being a teacher i.e. Guru is equally prestigious. For this one must have thorough knowledge of the practicai and theoretical aspects of the form with a perfect sense of rhythm, and some proficiency in music. Moreover, one needs to have an aptitude to teach, with a lot of patience and perseverance.

Dancers who take up teaching as a profession can find opportunities in schools, colleges, universities, dance institutes and even ope schools or academics of their own.

Choreography

The choreographer designs and composes dance sequences and co-ordinates the stage settings, music, costumes and supervises rehearsals. Choreographer must have creative or imaginative powers and an ability to interpret music and compose dance routines for solo as well as group performances. They must be able to work along with a team. Prospects in this field are expanding with more and more stage and TV shows.

Choreographers can find employment in troupes performing stage shows, TV shows and in films.

Job Prospects

One can find employment in Kala Kendras, Academics, TV channels, Dance troupes.

Eligibility and Course Areas

Though it needs to be an inborn talent, there is no doubt that it can be developed through professional training as training and guidance can only sharpen these talents. Training in Dance should start as early as age six or less.

Educational

To take up a course in this subject the basic requirement is 10 + 2. However, for post graduate level courses graduation in the subject is compulsory. Courses offered in this area are certificate courses, bachelor courses, diploma courses and postgraduate level courses. Duration of various courses, Certificate course is of one year, Bachelor courses is of three years, Diploma and Post Graduate level courses is of two years.

The Kathak Kendra in Delhi, the Kalakshetra in Chennai, Bharatiya Kala kendra in Delhi are some of the prominent institutes conducting courses in Dance. Course areas include history and evaluation of dance and dance forms, the characteristic features of the dance form one specializes in covering all aspects of dance as a performing art.

Personal Attributes

To excel in this field one needs to have love and devotion for the art, humility, grace, apart from talent, versatility, sense of rhythm, an expressive facial and body language, ability to interpret roles, creativity, physical stamina etc.

Another area that widens the horizons of dance and makes it something more than just a mere art form is its new found emergence in the field of Psychotherapy.

Taking the basics of dance as a medium of expression of ones deepest thoughts expressions it has evolved as a therapeutic took known as Dance therapy, or Dance movement therapy (sometimes referred to as choreotherapy). It is the psychotherapeutic use of movement (and dance) for emotional, cognitive, social, behavioural and physical conditions. It is a special form of creative therapy. Dance therapy is based on the premise that the body and mind are interelated.

Mental and emotional problems can result in muscle tension and constrained movement patterns compounding the original condition. Conversely the state of the body can affect mental and emotional wellbeing both positively and negatively.

The name Dance Movement therapy is more precise, because this form of therapy is not about achieving, defined forms of dance. Even standing still is considered a dance. Among therapists there is still a debate whether music should be used.

Dance therapy can be applied to all form of psychic and psychosomatic disorders. Through the experience in movement and dance, patients are not only touched physically but also emotionally, mentally and spiritually.

It is always said that there are no dearth of opportunities. It is just that one has to be extremely positive about oneself and life of course. What you need is to just clearly choose and define your goals, love yourself for your choice, take charge of your life and get going in no one can stop you from winning the world.

Dance as if you were born to dance......... make the world a better place...... happy dancing!!!

(c) MAGIC

Since time immemorial magic has been a part of our entertainment stream in India and the Magicians have been making the show as a remunerative economic activity. But in recent days magic as a profession is being used as a showpiece to attract gatherings and make money by using non-professional tactics and tricks. Such so-called magic shows lose their value and importance among the general public. In ancient time, magic was taught as a subject in Nalanda, Takshila and Avantipur Universities.

The field of magic survives today because of the efforts of a few magicians all over India. Prof. K.C. Pandey, President of Magical Academy of India and a practicing magician for 33 years, expresses his grief by saying that it is a "dying art". In India magicians have personally preserved this art without any support from the Government. The Government could have played a major role in promoting and developing, this art by opening academies/ museums/institutions. However, Mr. Sudhanshu Das a practicing magician from Guwahati feels that there is still scope. "These days it is difficult to find a magician who takes to the art of magic as a profession". Magic is an art based on science and techniques. Prof.Pandey takes immense pride in magic. It is beautified with the dexterity of hands and creates an illusion for eyes. One can do wonders with magic. It is a science of fun and frolic. The performance of magic eliminates superstition from the society and provides healthy entertainment, which is good for viewing of family members. It can be understood in spite of language barriers.

Of the younger lot, there are some who have the inclination to take magic seriously. However, they bear several misconceptions in mind. Once confronted with reality they wander away. Prof. Pandey says " Several young people come to learn magic since they believe that it's all about casting spells. They want to learn the magic to hypnotize a girl/boy of their choice. But when they come to know that magic is an art based on pure science and techniques, which requires investment in magical instruments and intensive practice, they disappear".

Competition in the entertainment industry is getting complicated day by day. Mr. Sudhanshu Says "with so much entertainment available, Magicians need to change and equip themselves suitably with latest magic materials and instruments, which involves huge expenditure. So any magician who has the talent of marketing his magic performance needs good sponsors to make the show with illusive items and costumes". He may also practise magic in the from of Magic Therapy. It has worked wonders in the field of medicine. Moreover, the Physically disabled person have gained lot through this therapy. If one has an innovative mind in this field, he/she has an attractive career even now. Prof.Pandey claims that it is good career option is these days and in metro cities like Delhi, a magician can make anywhere between Rs.5000/- to Rs.10,000/- for a simple small scale show at birthday parties etc. For corporate shows and other functions charges vary from Rs.40,000/- to Rs.3 lacks and in either case a good magician can easily make a minimum monthly income ranging between Rs.30,000/- to 50,000/-.

The younger generation generally gets training in magic personally form a magician. One can not expect to learn magic only through books Prof.Pandey adds." The practical training under the supervision of a good magician is a must to become a good performer and magic entertainer". He suggests that a bachelor's degree in the fine art of magic should be offered by the Indian Universities after seeking necessary approval from University Grant Commission". Aboard a Ph.D is available in the field of magic.

If disabled persons are given a suitable training with practical experiences by a Master trainer, who is otherwise a well known practicising Magician, they can perform magic shows in colleges, schools, corporate houses, hospitals, jails and even in birthday parties and wedding ceremonies. By realizing its economic potential, VRS, Guwahati approached NABARD to recognize magic as an economic activity under Rural Entrepreneurship Development Programme and succeeded in the attempt. The Training has two modules, one for solo performances and another for Group performance and the duration of performance ranges from 1-3 hours. The training programmes for the disabled is suitably designed by Shri Sudhansu Das, a well know practicing magician who is otherwise an Engineer by profession. Such training for the disabled gets the attraction of the media and they in turn popularize their magic skill and abilities. It is worth viewing a hearing impaired person do the magic by following the music tune accurately during training period. Advance booking of magic shows are being done by corporate houses, schools and colleges.

Magic troopes are also in use and practice of Govt. departments such as Song and Drama Division, Ministry of Information and Broadcasting for propagating various policies, programmes and themes such as peace, national integration and communal harmony. Health and Family Welfare, eradication of social evils, prevention and control of AIDS/ Malaria/ Leprosy/T.B., Rural Development education, women empowerment etc.

(d) MUSIC

Music is an art that fills the heart and soul with joy and happiness. It includes singing, dancing and playing on instruments. Singing is designated as Vocal Music while playing with instruments is known as Instrumental.

Music has its several branches ranging from pure classical to semi-classical and light music. In India, two types of music systems are prevalent. They are- South Indian Music also known as Carnatic Music System and North Indian Music also named as Indian Music System. In both the systems there are technical variations.

The Instruments that are generally placed under instrumental music are Sitar, Sarod, Sarangi, Santoor, Veena, Tabla and Pakharaj etc. These are played in the solo form as well as with vocal music to provide rhythm or background music.

There are several forms of dances that are popular in various States of India. In Northern India the notable style of classical dance is kathak while in Southern States Bharat Natyam, Kuchipudi, Odissi etc. have their roots. There are also other important dance styles like Manipuri.

MUSIC AS HOBBY

Many of us take to music as a hobby or pursue it for the sake of personal happiness without seeking any financial benefits while for some it becomes a profession in due course. There are several areas where a talent in music can be gainfully employed, such as teaching music, production of films, theatre, private performing clubs and other entertainment places, hotels, commercial recordings, broadcasting, band services in military and police etc. With the advent of multi-channels on the T.V. and government's support to organize music festivals in various parts of the country as well as abroad, the demand for Musicians, Dancers and other Artists has increased tremendously. Due to Western influence, the Western Music has also become very popular especially among youngsters. As a result Pop Music, Jazz, Rap, Brake Dance etc. are singing on the Indian soil.

One can learn Music and Dance through the traditional method learning i.e. from a 'Guru'. For this type of learning, no formal academic education is required but one should have the basic aptitude. Ultimately, it is the proficiency and the style of the artist that brings him recognition and fame.

In most of the Indian Universities and Colleges, Music is taught at graduation and post graduation level. There are several other Institutes and Academics that impart training in several fields of Music. With a view to creating awareness of music, Sangeet Natak Academy was set up at New Delhi. This Academy provides grants to various organizations relating to performing arts, promotes research, sets up training institutions, organizes seminar and festival and subsidises publications on music, dance etc. It has schemes for the grant of fellowships to performers and teachers of music. Similarly, there is the Jawaharlal Nehru Manipur Dance Academy at Imphal for training in Manipuri dance and Kathak Kendra at Delhi for providing training in Kathak dance.

There are several private Institutions and Organizations that impart training in music and dance.Sangeet Prayag Samiti conducts examinations in music. Gandharv Sangeet Mahavidyalaya, Bombay, Bhathkhande Sangeet Vidyapeeth, Lucknow and Madhav Sangeet Vidyalaya at Gwalior are very popular in the field of Music.

GOVERNMENT SUPPORT

The Ministry of Education provides financial assistance to young artists for advanced training in the field of Music and Dance. Travel subsidies are provided to deserving Musicians and other Artists for participation in International festivals, meets and seminars relating to Music and Dance. Ministry of Education and Ministry of Social Welfare sponsors the Artists to foreign countries for giving performances. The National awards such as Padama Shree and Padama Bhushan are also offered to renowned Artists. Many people regard performing arts as highly glamorous and fascinating. But one should be prepared for hard work and rigorous training before choosing a career in the field of Music.

Most of the Musicians are freelancers or casual artists. Salaried jobs are limited. The first few years are a struggle, unless you are exceptionally good. The best way to start earning is to start teaching. However, one needs a degree or diploma in music tc teach in a school or institute. It is also a choice for those who love music but do not want to brave the limelight. Giving private tuitions is an added advantage for teachers. Most of the girls prefer to learn music mainly dance at their homes.

Radio and TV offer contracts to artists-both established as well as emerging. The aspirant has to get in touch with the producer at the Radio or TV station responsible for producing such programmes. There is an audition test for Vocalists and performing test for other categories of artists. If they are found suitable they are called from time to time for performance. There is categorization of artists that determines the level of payments per performance. Artists who feature frequently on Radio or TV have a fair chance of being absorbed as and when vacancies arise in Radio/TV centres or other departments of government such as Song and Drama Division.

Singers present rhythmical melodies, either solo or in a group. As per their specialization they are termed as Classical Singers, Pop Singers, Opera Singers, Gazal Singers etc. The jobs are available in Radio, T.V., Musical Groups, Films etc. Several music agencies are producing audio and video cassettes. They require services of Singers. Renowned Musicians get handsome amount of money by participating in musical programmes.

The music composers make tunes for songs. Sometimes they themselves compose songs and set them to music. When they work for some Orchestra group they may plan compositions for several artists. Most of the music composers specialize in a particular form of music e.g. Camatic, Hindustani or Western. Modern Composition try to combine Indian melodies with a Western touch. These days computers are also being used for composing music. For this purpose, good knowledge of computer operation is needed. Music composers play an important role in films as musical effects are must in films. They are well rewarded for their work.

Music Director is a talented person who generally specializes in more than one area of music. For example he can compose a song or tune for it. He can set the song with other instruments and can direct it for recording. He is fully aware of the process of recording. A good Music Director can play several instruments. He also selects singers and instrumental musicians in consultation with Music Composer while directing a song for a film or stage. He plans background music effects as per the situations, events scenes etc. to provide a synchronized impact of the story. They are well paid in the film line or while working with the established Musical Group. They are generally well reputed Musicians.

Dancers are expected to express feelings through body movements and facial expressions. They can perform solo, with a partner or in a group. Rhythm and theme of a dance item has to be kept in mind before performing. A lot of stamina is needed to be a renowned dancer. Choreographers in the group design and compose dances. They select a theme for dance and plan its execution. They also choose which style of dance will be suitable for a particular theme. Choreographers may or may not participate in actual dance performance. They are the persons with knowledge of wide varieties of folk and classical traditions. This is also a highly paid work.

INSTITUTES

1. BHU, Varanasi
2. University of Bombay, Mumbai
3. University of Delhi, Delhi
4. University of Gorakhpur, Gorakhpur
5. University of Madras, Chennai
6. University of Mysore, Mysore
7. Patna University, Patna
8. Visva Bharti University, Shantiniketan
9. Ravindra Bharti University, Kolkata
10. University of Pune, Pune

(e) MUSEOLOGY

Museology is the science of Museum. It helps Museum professionals to understand the needs of Museum and know the procedures of Museum Organisation and Management viz. Museum Collection, Documentation & Research; Museum Education; Museum Exhibition; Conservation & Preservation; Museum Marketing; Museum Architecture; Museum Publication & Museum Security and Administration.

The term Museum is derived from the Greek word "Museion" which means temple of the Muses, the Goddess of protecting Arts and Sciences. Universally Museum are a place of learning, experience, preserving the old Culture and Heritage of a particular region and community presenting in its original evidence, its identity and development.

Eligibility

For Admission to Museology, a Graduate or a Post Graduate from Science, History or Art History or Fine Arts and Archaeology can join the courses.

Scopes and opportunities

Museology is a very wide subject and highly Professional field. After the completion of the course the persons can work in the Museum as a Curator, Conservator, Administrative Officer, Liaison Officer, Educator, Taxidermist and in the Teaching Profession.

Institutes Offering the Courses

Some of the Universities offering courses are : The Maharaja Sayajirao University, Baroda, offering P.G. Courses and Ph.D. Courses as well as 1 year Diploma Courses for Inservice people.

- The National Museum Institute of History of Arts and Conservation and Museology, New Delhi, offering P.G. Courses and Ph.D. Courses.
- Aligarh Muslim University, U.P.
- Jiwaji University, Gwalior (M.P.)

Most of these departments of Universities and Institutions have their own Museums and Laboratories. In India there are more than 700 Museums offering wide employment, starting from Central Government Museums to the District Levels and from Trust Museums to religious Museums according to the subject of the museum and specialization of the Candidates.

(f) THEATRE AND VISUAL ARTS

We have very little information about the origin of the theatre. The information we do have comes from wall paintings, decorations and artefacts that show the importance of successful hunts, seasonal changes, life cycles and stories of Gods. Early societies perceived connections between certain actions performed by the group of leaders in the group and the desired results of the whole society. Therefore, the formulation, repetition and rehearsal of these actions created ceremonies and rituals. Through these rituals, leaders, or actors of sorts, emerged. In ancient times, these acting/ leadership roles were filled by elders and priests. Rituals were practised not only because of duty to the gods, but because they brought entertainment and pleasure. The beginnings of acting spaces or auditoriums developed as a result of more elaborate rituals.

Drama has been practised in India from ancient times. Bharatha Muni helped establishing drama by incorporating the dialogue portion from Rig Veda, the music from Sama Veda, play acting from Yajur Veda and the rasa from the Atharva Veda, to help take the puranas, Ithihasaas, mythological tales to the common man. Aristotle believed human beings were naturally imitative and took pleasure from copying persons, things and actions. He also theorized that, humans wanted to be audience members to such play-acting. One of the first reported theatrical performances was traced to Abydos, the most sacred spot in Egypt. An annual performance dating from 2500 to 550 B.C. was called the Abydos passion play and was related to the god Osiris.

In ancient times Indian drama was spoken in Sanskrit which was the most commonly spoken language in India. Sanskrit drama emerged sometime between 1500 to 1000 B.C. and could not be classified as comedy, tragedy or melodrama, but was based on the concept of Rasa. All the Rasa relate to human emotions. The eight Rasa are- erotic, comic, pathetic, furious, heroic, terrible, odious and marvellous. Two famous Indian plays which deal with the Rasa were *The Little Clay Cart* by Bhasa and Shakuntala written by Kalidasa. Sanskrit performances were usually given on special occasions such as religious festivals, marriages, coronations or victory celebrations. No scenery was used but the stage had painting or carvings that would have symbolic value. The Modern Visual Art includes Painting, Sculpture, Architecture and Decorative arts. India , starting with the Indus period has developed heritage in all forms of arts, including architecture, literature, sculptures, painting, music dance forms, theatre, besides the contribution of the legendary 0 & infinity. Painting as an art form has flourished in India from very early periods as is evident from literary sources and also from the remnants that have been discovered. Decoration of the floor in geometric fashions, to narrate sequences of mythology on the walls of houses or buildings are the lesser known or acknowledged aspects of Indian traditional painting. The creations of the nature have been adopted by the artisans traditionally; may it be in making pots, plates, nutcrackers, hairpins, combs, vermilion & kohl containers or utensils. Deities were made both as solid casting and hollow casting and sastras, stating proportions were laid down to enable the artisans to create exquisite figures in proportion to human eyes' perception. In India, from ancient times, jewellery have not been mere ornamental or decorative items, but have gained the status of providing proof of various stages of a man/ woman's life like piercing a child's ear to signify his/her entry into the world, the man wearing the sacred thread made of gold strands from left to right shoulder to signify his entry into educational age, the thali for the women to signify her being married.

CAREER PROSPECTS

Theatre today has come a long way in India. However, theatre acting as a profession still remains neglected, perhaps as much out of ignorance as the lack of information. Graduates in Theatre and Drama have the skills to go on to a wide variety of careers. Allied to these skills, the practical experience they receive in performance and production projects provides them with an ideal springboard for further vocational training as actors, directors, theatre technicians, designers and administrators in institutions world wide. Their reading, oral and written communication skills, their advanced people skills and their capacity to improvise and think laterally equip them for careers in theatre administration, publicity and arts journalism, as well as in non-theatre related professions.

Theatre and Drama subjects include a variety of disciplinary approaches, some of which are, theatre theory, performance, theatre history, dramatic literature, genre studies and criticism. There is also some opportunity for performance-making and theatre production. These offerings are not intended as theatre arts training, however, many of its subjects include a substantial component of practical work. Play-going is an important part of all drama subjects and reviews of performances seen are part of the required written work. White choosing Visual Arts you need to assess your own character and talents. A freelance artist has to be self-motivated confident and organized and able to manage their own business. Working in a company has many benefits, such as superannuation and regular work hours. Graphic and industrial design pay well and are often creative and exciting, though creativity must serve a commercial purpose. As a hobby art is fun, but a professional in a competitive environment has to be 'a cut above' the rest, and you will need to develop original, real and marketable skills. Creative careers can be challeing and rewarding.

COURSES

A variety of courses are available in the institutes enlisted below, in the disciplines of Art. Theatre and Dance which offer certificate, diploma and degree. The contents of the courses include-Acting, Playwriting, Production, Direction, Modern Arts, Painting, Contemporary Art forms, Basic light design, Costume design, Modern dance, Dance composition, Theatre management, Monologues and Scene study, Persuasion and Public Controversy, solo performance, Choreography Technicalities in Mask and action, Space-harmony movement Physics, Body therapies, Jewellery designing etc.

WORK PLACE

Theatres, Animation centres, Movie companies, Fine Arts studios, Governments, Magazines, Museums, Jewellery and ornaments designing centres, Newspapers, Photographic studios, Publicity agencies, Publishing house, Retail trade, Self-employment, Teaching establishments, Archives, Art galleries, Entertainment sector, Advertisement companies.

INSTITUTE IN INDIA AND ABROAD

1. Film and TV Institute of India, Pune
2. Maya Entertainment Limited, Mumbai

3. National School of Drama, Bahawalpur House,Bhagwandas Road, New Delhi-1
4. Bhartendu Acaddemy of Dramatic Arts, A-2/58, Vishal Khand-2, Gomti Nagar, Lucknow-226 010
5. Film and TV Institute of Tamil Nadu, Chennai-600 113
6. Image Acting School, Brahma Studio, Film City, Noida-201 301
7. Ashok Kumar Academy of Dramatic Arts, Mumbai
8. National Centre for the Performing Arts (NCPA), Nariman Point, Mumbai
9. Sarojini Naidu School of Performing Arts, Fine Arts and Communication, University of Hyderabad
10. Vishva-Bharati, West Bengal, India
11. Trinty College of London's Speech and Drama
12. Tokyo National University of Fine Arts and Music
13. School of Dramatics, New York University
14. University of North Carolina, Chapel Hill
15. Department of Visual Arts, University of California, San Diego

5

Army

(a) ARMED FORCES

To get into the forces a person can opt for one of the two options:

Permanent Commission:

A Permanent Commission means a career in the Army till you require.

Short Service Commission:

You also have the option of joining the forces and serving as a Commissioned Officer for 5 years.

At the end of this period you have two options. Either to opt for a Permanent Commission or quit.

Those not selected for Permanent Commission have the option of a 5 year extension. They can resign at any time during this period.

A Short Service Commission empowers you with analytical thinking, planning skills, administrative and organizational abilities, which will make you an invaluable asset for any organization that you join after finishing your career in the forces.

RECRUITMENT IN THE FORCES

Through UPSC Exams,

For recruitment as Permanent Commissioned Officer in the Armed Forces, the UPSC conducts all India competitive examinations twice a year viz.

1. CDSE (Combined Defence Service Exam.)
2. NDA (National Defence Academy / NA (Naval Academy) Entrance Exam.

Through SSB/Air Force Selection Board

Through University Entry Scheme

Final/ Pre-final year students in the notified engineering disciplines are eligible to apply for commission into the Technical Arms/ Services.

Through Short Service Commission (Technical Entry)

Engineering graduate from notified disciplines of Engineering including those studying in their final year are eligible to apply.

Through NCC Special Entry Scheme

University Graduates possessing NCC "C" Certificate with minimum "B" grade and 50% marks in graduation are eligible to apply for commission into the Navy and the Air Force as Regular Commissioned Officers and as Short Service Commissioned Officers in the Army. These graduates are exempted from appearing in the CDSE conducted by the UPSC and are selected through the SSBs.

Medical Graduates

Armed Forces Medical College (AFMC), Pune: Directly inducted as permanent commissioned Medical Officers in the Forces.

***Other Medical Colleges (Civil)*:** The Director General of the Armed Forces Medical Services conducts all India competitive examination for recruitment of Graduates/Post-graduates from these colleges as Regular commissioned/ Short Service Commissioned Medical Officers.

WOMEN IN THE ARMED FORCES

Women have always been serving the forces with great pride through the Armed Forces Medical Services, Armed Forces Dental Services and Military Nursing Services. Apart from these cadres eligible women are recruited as Officers on Short Service Commission basis in the following branches of the Armed Forces:

ARMY: EME Corps, Signals Corps, Education Corps, Ordnance Corps, Military Intelligence Corps and Judge Advocate General Corps.

NAVY: Engineering (Naval Architects), Ligistics, Law, Education, Air Traffic Control.

AIR FORCE: Flying (Transport and Helicopters), Aeronautical Engineering (Electronics, Mechanical), Education, Administration, Logistics, Accounts and Meterology.

Tenure in the SSC is for 5 years, which can be extended to 14 years.

ENTRY :**After 10+2** : Only to the MBBS course at the Armed Forces Medical College, Pune or their Nursing School for B.Sc Nursing.

The B.Sc Nursing course is only for women, the MBBS course at AFMC, Pune has 25 seats for women.

After Graduation: Under Women Officers Special Entry Scheme women can entre the forces in the above mentioned Technical, Non-Technical and Specialized branches. (Those candidates holding NCC "C" Certificate with grade "B" or higher stand a brighter chance to get selected).

THE EXAMINATION **CDSE (Combined Defence Services Examination)**

Examination held twice a year. Age limits- 19-24 years for Indian Military Academy and 19-22 years for Naval Academy, 19-23 years Air Force Academy and 19-25 years for Officers Training Academy (OTA).

Educational Qualifications:

For IMA and OTA one needs a degree of a recognised University or equivalent.

For Naval Academy a BSc with Physics & Mathematics or Bachelor of Engineering.

For Air Force Academy one should have BSc with Physics and/or Mathematics or Bachelor of Engineering.

Examination is based on the knowledge of English, general awareness and elementary mathematics.

NDA (National Defence Academy)/ NA (Naval Academy) Entrance Examination

Examination held twice a year. Age limits- 16-1/2- 19 years

Educational Qualifications

For Army Wing of NDA candidate should be 12th class pass of the 10+2 pattern of school Education or equivalent.

For a course at Naval Academy, 12th class pass of the 10+2 pattern of school Education with Physics and Mathematics or equivalent.

Candidates appearing at the 12th Class Examination are also eligible to compete.

Examination is based on the knowledge of English and general mental ability.

(b) ARMY OFFICER

Many young men and women enquire as to how they could join the Indian Army as Officers? Well, this has spurred me into penning these lines for those aspiring to join one of the finest of all professions- the Indian Army and with the Annual Army Day on 15th January. I suppose it is an ideal time to do so.

You could opt for a permanent commission (serve till you retire) or for a short service one (five to fourteen years). You could choose to join immediately after leaving school (10+2) or after completing your graduation or post graduation. But before coming on to the specifics, why must you consider joining the Army?

WHAT YOU MAY EXPECT FROM A CAREER IN THE ARMY

When you join the Indian Army, you don't get just an ordinary career. You start an extraordinary life- you are blessed with a life that is full of adventure, honour and glory. Indeed, it is the life which makes of you an asset to the nation.

As an Army Officer, you are trained in the art, craft and technology of war and also of maintaining peace. You are also trained to meet the challenges of serving the nation in natural calamities such as earthquakes, floods and the like. You must have read about the extensive relief and rehabilitation operations launched recently by the Armed Forces. The services of the Army both within the country and abroad to mitigate the destruction and suffering caused by the recent tsunami disaster are too fresh to be recounted. For serving the nation, you pick up skills of management, computers and human nature. You also remain at par with your peers in educational qualifications. Even though you may have joined immediately after school, you go on to earn graduation in the National Defence Academy. Thereafter as you progress in your career, many avenues are available for various higher level degrees in IT, various streams of engineering, management, foreign languages and the like. Subject to certain conditions you can also apply for a sabbatical later in your career to study a subject of your choice including studying at IIMs, IITs or working for a doctorate, in India or abroad.

As for salary and perks, the Indian Army does compensate you well. In fact, you start drawing a package even while you commence your training at the Indian Military Academy, Dehradun and the Officers Training Academy, Chennai. Thus you earn even as you learn. You also get facilities such as medical cover, group insurance and schooling and professional courses for your children in some of the best educational institutes run by the Army for the children of their extended family.

You also get to travel widely, both within the country and abroad. You could be Army's representative as a peace keeper or an observer in the United Nations peace-keeping missions. You could also be nominated to various instructional courses abroad. I am certain that since your children would be exposed to life in various parts of the country, they would grow up to be better informed, more confident and adaptable. You surely see these traits in the Army kids- they indeed will be achievers of sorts. Thus by choosing to join the Army you would do good to your offspring too.

You could indulge in the finest of outdoor pursuits such as mountaineering, trekking, Para jumping, sky diving, river rafting and shooting. Do remember that it was an Army man- Major Rajyavardhan Singh Rathore who did the nation proud by earning a Silver in shooting in the last Olympics at Athens.

Every year thousands apply to become officers. But only actually make it through. The Indian Army wants men and women of intellect, determination and courage- those with a fire in their belly. If you feel you are the one, read on for what goes in the selection of officers.

PERMANENT COMMISSION

When you opt for 'Permanent Commission', you are basically looking at a permanent career in the army. A career till you retire. National Defence Academy and Indian Military Academy are the two institutions that you join for a Permanent Commission.

THE NATIONAL DEFENCE ACADEMY, PUNE

You can take the NDA Entrance Exam while in class XII. Once you clear this exam, the next step is Services Selection Board (SSB) interviews, which will last five days. The last step in the process is a medical test. After this, all you have to do is wait for your 10+2 results and NDA merit list. Once you clear these, you will be in NDA. Three years in NDA and you will become a Gentleman cadet.

INDIAN MILITARY ACADEMY, DEHRADUN

Here is yet another cradle of leadership that trains its men to lead from the front. Valour and Wisdom is its motto. Valour and wisdom is what exudes from every Army Officer who passes out of IMA. I was present at IMA last month watching the smart turnout of young Indians who passed out to start as Army Officers. There was something very special in their eyes and a unique élan in their steps. That's it. I remembered my days at the NDA and IMA too. Admission can be taken in your final year of college by clearing the Combined Defence Services Exam. If you are a Gentleman Cadet (Graduate from NDA or a Technical (Engineering Graduate), then your training at IMA will last one year. Alternatively, under the Graduate Direct Entry Scheme (if you are a Graduate in any other stream),your training will last one-and-a-half years.

You can also apply after passing the 10+2 examination with at least 70% marks in Physics, Chemistry and Mathematics. If you meet the eligibility criteria, you will be sent to the SSB. After the SSB interview, a merit list will be put up by the Recruiting Directorate.

Selected candidates are inducted for 1 year's Basic Military Training at IMA. This would be followed by a 4 years' degree course in engineering from College of Military Engineering, Pune/ Military College of Telecommunication Engineering, Mhow/Military College of Electronics and Mechanical Engineering, Secunderabad. The total duration of training is 5 years. On completion of 4 years of training, a commission in the rank of Lieutenant is granted. For a degree in engineering, however, you will need to successfully complete the stipulated 5 years of training. When you pass out of IMA, you will be commissioned as a Lieutenant in the Indian Army.

SHORT SERVICE COMMISSION

The Indian Army has a wonderful alternative for all those of you who aspire to serve it for a few years. It is called Short Service Commission. It gives you the option of joining the Indian Army and serving it as a 'Commissioned Officer' for 5 years. Once your tenure is over, you are allowed to opt for a Permanent Commission. Alternatively, you can also ask for a 5 years extension or another four years thereafter, and can choose to resign from your post any time during this period. With a Short Service Commission, you will have the best of both worlds. Even as it gives you the privileges and benefits of a full-fledged commission, you will be imbibing qualities that will make you an invaluable asset to any organisation that you join after the army. Analytical thinking skills, Planning ability, Administrative prowess, Organisation talent. The works, at the end of the day, the years fruitfully spent as an SSC Officer will make you a leader for life.

OFFICERS TRAINING ACADEMY, CHENNAI

OTA, Chennai is where you go once you are selected for the short Service Commission. The selection procedure is simple. A written exam followed by the SSB interview and medical test. It's slightly different if you are a Technical (Engineering) Graduate. You don't need to take the written exam. Once your application is screened and short listed by the Army Headquarters, you can directly go in for the SSB interview and medical examination.

Once in OTA, your training will last 10 months approximately. During this period, you will train to be a first class Officer and get ample opportunities to pursue interesting activities like skeet shooting, golf, riding and angling. Ultimately, OTA will equip you to take on the world with a broadened perspective once your leave the army.

SPECIAL SCHEME FOR WOMEN

If you are a women who wishes to be an Army Officer, there is good news for you. Indian Army recruits women officers through the Short Service Commission.

You need to be a Graduate/ Post Graduate in order to apply. All applications will be initially screened by the Recruiting Directorate of the Army Headquarters. If short-listed, you will appear for the SSB interview. Once selected, you will get trained at OTA, Chennai, very recently two of our women officers have been deputed as Military Observers in UN Peace Keeping in Congo.

ANTEDATD SENIORITY TO TECHNICAL GRADUATES

Antedated Seniority of two years is given to Engineering/ Technical Graduates inducted through technical entries. This is done in order to compensate you for the extra time and energy that you spent to earn the engineering degree before your training. With the Antedate Seniority, you will have opportunities for faster promotions in addition to pay benefits.

(c) DEFENCE SERVICES

The entry as a commissioned officer in defence services is through National Defence Academy examination conducted twice a year by Union Public Service Commission (UPSC). The candidates may give preference for different services, however, option depends on the rank in the merit list. Only unmarried male candidates between 16-1/2 and 19 years are eligible. For army wing of National Defence Academy, they should be 10+2, for Air Force and Naval Wings of NDA and for 10+2 Executive Branch of Naval Academy they should be 10+2 with physics and mathematics. The physical standards are also laid down. The minimum acceptable height is 157.5 cm (162.5 cms for air force). For pilots in their air force the leg length, thigh length and sitting height are also prescribed. The selection is through a competitive examination consisting papers on Mathematics (300 marks) and General Ability (600 marks). The papers are of objective nature. Those who qualify the written test are called for intelligence and personality test by the Service Selection Board. In addition to the interview, the candidates are put through intelligence tests designed to assess their basic intelligence. The candidates recommended by the Service Selection Board are required to undergo a medical examination. Only those candidates who are declared fit by the medical board are admitted to academy.The cadets on passing out are awarded B.Sc./B.A. degree from JNU, New Delhi. On completion of training, the candidates are granted commission in the rank of Lt.

Besides NDA, there are various other career options depending on your academic achievements. You may go for 10+2 Technical Entry Scheme if you have PCM and score at least 70% marks. You may also go for medicine and other options depending on your qualifications and interest.

MARINE ENGINEERING

Most marine engineers work in the merchant navy and are responsible for the ship's engine, boilers, electrical generating plant and all the technical aspects of the ship. Training of marine engineers for the merchant navy is conducted at the Marine Engineering Research Institutes at Kolkata and Mumbai. Selection for admission to these institutes is through the IIT-JEE after 10+2 with Physics, Chemistry and Maths. You can also join the merchant navy as a marine engineer through some private colleges which offer this course- Academy of Maritime Education andTraining, Chennai; International Maritime Institute, NOIDA, UP and Tolani Maritime Institute, Pune and others. If you are not interested in the merchant navy but want to work on design and construction of ships, or on offshore projects or with shipping companies, you can take up marine engineering at College of Engineering, Andhra University, Vishakapatnam or Sri Venkateshwara College of Engineering, Sriperumbadur, Tamil Nadu.

AERONAUTICAL ENGINEERING

You can do Aeronautical Engineering as a postgraduate programme after B.Tech in any specialisation. Institutes offering M.Tech. in Aeronautical Engineering include the Madras Institute of Technology and the Indian Institute of Science, Bangalore. Admission to the M.Tech.Courses is open to those who qualify in the GATE (Graduate Aptitude Test in Engineering). Applications are normally available in September and November and the test is held in February.

The Aeronautical Society of India, 13-B Indraprastha Estate, New Delhi-110 002, conducts an associate membership exam (section A&B) twice every year. Qualifying section A and B of this examination is recognised at par with a bachelor's degree in Aeronautical Engineering from an Indian University. As a degree holder in engineering, you can appear directly in section B. However, you will have to clear the "Princi;es of Flight" paper of Section A.

MASTER'S COURSE IN NETWORKING AND COMMUNICATION

There are a variety of courses ranging from diploma and certificate courses such as the IBM, SAP, Oracle and Microsoft to the formal degree programmes offered by IIITs (Indian Institute of Information Technology) at Gwalior, Allahabad, Hyderabad and Bangalore. The Dhirubhai Ambani Institute of Information and Communication at Gandhinagar, Gujarat also has a two year M.Sc. in Informatics and a three year Master of Information Technology. You may go for an M.E. or M.Tech. in Electronics and Communications Course. To pursue a master's course in any engineering field, you have to clear your Graduate Aptitude Test for Engineering (GATE). Another option is a three year MCA programme available at several universities. Admission to the course is through the AIMCET conducted by IIT Roorkee.

After acquiring a master's degree, you can work in the field of design, invention and operation of electronic systems. Job opportunities exist in computer companies and in the telecom and communication sector.

(d) MERCHANT NAVY

A Sailor keeps his eyes on the Horizon. To achieve ambition, one has to be focussed and dedicated, irrespective of all difficulties and failures. A career on the High Seas is full of adventure and thrill. Merchant Navy is different career in comparison to others. The compensation package is enormous and lucrative but the life is not bed of roses. But before that we must understand the difference between Navy, Coast Guard and Merchant Navy.

Indian Navy is a part of Armed Forces, its employees are combatants. Its role is to defend the coast line of the country in times of aggression/ hostilities and safe-guard maritime interests of the country.

Coast Guard is a para-military force entrusted with the task of protecting Maritimes Zones of Indian besides assisting in anti-smuggling operations. Its role is primarily in peacetime.

Merchant Navy is a non combatant commercial fleet comprising of : (a) Passenger Vessels (b) Cargo liners (c) Tankers (d) Carriers

India has a coastline of 4500 km and 97 per cent of India's national trade is carried though sea-routes. The main areas of Merchant Navy's work are as follows:-

(1) **Navigation**. Navigating officers are responsible to navigate ship, loading and off-loading of cargo and adherence to international rules of navigation.

(2) **Engineering**. Engineers are to ensure smooth and safe operations and maintenance of machinery and running of ship.

(3) **Radio and Wireless Communication**. They operate and maintain wireless equipment.

QUALIFICATION REQUIRED

Entry procedure in Merchant Navy is stringent, as the nature of job requires the candidate to be confident, focussed with adequate ability to withstand work-stress. Minimum qualification for courses in nautical science and marine engineering is 10+2 with 60 per cent marks in Physics, Chemistry and Mathematics. The applicant must be below 20 years of age. A joint entrance examination is conducted by Indian Institute of Technology, followed by personal interview, wherein the candidates' ability to withstand rigors of merchant navy and suitability is assessed.

For Navigation branch, 3 years B.Sc in nautical science training is imparted in TS Chanakya. The training encompasses navigation, rules of the Sea, Cargo work and ship maintenance and architecture. The certificate of training from T S Chanakya is recognized which is equivalent to one year of sea service.

The four year course of Marine Engineering at MERI has a comprehensive syllabi, which includes repair and maintenance of ships, marine engineering and technology.

Another method of getting inducted in Merchant Navy is through the direct route i.e. individuals who have completed BSc in Nautical Science or BE in Marine or Mechanical Engineering can join Navigation and Engineering Branch. Even the candidates who have completed 10+2 with PCB can join as deck cadets on board and complete on the job training for three years and acquire competency certificate as laid down by Ministry of Surface Transport.

PHYSICAL STANDARDS

The candidates aspiring to join must be mentally and physically alert and fit. The navigators should have perfect eye sight and should not be a habitual wearer of glasses. The engineers are permitted to wear glasses with eyesight of plus/minus 2.5 For both jobs, colour blind candidates are not acceptable.

Since Merchant Navy has long voyages on high seas, team spirit and ability to work in group is very essential. Love for travelling, self-confidence, practical intelligence and ability to withstand stress due to monotony of work is of paramount importance. Mental and physical stamina is essential.

The pay structure is very lucrative. Foreign companies offer attractive salaries. Most professionals in shipping companies work on a contractual basis normally for a period of six months. After break the contract is again renewed.

INSTITUTIONS' NAME

Prominent Institutions and imparting trainings are:-

1. ***Training Ship Chanakya*** – Mumbai formerly known as TS, Rajendra conducts 3 years course in Nautical Science.
2. ***Marine Engineering Research Institute*** (MERI)-Calcutta offers 4 years Marine Engineering Course.
3. ***Birla Institute of Technology & Science*** (BITS), Pilani offers Bachelor of Science in Marine Engineering.
4. ***Tolani Maritime Institute Sharda Centre, Karve Road, Pune-*** 411 004 (4 years degree course in Marine Engineering).
5. ***Chennai School of Ship Management, 37, Perambur High Road, Chennai***-600 012 (3 years Marine Engineering Course)

6. ***International Maritime Institute, 13, Institutional Area, Greater Noida***, U.P. conducts course for Diploma in Nautical Science and Pre-Sea Deck Cadet Course.
7. ***Chidambaram Institute Maritime Technology No.6, Second Line Beach, Chennai***-600 001. It conducts 1 year course in Marine Engineering for Mechanical Engineers.

JOB AVENUES

Trained Navigation and Marine Officers have very good career prospects in shipping companies with a starting salary between Rs. 25 to 30 thousand. The experienced persons even get more than Rs. 1 lakh per month. The attrition rate is very high due to shortage of trained personnel as they keep switching over from one company to another. Most of the modern ships provide luxurious environment with all facilities to off set monotony of long voyage and lack of social life. Foreign companies even provide accommodation to the families of senior crew members.

(e) NAVY

Life in the Navy is full of travel, adventure, variety, education and friendship that last through life, even after you have retired from the service. And what's more, these days, the Indian Navy is hiring all kinds of people- from Computer Operators to Engineers; from Naval Airmen to Radar Operators; from Medical Assistants to Cooks; from Divers to Surveyors and many more.

LIFE AT SEA

It's a far cry from duty ashore- a real test of your physical and mental endurance. Nonetheless, sea duty does not mean that you will be spending all your time riding the waves. For one thing, while at sea, you'll be putting all your skills and determination to the actual test. Life can be a bit demanding when you have to sleep in bunkers, eat mess food and get used to the cramped life on a small vessel. However, in some cadres like naval architecture, there is no sea posting. In all other cadres, your ship will have its own "home-port" where you will spend quite a bit of your time in or close by, where your family could be staying. And when you do head out to sea, you will find excitement in visiting far-flung places in India and abroad, which you had only read or heard about.

AN ARTIFICER IN THE NAVY

Responsibility, good pay and good technical training- that's the hallmark of an artificer in the Navy. His responsibilities include operating and maintaining some of the most complex naval systems and equipment, ranging from steam- powered machinery, diesel and gas turbine, guided missiles, besides other automatically controlled weapons, sensors, computers and highly advanced radio and electrical power systems.

The Navy trains its own artificers, through a three-year diploma programme recognised by the Ministry of Human Resource, after which candidates are enrolled in the engine room, electrical, shipwright, aviation (engineering/ electrical) or submarine divisions.

RANKS, RATINGS AND PROMOTIONS

Sailors who possess unique leadership abilities and fulfil all the requisite conditions in terms of age, education etc. can aspire to become Commissioned Officers through the Commission Worthy (CW) and Special Duty (SD) schemes, going up the ladder to command ships and units and even become Admirals! The retirement age varies according to the rank.

WHAT THE NAVY OFFERS YOU

Besides adequate leave benefits and travel concessions, a Naval Officer is also entitled to free accommodation, medical, clothing, ration benefits, schooling and transport for children, group insurance scheme, naval housing scheme, soft loans for house/car/scooter/PC etc. What's more, the government has now introduced several resettlement schemes for retired sailors in the government, public and private sectors. Although, the starting pay for a recruit (Combatant Group 'Y'(Metric) and Combatant Group 'Z' (Non Metric) is small: Rs.2750 and 3200, respectively), there are various other allowances, such as Sea Duty Allowance, Transport Allowance, City Compensatory Allowance etc. to more than make up for the monetary shortfall. In the end, nobody is short changed. The total emoluments for a new officer in the first year are about Rs.12500-13000.

THE SELECTION

Sailors are inducted on the basis of an 'All India Merit List' drawn after a written test, Physical Fitness Test (PFT) and medical examination. The second route is through direct entry if you hold a Naval Officer's diploma. Training is conducted at INS Chilka, which includes nine weeks basic training, followed by four weeks of sea training and 80 weeks of technical training. Recruitment takes place twice a year in January-February and again in July-August. Officers can enter indirectly through the NDA and the Naval Academy or directly through the Service Selection Board (which only comprises of an interview). All officers are required to be degree holders.

WRITTEN TEST

This is an objective type, bilingual, Matric level paper, which carries questions from English, G.K. Science and maths. The question paper for Direct Entry (DE) recruits has additional sections. A DE candidate will be required to attempt only one of the sections which will be as per the choice of the Branch/ Trade indicated by him in his application. This Branch/Trade will also be indicated in the call letter issued by NHQ viz. K for Mechanical, E for Electronics and L for Electrical.

PHYSICAL FITNESS TEST(PFT)

Qualifying this test is mandatory. It comprises a 1.6 km run that has to be completed in seven minutes, 20 squat-ups and 10 push-ups.

MEDICAL STANDARDS

Weight correlated with height and proportionate chest with a minimum expansion of 5 cms. Good medical and physical health, no cardio-vascular, surgical deformities or infection of the ears. No history of fits or psychiatric ailments. The minimum height requirement is 157 cms (relaxable to 152 cms for artificer apprentices).

COLOUR PERCEPTION / VISUAL STANDARDS

CP II Candidates detected with colour blindness will not get a clearance from the Navy medical board. Candidates must also have excellent vision.

RECRUITMENT CENTRES

There are 30 exam. centres. For further enquiries contact: The Director, Manpower Planning and Recruitment, Naval Recruitment Organisation, Room No. 2323, C Wing, Naval HQ., Sena Bhavan, New Delhi -110 011.

6

Aviation

(a) AIR-HOSTESS & FLIGHT STEWARD

All commercial aircraft have two sets of people. Firstly those responsible for flying the aircraft and secondly those who are responsible to look after an equally important aspect, its customers-the passengers. The former, male or female, are in the cockpit and are represented by the Pilot, Co-pilot and Flight Engineer. The latter are known as cabin-crew or flight attendants: The male crew are referred to as flight stewards/ pursers while the female crew are called Air hostesses.

WORKING ENVIRONMENT

An Air Hostess has to work continuously and efficiently in the confined and restricted space of the aircraft. Their duty starts much before take off. They have to report one –and-a-half-hour before take off time and undergo briefing by senior flight attendant. Cabin crew has to run a safety check on the aircraft including testing safety equipment, life jackets and mikes etc. They have to ensure that pillows, blankets, books, newspapers, food plates, glasses, napkins and medicines are in stock. Final check before passengers are allowed to move in, includes making sure that the aircraft has been cleaned and is ready for boarding. A cabin crew has to spend up to one-half of the working hours preparing the cabin for flight, writing reports and doing other flight related work on the ground.

As airlines operate round the clock and the year around, cabin crew may have to work at night, and also on holidays and weekends. The longest stretch on domestic flights can be of 5-6 hours duration. This duty, on an international flight can be 10-15 hours at a stretch. Now that can really be trying and tiring. But it can turn out to be even more strenuous in case the weather is bad and the flight is turbulent. Serving meals and drinks in such a scenario can be well imagined.

At times there is additional work in taking special care of air sick travellers, sick children, the babies, the elderly or the very young who are travelling alone. In addition, one has to be mentally alert and cope with the likely possibility of a hijack or any serious problem with the aircraft. Imagine handling more than 200 distraught passengers in such a scenario! Cabin crew can, at times, become prone to medical problems that occur from working in a pressurized environment and breathing recycled air, irregular sleeping and eating patterns and dealing with stressful passengers.

GENERAL REQUIREMENTS

The airlines recruit air hostess and flight attendants on the basis of following broad eligibility criteria:-

Age	:	19-27 years
Height	:	
Men	:	167 cm and above (barefoot)
Women	:	154 cm and above (barefoot)
Weight	:	Proportionate to height
Marital Status	:	Unmarried
Vision	:	Normal eyesight withoutglasses. However, Minimum uncorrected vision (distant) should Be 6/24 in each eye.
Complexion	:	Clear
Languages	:	Fluency in English and Hindi
Education	:	Graduate degree from a recognised university Or Plus Two with a diploma in catering/ Hotel Management from a recognised institute.

SPECIFIC REQUIREMENTS

An air hostess or a flight attendant, in addition to the above minimum requirements must possess few more specific qualities. One must have an attractive appearance and a well modulated pleasant voice. In addition, one ought to be confident, intelligent and patient with lots of common sense. One must also be capable of keeping calm in crises and taking initiative in stressful and uncommon situations. A keen interest in people and places along with being dedicated and contentious is what makes an ideal cabin crew. One needs to be creative, enthusiastic, committed and sensitive to anxious passengers needs.

SELECTION PROCESS

Airlines, as per their requirement arising from time to time, release advertisements in the prominent newspapers calling for applications. In such an advertisement, eligibility criteria are specified. Those who are interested and fulfil the eligibility criteria can apply.

After the initial screening of applications is completed by the Airlines, the company calls the shortlisted candidates for a four stage selection process as indicated below:

1. Written examination, usually objective type, multiple choice type. It is generally for English proficiency and general awareness.
2. Group discussion
3. Personal Interview
4. Medical Examination

Some of the private and international airlines follow a procedure of organizing walk in interviews in some prominent cities. Interested candidates who fulfil the criteria laid down in the advertisement appear with their bio-data in a prescribed dress. There are elimination rounds followed by crucial selection interviews.

ACADEMIC COURSES

The jobs as cabin crew are never too many, but aspirants are always too many. The selection therefore, is always tough. In such a scenario, to increase the probability of selection, one has to prepare really well and develop a "Personality".

TRAINING

Once a person is selected, he/she is trained extensively by the airlines. During the period of training various subjects are taught such as catering, first-aid, general airborne procedures, flight documentation, use of public address system and technical details of various important aspects of aircraft such as pressurization and ventilation systems. Cabin crew is also given lessons in the use of safety equipment and emergency drill. After the theory classes, the practical work is first taught on the ground and then they are given training in the air.

QUALITIES FOR AIR HOSTESS

An airhostess should be patient, committed and have a cheerful demeanour. The person should be prepared to work hard and be polite under all circumstances. At training centres, training relates as students to become accustomed to international standards. Many company offer training workshops in Customer Care, Time Management, Personality Development and Communication Skills.

TO BE INCLUDED IN CURRICULUM

The curriculum has been designed in such a way that students are able to face the toughest interviews in Aviation, Hospitality and

Travel. The curriculum also includes swimming and training in the Computerised Reservation System (CRS) of Airlines/ Travel and Hotel Industries. Much emphasis is given to extra-curricular activities. The idea is that a candidate who graduate from training centre should be able to perform well in any industry.

PROMOTIONAL AVENUES

Air-Hostesses can look for monthly emoluments (salary and allowances) starting at about Rs.15,000 per month. The emoluments increase gradually with experience and the length of service. Senior Air-Hostesses in Air India/ Indian Airlines get up to Rs.75,000/- per month whereas air hostesses with almost same experience in international airlines get up to rupees two lakh per month.

There are promotions in a limited manner. In the beginning, one is put in economy class. After one/ two years, one graduates to business class. After satisfactory service and another year or so one moves in to First Class. Along with this progression from "Economy to First Class", one becomes a supervisor and then Chief Air Hostess or steward, incharge of the whole aircraft. It usually takes 7-8 years and a good service record to reach that level.

There is however a need to mention something that is not common knowledge and it can be stated with the help of an interesting paragraph about their job profile pasted on a website:

"Let's clear your head of some glaring misconceptions. Air hostesses do not lead glamorous lives. Nor is it cakewalk in the air. The job profile ranges from passenger safety to good public relations. It is your job to make people feel comfortable during the flight and ensure their safety at all times. You've got to be strong enough to lift heavy containers and slim enough to glide through the aisle in between foodcarts".

(b) ASTRONAUT

Good luck to you- we need another Kalpana Chawla! Yes, you can become an astronaut after doing aerospace engineering, which is offered at the IITs in Kharagpur, Chennai, Mumbai and Kapur and also at Punjab Engineering College, Chandigarh. You need to be good at Maths and Physics, have good analytical ability and scientific acumen. You also require physical stamina to become an astronaut. However, Aerospace Engineering is not the only on specialists from different disciplines including biomedical engineering , industrial engineering, materials engineering, optical engineering and oceanography. You can specialise at the master's level in any of these disciplines and then do a Ph.D. to qualify for NASA.

The culture in which we live does not value silence. It becomes habitual to turn on the TV or Radio as one of the first things we do when we get home, just to have something familiar going on in the background. But silence is not just the absence of talk. Silence has substance. It is the presence of something.

We can be reduced to silence in times of doubt, uncertainty, nothingness and awe. When we have exhausted all our human efforts, experience the limitations of human justice, or the finitude of human relationships, we are left with silence. Those who have experienced the sacrement of failure are more likely to know the emptying power of silence.

There is a relationship between outward silence and interior silence. Merton notes that even the overuse of sign language within the material silence of the monastery promotes the busy mind. The more silence becomes part of our lives, the less impulsive we become. We are slowed down.

(c) AVIATION

Most of the people think that the only job associated with aviation is that of flying an aircraft. Just a few know that there are additional jobs as air hostess. Beyond that very few are aware of any other avenue. The reality is miles away from such a scenario. There is a plethora of jobs I the aviation sector. And that is not all. An increase in aviation activity in the country, that has already set in, will spur a growth in all fields. The investment in aircraft procurement is going to be of the order of Rs.1,00,000 crore whereas about Rs.15,000 crore would be required in upgradation of airports and airport facilities. Equally large amounts would be required for improving aircraft safety and handling systems. All these would generate additional jobs in various field and activities related to aviation, which can basically be divided into two major categories.

DIRECT- As Pilots, Cabin-crew, Air traffic Controllers, Aircraft maintenance engineers and Support services.

INDIRECT- Such as Research, Design & Development, Aircraft Manufacturing Industry, Aeronautical Education and Space Systems.

THE PILOT

Flying is a thrilling activity. A Boeing 747 aircraft, carrying 500 passengers, weights some 500,000 kg. This is equivalent to the weight of more than 30 fully loaded trucks. The Aircraft flies at a speed of more than 900 kmph which is about seven times faster than our fastest train Shatabdi Express. The scenario in a military aircraft is even more fascinating. These aircraft fly at even faster speeds, at times as much as 2,000 kmph and while doing so, the Pilot is busy looking for the enemy aircraft, tracking him down and preparing himself to shoot the enemy aircraft with his guns, rockets and missiles. Well, the scene is much more real and thrilling than in the best of the movies for a real fighter pilot. Thus there are two types of flying careers.

1. **Commercial Pilot**—To become a pilot, one has to go through three stages of acquiring Student Pilot License (SPL), Private Pilot License (RPL) and Commercial Pilot License (CPL).
2. **Military Pilot in the Air Force, the Navy, the Army or the Coast Guard**—The route is either through NDA or Combined Defence Services Examination. In addition, there is Short Service Commission for women in the Indian Air Force.

CABIN CREW

These are the people who are responsible to look after the passengers. The male crew is referred to as flight stewards/ pursers while female screw is called air hostess. The job of a cabin crew demands attention, responsibility and a pleasing personality complimenting with glamour and excitement. But their job is tough as well. A cabin-crew has to work continuously and efficiently in the confined and restricted spaces of the aircraft. As airlines operate around the clock and the year around, cabin crew may have to work at night and also on holidays and week ends. Cabin-crew get handsome salary and allowances. With the expansion in aviation industry, a lot of vacancies are being generated on a regular basis.

AIRCRAFT MAINTENANCE ENGINEERS

Aircraft is a fascinating piece of engineering. It has a multitude of systems. Each system is further divided into many sub-system and each of these sub systems in turn has a large number of components and parts. Thus an aircraft will have tens of thousands of parts, each one having a distinct and important role to play just like each system of your scooter or car is expected to do. The major difference being that an aircraft is a much more complex and bigger machine. However, there is yet another difference. The aircraft, once it gets started and goes up in the air, must not fail, come what may. Though, it is a tough task and a daunting requirement, but it is an absolutely essential one to be fulfilled. Such a challenge is met by a breed of people in aviation industry Maintenance Engineers.

There are jobs both in Commercial airlines as well as in all the four arms of the Defence Forces. To work in commercial airlines, one has to acquire Aircraft Maintenance Engineer (AME) License which is issued by Director General Civil Aviation. A job of Maintenance Engineer in the Defence forces is through selection by the Services Selection Board (SSB).

AIR TRAFFIC CONTROLLERS

Pilots fly the aircraft, but Air Traffic Controllers supervise and control their movements so as to ensure that it operates safely without any untoward accident/incident. Their job is highly skilled, carries a great responsibility and demands alertness and dedication of the highest order. There are two different avenues for jobs as Air Traffic Controller : In Civil sector and in the Defence Forces (The Air Force and the Navy).

SUPPORT SERVICES

The airline industry is one of the most dynamic industries today with a variety of operations in many fields. The multi-billion dollar industry worldwide has risen from a humble beginning since 1903. Today, there are more than 10,000 aeroplanes offering more than twenty lakh seats every day. With new developments on the board as well as in the pipeline, the commercial aviation industry is expected to throw up new challenges and career opportunities in the current decade. There are various types of job prospects in various fields of aircraft operations and airlines management like Airport Manager, Public Relations Officer, Commercial Superintendent and Assistants, Flight Handling Officers, Crew Schedulers, Ticketing and Reservation Staff and Tourist Information Centres.

RESEARCH DESIGN AND DEVELOPMENT

Today, more than 30,000 skilled scientists and technologists are working in 51 laboratories located nationwide and are working for the development of aviation related equipment and systems. It can accommodate qualified personnel from various disciplines of engineering and science. Prominent aviation related agencies are Gas Turbine Research Establishment, Aeronautical Defence Establishment, Aerial Delivery Research and Development Establishment, Aeronautical Development Agency, National Aerospace laboratories

MANUFACTURING INDUSTRY

There are technicians and engineers who manufacture aircraft which contain as many as few lakh components, the safely and reliability of these components being beyond imagination. Well, the requirement is fail-safe components and systems. Presently, the agencies involved in this task are Hindustan Aeronautics Limited and Taneja Aerospace and Aviation Limited.

CONTROLLING ORGANIZATIONS

Aviation industry is unique in one respect. It has to be strictly regulated and controlled since it demands high levels of skills and warrants even higher levels of security. Thus, there are certain agencies which control and govern various aspects related to flying. Two of the important organisations that do so and offer a variety of jobs are:-

AIRPORTS AUTHORITY OF INDIA(AAI)

AAI manages, 11 international, 89 domestic airports and 26 civil enclaves at Defence air-bases, a total of 126 in the country. It also manages air –traffic services in the entire Indian Airspace extending beyond the territorial limits of the country as per the requirements of International Civil Aviation Organisation (ICAO). It is manned by a dedicated team of professionals including managers and engineers.

DIRECTOR GENERAL OF CIVIL AVIATION (DGCA)

It is responsible for, laying down rules, regulations and their implementation for ensuring the safety of aircraft operations. The Aircraft Act, Aircraft Rules and the Civil Aviation Requirements issued from time to time by the DGCA, broadly stipulate the various safety requirements. The work of DGCA is discharged by various personnel technical and non technical engaged in the various areas such as Air-Worthiness, Safety, Flight Inspection, Aerodrome Standards and Administration.

The years to come are going to throw open a large number of job opportunities in the interesting field of aviation. This will be partly due to the increasing thrust on Tourism and partly due to the fact that air-travel is becoming cheaper day-by-day. Obviously more passengers mean, more aircraft in the skies thus leading to increase the number of jobs.

SELECTED LIST OF PILOT TRAINING

1. Indira Gandhi Rashtriya Udan Academy (IGRUA) Fursatganj Airfield, Rae Bareli –229 302 Website: www.igrua.com
2. The Honorary Secretary, Bombay Flying Club, Juhu Aerodrome, Santa Cruz, Mumbai-400 054
3. The Honorary Secretary, Delhi Flying Club Limited, Safdarjung Airport, New Delhi-110 003
4. The Principal, Government Flying Training Institute, Jakkur Aerodrome, Yelahanka, Bangalore-560 054
5. The Honorary Secretary, North India Flying Club, Civil Aerodrome, Jalandhar Cantt., Ludhiana, Patiala-147 001
6. Orient Flight School, 40, GST Road, St.Thomas Mount, Chennai-600 016, email-hetc@vsnl.com
7. Ahmedabad Aviation and Aeronautics Ltd.,AAA Hanger, Near Old Terminal, Airport, Ahmedabad-380 012

8. TAAL Flying Academy, 1010, 10th floor, Prestige Meridian-129, MG Road, Bangalore-560 001
9. Tatanagar Aviation Pvt Ltd.,Sonari Aerodrome Jamshedpur-831 011
10. Rajputana Aviation Academy Pvt.Ltd., 6-B, Ganga Path, Suraj Nagar (West), Civil Lines, Jaipur-302 006

SOME SELECTED LIST OF AME TRAINING INSTITUTES

1. School of Aviation Science and Technology, Delhi Flying Club, Safdarjung Airport, New Delhi-110 003
2. Flytech Aviation Academy Road No.10, Maredpally West Hyderabad-500 001
3. Institute of Aircraft Maintenance Engineers, Old Airport Road, Gautam Nagar, 4-71/1, Ferozguda, Secundarabad-500 011
4. Aeronautical Training Institute, Lucknow Airport, Lucknow-226 001
5. Rajiv Gandhi Aviation Academy, 190, Plassy Lane, Bowenpally, Secunderabad-500 011
6. Bombay Flying Club, Juhu Aerodrome, Santacruz(W), Mumbai-400 059

(d) **PILOT**

Train to be a commercial pilot!

The basic prerequisites

(i) You must complete your Class XII under the 10+2 system or its equivalent with a minimum of 50 per cent marks in Mathematics and Physics.

(ii) You must be minimum 16 years of age to be eligible for a Private Pilot License and 17 for a Commercial Pilot License.

(iii) Your vision in one eye must be perfect. In general medical terminology, it is called 6/6 eyesight. In the other eye, you could have an imperfection of 6/9, which must be correctable to 6/6.

(iv) General physical fitness is mandatory. You must be free of any disease that can hamper normal function.

The route to being a commercial pilot

First, zero in on a good flying club.

Then you begin the stepwise training process.

Student Pilot License

(i) You must appear for a written theory examination in Air Regulations, Aviation Meteorology and Air Navigation and Air Technical.

(ii) You must obtain a medical certificate of fitness from doctors designated by the Director General of Civil Aviation. Only two bodies in India — Air Force Central Medical Establishment in New Delhi and the Institute of Aviation Medicine, Bangalore — are authorised to give you a medical fitness certificate.

(iii) You have to get a security clearance.

(iv) You will need to appear for an oral examination and an aptitude test.

(v) If the medical clearance comes through and you clear the exams, you will be granted the SPL.

Damages: You must furnish a bank guarantee of Rs . 10,000.

Private Pilot Licence

(i) Post attaining the SPL, you will be assigned an instructor to start flying lessons. You will be taught the basics of flying and your instructor will accompany you on flights.

(ii) After about 15 hours of flying with an instructor, ie dual flying, you can fly solo and go cross-country as well.

(iii) To obtain a Private Pilot License, you have to fly a minimum of 60 hours. Of this, at least 20 hours should be solo flying and 5 hours should be cross-country flights.

(iv) You will also need to appear for the written theory examinations in subjects like Air Regulations, Aviation Meteorology, Air Navigation, Aircraft Engines and Seamanship.

(v) You will need to obtain the medical fitness certificate from the AFCME or IAM.

(vi) You must be at least 17 years old.

(viii) You must have passed Class XII or equivalent exam with Physics, Maths and Chemistry as your subjects.

Damages: The per hour cost of flying is quite steep: about Rs 3,500.

To get a PPL, you need at least 60 hours of flying. Thus the total cost of obtaining a PPL will be a cool Rs 2 lakh (Rs 200,000)!

Commercial Pilot License

This license is the most important license to become a commercial pilot.

(i) The age bracket for getting a CPL is between 18 years and 30 years.

(ii) You need a minimum of 250 hours of flying to get this license. Of this, 150 hours have to be solo flying, 25 hours of cross-country flying, 10 hours of instrument flying (which means you rely only on the plane's instruments for flying without looking at the horizon or external assistance), and 5 hours of flying in the night.

(iii) A medical certificate from ACFME or IAM and theory tests in Air Regulations, Aviation Meteorology, Air Navigation, Technical and Planning are other important parts of the process.

(iv) You can get the Private Helicopter License if you complete 40 hours of flight training with 15 hours of solo flying. Written exams on basic aviation subjects have to be taken.

(v) To get a Commercial Helicopter Pilot License, you need 60 hours of flight training as well as appear for a written exam.

(vi) Helicopter pilots are hired by public and private sector corporates as well as security agencies.

Damages: A steep Rs 9 lakh (Rs 900,000). For Commercial Helicopter Pilot License, the cost could go up to Rs 13 lakh (Rs. 1.3 million)!

Airline Transport Pilot's License

The above mentioned licenses can only allow you to fly as a co-pilot. If you want to take over as captain, you need the Airline Transport Pilot's License, which is the highest aviation license available.

Along with clearing written papers, you also need to clock a total of 1,500 flying hours and take medical tests.

Damages: It costs Rs 30,000 to Rs 40,000 per hour. Often, the airline you work for may sponsor the training costs.

Additional training and information

Once you get the CPL, you may want to go in for multi engine training. After seven to 10 hours of multi engine training on a certain aircraft, your license will carry an endorsement of the aircraft you have flown. All the above licenses need to be renewed regularly. You must adhere strictly to medical tests. Fly one hour after your license expires, and you will be banned from flying ever again! Medical conditions and regular exam clearances notwithstanding, a pilot can continue in this career till 61 years. These days, you could even try for a scholarship. Please visit www.scholarshipsindia.com for details.

Damages: Multi engine flight training is very expensive and can cost anything between Rs 15,000 and Rs 25,000 per hour.

List of Flying Clubs in India

State-owned

1. Indira Gandhi Rashtriya Udan Akademi, Rae Bareilly, Uttar Pradesh
2. Andhra Pradesh Aviation Academy, Hyderabad, Andhra Pradesh
3. Amritsar Aviation Club, Amritsar, Punjab
4. Bihar Flying Institute, Patna, Bihar

5. Bombay Flying Club, Mumbai, Maharashtra
6. Gujarat Flying Club, Vadodara, Gujarat
7. Government. Flying Training Institute, Bhubaneshwar, Orissa
8. Government Flying Training Institute, Kolkata, West Bengal
9. Government. Flying Training School, Bangalore, Karnataka
10. Haryana Institute of Civil Aviation, Karnal, Haryana
11. Haryana Institute of Civil Aviation, Hissar, Haryana
12. Haryana Institute of Civil Aviation, Pinjore, Haryana
13. Ludhiana Aviation Club, Ludhiana, Punjab
14. Madhya Pradesh Flying Club, Indore, Madhya Pradesh
15. Madhya Pradesh Flying Club, Bhopal, Madhya Pradesh
16. Madras Flying Club, Chennai, Tamil Nadu
17. Northern India Flying Club, Jallandhar, Punjab
18. Patiala Aviation Club, Patiala, Punjab
19. Rajasthan State Flying School, Jaipur, Rajasthan
20. UP State Flying Training Institute, Kanpur, Uttar Pradesh
21. Andaman and Nicobar Flying Training Institute, Port Blair, Andaman and Nicobar Islands
22. Assam Flying Club, Guwahati, Assam
23. Banasthali Vidyapith Gliding and Flying Club, Coimbatore, Tamil Nadu
24. Aviation Training Academy, Coimbatore, Tamil Nadu
25. Delhi Flying Club, New Delhi
26. Kerala Aviation Training Centre, Thiruvananthapuram, Kerala
27. Nagpur Flying Club, Nagpur, Maharashtra
28. Jamshedpur Cooperative Flying Club, Jamshedpur, Jharkhand

Private

1. Ahmedabad Aviation and Aeronautics, Ahmedabad, Gujarat
2. Academy of Carver Aviation, Belgaum, Karnataka
3. Flytech Aviation Academy, Hyderabad, Andhra Pradesh
4. Garg Aviation, Kanpur, Uttar Pradesh
5. HAL Rotary Wing Academy, Bangalore, Karnataka
6. Rajputana Aviation Academy, Kota, Rajasthan
7. Orient Flight School, Pondicherry
8. Wings Aviation, Hyderabad, Andhra Pradesh
9. Yash Air, Indore, Madhya Pradesh
10. Frank Airways, Indore, Madhya Pradesh
11. Bangalore Aeronautics and Technical Services, Bangalore, Karnataka

7

Clerical Job

(a) ADJUSTMENT CLERK

Description

Investigate and resolve customers' inquiries concerning merchandise, service, billing, or credit rating. Examine pertinent information to determine accuracy of customers' complaints and responsibility for errors. Notify customers and appropriate personnel of findings, adjustments, and recommendations, such as exchange of merchandise, refund of money, credit to customers' accounts, or adjustment to customers' bills.

Experience

Some previous work-related skill, knowledge, or experience may be helpful in these occupations, but usually is not needed. For example, a drywall installer might benefit from experience installing drywall, but an inexperienced person could still learn to be an installer with little difficulty.

Education

These occupations usually require a high school diploma and may require some vocational training or job-related course work. In some cases, an associate's or bachelor's degree could be needed.

Training

Employees in these occupations need anywhere from a few months to one year of working with experienced employees.

Tasks

1. Writes work order.
2. Examines weather conditions, number of days in billing period, and reviews meter accounts for errors that might explain high utility charges.

3. Trains dealers or service personnel in construction of products, service operations, and customer service.
4. Compares merchandise with original requisition and information on invoice and prepares invoice for returned goods.
5. Reviews claims adjustments with dealer, examines parts claimed to be defective, and approves or disapproves of dealer's claim.
6. Notifies customer and designated personnel of findings and recommendations, such as exchanging merchandise or refunding money, or adjustment of bill.
7. Orders tests to detect product malfunction and determines if defect resulted from faulty construction.
8. Prepares reports showing volume, types, and disposition of claims handled.

(b) MEETING AND CONVENTION PLANNERS

Description

Coordinate activities of staff and convention personnel to make arrangements for group meetings and conventions.

Experience

A minimum of two to four years of work-related skill, knowledge, or experience is needed for these occupations.

Education

Most of these occupations require a bachelor's degree, but some do not.

Training

Employees in these occupations usually need several years of work-related experience, on-the-job training, and/or vocational training.

Tasks

1. Directs and coordinates activities of staff and convention personnel to make arrangements, prepare facilities, and provide services for events.
2. Evaluates and selects providers of services, such as meeting facilities, speakers, and transportation, according to customer requirements.
3. Inspects rooms and displays for conformance to customer requirements and conducts post-meeting evaluations to improve future events.
4. Obtains permits from fire and health departments to erect displays and exhibits and serve food at events.

5. Speaks with attendees and resolves complaints to maintain goodwill.
6. Reads trade publications, attends seminars, and consults with other meeting professionals to keep abreast of meeting management standards and trends.
7. Maintains records of events.
8. Reviews bills for accuracy and approves payment.
9. Negotiates contracts with such providers as hotels, convention centers, and speakers.
10. Plans and develops programs, budgets, and services, such as lodging, catering, and entertainment, according to customer requirements.

Consults with customer to determine objectives and requirements for events, such as meetings, conferences, and conventions.

(c) PRECISION PRINTING WORKERS

Description

Perform variety of precision printing activities, such as duplication of microfilm and reproduction of graphic arts materials.

Experience

Some previous work-related skill, knowledge, or experience may be helpful in these occupations, but usually is not needed.

Education

These occupations usually require a high school diploma and may require some vocational training or job-related course work. In some cases, an associate's or bachelor's degree could be needed.

Training

Employees in these occupations need anywhere from a few months to one year of working with experienced employees.

Tasks

1. Immerses exposed materials into chemical solutions to hand-develop single or multicolor proofs or printing plates.
2. Reviews layout and customer order to determine size and style of type.
3. Hand-rubs paper against printing plate to transfer specified design onto paper for use in etching glassware.
4. Compares test exposures to quality control color guides or exposure guides to determine data for exposure settings.
5 Positions and aligns negatives to assemble flats for reproduction.
6. Sets up and operates bindery equipment to cut, assemble, staple, or bind materials.

7. Sets up and operates various types of cameras to produce negatives, photostats, or plastic or paper printing plates.
8. Prints paper or film copies of completed material from computer.
9. Scans artwork, using optical scanner, which changes image into computer-readable form.
10. Measures density levels of colors or color guides on proofs, using densitometer, and compares readings to set standards.
11. Prepares microfiche duplicates of microfilm, using contact printer and developing machine.
12. Maintains printing machinery and equipment.
13. Examines and inspects printed material for clarity of print and specified color.
14. Operates offset-duplicating machine or small printing press to reproduce single or multicolor copies of line, drawings, graphs, or similar materials.
15. Operates automatic processor to develop photographs, plates, or base material used in single or multicolor proofs.
16. Mixes powdered ink pigments, using matching book and measuring and mixing tools.
17. Puts flats into vacuum frame to produce aluminum plate, microfiche print, or single or multicolor proof.

Enters, positions, and alters size of text, using computer, to make up and arrange pages to produce printed materials.

(d) PURCHASING MANAGERS

Description

Plan, direct, or coordinate the activities of buyers, purchasing officers, and related workers involved in purchasing materials, products, and services.

Experience

A minimum of two to four years of work-related skill, knowledge, or experience is needed for these occupations.

Education

Most of these occupations require a bachelor's degree.

Training

Employees in these occupations usually need several years of work-related experience, on-the-job training, and/or vocational training.

Tasks

1. Directs and coordinates activities of personnel engaged in buying, selling, and distributing materials, equipment, machinery, and supplies.

2. Develops and implements office, operations, and systems instructions, policies, and procedures.
3. Conducts inventory and directs buyers in purchase of products, materials, and supplies.
4. Determines merchandise costs and formulates and coordinates merchandising policies and activities to ensure profit.
5. Represents company in formulating policies and negotiating contracts with suppliers.
6. Prepares, reviews, and processes requisitions and purchase orders for supplies and equipment.
7. Analyzes market and delivery systems to determine present and future material availability.
8. Prepares report regarding market conditions and merchandise costs.

(e) RECEPTIONISTS & INFORMATION CLERKS

Description

Answer inquiries and obtain information for general public, customers, visitors, and other interested parties. Provide information regarding activities conducted at establishment; location of departments, offices, and employees within organization.

Experience

No previous work-related skill, knowledge, or experience is needed for these occupations. For example, a person can become a general office clerk even if he/she has never worked in an office before.

Education

These occupations may require a high school high secondary pass certificate. Some may require a formal training course to obtain a license.

Training

Employees in these occupations need anywhere from a few days to a few months of training. Usually, an experienced worker could show you how to do the job.

Tasks

1. Analyzes data to determine answer to customer or public inquiry.
2. Types memos, correspondence, travel vouchers, or other documents.
3. Operates telephone switchboard to receive incoming calls.

4. Enrolls individuals to participate in programs, prepares lists, and notifies individuals of acceptance in programs, and arranges and schedules space and equipment for participants.
5. Answers telephone to schedule future appointments, provide information, or forward call.
6. Provides information to public regarding tours, classes, workshops, and other programs.
7. Registers visitors of public facility, such as national park or military base, collects fees, explains regulations, and assigns sites.
8. Collects and distributes messages for employees of organization.
9. Provides information to public concerning available land leases, land classification, or mineral resources.
10. Greets persons entering establishment, determines nature and purpose of visit, and directs visitor to specific destination, or answers questions and provides information.
11. Records, compiles, enters, and retrieves information, by hand or using computer.
12. Calculates and quotes rates for tours, stocks, insurance policies, and other products and services.
13. Receives payment and records receipts for services.
14. Performs duties such as taking care of plants and straightening magazines to maintain lobby or reception area.
15. Hears and resolves complaints from customers and public.
16. Transmits information or documents to customer, using computer, mail, or facsimile.
17. Monitors facility to ensure compliance with regulations.
18. Files and maintains records.

Conducts tours or delivers talks describing features of public facility, such as historic site or national park.

(f) TELLERS

Description

Receive and pay out money. Keep records of money and negotiable instruments involved in a financial institution's various transactions.

Experience

Some previous work-related skill, knowledge, or experience may be helpful in these occupations, but usually is not needed.

Education

These occupations usually require a high school diploma and may require some vocational training or job-related course work. In some cases, an associate's or bachelor's degree could be needed.

Training

Employees in these occupations need anywhere from a few months to one year of working with experienced employees.

Tasks

1. Enters customers' transactions into computer to record transactions and issues computer-generated receipts.
2. Cashes checks and pays out money after verification of signatures and customer balances.
3. Examines coupons and bills presented for payment to verify issue, payment date, and amount due.
4. Issues checks to bond owners in settlement of transactions.
5. Quotes unit exchange rate, following daily international rate sheet or computer display.
6. Removes deposits from automated teller machines and night depository and counts and balances cash in them.
7. Receives checks and cash for deposit, verifies amount, and examines checks for endorsements.
8. Counts currency, coins, and checks received for deposit, shipment to branch banks, or Federal Reserve Bank by hand or currency-counting machine.
9. Explains, promotes, or sells products or services, such as travelers checks, savings bonds, money orders, and cashier's checks.
10. Prepares daily inventory of currency, drafts, and travelers' checks.
11. Composes, types, and mails correspondence relating to discrepancies, errors, and outstanding unpaid items.
12. Gives information to customer about foreign currency regulations and computes exchange value and transaction fee for currency exchange.

Balances currency, coin, and checks in cash drawer at end of shift and calculates daily transactions.

8

Educational Courses

(a) ECONOMICS

Economics has a bold approach to solve the multi dimensional problems facing the nation. It is useful for eradicating, poverty, unemployment and overcome problems such as inflation, stagnation, recession, population explosion and adverse balance of payments etc. Knowledge of economics is being used for accelerating growth in the economics of world. Economics is a social science concerned with the use and allocation of resources for achievement and maintenance of growth with stability. Over the years economics has produced many fascinating fields such as :-

- Agricultural Economics
- International Economics
- Business Economics
- Labour Economics
- Development Economics
- Natural Resource Economics
- Econometrics
- Rural Economics and Rural Development
- Financial Economics
- Welfare Economics
- Industrial Economics

Educational and Research Facilities

Almost all colleges and Universities in India offer the main subject "Economics" at the graduate and postgraduate level. Economics can be taken up as a subject at the 10 + 2 level. It may be studied at the under graduate level in various courses such as BA/B.Com. BBA/ BBS, BBE (Bachelor of Business Economics) and BFIA (Bachelor of Financial and Investment Analysis). All these courses are of three years duration. Many Universities offer BA(Hons.) in Economics to those students who had Maths. as a subject at the 10+2 level.

MA (Economics) is available in most of the Universities. A student after completing postgraduate studies can step ahead for M.Phil or Ph.D. Economics is a comer stone for advanced professional degree in areas of management, law, finance, public affairs and so on.

Prominent Institutes for higher learning

- Institute of Economic Growth, University of Delhi, North Campus, Delhi-110007 Web.-www.iegindia.org
- Indian Council of Social Science Research, JNU Institutional Area, Aruna Asaf Ali Marg, New Delhi-110 067 Web-www.icssr.org
- National Council of Applied Economic Research (NCAER),Parisila Bhawan, 11,Indraprastha Estate, New Delhi-110002, Web-www.ncaer.org
- National Institute of Rural Development, Rajendranagar, Hyderabad- 500030 Web.-www.nird.org.in
- Institute of Applied Manpower Research, New Delhi-110002
- Indian Statistical Institute, 203 BT Road, Kolkata-700108, Web.-www.isical.ac.in
- Institute of Studies in Industrial Development, PO Box 7151, Narendra Niketan, Indraprastha Estate, New Delhi-110002 Web.-www.icssr.org
- Indira Gandhi Institute of Development Research, Gen.AK Vaidya Marg, Film City Road, Goregaon(East), Mumbai-400065 Web.-www.igidr.ac.in
- Institute of Development Studies, B-8, Jhalana Institutional Area, Jaipur-302004, Web.-www.idsj.org
- Centre for Economic and Social Studies, Nizamia Observatory Campus, Hyderabad-500016 Web.-www.cess.ac.in
- Institute for Social & Economic Change, Nagarbhavi, Bangalore-560072 Web.-www.isec.ac.in

Job Opportunities

There are a few broad areas in which a graduate in economics can get jobs. These are: Services in the Central, State, Local Government, Public Sector Undertakings, Private Sector, NGOs in fields of agriculture, labour, housing, transportation finance etc. Business in marketing, advertisisng, insurance, training, real estate and personnel work. Teaching in educational institutes, secondary and elementary schools. In Journalism and writing reports on economic and business events in Newspapers and editing etc. are some other areas.

After Postgraduation one can be eligible to apply for the National Eligibility Test (NET) which is conducted by UGC. A postgraduate student can expect a financial assistance of approx. Rs.8000/- as a junior research fellow in the field of research. UPSC conducts Indian Economic Service Examination for postgraduate in economics, econometrics, applied economics and related disciplines. Besides, any student interested in academics can get a job as a teacher, researcher, supervisor in business, as a sales manager, sales representative, advertising officer, insurance officer, production manager, project coordinator, labour relation officer, journalist etc. Apart from these, International Organisations such as World Bank, International Monetary Fund (IMF), International Labour Orgnisation (ILO) and World Trade Organisation (WTO) provide job opportunities to well known economists. Economics is the only social science discipline for which, a Nobel Memorial Prize in Economics has been instituted in 1967 (but awarded for the first time in 1969) by Bank of Sweden.

(B) FASHION BUSINESS EDUCATION

We get fascinated seeing elegantly dressed people, fabulous accessories, splendid home furnishing, bags, leather garments, computer generated designs, presentations, visual merchandising of stores and shopping mails. All these are categorized under Fashion Industry. The growth in this sector is immense and right assessment of market trend and a creative art can fetch you a fortune. Fashion has many streams and thus has similar career options. You may not be good in a field but that does not stop you in pursuing your career in fashion. As per your interest you can choose a right option. National Institute of Fashion Technology (NIFT) is a premier institute in fashion industry.

The programme and the career option after completing the programme are:-

Programme : **Undergraduate Programme in Fashion Design**

Duration : 4 years

Eligibility : 12th Pass (students appearing for final examination can also apply)

Career Options : The most coveted profession by most of the aspirant fashion students for career as:- Designers, Design merchandisers, Freelance Design Consultants, Stylists, Exhibition & Visual Display Experts, Forecasting & Fashion Trends Forum Organizers, Fashion & Lifestyle

Journalists, Constume Designers and Illustrators.

Programme : **Undergraduate Programme in Leather Design**
Duration : 4 years
Eligibility : 12th Pass (Students appearing for final examination can also apply)
Career Options: Leather Design Programme offers study in fashion illustration, pattern making & construction, leather processing & surface techniques, field studies, liberal arts, branding & retailing, design projects, merchandising & supply chain, production systems & analysis, portfolio development, to name a few.

Programme : **Undergraduate Programme in Fashion & Lifestyle Accessory**
Duration : 4 years
Eligibility : 12th Pass(students appearing for final exam. can also apply)
Career : This programme gives career options in :- Accessories, Designers-in different areas of interest, Brand Managers, Visual Merchandisers, Product Managers, Consultants, Entrepreneurs, etc.

Programme : **Undergraduate Programme in Fashion & Lifestyle Accessory**
Duration : 4 years
Eligibility : 12th Pass (students appearing for final exam. can also apply)
Career : This programme gives career options in :- Accessories, Designers-in different areas of interest, Brand Managers, Visual Merchandisers, Product Managers, Consultants, Entrepreneurs, etc.

Programme : **Undergraduate Programme in Textile Design**
Duration : 4 years
Eligibility : 12th Pass (students appearing for final exam can also apply)
Career : Textile Designers, Design Managers, Fabric Managers, Opening in Design Studio, Opening

in Textile Mills, Opening in Export Houses, Merchandisers, Consultants, Entrepreneur etc.

Programme : **Undergraduate Programme in Knitwear Design**
Duration : 4 years
Eligibility : 12th Pass (student appearing for fina exam can also apply)
Career : Knitwear Designers, Creative Managers, Merchandisers, Production Managers, Consultants, Entrepreneurs.

Programme : **Undergraduate Programme in Fashion Communication**
Duration : 4 years
Eligibility : 12th Pass(students appearing for final exam can also apply)
Career : If you wish to be the part of Fashion Events, Retails, Styling, Photography, Fashion Journalism, Visual Merchandising, Graphic Designing, multimedia presentations and wish to Acquire communication skills, than Fashion Communication is The right programme for you.

Programme : **Undergraduate Programme in Fashion Technology**
Duration : 4 years
Eligibility : 12th Pass with Physics, Chemistry and Maths (students appearing for fina exam can also apply)

The programme in Fashion Technology offers in-depth study in fabric properties, manufacturing process and machinery, statistical tools, software related to apparel industry, production planning, construction of garment, processing techniques, production planning and control, management of trade, supply chain, IT applications, to name a few.

Programme : **Postgraduate Programme in Fashion Management**
Duration : 2 years
Eligibility : Graduate/Diploma from NIFT. Students appearing for qualifying Exam can also apply.
Career : By doing Postgraduate Programme in Fashion Management, One can build career in.

Brand Management, International Marketing, Fashion Merchandising, Retail Buying and Global Sourcing. Product Development, Retail Management, Visual Merchandising, Export Merchandising, etc.

The 2- years programme in Fashion Management offers professional education in basic product and manufacturing, fashion marketing, export, economic analysis, statistical fabric knowledge and analysis.

Programme : **Postgraduate Programme in Fashion Technology**

Duration : 2 years

Eligibility : BE/B.Tech.(Textiles/Apparel/Mechanical/ Industrial Production/ Electronics/Computer/ Information Technology)- Students Appearing for qualifying exam can also apply.

Career : The two years Fashion Technology Postgraduate Programme Builds career in:-

. Apparel Technology Management, Industrial Engineering, Quality Management, Production Management, Research and Development Consultancy in Global Fashion Industry.

The programme is aimed to motivate and facilitate students to excel in understanding and integrating the areas of technology and management for apparel manufacturing and develop capability to offer strategic solutions.

(c) FILM DIRECTION

The film and television direction course at FTII, Pune is a diploma course for three years for which a bachelor's degree is required. Admission is on the basis of an entrance test followed by an interview. The written test can be taken at a number of examination centres around the country, but the interview will be conducted at the FTII campus. Allahabad is one of the centres for the written test. Applications should be sent by early April and the test is normally held in early May. Tuition fees for the course is Rs.20,000/- per year. The application form can be procured from the Registrar, Film and Television Institute of India, Law College Road, Pune- 411 004.

Do not be afraid to shine. This world needs what you have to give. Open up the areas of your beings.Expose them to yourself to others. You are valuable. You are unique. You have much to give. Do not be afraid to give it. As we risk ourselves, we grow.

Each new experience is a risk. We can try and may be fail, And, as a result, grow.

Some useful courses are:-

DIPLOMA AND CERTIFICATE COURSES IN FILM AND TELEVISION

Course	*Duration/Title*	*Qualification*
Direction	Three Year	Bachelor's Degree
Cinematography	Three Year	Bachelor's Degree
Audiography	Three Year	Bachelor's Degree withPhysics as a subject at (10+2) Level
Editing	Three Year	Bachelor's Degree
Acting	Two Year	Bachelor's Degree
Art Direction	Two Year	Bachelor's Degree
Animation & One and a Half year Computer Graphics		(10+2) pass
Feature Film Screen Play Writing	One year	Bachelor's Degree
COURSES IN TELEVISION		
Direction	One Year	Bachelor's Degree
Electronic Cinematography	One Year	Bachelor's Degree
Video Editing	One Year	Bachelor's Degree
Audiography and TV Engineering	One year	10+2 level with Physics

(d) INTERNATIONAL BUSINESS

International business, foreign trade or international marketing as the course is often termed is taught as part of the MBA curriculum at most B-schools. However, a number of such institutes also offer a specialised master's degree in International Business or Foreign Trade. While the major part of the programme is similar to the marketing modules of business management, it also includes procedures and documentation of international trade operations, international law and taxation, quotas and restrictions, relevant treaties, various aspects of international business practices and so on. A Master's in International Business, or Foreign Trade is offered by the following: Indian Institute of Foreign Trade, New Delhi; Delhi University, Punjab University, Chandigarh; Kurukshetra University, Aligarh Muslim University, Sumbiosis Institute of Foreign Trade, Pune, Fore School of Management, Delhi, and several other management institutes. There are also PG diploma programmes in foreign trade, such as those offered by International Management Institute, New Delhi and Amity Business School, New Delhi and some courses through distance learning too, such as those from All India Management Association and IGNOU. Admission to all these courses is through admission tests.

(e) JOURNALISM

Post Graduate Diploma in Journalism

The post-graduate diploma in journalism is a one-year intensive vocational programme for graduates who wish to train for careers in the exciting world of print, television, radio or online journalism. The course is spread over two semesters and is so designed that every student grasps the fundamentals in every strain of media and to thereafter choose an area of specialisation.

The course has the right mix of theory and practice which enable students to not only learn reporting, interviewing, writing and researching reports but also acquire production skills that puts them firmly ahead of their peers. Students at the Pioneer Media School are taught by a distinguished array of media teachers and professionals who will bring their rich experience to the classroom. The School's Visiting Faculty, which comprises the best media practitioners in the country, provides valuable insights into journalism practice.

COURSE STRUCTURE

The course is spread over two semesters and is so designed that every student grasps the fundamentals in every strain of media and to thereafter choose an area of specialisation.

The units taught in each semester:
Semester -I

Mass Communication Theories, Communication Research, Media History,Fundamentals of Audio Visual (AV) Journalism, Print Journalism – I, Radio Journalism – I,Television Journalism- I

Semester -II

Media Law and Ethics, Print Journalism – II,Radio Journalism – II, Television Journalism – II, Internet Journalism, Project Work

THE COURSE IN DETAIL
Semester I

Mass Communication Theories

This is a basic unit that outlines the theories and forms of communication and their relevance to journalism practice. It deals with models of communication and relevance of communication theories to practice. It enables students to understand the relationship between media and society and the impact the former has on the latter. Students are also exposed to various political systems as also the role and power of media in them.

Communication Research

This unit deals with the fundamentals of research, types of research, the nature and purpose of social research and research methodology. Students will learn about research tools and techniques, data analyses methods, statistical analyses and report writing. They are introduced to communication research and to the deployment of this research method in reporting. This will enable them to understand how quality research is crucial. The unit also exposes students to the fundamentals of marketing and public opinion research as also to readership and audience surveys in India.

Media History

An understanding of the history of the media and the development of radio, television and online journalism enables students to acquire a global perspective.

This unit deals with the story of newspapers and other media and their impact on society. It also focuses on the history of the Indian media and the role of newspapers in the freedom struggle.

Other elements in this unit include the history of broadcast journalism in India and the growth of television and web journalism.

Fundamentals of AV Journalism

This unit gives students their first look-in on the audio-visual media. Students learn about broadcast equipment, formats of production and the different kinds of programming in radio and television. They are introduced to skills needed in contemporary multimedia journalism and to the application of these skills across media. They also get the first feel of the skills needed to make them technically competent to produce radio and television programmes. This includes an understanding of the principles of sound, microphones, stereo and hi-fi sound, characteristics and features of the video camera, basic shots, television lighting, basic audio for television, satellite and terrestrial transmission.

Print Journalism – I

This unit deals with basic concepts like - what is news, the structure of news reports, news sources and news reporting. Students learn writing styles and pick up skills in writing news features, news analyses and opinion pieces. They learn about specialised areas of reporting like politics, business, sports, crime, cinema etc., and about investigative journalism. They also go out on assignments to report real events in the municipal council, city courts, the Delhi legislature and on the sports arena. Members of The Pioneer staff act as their mentors.

Radio Journalism – I

This unit explains how radio news is different from news in print or on television. Students learn skills needed to report for radio and about field and investigative reporting for radio. They pick up skills relating to structuring radio copy, use of ambient sound and sound bytes, voice dispatches, writing lead-ins and interviewing for radio news. Other elements in this unit include editing agency and reporters' copy for radio and content, delivery of news on FM radio, radio jockeying skills, presentation of music programmes and talk shows.

Television Journalism - I

Students learn about the concept, process and functions of visual communication in this unit. Understanding a story in visual terms is critical to quality television journalism and this unit helps students grasp this fundamental principle. They learn to visualise television news and pick up skills relating to writing to video, stills and graphics. This is followed by an understanding of television reporting, doing piece to camera and voice overs as also presentation of soft news and entertainment programmes.

Semester II

Media Law and Ethics

A sound understanding of media law and ethics is essential for every journalist. This unit equips students to avoid legal pitfalls in their careers. They learn about constitutional safeguards relating to freedom of expression and also acquire a firm grasp of the legal system and about laws pertaining to defamation, libel, contempt of court, contempt of legislature, court reporting etc. The unit covers laws relating to intellectual property and copyright and discusses issues like personal privacy versus press freedom, legislature privilege versus public interest etc. Students also learn about a wide range of laws that have a bearing on the media.

Print Journalism – II

Having learnt to report events for a newspaper and to write for different sections of a newspaper in the earlier unit, students acquire skills in editing and newspaper production in this unit. They learn the basic principles of editing, the art of headline writing, newspaper vocabulary, the flow of news copy from across the globe and the structure of a news desk. They are taught newspaper design, page visualisation, designing the front page and other special pages. Most importantly, students acquire computer skills and an understanding of computer software essential for quality newspaper production.

Radio Journalism - II

This unit of radio journalism teaches students to apply the principles of sound, sound recording and their understanding of microphones to produce radio programmes. They learn about editing sound and using special effects, digital sound recording and editing. Armed with this technical knowledge, students get down to editing and compiling radio news capsules and produce different types of radio programmes as class work.

Television Journalism – II

Students learn production and post-production skills in this unit. They learn to plan and research for field reportage and for studio productions in this unit of television journalism. They are taught single camera and multi-camera shoots, television news capsuling and news anchoring. Finally, they learn editing skills on non-linear editing systems.

Internet Journalism

This unit introduces students to online or web journalism, the newest form of journalism. Students are taught a short history of the web and its creation, web technology, emergence of web journalism on the web and E- publications. They are taught to apply design principles and journalistic disciplines in web publications as also online narratives and use of hyper-links. They learn about web writing as distinct from print, radio or television. The final step is learning production of a web newspaper.

ENTRY REQUIREMENTS AND SELECTION PROCEDURE

Anyone who has a basic degree in any subject with a minimum of 50 per cent marks and a flair for journalism is eligible to apply for admission to this post graduate programme.Candidates will be selected on the basis of their performance in the entrance test and the interview.

Learning Facilities

The Pioneer Media School has state-of-the-art equipment to train students in Print, Radio, Television and Internet Journalism. This includes a computer lab, digital cameras, high-end non-linear editing systems and graphics workstations. In addition to the facilities at the school, students will gain hands-on experience in different facets of print journalism and newspaper production at The Pioneer itself. The students' internship would make all the difference with all students being assigned to The Pioneer and its respective staff for hands-on experience in newspaper work. During this period, the students will be taught and trained by experienced desk, reporting staffers and feature writers at The Pioneer. Every student gets an opportunity to make it to the news and opinion pages. Many students will thus have a portfolio of published work before they leave the school. The school will also organise internship facilities in other established newspaper and television companies and news channels.

The school's placement cell will be in touch with leading media organisations to provide the students the best career options even before the course ends. In view of the growth in Hindi language media — TV, Print and Radio — special training will be given to equip students with the necessary language and attitudinal skills needed to excel in Hindi-oriented organisations.

(f) MASS COMMUNICATION

A course in mass communication will give you an overview of each of these fields, after which you can choose to specialise in the area that interests you. If you have good communication skills and write and speak well you can take up journalism which is about providing information through the print media- newspapers and magazines, or the electronic media- television, radio and films. If you are interested in the electronic media and have good presentation skills and creative ability you can take a plunge in this line. Working for radio and TV entails planning, directing or producing programmes of all kinds, or even presenting or performing in them.

Advertising is the most creative of the different media as it involves selling a product or service through the communication of ideas. So if are creative and full of ideas and good communication skills you can get into the ad world. There are many institute and polytechnics offering PG diplomas in mass communication. These include Indian Institute of Mass Communication , Delhi; Bharatiya Vidya Bhavan, Delhi; YMCA, Delhi; National Institute of Advertising, Delhi; Wigan & Leigh and Amity School of Communication.

(g) MEDICAL ENGINEERING

There is a growing demand for biomedical engineering professionals particularly in new technology fields such as lasers, cryosurgery and ultrasonics. Biotechnology companies involved in research are employing biomedical engineers for research and design work. Biomedical instrumentation, which applies the principles of electronics and measurement for the development of devices for the use in diagnostics and treatment of disease, is another area you could consider.

Meerut Institute of Engineering and Technology, Meerut; Mahatma Gandhi College of Engineering and Technology, Navi Mumbai; College of Engineering, Vishakapatnam, Osmania University College of Engineering, Hyderabad and BMS College of Engineering, Bangalore are among the few institutes offering biomedical engineering, VPK Mandal College of Engineering, Mumbai, offers B.Tech. in biomedical instrumentation. Admission is based on the results of an entrance test conducted by each state government according to the prevailing regulations.

(h) PACKAGING

Marketing, in the simplest language, may be known as an interplay of 4 Ps i.e. P1- product, P2-price, P3-physical distribution and P4-promotion. Apart from these Ps, there is one more P that does not have a separate identity of its own but has an important role to play in the marketing mix. That another P stands for Packaging. Packaging, although an integral part of P1 (product) has established itself as a powerful marketing tool. Packaging is not merely the carrier of the product, as it is generally understood to be. Modern packaging has come up as a bundle of the features and functions. An unaware consumer can never realise the hidden potential of packaging that influence the image and life of a brand in the market in several ways.

Favourably positioning a product in the consumer's mind, the right packaging carries with it an air of distinction, which sets it apart from the competitor. In fact, very often small details in the packaging influence buyer's decision to select or reject a product. Attractive designed packaging has an enhanced appeal to draw an onlookers attraction and convert him/her into a customer the brand values are communicated and confirmed by packaging. The stature of the brand and its intrinsic value are conveyed by the manner in which the packaging is done. It also enhances the shelf-life ,self appeal and image of the product.

Packaging holds special prominence in the FMCG (fast moving consumer goods) sector because of the stiff competition. Soft drinks, detergents, shampoos and such other luxurious items are reaching the remote areas and are being afforded even by low-income group because of the special-small packs promoted by the manufactures as a part of their affordability strategy. The advancements in the packaging technology have facilitated the production and round-the-year availability of such products as ready to serve meals, frozen vegetables and delicate diary products. In a way, packaging has been one of the factors leading to the growth and expansion of the market.

Packaging has recently been given an additional task of popularising and advertising the brand. All the promotional efforts like price reduction, gift or any other offer available with the brand are reflected silently by the packaging. That is why; packaging has now come to be used as a potential advertising tool. With the contributed efforts of advertising agencies and packaging technologists, the Indian packaging is taking a new shape indicating a bright future of this sector. The attention, emphasis and expenditure on packaging have as a separate industry calling for expansion and advancement efforts. Major players of the packaging industry are- Tetra Pack, Neo Sack, Sandico Packaging, Machinery Limited, India Foils, Ashahi India, Essel Packaging etc. that are providing their packaging services to different sets of manufacturers.

The recent marketing trends are suggestive of the fact that packaging industry will also flourish along with the growth of the market and will be one of the most developed industries of the country in the days to come. Even at this 'miles to go' stage, packaging industry has immense potentialities in terms of employment opportunities. Following employment opportunities are available in this sector:-

1. **Packaging Technologists**

Packaging technologists are the persons responsible to prepare eco-friendly and standardized packaging (appropriate according to the set standards and quality control) for the product of their client. Their work includes designing the type of packaging needed by a specific product which would ensure that the product reaches the hands of the consumer in proper condition. Packaging technologists are the persons having high level of technical know-how.

2. **Packaging Managers**

Packaging Managers are responsible for the overall management of the packaging unit.

3. **Packaging Supervisors**

Packaging Supervisors are responsible for monitoring the manufacturing process of the designed product (the package) and ensuring a smooth supply of finished product to the client. Their work also includes sealing , labelling etc. of the product.

Need of professional courses of packaging in India

With packaging on the threshold of becoming an independent P of the marketing mix, there is now a demand of professionally qualified cadre of people who can undertake design, development, production, quality control and other aspects of packaging. There are over 7,000 organised industrial units and nearly 4,50,000 small industries in India who use packaging material but do not have at their disposal qualified technical persons of packaging. In the global scenario governed by WTO, it is imperative to upgrade the packaging standards to be at par with the best at optimum cost through innovative latest technologies to meet the requirement of Indian as well as International consumers' demand. Advancement in packaging technology and standards is essential to accelerate the growth of the Indian market. Here comes the role of professional courses of packaging in order to professionalise and develop this sector.

Institutes offering Professional Courses on Packaging

Number of institutes offering courses in packaging is very limited but is expected to increase along with the expansion of the packaging industry. At present two institutes namely, The Indian Institute of Packaging (IIP), Mumbai and SIES School of Packaging, Nerul, Navi Mumbai are offering different types of courses of packaging. The Ministry of Commerce established the Indian Institute of Packaging, Mumbai, the apex body of the packaging industry in Indian in 1966. IIP encompasses the entire spectrum of packaging including : Research, Development, Education, Testing and Information. Exhibitions and Design , Publication and other related activities. At present following courses are offered by IIP:

1. Post Graduate Diploma in Packaging (full time)

This two years' course consisting of four semesters is available at Mumbai and Delhi centres of IIP.

Minimum Eligibility:- Graduate in science (12+3 years Degree) with Physics/ Chemistry/ Mathematics or Microbiology as the main subjects or Agriculture/ Food Science or Engineering Technology degree of a recognized university with a minimum second class.

Admission Procedure:- Candidate for the Post Graduate Programme are selected on the basis of performance in the entrance examination comprising a written test and interview. The test are conducted in selected cities like Mumbai, Kolkata, Delhi and Chennai usually in the month of June every year. The form can be obtained from middle of April on sending a demand draft of Rs.500/- drawn in favour of "Indian Institute of Packaging". The seats for each academic year for Post Graduate Diploma in Packaging are as follows:- Mumbai-40, Delhi-40; **Course Fee:-** 18,000 per semester.

2. Graduate Diploma in Packaging (Correspondence Course)

This 18 months course is accredited by Asian Packaging Federation and is recognized internationally. The course commences on 1st January every year and the registration is done in November-December.

Admission Eligibility:- Admission to the Graduate Diploma in packaging requires:-

1. Bachelors degree in Science/Commerce/Arts or a related field with one year of working experience
2. Engineering /Pharmacy/ Technology graduates with minimum one year of experience.
3. Diploma holders (10+3) with 2 years of working in packaging or related field.

Course Fee:- Rs. 22,000/-

3. Certificate Course of Packaging

The three months' course is available at Mumbai as well as regional centres of IIP in almost every quarter of the year.

Minimum eligibility for the Certificate Course:- Graduate in Science or Technology/ Economics/Commerce/ Mathematics/ Diploma from Polytechnic/ persons working in packaging or related fields.

Course Fee:- Rs.15,000/-

Addresses of Institutes Offering Courses of Packaging

1. Indian Institute of Packaging, E-2 MIDC Area, Post Box no. 9432, Andheri(E), Mumbai-400 093 (Phone- 28219803,28216751, 28219469,28254631, FAX- 28375302, Email- rneiip@iip-in.com, Website- www.iip-in.com

Regional Centres of IIP

1. Indian Institute of Packaging-Delhi, Plot no.21, Functional Industrial Estate, Patparganj, Opp.-Patparganj Bus Depot, Delhi-110 092 (Phone-221666703- 05, FAX- 22169612), Email-iip@bom4.vsnl.net
2. Indian Institute of Packaging –Kolkata, Block C.P. Sector-V, Salt Lake, Bidhan Nagar, Kolkata-700091 (Phone- 23670763/ 23676016, FAX-23679561) Email- iipcal@cal.vsnl.net.in
3. Indian Institute of Packaging-Chennai, Plot no.169, Industrial Estate, Perungudi, Chennai-600 096 (Phone- 24961077/ 24961560,Fax-24961077), Email iipche @giasmd 01. vsnl.net.in
4. Indian Institute of Packaging-Hyderabad, Lux-3, Industrial Estate, Hyderabad-500 001 (Phone- 23814321, FAX-23814321 Email-karnaipa@yahoo.co.in)
5. SIES School of Packaging- Mumbai, Shri Chandrashekaharendia Saraswati Vidyapuram, Sector V, Navi Mumbai (Ph-27716969)

(i) PhD

If you don't get a huge kick out of seeing a Dr. prefixed to your name, junk that idea of a doctoral programme. If recruiters are to be believed, it does not add any real value to your resume, in fact, over qualification can hurt, rather than help your job prospects in the real, experience-driven world. Employers may conclude, you are another armchair empiricist, not an action man for combating ground realities.

Consequently, although the number of universities and deemed universities have almost doubled in the country between 1980 and 2000, granting a staggering 11,534 doctoral degrees a year, fewer engineers, doctors and veterinary science post graduates are opting for a Ph.D degree while the trend is just the reverse for general Arts/ Science and Commerce students, who do not belong to any definite job oriented field.

Worse, the growing perception is that the quality of doctoral programmes has been steadily falling over the years (Source:PhDs: A need for quality control, Current Science, Volume 8, No.6, March 2000 and the AICTE report on Post-Graduate Education and Research in Engineering and Technology, 1999). The only exception is in the field of Biotechnology and Bio Informatics, where a doctoral degree is still hot.

Five years ago during the Infotech boom, with a steep rise in the wages in the IT sector (20-30 percent per annum, according to NASSCOM) the number of Ph.Ds started falling at an alarming rate to a mere one-third of the capacity of the engineering colleges. The exodus in most job oriented disciplines, it appears is still unstoppable with all the bright ones being weaned away by the industry.

"Less than 6 percent of our data base may actually comprise of Ph.Ds," says Alok Mittal, Co-founder and Vice Chairman of JobsAhead.com, who says that except for hi-end research work, "Corporates are not looking beyond Bachelors or MBAs for midrun IT, sales or marketing divisions".

"I don't think a PhD. Enhances your value in the job market in any major ways", maintains Dr.Yasho D.Verma(VP) HR, who earned his Ph.D in Organisational Behaviour from IIT, Kharagpur in 1996, after completing Engineering and Business Administration from Chandigarh. "I could have done without the doctoral degree, my job didn't specifically demand it, but I liked the Dr.prefix to my name, he confesses candidly.

Even in the field of academics, don't go for a Ph.D. unless you only want to get into the government sector. Otherwise, there are plenty of private colleges and coaching institutes, which could be glad to have you on their rolls if you have a natural inclination towards teaching.

"We have experienced that graduates from RECs (now NITs) are often better teachers than retired Dons from IITs and IIMs, because teaching is an art, which they don't teach in a doctoral programme," says the spokesperson of a private leading coaching institute, which has branches all over India and which is considered one of the best pay masters in the industry.

"If a candidate has the knack of coming down to the level of the students, empathising with their problems and committing his time to solving them, we won't care if he is armed or not armed with a Ph.D," he explains, adding that their institute by design has more MCAs,M.Sc and M.Techs on board than Ph.Ds and they draw on par with the Ph.D faculty. " Qualification is just a 'hygience' factor. What matters is performance," he quips.

However, Professor of Communications at the Indian Institute of Management, Ahmedabad, M.M.Monipally admits that "Some brilliant Ph.Ds make very bad teachers, this is not the only avenue open to them." Any setting that needs high quality research should benefit from Ph.Ds, who are after all the Brahmins of the academic community.

STEPS TO BEEF UP DOCTORAL PROGRAMMES

1. All Masters degree programmes should be increased from 18 to 21 months for high quality project work.
2. There should be an entrance test to all doctoral programmes akin to the Graduate Aptitude Test.
3. The scholarship value should be enhanced to Rs.5,000 per month for post-graduate studies and Rs.7,000 per month for doctoral studies with an annual increment or Rs.500 for four years (max).
4. All obsolete curricula should be gradually phased out.
5. Vacant faculty positions should be immediately filled-up, even if it means filling those up with non-PhD, meritorious post-graduate students.
6. A National Doctoral Programme with a scholarship of Rs,12,000 per month and a contingency fund of Rs.25,000 per year must be established to increase motivation of high calibre, prospective doctoral candidates.
7. A manpower information system should be built in the country.

An assured placement scheme should be introduced as in the Department of Atomic Energy.

(j) PHOTOJOURNALISM

If you are planning to pursue a career in photojournalism, you should have keen interest in journalism which is also described in this book.

Photojournalists may work side by side with a reporter to decide which photograph will accompany with the news item.

There are many different structures of photo department management in a publication. A large newspapar or magazine may have a managing editor or photography and graphics that supervises a team of photo editors who work with the photographers, page designers and lab technicians.

The primary duty of the photojournalist is to take pictures. They are responsible for providing clear, easy-to-read, high quality, truthful images, that communicate a meaningful message to the readers of the publication they work for.

Most newspapers also give the photographer other duties such as developing their film, editing film, scanning their pictures in the computer, adjusting the tone and colour of the pictures.

Salaries for photojournalists vary depending on the location, size and type of the publication, experience of the photographer.

Eligibility Criteria

In India there is no institution or university specifically offering degree or diploma course in photojournalism. The course is offered through different programmes of journalism and mass communication, art & craft, film and television and advanced information technologies. This education is recognized as professional education, usually referred to by different nomenclatures, viz. photo editing, layoutf and design, fundamentals of photography, electronic editing, advanced photography, digital imaging, fundamentals of digital technology, basic and advanced photojournalism, film editing, fundamental principles and practices on videography, moving and still photography, etc. depending on the emphasis on different aspects of photojournalism.

Graduates from any stream can join the above courses offered by various universities and media institutes. Almost all institutions and universities prefer to take the candidates through written and personality test (interview) examinations due to limited seats.

Institutions Offering Courses on Journalism and Photography

- Amity School of Journalism & Communication, Saket, New Delhi-110024
- Amrit College, Railway Colony, Poojappura, Trivendrum-695012
- Asian College of Journalism, Kasturi Centre,2-Anna Salai,Chennai-2
- Bhartiya Vidhya Bhavan Units at Trivandrum, Kottayam, Thrissur, Kochi, Kozhikode and other cities of India
- Bhavan's Institute of Communication & Management, Andheri West, Mumbai-400058
- Bhavan's PDN College of Communication and Management, Somani College, Chowpatty, Mumbai-400007
- Biju Patnaik Film & Television Institute, Bhubaneshwar
- Centre for Convergence Media Studies (Kerala University), Senate House Campus, Trivandrum-695034

- Centre for Development of Imaging Technology, Chitranjali Studio Complex, Thiruvallom,Trivandrum-695027
- DCSMAT Media School, Kinfra Film and Video Park, Kazhakkoottam, Trivandrum
- Film & Television Institute of India, Pune
- Garware Institute of Career Education & Development, Vidyanagri, Kalina Campus,Santa Cruz (East) Mumbai-400098
- IILM Film & Media School, 3 institutional area, Lodhi Road, New Delhi
- Indian Centre for Media and Communication, Agrasen Campus, S.No.239/2, Yerawada, Pune-411006
- Indian Institute of Mass Communication, Aruna Asaf Ali Marg, JNU Campus, New Delhi-110067
- Indian Television Training Institute, C-41 Gulmohar Park, New Delhi-49
- Institute for Integrated Learning in Management, Lodhi Institutional Area, Lodhi Road, New Delhi-3
- Jaipuria Institute, Lucknow and Noida
- Manipal Institute of Communication, Old Tile Factory Road, Press Corner, Manipal-576104
- Mother Teresa Institute of Communication and E-Journalism, TC16/38 EVRA-29, Cotton Hill, Trivandrum-695014
- Pioneer Media School, 6, Toder Mal lane, Bengali Market, New Delhi-1
- Ranade Institute, Fergusson College Road, Pune-411004
- School of Convergence, 208A, Savitri Nagar, New Delhi-17
- Satyajit Ray Film & Television Institute, EM Bypass Road, Kolkata
- The Manorama School of Communication, PB No.229, Kottayam-686001
- Rai Media Lab, B-II/58, MCIE, Mathura Road, New Delhi-44
- School of Broadcasting and Communication, 108, Building, 4,Kamdhenu Centre, Lokhandwala Complex, Andheri (West), Mumbai-53
- School of Communication and Management Studies, Management House, South Kalamassery, Kochi-682033
- Sri Aurobindo Institute of Mass Communication, Sri Aurobindo Marg, Near IIT, New Delhi-16
- St.Xavier's Institute of Communication, St.Xavier's College, Mumbai-1
- Times Centre for Media Studies, 10-Daryaganj, New Delhi-23
- National Institute of Social Communications, Research and Training, A-2, Sector-1, Vaishali, Ghaziabad, UP-201012
- Symbiosis Institute of Communication, Pune-411004
- YMCA, Jai Singh Road, New Delhi

(k) PHYSICAL EDUCATION AND SPORTS

From time immemorial, Physical Education has been used by human communities all over world to deveoop fitness for survival. Set of exercises, combative activities, endurance training, defensive and offensive arts and the like have been practiced from ancient times to prepare youth for the defence of the country and for developing and ensuring loyalty to the society. Gymnastics, dances and many games were also included in schemes of training so as to develop not only fitness, but also to promote group feeling and provide leisure-time occupations.

India has a great tradition in physical education as a means of ensuring physical development, martial valour and recreational competence; and the Indian system of exercises includes variety of physical activities such as *dands*, *baithaks*, *namaskars*, *yogic asanas* etc. which formed the integral part of physical education such as *Kho-Kho* and *Kabbadi* now promoted as National Games.

Physical education is an integral part of the total education process.

The Aims and Objectives of Physical Education

The aims and objectives of physical education depend to a great extent on the political, economical and social changes that take place in a society. India has achieved political freedom and chosen to become secular democratic republic. The aims are:-

1. The development of organic fitness
2. The development of neuromuscular skill
3. The development of character and personality
4. To prapre highly qualified leaders in the field of physical education and sports.
5. To provide professional and academic leadership to other institution in the field of physical education.
6. To provide vocational guidance and proper job placement to the people in this field.
7. To promote mass participation in physical education and sports.
8. To develop and promote programmes of physical education and sports in schools and colleges.

Need of Physical Education

There is a great need for physical education in the present era in the interest of total well-being of a child. This is an age of automation and industrial revolution. Life has become much more inactive than before which is detrimental to the health, growth and development of a child. Radio, Television and other devices have made our life sedentary. The Youth are inclined to be onlookers rather than participants in various activities. Physical activity in a planned manner is, therefore, essential to overcome the evils of modern era. Physical education has also an important role to play to overcome the problem of juvenile delinquency. Diseases concerned with the heart, blood vessels,kidneys and the like are on the increase and physical education activities can contribute considerably in safeguarding the child from the tension of modern day living. Play and exercises are absolutely essential for a youth during the period of child-hood which is period of growth and development. Good health and wholesome experience through recreative games regardless of age will certainly contribute to make life worth living.

Courses offered and duration

1. Bachelor of Physical Education (B.P.E. 3 years)
2. Bachelor of Physical Education (B.P.Ed. 1 year)
3. Master of Physical Education (M.P.E. 2 Years)

Scope of Courses Offered

On completion of the course the graduates are eligible for appointment as Supervisors, Administrators, Lecturers, Teachers of Physical Education, Coaches and Recreation Leaders in Universities, Colleges, Schools, Industrial Establishments, Commercial Firms, Governmental and Non-Governmental agencies which are engaged in promoting physical education, sports and recreation.

Admission Requirements and Procedures

(a) Bachelor of Physical Education (B.P.E. 3 years degree course) Eligibility: 10 + 2.
(b) Bachelor of Physical Education (B.P.Ed. 1 Year degree course) Eligibility : Graduation
(c) Master of Physical Education (M.P.E. 2 year degree course) Eligibility : B.P.E. / B.P.Ed.

List of Well-Known Colleges and Courses in Physical Education and Sports in India

1. B.N.College of Physical Education, Udaipur (Rajasthan) Courses Offered – B.P.E. (Three years, Eligibility 10+2), B.P.Ed. (One year, Eligibility- Graduation), M.P.E. (Two year, Eligibility B.P.E. / B.P.Ed.)
2. Mumbai University, M.G. Road, Fort, Mumbai-400 032. Courses Offered BA (Physical Cultural and Yoga Study) (Three Years, Eligibility – 10+2)
3. Amravati University, Guru Hanuman Vyayam Nagar, Amravati-444 605. Courses Offered- Bachelor of Physical Education

(Three Years, Eligibility 10+2), B.P.Ed.(One year Eligibility-Graduation), M.P.E. (Two year, Eligibility- B.P.E./ B.P.Ed.)

4. Faculty of Arts, Banaras Hindu University, Varanasi- 221 005. Courses offered- Bachelor of Physical Education (Three Years, Eligibility- 12th Passed) M.P.E.(Two year, Eligibility-B.P.E./ B.P.Ed.)
5. Indira Gandhi Institute of Physical Education and Sports Science (University of Delhi), "B"Block, Vikaspuri, New Delhi-110 018. Courses Offered- B.Sc. (Physical Education Health Education and Sports) (Three Years, Eligibility 10+2, Age 17 to 20 years).
6. School of Physical Education, Devi Ahilya University, Indore-452 001. Courses Offered- Bachelor of Physical Education (Three Years, Eligibility 10 +2), M.P.E. (Two year, Eligibility- B.P.E./ B.P.Ed.).
7. Punjabi University, Patiala-174 002. Courses Offered- Bachelor of Physical Education (Three Years, Eligibility- 10+2)
8. Laxmi Bai National Institute of Physical Education, Gwalior. Courses Offered- Bachelor of Physical Education (Three Years, Eligibility- 10+2), M.P.E. (Two year, Eligibility – B.P.E./ B.P.Ed.)
9. Choudhary Charan Singh Agriculture University, Hisar (Haryana). Courses Offered- Bachelor of Sports Humanities (Three years, Eligibility 10+2)
10. Yasvant Rao Chouhan College of Physical Education, Akola (Maharashtra). Bachelor of Physical Education (Three years, Eligibility- 10+2)
11. Department of Physical Education, Jiwaji University, Gwalior. Courses Offered- B.P.E.(Three years), B.P.Ed. (One year), M.P.E.(Two years).

(I) SOCIOLOGY

Sociology is a discipline emerged during the early part of the 19th Century in France. It was August Comte who is considered as the 'father' or 'founder' of sociology. At one time he ' regretted the hybrid character' of the word 'sociology' derived from the Latin socius and the Greek logos, but later suggested that there is a compensation..... for this etymological defect. In the fact that it recalls the two historical sources- if one intellectual, the other social- from which modern civilization has sprung. The intellectual climate from which the discipline originated can be categorized under four headings: Political philosophy, the Philosophy of History, Biological theories of evolution, and the movements for social and political reform which found it necessary to undertake a survey of social conditions.

As a discipline, sociology engages in the description and explanation of social structures and processes. These range from two person interactions to relations between large social institutions, such as politics and the economy, to relations between nations. Sociology also ranges across time and serves as a useful complement to history. Studying sociology not only increases the understanding of human society but also helps to classify human social behaviour systematically. It also helps to understand the social, religious, political, economic and governmental institutions in society, their changing nature and impact on everyday life.

Over the years the discipline produced many fascinating subjects for discussion and study such as : social stratification, social change, social movements, industrial sociology, sociology of gender, sociology of culture, sociology of religion, sociology of science and technology, sociology of inter-ethnic relations, sociology of education, sociology of backward class, sociology of communication, rural sociology, sociology of law, industrial sociology, sociology of health, military sociology, environmental sociology, sociology of migration and diaspora, clinical sociology and so on and so forth. Almost all colleges and universities in India offer either of the above or new courses besides the core courses such as theory, method and data- in the graduate and post-graduate level under the main subject 'sociology'.

A student can choose a specialisation within the field of sociology later such as family; adolescence; the urban community; education; health and medicine; ageing; work and occupations; environment and ecology; science and technology; social inequality and social class; race relations; ethnicity; migration and diaspora ; sex and gender; sports; culture; and arts; politics; the military; peace and war; crime and delinquency; law and justice; social change and social movements and any other area of human organisation.

SOCIOLOGY AS CAREER

Most students, after a Bachelors Degree or Masters Degree in Sociology in the Arts stream worry about their future. Thus comes the question of the relevance of the discipline and its future possibilities. The following section will present a plethora of choices for a career in sociology for a candidate who opts either for graduation or post-graduation in the subject.

Students often think that with an advanced degrees such as Masters or M.Phill or PhD may lead one only to make a career in academics but in reality the opportunities are wide enough. A post-graduate in sociology will provide knowledge about the research design, data analysis, statistics, theory and sociological concept which enables students to opt for job such as program, administrative or research assistant in government and non government sectors for policy analysis, program evaluation, and several other social science endeavours such as directors of research, fieldwork analyst , human resource officers and so on besides giving scope for pursuing higher research, demographer, statistician, urban planner, and community counsellor.

CAREER AFTER B.A. IN SOCIOLOGY

Taking sociology as a subject at the graduate level in colleges and universities in India is different than taking it outside India specially in Europe and America where job prospects vary because of the curriculum and evaluation pattern. In India, at graduation level most of the colleges offer sociology as a major subject. There are a few broad areas in which a sociology graduate can undertake jobs. The following list of possibilities is only illustrative- many other paths may be open for a student of sociology.

1. **Social Service**- in rehabilitation, case management, group work with youth or the elderly, recreation or administration.
2. **Community work**- in fundraising for social service organisations, child-care, or community development agencies, or environmental groups.
3. **Corrections**-in probation, parole or other criminal justice work.
4. **Business**-in advertising, marketing and consumer research, insurance, real estate, personnel work, training or sales.
5. **College settings**- in admissions, alumni relations or placement offices.
6. **Health services**-in family planning, rehabilitation counselling, health planning, hospital admissions and insurance companies.
7. **Publishing, journalism and public relations**-in writing, research and editing.
8. **Government service** –in central, state and local government jobs in such areas as transportation, housing, agriculture and labour.
9. Teaching-in elementary and secondary schools, in conjunction with appropriate teacher certification.

CAREER AFTER MA, M.PHILL OR PhD IN SOCIOLOGY

The Doctorate in Philosophy (Ph.D) is the highest degree in academics, while the Master's degree is a preliminary effort to become an academician or researcher. It also gives an opportunity to write examinations (for instance UGC's NET and other state service exams) for teaching posts in universities and colleges. Masters degree generally takes two years (or four semesters) in India, for that one should have a three-year degree course in any discipline. M.Phil is the sandwich between M.A. and a Ph.D degree. It is a further extension of research in sociology, which normally takes one year to two years depending upon the university curriculum and exam patterns, and for that one needs to have a Masters degree in sociology. These courses generally cover sophisticated knowledge of the field's perspectives and methods. The Ph.D, however, requires qualifications like Masters with a fellowship (such as junior Research Fellowship of UGC or any other)or an M.Phill degree or two to three years of teaching experience in colleges and universities. A student after completing M.A. can step further for M.Phill or Ph.D. or make it an end in itself.

However, a student of sociology after finishing any of the above degrees can get jobs- besides being I the academics as a teacher, researcher or supervisor- in business for instance, as an advertising officer, sales representative, sales manager, market analyst, real estate agent, journalist, public relations officer, human resource manager, production manager, labour relation officer, publishing officer, project manager etc. In research for instance, a student can become a data analyst survey researcher, data entry manager, census officer, demographer etc. Besides this one can also get jobs in government organisations as personnel coordinator, community affairs officers, urban/regional planning, legislative aide, affirmative action worker, foreign service officer, human rights officer and so on.

To sum up, as an emerging discipline, sociology gives enough choices in building one's career. It offers students an outlook to not only explore the processes that are shaping current trends, but also to develop an understanding of the complexity and diversity of human societies and their continuities with the past. It also stimulates awareness of contemporary social, cultural and political issues, and focuses on the importance of examining these issues in a rigorous, reasoned and analytical way.

(m) SOME USEFUL COURSES AFTER PASSING 10+2 EXAM

Course	*Name of the Institutions*	*Eligibility*
Actuarial Science		
BA(Pass)Insurance	University of Delhi	10+2
BA(Vocational) Insurance and Economics & Commerce	University of Delhi	10+2
Vocational Course in Insurance	The College of Vocational Studies, New Delhi	10+2
B.Sc. (Actuarial with Science a	Goa University	10+2

(Contd.)

(Contd.)

Course	*Name of the Institutions*	*Eligibility*
Subject. In an approved Combination)	University of Mumbai	
BA in Actuarial Science	Kurukshetra University Haryana	10+2
Advertising-Art Course		
Fine Arts/Applied Arts	Collegeof Art, New Delhi College of Art,Chandigarh College of Arts & Crafts, Lucknow Govt. College of Arts & Crafts, Chennai	10+2, Admission test
Diploma Course in Graphic Art & Design	Kala Bhavan,Viswa Bharti, West Bengal Aptitude test	10+2 with
Archaeology and Art Restoration		
BA(Archival Science)	University of Ajmer	10+2
BA Archaeology	MS University of Baroda,Gujarat Bangalore Univ.,Bangalore Dr.Babasaheb Ambedkar Univ.	10+2
Maharashtra		
Architecture		
B.Arch Hyderabad	College of Fine Arts & Arch. aptitude with PCM	CET and test 10+2
	Bihar College of Engineering 50%	CET for
Seats	Chandigarh College of Arch. Eng.With a	PCM & Min.of 55% in aggr.
	College of Engineering,Goa 45% aggr.	10+2,min.
	D.C.Patel School of Arch. Gujarat	10+2 with Science
	PDA College of Engineering 50%	CET &

(Contd.)

(Contd.)

Course	*Name of the Institutions*	*Eligibility*
	Karnataka	PCM
	Jagadguru Malikarjuna Murug-Harahebdra Institute of Technology,Karnataka	
	Manipal Instt.of Technology	10+2 with
Karnataka	50% marks	
		In PCM, Interview
	University Visvesvaraya, Karnataka	10+2 with PCM(min. 50% CET
	Govt. Engineeringk College,M.P.	10+2 with PCM
	B.K.P.S.College of Arch. Maharashtra	10+2 with PCM
EntranceTest	College of Fine Arts &	10+2
	PCM	
	Architecture, A.P.	
	School of Planning and Architecture,New Delhi	60% in 10+2 PCME
Agriculture/Horticulture/Floriculture		
B.Sc.Agriculture	AP Agricultural Univ.A.P.	10+2 with Phy.Sc. or Natural Sci. Or Agri. EAMCE Tent. Exam.
	Assam Agriculture Univ.	50% in 10+2 PCMB or Equivalent Entr.exam.
Gujarat Agriculture Univ.		55% in 10+2 Equiv.in Sc. With Engg.

(Contd.)

(Contd.)

Course	*Name of the Institutions*	*Eligibility*
		Entr.exam.
	Haryana Agriculture Univ.	10+2 with Science Exam.& Interview
	Konkan Krishi Vidyapeeth College of Agriculture	12th or equiv. PCB
B.Sc.In Agriculture And Allied Science	Indian Council of Agricultural Research, New Delhi	10+2 with Science
B.Sc.Horticulture	College of Agriculture, AP	
Deptt. of Horticulture, Maharashtra		
College of Agriculture, Maharashtra		
Anthropology		
B.Sc.		
	Sri Venkateshwara Uni.,AP	10+2
	Guwahati Uni.	
	University of Delhi	
	Kurukshetra University	
	Vidya Sagar University,WB	
Aquaculture		
B.Sc. Fisheries	College of Fisheries,Bihar	10+2 Sc.
B.F.Sc.	College of Fisheries, Kerala	
B.Sc.in Aquarial	University of Mumbai	10+2Sc. Science
Banking		
Short term certificate course	Marathwada University Maharashtra	10+2
BA(Bank Management)	Bharathidasan University,TN	10+2
Business Management		
BBA	Garhwal University,Uttaranchal	10+2
	Guru Ghasidas University,CG	
	Dr.B.R.Ambedkar Univ.,UP	
Degree Course	Jamia Milia in Islamia,New Delhi	10+2,

(Contd.)

(Contd.)

Course	*Name of the Institutions*	*Eligibility*
BBS		50% marks
BBS	College of Business Studies Delhi	10+2 min. 60% marks
Biotechnology		
B.Sc.	Kakatiya University AP Patna University,Bihar	10+2 PCM
B.Tech.	All India Institute of Medical Sci.	-do-
B.Sc.Microbiology	University of Delhi Punjab University Guru Nanak Dev University Gurukul Kangri Vishwavidyalaya,UP	
Counselling		
Certificate in guidance	IGNOU	10+2
Dentistry		
BDS/MBBS	All State Dental Colleges and Hospitals	10+2 with
PCBE		
Design		
Designing Ahmedabad	National Instt. Of Design entrance test	10+2
Diploma Course in Industrial And Communication design	-do-	10+2
Undergraduate course in Accessory Design	National Instt. Of Fashion Tech. New Delhi	
Diploma Course in Furniture & Jewellery design	South Delhi Polytechnic for Women, New Delhi	
Diploma in Art & Book Illustration & Graphics	Shankar's Academy of Art and Book Publishing,New Delhi	

(Contd.)

(Contd.)

Course	*Name of the Institutions*	*Eligibility*
Fashion Design Courses		
Diploma course in apparel	National Institute of Design Ahmedabad	10+2
Diploma in Fashion designing	South Delhi Polytechnic, N.D.	10+2
	National Institute of Fashion Design, New Delhi	Written test
Film,TV & Radio		
Training for News Readers in English	Film & Television Institute of India(FTII),Pune IIMC, New Delhi	10+2
Finance		
Cert.in Financial	Gujarat University	10+2

(Contd.)

Course	*Name of the Institutions*	*Eligibility*
Management		
Diploma in Cost and Works Accountancy	University of Jodhpur	10+2
Fine Art and Commercial Art		
Diploma in Drawing, Painting	Govt.College of Fine Arts &	Xth/
Modelling and Sculpture	Architecture,Hyderabad	Higher Sec.
BFA	Jawaharlal Nehru Univ.Hyd.	10+2
	Delhi College of Art	XIIth & Entr.Exam.
	University of Bombay	
Diploma in Commercial Art	Central School of Art and Crafts, AP	Xth/Higher Secondary
	Sophia Polytechnic for Women	10+2
Mumbai		
BA(Hons)in Art & Art Education		Jamia Milia

(Contd.)

(Contd.)

Course	*Name of the Institutions*	*Eligibility*
	Islamia, New Delhi	10+2
Hotel Management		
Diploma in Hotel Management	All State Instt.of Hotel Management	10+2 with 50% any Discipline
Journalism		
Degree Course in Journalism	Lalit Narayan Mithila Univ. Darbhanga, Bihar Bangalore University Bombay University Marathwada University	10+2
BA.LLB	State Universities	10+2
Painting and Publishing		
Vocational Course in Book Publishing	College of Vocational Studies New Delhi	10+2
Course in Book Publishing, Editing,Introduction and Sales	Delhi University	
Photography		
Integrated degree course in Photography	Jiwaji University,M.P. University of Pune	10+2
Social Work		
BSW/BA	Universities of Andhra,Osmania Baroda etc. Jamia Milia Islamia,New Delhi	10+2
Sports		
Bachelor of Physical Education	Lakshmibai National College of Physical Education,Gwalior	10+2/ HSC
Diploma Course in Cricket,handball,hockey,	SAI-NSNIS,Gujarat	10+2/ HSC

(Contd.)

(Contd.)

Course	Name of the Institutions	Eligibility
Kabaddi/Kho-kho & Swimming		
Courses in athletics,	SAI-NSNIS, Calcutta	-do-
Basketball,		
Volleyball,Judo,football,hockey		
Diploma courses for-do-		-do-
Training of coaches		
Teaching		
Diploma in Pre-school Education	M.S.University of Baroda	10+2
Early Childhood Education	Osmania University,Hyderabad SNDT Women's Univ.,Mumbai	
BA B.Ed/BA(Hons), B.Ed. B.Sc.,B.Ed., B.Sc.(Hons.), B.Ed. B.Com., B.Ed.	Barkatullah Vishwavidyalaya, M.P.	10+2
Garment Manufacturing Technology		
NIFT	10+2 with	Maths.

9

Engineering Courses and Profession

(a) AGRICULTURAL ENGINEERING

Agricultural engineering is the discipline of engineering in agriculture, food and biological systems. Agricultural engineers develop engineering science and technology in the context of agricultural production and processing, and for the management of natural resources. They apply their engineering knowledge and skills to solve problems relating to sustainable agricultural production.

Role of Agricultural Engineers

Agricultural engineers are trained to deal with soil, water, crop and engineering principles applications to agriculture. They provide inputs for mechanization of agriculture, conservation of produce and by-products, minimization of losses, value addition and agro-processing enterprises for additional income and employment generation, energy management in agriculture and rural living. They act as knowledge binding agents between traditional agriculturist and engineers because of their knowledge in the field of farm machinery and power, dairy and food processing and agricultural structure; land and water management engineering, energy and aquaculture.

Career Opportunities for Agricultural Engineers

There is tremendous scope for qualified engineers having professional degrees in agricultural engineering. Agricultural engineers work in production, sales, management, research and development, or applied science in agriculture. A large number of agricultural engineers work in academia or for research and developmental activities in private and government agencies such as Central and State Agricultural Universities (SAUs), Indian Council of Agricultural Research (ICAR), Council of Agricutural Research in various states at different capacities.

Opportunities with UG Degree

Agricultural engineers with UG degree have job opportunities in private and government sectors. Private sectors include tractor industries for sales, R&D and management; Irrigation equipment companies for sales, R&D and maintenance; Dairy and Food industries for quality control, R&D, and maintenance of processing machineries; Computer applications for software development; Instrumentation for automation and control; Consultants to many organizations; Agri-clinic, agribusiness; and NGOs. The Government sectors include field executives and engineers, training assistants and organizers in areas of mechanization of agriculture, irrigation, drainage, soil and water conservation engineering, command area development, watershed management, rural development; and also in SAUs, ICAR, Krishi Vigyan Kendras (KVKs), Universities, Colleges and other organizations for teaching, research & development, extensions and other scientific and technical jobs. Nationalized banks also, recruit Agricultural Engineers for agriculture officers and managerial level posts.

Opportunities with PG Degree

Post Graduate agricultural engineers specialized in different disciplines have job opportunities in both private and government sectors. Private sectors include Tractor Industries; Irrigation Equipment Companies; Dairy and Food Industries; Computers; Instrumentation; Agri-clinic and Agribusiness. In private sectors they work as subject specialists for R& D, management and consultants to many other organizations including NGOs. The job opportunities in government sectors include teaching, research & development, and extension activities as Scientists, Assistant Professors, Training Organizers, Research Officers, Subject Matter Specialists (SMS), Engineers, in universities, SAUs, KVKs, ICAR and other organization such as DRDO, BARC etc. and also as executives and managers in areas of mechanization of agriculture, irrigation, drainage, soil and water conservation engineering, watershed management , Command area and rural development.

Opportunities with Ph.D Degree

Agriculture engineers with doctorate degree have job opportunities in teaching, research & development, and extension activities as Scientists, Assistant Professors, Research Officers, SMS and Engineers at senior levels in various Universities, SAUs, KVKs, ICAR and other organization involved in high level research, development, extension, consultancies, planning and policy framing activities.

Professional Degrees in Agricultural Engineering

Professional degrees at various levels UG, PG and Doctorate programs in Agricultural Engineering are offered by State Agricultural Universities (SAUs), Deemed Universities(Dus), Central Agricultural University (CAU) & Central Universities (Cus).

Under Graduate Degree Programs

Different Universities and Institutes offer Under Graduate (UG) degree (B.Tech.) in agricultural engineering. Eligibility for UG is 10 +2 pass with Physics, Chemistry and Mathematics or equivalent. The mode of admissions is through entrance test conducted by IITs, state governments, universities, Institutes and Indian Council of Agricultural Research (ICAR). ICAR conducts All India entrance examinations for 15% of UG seats in SAUs, Dus, CAU & Cus.

Post Graduate Programs

Eligibility for admission to post graduate (PG) degree (M.Tech./ M.Sc.) programs in agricultural engineering is B.Tech. in the discipline. Mode of admissions is through entrance cum academic performance (entrance test and/ or interview). Entrance test conducted by the universities and/or qualified in Junior Research Fellowship (JRF) conducted by ICAR for 25% of seats in SAUs, Dus, CAU and Cus through all India entrance examination or Graduate Aptitude Test in Engineering (GATE). The specializations offered for post graduation are : Soil and Water Conservation Engineering; Irrigation and Drainage Engineering; Farm Machinery and Power Engineering; Dairy Engineering , Food Technology, Food Processing and Agricultural Structural Engineering; Aquaculture Engineering; Renewable Energy Sources; and in other multidisciplinary branches in Civil Engineering, Mechanical Engineering, Biotechnology, Computer Applications, Management and Humanity disciplines.

Doctoral Degree Programs

Eligibility for admission to Doctorate degree (Ph.D.) program in various disciplines of agricultural engineering is M.Tech or M.Sc. in that respective disciplines or equivalent. Mode of admissions is through entrance cum academic performance (entrance test and/or interview) conducted by various universities and IITs including those qualified in Senior Research Fellowship (SRF) conducted by ICAR for 25% of seats in SAUs, Dus, CAU and Cus through all India entrance examination.

Universities offering Courses in Agricultural Engineering

Name of important universities and institutes in the country offering courses at various levels UG, PG and Doctorate programs in Agricultural Engineering are given below.

1. Acharya N.G.Ranga Agricultural University (ANGRAU), Hyderabad(A.P.).
2. Allahabad Agricultural Institute Deemed University, Allahabad, U.P.
3. Anand Agricultural University (AAU), Anand, Gujarat
4. Bidhan Chandra Krishi Vishva Vidyalaya (BCKVV), Mohanpur, Nadia, W.B.
5. Birsa Agricultural University (BAU), Kanke, Ranchi, Jharkhand
6. Central Agricultural University (CAU), Jroisemba, Imphal, Manipur
7. Chandra Shekhar Azad University of Agric. & Technology(CSAUT), Kanpur, UP
8. Ch.Charan Singh Haryana Agricultural University (HAU), Hisar, Haryana
9. Dr.Balasaheb Sawant Konkan Krishi Vidyapeeth(KKV), Dapoli, Maharshtra
10. Dr.Panjabrao Deshmukh Krishi Vishwa Vidyalaya (PKV), Akola,Maharashtra
11. Govind Ballabh Pant University of Agric. & Technology, Pantnagar, Uttaranchal
12. Indian Agricultural Research Institute, New Delhi
13. Indian Institute of Technology (IIT), Kharagpur, West Bengal
14. Indira Gandhi Krishi Vishwa Vidyalaya, krishak Nagar,Raipur, CG
15. Jawaharlal Nehru Krishi Vishwa Vidyalaya, Jabalpur, M.P.
16. Junagadh Agricultural University (JAU), Junagadh, Gujarat
17. Kerala Agricultural University (KAU), Vellanikkara, Trichur, Kerala
18. Maharana Pratap University of Agric. & Technology (MPUAT),Udaipur,Rajasthan
19. Mahatma Gandhi Gramodaya Vishwavidyalaya, Chitrakoot, M.P.
20. Mahatma Phule Krishi Vidyapeeth (MPKV),Rahuri, Maharashtra
21. Marathwada Agricultural University (MAU), Parbhani, Maharashtra
22. Narendra Dev University of Agriculture and Technology, Faizabad,UP
23. Navsari Agricultural University (NAU), Navsari, Gujarat
24. Orissa University of Agriculture & Technology(OUAT), Bhubaneshwar,Orissa

25. Punjab Agricultural University (PAU), Ludhiana, Punjab
26. Rajendra Agricultural University (RAU), Pusa, Samastipur, Bihar
27. Sardar Vallabh Bhai Patel University of Agriculture & Modipuram, Meerut, U.P.
28. Tamil Nadu Agricultural University (TNAU), Coimbatore, Tamil Nadu
29. University of Agricultural Sciences (UAS), Bangalore, Karnataka
30. University of Agricultural Sciences (UAS), Krishi Nagar, Dharwad, Karnataka.

(b) BORDER ROADS ORGANISATION

As of now there is a lot of unemployment in India. More so for employment in State Government and Central Organizations. Even technically qualified youth are unable to find appropriate opportunities to have their expertise and talent utilized in the form of cherished government service. As per available statistics, on an average nearly fifty lakh new youth are getting their names registered in the country's Employment Exchanges every year for employment. Many unemployed youth may even not be able to do that either for a variety of reasons. As against that the country is able to generate only about three lakh jobs a year And, whereas ultimate solution for ending the menace of unemployment amongst youth may lie in their going in for self employment in larger and larger numbers, limited openings in state employment will certainly remain available for really suitable and deserving youths. Accordingly, competent youth who have a mind for working outdoors and possess zeal for adventure may find the General Reserve Engineer Force and Border Roads Organization— BRO for short—quite interesting and worthy of giving a try.

Nature of Organization

Border Roads Organization is a fine young satellite of the Armed Forces of India. In fact it is an integral part of theirs. A road building civil engineering organization, it is similar to Central Public Works Department or provincial PWDs in its outward appearance. But its role in akin to that of Corps of Engineers of the Army. It constructs and maintains roads, bridges, airstrips and airfields. It is assigned even buildings in certain strategically sensitive areas where other construction agencies are unable to operate. The officers and men of this organization are partly drawn from other wings of the Armed Forces and partly commissioned and enrolled exclusively for this Force only. The troops enrolled exclusively for this organization are collectively known as General Reserve Engineer Force, or GREF. The personnel drawn from the other Corps of the Army are considered on normal military duty only. The technical head of the organizatios, located at

New Delhi, is addressed as Director General Border Roads. The officer has necessarily to be a civil engineer Lt. General of the Corps of Engineers. The administrative control of the organization as its Head, is vested in the Secretary, Border Roads. The officer is generally an incumbent of an organized cadre of Central Civil Services, like IAS, Central Secretariat Service, etc. The organization is an important constituent of the Orbit Chart of Armed Forces. While for administrative control it is placed under Ministry of Highways for strategic and technical deployment it comes under Ministry of Defence.

Organisation of Units

The lower most independent road construction unit of BRO is called Road Construction Company of RCC. It functions like a Division of the provincial PWD, and is commanded by a civil engineer officer of the rank of Executive Engineer or a civil engineer Major of the Corps of Engineers. The Unit comprises of smaller functional platoons like Formation Cutting Platoon, Permanent Works Platoon, Surfacing Platoon etc. The first mentioned sub-unit cuts new formations i.e. it cuts hill slopes to make a just passable fair weather kucha road. The next one constructs culverts, retaining walls, breast walls, drains, parapets, etc. The last one is charged with metalling the driveway and keeping the finished roads in good repairs. These platoons are placed under the charge of a platoon officer of the rank of Assistant Engineer or Assistant Executive Engineer or a Captain, who reports to the OC, RCC for all executive, administrative and financial matters. Two or three RCCs make a Border Roads Task Force, or BRTF, it functions like a Circle of the provincial PWD or an Engineer Regiment of the Army. Two or three BRTFs put together form a BRO Project.

With a view to assisting the BRTFs to produce optimum results, the Organisation has certain common service units, like Engineer, Stores and Transport Companies, Field Workshops, Medical Staging Sections, Medical Inspection Room(s), Dental Unit(s), Signal Unit(s), Provost Unit(s), Postal Unit(s), GREF Pioneer Companies etc. The ES & Tpt Coy caters all kinds of resources, stores, engineering's equipment, rations, vegetables, fruit etc. A Field Workshop looks after the repairs and maintenance of the departmental vehicles and assorted machinery. The Medical Staging Sections and Medical Inspection Rooms take care of the health of sick troops. The Dental Officer and his team move from camp to camp for checking and treating the dental problems of the road building personnel, wherever they are deployed. Every Project has one Signals Officer for meaning the wireless communications network. A Postal Unit is there to look after movement of dak of the troops, as also units. Provost Unit is a set up for internal security. The remaining units undertake jobs suggested by their respective names.

The GREF Pioneer Companies, hold about 300 to 400 Pioneers. They (pioneers) are combined with casual daily wagers to provide non-technical manual assistance for execution of the civil engineering works on the ground. These Coys are generally commanded by non technical officers, earlier called Civilian Officer, but now called Administrative Officers. Further, BRO borrows a few Army Pioneer Companies also for armed security cover for a safe movement of cash, sensitive documents and attractive materials etc. Officers having expertise in respective specific fields man the remaining common service units.

A Superintending Engineer (Civil Engineer) or Colonel or Corps of Engineers commands a Task Force. A Chief Engineer (Civil) of GREF or a Brigadier of the Corps of Engineers commands a BRO Project.

Governing Regulations

The GREF officers and personnel are governed by Civil Service Regulations of the Govt. of India for the purpose of recruitment, leave, pay and allowances and retirement or discharge etc. For discipline, however, they are governed under Army Act 1950, but with certain essential modifications.

Tradesmen

Bulk of BRO's man power comprises troops required for and deployed on constructing of roads, bridges, buildings, etc. They are pioneers, masons, drillers, dozer operators, compressor drivers, mechanics, electricians, carpenters, mates, leading hands, overseers etc. They (road building troops) are helped by clerks, nursing assistants, wireless operators, safaiwalas, cooks, etc. i.e. those responsible for running the administration in offices and camps.

Recruitment

Of the officers, the Civil Engineers comprise bulk of the officer cadre, followed by Electrical and Mechanical Engineers, Administrators, Medicos, etc. The recruitment of GREF Officers is conducted by Union Public Service Commission based on the recruitment projected by the Head of the Organisation. A number of officers also rise from lower ranks through departmental promotions as per standard norms. The vacancies available in officer cadres are advertised by Union Public Service Commission through leading Newspapers. Many of the allopathic doctors, all Dental Officers, Signal Officers, Postal Officers etc. required in insignificant small numbers, are drawn from respective Corps of the Army.

The recruitment to various categories of GREF subordinates is done centrally by the Commandant, GREF Centre and Records, located at Pune in Maharashtra. Their vacancies are advertised by GREF Records through Employment News.

Pay and Allowance

In matter of pay and allowances, the officers and personnel drawn from other Corps of the Army, retain their usual terms and conditions as in their respective parent Corps. The GREF Officers are, however, paid as per Central Govt. rules and scales of pay. The rank and category-wise emoluments entitled to the GREF officers and personnel, are as per the latest recommendation of the Central Pay Commission (s) as revised from time to time. Various central allowances are also paid to them like those in any other Central Govt. Department.

Service Benefits

All benefits of service available to Central Government servants are applicable to GREF personnel as well. Therefore, benefits like Children Education Allowance, Leave Travel Concession, Central Govt. Employees Group Insurance Scheme, General Provident Fund, House Rent Allowance, Allotment of Govt. accommodation, Pension and Gratuity etc. all are applicable to GREF nearly at par with other Central Govt. Employees. Rather, the BRO's fields of work being in remote areas, the troops deployed in difficult places of work like remote tribal areas, are entitled to difficult locality allowance or special compensatory allowance at variable rates according to one's pay scale. Those posted to North Eastern Region, thus, get a special duty allowance as applicable for that areas at the rate of 12 ½% of basic pay.

In addition, the GREF personnel are also entitled to following special concessions—more or less similar to those available to personnel of other Corps of Armed Forces:-

(i) *Free Ration*:- for self only, while posted to field units.

(ii) *Canteen Stores*:- All GREF units run their own CSD canteen, where essential general merchandise i.e. items of daily necessity are available at concessional Army Canteen rates. Utility items like watches, household appliances, crockery, cutlery and kitchenware etc. are also available in these canteens.

(iii) *Uniform and uniform Allowance*:- The GREF officers and personnel have to put on specified uniform which is Khaki in colour. The same is issued free to lower rank subordinate officials including supervisors. Group A Officers, on their first appointment, are instead paid a cash grant of Rs.7000=00 for equipping them with the prescribed items of uniform for the first 5 years of service. In case of GROUP 'B' Officers, a similar grant of Rs.3000/- is paid. Subsequently, this grant is replenished every year at the rate of Rs.4000/- for group 'A' and Rs.2000/- for group 'B' officers. In addition, group 'A' officers are paid at the rate of Rs.80/- and group 'B' officers at Rs.30/- per month for upkeep of their uniform.

(iv) *Free Accommodation*:-BRO provides free hut type accommodation to all of its employees. The organization also bears the cost of water and electricity charges as long as the individual lives single in the unit lines.

(v) *Mess*:- The BRO units run separate messes for officers and supervisors. The lungers cater food/boarding etc. for the other ranks.

Needless to say that any individual deployed in field areas is not to worry about procurement of rations and or cooking of his food, which is provided free centrally under unit arrangement.

(vi) Medical Aid:- All BRO units either have a Medical Staging Section or a Medical Inspection Room, where common ailments are treated. Troops suffering from serious medical problems are referred/ evacuated to the nearby military hospitals or civil hospitals, on as required basis.

(vii) On the Job Training:- GREF personnel are afforded liberal opportunities to improve their qualifications. Matriculate non gazetted GREF personnel are encouraged to compete for entrance to departmental diploma course(s) in Civil or Mechanical Engineering or Draughtsman ship or Nursing Assistant Course depending upon an individual's aptitude. Graduate Civil Engineer Officers are encouraged to take up postgraduate studies in Engineering. The doctors are allowed to do post-graduation in medical sciences. The incumbents of generalist cadres can, however, only improve their qualifications by enrolling in evening sessions of professional courses run by nearby govt./private institution or through correspondence courses.

(viii) 50% concession in Air fare:- The GREF troops and their dependents are entitled to 50% concession in air fare for travel by IA and allied air service aircraft.

(ix) Free remittance:- An individual posted to any field units can remit upto Rs.4000/- out of his monthly salary to his dependents through field post office whereon no money order commission is charged.

Promotion Prospects

A Competent Civil Engineer Youth who joins the Organisation as Assistant Executive Engineer can hope to reach the level of Chief Engineer and even Additional DGBR. The Electrical and Mechanical

Engineers too have fair chances of promotions. A graduate in Mechanical Engineering who joins the organization as Asstt. Executive Engineer(E&M) can hope to rise upto Chief Engineer (Mech.) level.For non-technical officers, however, promotional avenues are limited. Though certain individuals have been making earnest endeavors to have their group encadred in an organized cadre for proper promotional avenues, the proposal/case has so far made little headway.

CAD/CAM

General engineering design is divided into two caegories aesthetic design and functional design. It is necessary to use modern CAD system to eliminate all possible error. The first creative stage of any design is to generate concepts and then select the best by doing brain-storming session. The engineers are expected to actively participate in the session to "freeze" the design. Then the design is put in the CAD system for feedback in the design development team.

What is CAD?

Computer Aided Design supports the Design Engineering activity, that includes creation of 2D/3D Geometric models, doing engineering analysis, evaluating the design by simulation and Produce Rapid Drafting for Manufacturing with the help of computers. The traditional CAD System offers 2D Drafting, 3D Modeling with Limited Modification Capability. This System substitutes Drafting Board completely. The high end 3D CAD Tool Provides many solutions under one platform. If alteration is made in one feature then it will automatically change other related (dependent) features. Dimensional and Geometrical constraints play a major role in this parametric design Technology. Testing the designs on the computer instead of expensive and time-consuming field tests leads to significant reduction in Product Development Cycles (PDC). Cost and time-to-market is another advantage. The modern CAD System helps Product Design under practical constraints, helps enormously imaginative concepts.

What is CAM?

CAM (Computer Aided Manufacturing) is defined as "the effective use of computer technology in manufacturing planning and control". Often there is confusion between the term manufacturing and production. Providing the component that is to be produced in large quantity is called manufacturing technology.

What is CIM?

Computer Integrated Manufacturing is an integrated approach to maintain a Common Database for CAD, CAM and Business control,

CIM includes CAD/CAM, R&D, e-Publishing and also embraces the business functions of manufacturing. CIM implements computer technology in all the operational and information processing activities related to manufacturing.

Emerging Trends in CAD/CAM

Product development cycle, Reverse Engineering, Rapid prototyping Product life cycle management, Virtual Manufacturing are emerging trends in CAD/CAM Technologies. Reverse Engineering is the process of duplicating an existing part, component of product, without the aid of drawings, documentation, or computer model. Reverse engineering involves acquiring 3D position data in laser scanners.

A fresh and CAD/CAM trained Engineer can get salary of 10000 INR to 20000 INR and with two/ three years experience professionals can get a salary of as high as 35000 INR.

The chart show some of the institutions offering courses in CAD/ CAM.

National Institutes offering CAD/CAM

Sl. No.	*Institution*	*Courses Offered*	*Duration*
1.	CITD Hyderabad (An UNDP Pro.) SIDO TR and Extension Centre Across AP	ME/Mtech (IIPP) Short Term Long Term	3 Years 6 Months 01 Years
2.	Central Tool Room (Indo-German) Ludhiana, SIDO TR	Short Term Rapid Prototype	01 to 06 Months
3.	CTTC (An Indo-Danish pro.) SIDO Organization, Ministry of SSI Bhubaneshwar	Post Dip. CAD/CAM Adv. CNC Tech Master Certificate CAD/CAM Summer Pro. CAD, CAM, IA Mtech-IIPP (Proposed)	01 Yr. 6 Months 5 Months 30 to 45 Days 2 Years

(Contd.)

(Contd.)

Sl. No.	*Institution*	*Courses Offered*	*Duration*
4.	IDTR, Jamshedpur, CTTC Kolkata SIDO Organization, Min. of SSI	PD in CAD/CAM Short Course	6 Months 1 to 6 Months
5.	IGTR Indore, Ahmedabad, Aurangabad SIDO Organization, Min. of SSI	PD in CAD/CAM Short Course	1 Year 01-06 Months
6.	NSIC-Training Centre Across the country, Ministry of SSI	CAD/CAM Short Course	01 to 06 Months
7.	PPDC-IDEMI, Mumbai-ESTC, Nainital SIDO Organization, Ministry of SSI	PD CAD/CAM Short Course	1 Year 01 to 06 Months
8.	A TI/CTI-National Institues -Across the Country Ministry of Labour	Short course CAD/CAM	01 to 06 Months
9.	CIPET (An UNDP Pro.), Ministry of Chemical & Fertilizer, Chennai and its Extension Centres	CAD/CAM Short Course	1 to 6 Months
10.	Anna University, AU-FRG Initiative, Chennai	CAD/CAM Short Course And Part time CAD course	1 Month onwards
11.	IITs-Naional Institutes Across the Country	M.Des	3 Years

University Engineering Subjects and their Respective Computer Based Tools

Sl. No.	*Engineering Subject*	*CAD/CAE/CAM*
1.	Strength of Material	Finite Element Analysis
2.	Theory of Machines	Digital Mock-up, Kinematics Simulation

(Contd.)

(Contd.)

Sl. No.	*Engineering Subject*	*CAD/CAE/CAM*
3.	Fluid Power	Computational Fluid Dynamics,Pipe design
4.	Production Tech	NC,CNC,DNC,CAM CIM,RP
5.	Machine Design	CA Design, PLM
6.	Machine Drawing	CA Drafting
7.	Industrial Engineering	CAPP,layout design for a manufacturing plant
8.	Equipments & System	Electrical Harness, Cable system, PCB Design
9.	Heat transfer,fridge & AC	HVAC Tools
10.	Engineering metrology	Tolerance & Interference Analysis Tools,CMM,RE
11.	Tool Engineering	Mould Flow Analysis, PT Design
12.	Power Plant Engineering	Thermal analysis
13.	Electrical M/Cs	Electro magnetic Field Analysis coupled-field Analysis
14.	Element of M/C Design	Mech CAD

(d) CHIP DESIGNING

It's no new story that the Indian IT sector has been on a high growth path, even while the rest of the world was reeling under recessionary pressures, thanks to the vast pool of skilled manpower available in India. However, two IT sectors that have been growing rapidly, yet quietly, are embedded technology and semi-conductor designing. Again, thanks to the technical skills of Indian engineers.

EMBEDDED TECHNOLOGY

The term embedded technology usually refers to different forms of technologies that go into building an electronic system. This covers the design of integrated circuits, operating system, firmware (software), test schemes and the system itself. This has been one of the fastest growing career opportunities in the past five years and is expected to grow even higher in the coming years. A trend that is being driven by electronic systems becoming more and more digital, mobile, portable and convergent.

Career opportunities in sectors like VLSI architecture, algorithm and software development and system architecture and end equipment design are huge. Says Srini Rajam, Chairman and CEO, Ittiam Systems Pvt. Ltd., “The growth prospects are very good and one can aspire to build a career spanning technology, marketing and management”.

As far as qualifications go, the ideal combination is Engineering in the Electrical/Electronics field with a strong inclination for development and application of software in design. “Alternatively, a very strong engineering background in Computer Science with application skills in electronic systems will also be very suitable, “says Rajam.

However, Rajam feels that to be successful in this field, students must be very strong on their fundamentals. They should also develop a flair for visualising new algorithms/techniques/products and apply them in practical, real life problem areas”.

CHIP DESIGNING

Says Pradeep Kumar, Country Director; ST Microelectronics India,"Semi-conductor chips, which are at the heart of the IT revolution, have found applications in almost everything. They are used in computers, mobile phone handsets, consumer electronic goods, consumer durable goods, industrial automation, automobiles, etc.etc. This kind of diversity in their applications has resulted in a positive boost for their demand as well. Many industry analysis believe that this will become the fastest growing segment in the years to come”.

NASSCOM predicts that the chip design industry will grow to US $ 808 million by 2005. According to a MAIT- an Ernst and Young study. It is estimated that the semi-conductor chip design market in India will require around 1,40,000 engineers by the year 2010 translating to a US$7 billion industry. On the global front, another report suggests that the international market expects product development to be worth US$75 billion and will require nearly 1,50,000 trained professionals by 2005.

It is no wonder, therefore, that many global corporations have set up design centres here in India. Global semi-conductor majors Texas Instruments and ST Microelectronics being amongst the first. They set the trend for more and more semi-conductor companies and OEM organisations, which began to outsource the development of complex technologies such as system on chip to Indian start-ups and established companies with design expertise. Today, India houses more than 60 chip design firms that are “undertaken cutting edge design work”. This number, incidentally, has only been rising and includes some big names such as Motorola, IBM, Cisco, Lucent and Sun, among others, besides some Indian names like Accel, C-DAC, Ittiam Systems, Wipro Infotech, Tata ELEXSI and Tejas Networks.

Says Kumar; "India has got enough talent and technical skill to become a global chip design hub. The industry is growing at a phenomenal rate and companies who have invested in chip design facilities in India are reaping substantial benefits".

According to a research based on primary and secondary data collected by NASSCOM to ascertain manpower skill requirements in the Indian software sector; the demand for EDA/ASIC/VLSI skills are growing rapidly. And considering the target of US$1 billion in revenues in chip design exports by 2004 set by the Indian government. India would need to produce almost 5,000 chip designers every year; as against the current output of 400 chip designers, according to a report brought out by Tata Consultancy Services.

Going by the statistics there is an immense requirement for manpower in this sector: Chip design is a highly specialised area and the field is open to all those who have done BE, B.Tech., MCA, BCA, M.Sc, B.Sc (Computer Science/ Electronics). "Finding the right kind of skills in this highly specialised field is very difficult. The skills required are related to the recruit's understanding of the vertical domain (Telecom, DSP etc.) coupled with a deep understanding of the complexities involved in chip design. These could range from dealing with issues like speed, size, full system integration within a single chip, low power consumption, etc. "says Praneet Mehrish, Country Human Resource Manager, STMicroelectronics India.

"While entry into this specialised industry is not easy and it would require very special skills, the requirement scene is somewhat ambiguous. Some companies think that freshers with a basic aptitude can be recruited and trained specifically to suit to their needs. Whereas others prefer hiring out of institutes that offer specialised courses in semi-conductor design.

In terms of specific skills, knowledge is required in digital design fundamentals. VHDL/ Verilog simulation and synthesis tools and computer architecture. Some specialised areas would require additional skills, for example, mixed signal design, which requires analogue design skills as well, "he says, There are many educational institutes like the IITs and the regional engineering colleges offering specialised VLSI courses.

So, with the kind of demand and supply gap of skilled manpower in the semi-conductor design industry, the time certainly holds a lot of promise for these who want to build a career out of chip designing.

(e) FIRE TECHNOLOGY

Incidents of fire have, in recent years, been mounting and the loss to property as well as life has been high. As a result, the demand for trained and qualified persons in field of fire protection in India is escalating. An education in fire technology offers an excellent career opportunities with tremendous scope for growth.

The local fire fighting resources in almost every Indian city are inadequate. This coupled with the fact that fire teams do not have the appropriate expertise to handle complex fire problems, has resulted in more and more companies investing in their own fire equipment and staff so that fire related problems are immediately responded to and routine fire prevention systems are in place.

The College of Fire Technology is the first fire training institution in the country to offer a B.Sc. course in Fire. Located at 86, Village Khoda on Sanand Viramgam High Way, the college which is 32 kms from Gandhigram (Ahmedabad city) also offers specialised Fireman and ITI courses. The first batch of B.Sc. (Fire) students is awaiting their results. One of the key strengths of the college is its emphasis on practical training- taught by thoroughly experienced fire experts using modern fire fighting equipment. To enhance the value of the syllabus, the college also provides personality development workshops, industrial visits, AutoCAD training and an interaction with various fire experts. All this is geared to enhance the entire learning process.

The college is also the first in its field to establish a job placement cell for Fire Graduates. Several of its successful students have been absorbed as firemen in the Army, as local fire brigade staff, or as fire officers in prestigious plants and offices with lucrative salaries and steady careers. Encouraged by a recent contract from a foreign company to train its personnel in India, the College will also be introducing a course for foreign students this year.

The college offers a Bachelor of Science (Fire), {The degree is awarded by the Gujarat University} for the students to pursue a career in Fire Technology. The eligibility is 10+2 or its equivalent with Science and Maths and the course fee is Rs.15,000 per year.

Fore the fireman's course, the eligibility is a SSC or its equivalent and the course fee is Rs.28,000/- for a one year programme. This course is approved by Directorate of Employment and Training, Gandhinagar, Gujarat.

Yet another module offered is the Safety and Security Course (ITI). The eligibility for this is an SSC or its equivalent and the duration is one year (nine months training at college and three months attachment training). The fee is Rs.20,000/-.

The college of Fire Technology, located at Khoda Village on the outskirts of Ahmedabad is run by the Champaben Bhagat Education Trust, which is dedicated to promoting professionalism among students through education, training and research. The college has the capacity to train 120 students for the B.SC. course and 200 for the ITI courses.

At present, at the national level, there are only a few fire fighting establishments, the most important of them being the National Fire Services College in Nagpur, under the Ministry of Home Affairs which solely caters to the needs of State/Municipal fire services as it conducts courses for Divisional Officers. The college intakes around 30 students per academic year and awards Diplomas to its students. Of late the college has also started a B.E.(Fire) course of a three to five year duration under the affiliation of the University of Nagpur. This was the only college in India, before the establishment of the College of Fire Technology to offer any module dealing with fire technology.

(f) FOOD TECHNOLOGY

In today's busy world people do not have enough time to stay in the kitchen. With changing food habits and job profile the ready to cook, ready to serve, and fully processed packaged food and beverages are becoming popular. With the introduction of modern technology in the production and processing of livestock and agricultural food produce, the concept of food is shifting from survival to value added food business. The agro based food industries have opened up new avenues for employment and economy. It is estimated that food processing industry is growing and generating new jobs to the extent of 2.5 lakhs every year. Agro processing sector is further expected to grow faster and generate more employment in the near future. It is estimated that the Indian food business will increase more than Rs.5,00,000 crores by the end of the year 2005. The market of the value added specialized processed packaged food product will grow to Rs.2,30,000 crores at the end of 2005. Developing the food chain is likely to have strong benefits to economy, both in terms of income and employment.

Role of Food Technologist

The increasing world population and limited agricultural land has widened the gap between food requirement and production. This gap can be fulfilled by better post harvest management, by applying appropriate food processing techniques and qualified Food Technologist. Adoption of the latest and advanced processing technology can minimise losses, provide better quality and nutrition, more employment opportunities and ensure better relation with producer as well as consumer.

The Processing of food industry in India which made humble beginning in the early 30's are still lagging behind, as compared to its counterpart in the advanced countries. The progress of Indian food industry has been quite tardy, but the industry will get a boost after the WTO regime. More units with advanced techniques are coming up in the food processing.

List of Institutes offering various food technology courses:

College/Institute	*Courses offered*	*Website*
CFTRI, Mysore, Karnataka	M.Sc.Food Tech. & Phd	www.cftri.com
IIT, Kharagpur,WB	M.Tech & Phd	www.iitkharag.org
HBTI, Kanpur,UP	M.Tech & B.Tech	
GNDU, Amritsar,PB	B.Tech & M.Sc. &Ph.	www.gndu.ernet.in
PAU, Ludhiana,PB	M.Tech & Ph.D	www.pau.org.in
Santiongwal Institute Of Food & Tech.Longwal, Sangroor,PB	B.Tech & M.Tech	
CCSHUA, Hissar,Hry	M.Sc Food Tech.	www.hau.in
CCSU, Meerut,UP	M.Sc Food Tech	www.ccsu.in
Guru Jambheswar University, Hissar, Hry	M.Sc Food Tech	
Osmania University Hyderabad,AP	M.Sc Food Tech	www.osmania. tech.ac.in
Bundelkhand University Jhansi, UP	B.Tech & M.Sc Food Tech	www.bundelkhand university.org
AAI-DU, U.P. FoodTech	B.Tech & M.Tech.	www.aaidu.org.in
University of Allahabad,UP	M.Sc Food Tech	
Jiwaji University,Gwalior,MP	M.Sc Food Tech	www.jiwaji.edu
Sahid Rajguru College Of Applied Science for Women, Vivek Vihar,Delhi	BASC Food Tech	www.rajguru college .org
Bhasker Acharya College Of Applied Science, Sector-2, New Delhi	BASC Food Tech	

Status of Food Processing at a glance

India is the largest milk Producing Country with 88 MT milk productions. India is first in vegetable production and second in fruit production and has the world highest percentage of arable land to the total geographical area. India grows more than half of the world's mangoes and leads all countries in the production of cauliflower, onion, rice, sorghum and sugarcane. India is the major producer of banana, apple, coffee, coconut, oranges, potatoes, rapeseeds, tobacco and wheat. India is also leading producer of spices such as cardamon, ginger, pepper and turmeric. Agriculture provides livelihood to 65% of India's labour force. Agriculture contributes nearly 33% of the total GDP. Agricultural produce account for about 10% of India's export.

Indian Packaged Food Industry

Sector	*Monetary Worth*
Packaged Foods (Domestic Market)	Rs.336 billion
Primary Products (Cereals, Edible Oils)	Rs. 48 billion
Dairy Processing	Rs. 24 billion
Backery and Culinary Product	Rs. 77 billion
Beverage and Alcoholic Drinks	Rs.139.2 billion
Impulse	Rs. 48 billion

FOOD CONSUMPTION PATTERN IN INDIA

Items of expenditure	*Monetary Worth*
Domestic expenditure on Food	Rs.6270 billion
Processed food sector	Rs.1262.4 billion
Per capita consumption/ year	Rs.6720

Epilogue

The Innovative use of appropriate technologies can help the industry produce high quality products at lower cost while professional management can ensure a more optimal utilization of industry's human and financial resources. The Indian food industry should set higher standards of products quality, usher in greater product variety, compliance with tougher environment and labour standards, just-in-times delivery and quick turnaround time. Increasing competition at domestic front, from cheaper imports at home and better quality, higher value- added imports from developed countries.

(g) GEMMOLOGY

Kings have coveted them, legends revolve around them. Epics like the film King Solomon's Mines have portrayed man's greed to possess them. Yes, we are talking about gemstones: emeralds, rubies, sapphires, diamonds..... But have you ever stopped to think as to who identifies the gemstones and sets apart the glittering, less valuable ones from the really precious ones? As the coloured gem specialist and well-known jeweller Ralph Esmerian said when he beheld the famous Australian pink diamonds, "A designer has ideas and makes sketches, then finds the gems. But a jeweller takes the opposite road. He buys the stones and then realises there is a jewel-it arises from the gemstones".

Today, we call him a gemmologist- some one who has undertaken a scientific study of precious and semi-precious gemstones including their origin, characteristics and distinguishing features. The word "gemmology" is derived from the Latin word gemma meaning "gem" and ology meaning logic. Gurmeet Singh, Director, Indian Institute of Gemmology, says, " It is an applied branch of science which deals with topics like how gems are recovered from the mine, how they are cut and polished, assorted, graded and "evaluated".

The study of gemmology is relevant to the trader, the dealer, the artisan or simply a layman who is fascinated by gemstones. From the point of view of the trade, gems and jewellery has been one of India's biggest foreign exchange earners. If the potential is tapped further then the earnings could skyrocket. Hence, it is imperative that the people associated with the trade receive full-fledged training so that they are able to carry out their work in a scientific and professional manner.

Gemmology is often mistaken for jewellery designing. K.K.Sharma, Executive Director, Indian Diamond Institute (IDI), Surat, says, "Though Jewellery Designing and Gemmology are two different subjects, they are complementary. It is, therefore, advisable for a jewellery designer to have a profound knowledge of gemstones as they are always used in ornaments. If you do not have a sound knowledge of diamonds or of gemmology you can not become a jewellery designer". Echoes Singh, "Gemmology and Jewellery Designing are linked. If a designer has no knowledge of gems, he will not able to put a price to a jewellery piece. He can also embellish his designs by combining stones of various sizes, shapes and colours and this is only possible if he has an idea about gemmology".

Take the example of Frederic Boucheron, the famous innovator in gem design and technology. Or of Charles Lewis Tiffany called the 'King of Diamonds", who was known for his knowledge as well as design of diamond jewellery. Or of the jewellers and designers of the 20th Century: Bulgari, Cartier, Van Cleef & Arpels and Harry Winston- all of whom are household names today.

COURSES ON OFFER

So if you want to join the big league, there are a number of courses on offer: IDI offers two courses- a regular one and a correspondence course. There is the Diploma in Gemmology (DG), which is a 16 week programme with a tuition fee of Rs.15,000/-. A study of all the important gemstones are covered in this course.

Then there is the certificate course in gemstone identification, which includes the study and identification of stones that are important from the point of view of astrology. The duration is eight weeks and the fee is Rs. 8000/-. IDI is the Allied Teaching Centre (ATC) of Gem. A, London, a gemmological association based in UK. On its behalf, IDI conducts exams for two internationally recognised diploma programmes: Fellow of Gemmological Association (FGA) (Gem.A) and Diamond Merchant of Gem.A(DGA). The Indian Institute of Gemmology(IIG), Delhi offers a course in Gems and Gem Identification, which is of a three month duration and the course fees are Rs.12,500/-. There is another course on Diamonds and Diamond Grading which is of a two month duration and the fees are Rs.12,500/-. The third course is an Advanced Gem Identification programme, a three month course which comes at Rs.15,000/-.

The recently launched Gemmological Institute of America India in Mumbai is conducting a Graduate Diamond Diploma Programme that began on September 16 and will continue till November5, 2004. The Graduate Gemmologist Programme will be conducted from mid-April, 2005.

THE OPTIONS

There are a number of career options for students of Gemmology. Deepak Bagai, Director, Indian branch, Gemmological Institute of America(GIA), says "The sky is the limit for students of Gemmology. It all depends on the individual's aptitude and preference". One can set up a business, be a consultant, a gem tester, appraiser, grader, cutter, jewellery designer or even a manufacturer".

Adds K.K.Sharma, "After completing a Diploma in Gemmology, you can be absorbed as a gemmologist with a jeweller or a gemstone trading company. You can also get a job abroad or work with a mining company. Or you can venture into the business of coloured stones, especially in the range of Navratnas, because they are in great demand". Other options include starting a gem-testing laboratory or practicinge gem therapy treatments.

THE SCOPE

Jewellers require trained personnel to identify, grade and evaluate gems and diamonds. Consumers want a certificate of authenticity when they make their purchases. The USA, Japan, Hong Kong, Belgium and other European countries are prime markets for Indian gems and jewellery. Many grading and certification laboratories have also come up.

Gemmology can be a lucrative career option. After all, India is one of the biggest consumers of gold, silver, diamonds and other precious stones. We consider jewellery to be not only an item of fashion but also a form of investment.

In a nutshell, as long as man remains fascinated with gems, the profession has a bright future.

INSTITUTE WATCH

1. Indian Institute of Gemmology, New Delhi
2. Gemmologial Institute of America India, Mumbai
3. Indian Diamond Institute, Surat
4. Indian Gemmological Institute, New Delhi
5. The Geology Department of St.Xavier's College, Mumbai

(h) INDUSTRIAL ENGINEERING

As industry evolved, so did the role of industrial engineer. Before World War-II, the industrial engineer performed layout studies, did work measurement and time and motion analyses, and provided technical expertise in such manufacturing areas as statistical quality control, production control, and inventory control.

Industrial Engineering as the name is used in industry, business and government throughout the world, may be broadest of all the modern management functions. Time study people may consider themselves to be industrial engineers, as might process planners, manufacturing systems analysts or rate setters. All of them, no doubt, are performing duties which fall within the broad range of activities generally considered to be part of industrial engineering function. In fact, the range of industrial engineering activities is so broad that one prominent industrialist said that 'industrial engineering consists of all of the engineering and management control activities or accounting functions'.

The truth is that the field of industrial engineering is a large umbrella that includes a wide variety of tasks established for the purpose of designing, implementing and maintaining management systems for effective operations. Mechanical engineers are generally perceived as individuals who design mechanical products or improvements to equipment and their technical training is pointed largely toward that end. Similarly, electrical engineers design electrical systems or apparatus and they are trained accordingly. Many people who call themselves industrial engineers, on the other hand, may never design anything. They may spend a whole career taking time studies, making, developing methods studies, or conducting layout studies of factories or offices. Still, they are all involved in performing some aspect of Industrial Engineering work and may rightly feel justified in using the title industrial engineer in describing their jobs.

INDUSTRIAL ENGINEERING AS A CAREER

Industrial Engineer are the people who select the right combination of human resources, natural resources and man made structures and equipment and also bridges the gap between management and operations. Industrial Engineer deals with motivating people as well as determining what tools should be used and how they should be used. The most distinctive aspect of industrial engineering is the flexibility that it offers. The current emphasis of Industrial Engineering is on the integration of information and technology to operate and control complex system. The definition of industrial engineers has thus changed from that of 'efficiency experts' and 'productivity people' to ' knowledge workers'. Industrial Engineering has evolved with three 'S' principles i.e. Simplification, Standardization and Specialization. Even today the strength of Industrial Engineering lies with the application of these principles in organizational work systems planning and design. Consequently industrial engineering draws upon a variety of disciplines, from mathematics to psychology, from communications to computer science, from production management to process control. Industrial engineers are viewed as people who can contribute greatly to improve productivity and establish a competitive position in the world marketplace.

WHERE INDUSTRIAL ENGINEERING CAN BE USED

Industrial engineers design integrated systems combining people, machines and material resources for greater effectiveness. In these integrated systems, the person involved can be a machine operator, hospital administrator, production scheduler, dentist, banker or construction foreman. The resource can be a hospital, steel rolling mill, commercial loan department, subway transportation fleet, or road paving machine. The material resource can be the physical substances being processed or the persons using the system, such as metal for machining, patients, steel slab, teeth, money and mortgages, passengers or concrete.

Industrial engineers can be involved in ergonomics/ work design to improve work environment; in developing mathematical and computer models to provide better information for managers; in planning facility layouts and material handling systems; in using statistical and mathematical methods to improve service and product quality; in forecasting, scheduling and managing production and / or in investigating and evaluating investment alternatives.

WHAT INDUSTRIAL ENGINEERS CAN DO

1. Analyses complex business problems using tools of operations research

2. Design a computer based management information system for an organization.
3. Identity, formulate and solve engineering problems.
4. Improve planning and allocation of scarce resources.
5. Help in installing and maintaining advanced manufacturing systems.
6. Develop quality systems, documentation for ISO 9000/ QS 9000 and implement TQM program.
7. Install data processing, management information, wage incentive systems.
8. Conduct organisation studies, plant location surveys and system effectiveness.
9. Design facilities, management systems and operating procedures.
10. Develop management control systems to aid in financial planning and cost analysis.
11. Develop performance standards, job evaluation, wage and salary programs.
12. Evaluate reliability and quality performance
13. Design ergonomically sound tools and workstations.
14. Select operating processes and methods to do a task with proper tools and equipment both effectively and efficiently.
15. Use the techniques, skills and modern engineering tools necessary for engineering practice.
16. Visualize and simulate various through computer aided tools.

PROGRAMME AND ELIGIBILITY CRITERIA

To take up the four year course leading to B.Tech/B.E. degree in Industrial Engineering/ Industrial and Production Engineering, candidates need to qualify in the All India Engineering Entrance Examination (AIEEE) conducted by Central Board of Secondary Education, New Delhi. They should have a minimum aggregate of 50% in Physics, Chemistry and Mathematics at Senior Secondary level. Admission to postgraduate programme (M.Tech./M.S.) in Industrial Engineering/ Industrial and Production Engineering, candidates need to qualify GATE Examination organized by I.I.T/ I.I.Sc. The dates and other details of the examination are advertised prominently in the leading newspaper of the country.

STUDY CENTRES

Related branch in IIT's and NIT's Allahabad, Calicut, Jamshedpur, Jalandhar, Surat, REC Tiruchirapalli, BIT Ranchi, MAHE Manipal, SIST Chennai, DIT Dehradun(UA), GLAIT&M, Mathura, Ideal IT Ghaziabad, IE&RT, Allahabad, SRMSCE & T, Bareilly.

JOB OPPORTUNITIES

Candidates with a degree in Industrial Engineering/ Industrial and Production Engineering from an engineering college recognised by the AICTE (Ministry of Human Resource Development) have various types of job opportunities available in all manufacturing, service and software companies. The following are the industries involved in using of Industrial Engineering branch: ACC, Andersen Consulting, ANAND Group, Apollo Tyres, Ashok Leyland, ABB India Limited, Aptech, Andersen Consulting, Atlas Cycles, Bajaj Auto Limited, BPL India, BEL, Bharti Telecom Limited, BHEL, Boeing, Banking, Cadbury, Defence Services, Dabur India Limited, Eicher Escorts Group, Ernst and Young Engineering India Limited, Goodyear Limited, Hero Group, Hospitals, HAIL, HCL Infosystem, ISRO, ITC, IBM, Indian Oil Corporation Limited, Kelvinator, LML, Modi Tyres, Nestle, National Fertilizers Limited, SAIL,TIMEX,TVS Group,Infosys, 12 Technologies,GSSL, MAIT, Mahindra and Mahindra, MUL, Modi Rubber, NHPC, NTPC, Oracle, Oswal Group, Ordnance Factory, ONGC, Parametric Software, Pepsi, Railways, Siemens India Limited, TCS, Tata, Udyog etc.

Industrial engineering's role in business in expanding rapidly today. With the changes in favoured motivational theories moving from classical to human resource to even more participative management styles, the skills of the industrial engineer have been in great demand. Increased competition, the broader spectre of a world economy, changes in demographics, technological advances and the higher educational levels of the workplace have all combined to create broad sweeping changes in organisation strategies in the last decade. The industrial engineering focus has always been on the controlled management of change with the purpose of creating a continuously improving environment.

(i) INFORMATION TECHNOLOGY

Hardware and software sectors of the IT Industry offer technical work options which require a science background and good mathematical skills. Programmers require analytical acumen and above average mental ability. IT enabled industries require professionals with a range of skills- creative, problem solving, technical, organising, communicating and programming.

Introduction

The Ministry of Information Technology responding to the growth of the IT sector has planned adequate growth of the educational facilities. By 2008 there are going to be 2.63 lakh postgraduates including MCA's, 7.85 lakh graduates, 7.42 lakh diploma holders, 10.5 lakh in hardware and 7.5 in IT enabled services. At the higher and we produce only 25 PhDs and 300 M.Techs as compared to 800 PhDs and 10,000 postgraduates in the US. Quality institutions will be doubled by next academic year and tripled by 2005-06. Another 205 government aided institutions will be added to the list. There will be a cluster of 65 institutions, the IITs, IIITs, IIMs, IISc included to share instructional material, coursework, faculty for an integrated approach to IT education.

Nature of Work

Computer Scientists- People who work on the elements of chip design, mathematical modelling, reliability aspects of chip design are the scientists. How a computer is required to respond is what the scientists conceive. The study route in BSc in computers, MSc in computers and a Ph.D in the subject. Those who opt for studying abroad do a BS in Computer Science, MS in Computer Science and a doctoral programme. IIT offers a 5 year programme in Computer Science and Mathematics. This course covers scientific aspects required for chip design.

Computer Engineers: These are the hardware professionals who work on three major areas- Computer manufacture, computer repair and maintenance and System integration.

Designing of computer implies the basic development of computers, computing equipments and ancillary units. People from electronic and computer engineering work in this field. Manufacturing of computers is managed by engineers.

Maintenance is essentially the work of hardware professionals. BE/ B.Tech or M.Tech in computers is the required qualification. A computer hardware specialist is an expert in IT related hardware. They are trained to dismantle, identify, troubleshoot and assemble various parts of a computer.

System integration has two facets. The first deals with integrating various peripherals to form an independent system which works as per user requirement. The second deals with integration of different platforms with different operating systems environment so that they can communicate.

In the hardware sector, with the internet boom, increased PC penetration and the new exim policy, more hardware professionals will be required.

Information Technologists

Information Technology span an enormous range of jobs from software designing to consultancy. It is basically about how a computer can be exploited in different fields.

Information Technology has pervaded virtually every sphere of life and hence offers a variety of options. It has the potential to absorb

7 million people by 2008 with software accounting for 2.2 million, hardware sector direct employment 1.6 million and indirect employment of 3.2 million professionals. India has set a target of $50 billion in software exports.

Software Engineers/ Systems Programmers

Software designing is a technical task. It involves writing a set of instructions for the operating systems which control the operations of the entire computer system. The job involves research, development and adaptation of application programmes for use with computer systems.

Systems programmers have good technical acumen and knowledge of the parts of a computer and their operations. A degree in computer science and excellent knowledge of computer architecture is required.

System programmers are employed with IT end users, computer manufacturers and service centres and also consultancy firms. Systems programmers with telecommunication and database concepts will find many opportunities.

Over 70,000 people join the software sector every year. Jobs will touch 85,000 by 2002 and 2.2 million by 2008.

System Analyst

Computerisation within any organisation involves analysing its informational needs and the problems related to it and designing patterns for the flow to the computer users. The job also involves planning the distribution of information within the organisation which requires discussion with departmental heads to determine their information needs and problems.

Analyst Programmers

When computerisation has to replace manual procedures analyst programmers study how work is manually carried on to design and develop computerised processes to replace these manual processes. The job requires excellent analytical skills, the ability to define the elements of a task devise alternative and innovative solutions and select the best alternative. The job requires communicating with the various departments in an organisation to design the most efficient flow of information. The academic background required is BE/B.Tech/ MCA/M.Tech. Generally programmers with a couple of years experience can upgrade themselves to become analyst programmers.

Application Programmers

When the System Analyst defines a system, a series of logical steps which a computer would do to process information for use have to be written. This involves using programming languages. Application programmers write , debug and test computer programmes. They work with analyst programmers to follow the guidelines given in the form of flowcharts or tables by System analyst.

Consultants

Consultant specialise in one of the many fields eg. Optimising computer performance, computer/net security, projects, hardware and software selection and installation, management of database or telecommunications. These are primarily aimed at solving IT related problems of the client. Consultants are experienced professionals with 5-7 years of experience and a postgraduate degree related to computers.

Operators

Data Entry Operators, Desk Top Publishing Operators, generally have a +2 qualification and a computer certificate/ Diploma.

Information Systems Designers

Systems designers design alternative systems as per the system requirements which has been determined by the analyst. In an industry, business, commercial or professional set up computerisation implies that the data stored in the system must have a systems design and application design.

BE/MCA/BIS/MIS are desirable qualification. Software developers and IT end users are potential employers.

Information systems Managers

Information systems managers provide ready access to decision making information. This is used by the organisational decision makers. Information managers can be from diverse backgrounds such as computer science, physical or social sciences, business, finance, management, engineering etc. Information systems jobs are with IT end users.

WORK CONDITIONS

Hardware Engineers-

Shopfloor

Client's premises when installation work is being done

Manitenance

Assembly line

Client's premises

Software Engineers-

Computer stations

Clients office on project assignments

Team work

Analyst

Analyst work from office
Consultants require to travel

Internet

In dot com offices
With teams of professionals
Considerable interaction with team members

Personal Qualities

Technical acumen for hardware jobs
Analytical skills
Programming skills
Patience
Perseverance
Ability to keep updated with the latest technology

JOB PROSPECTS IN IT:

Business and Industry- Large and medium sized businesses have computer networks information systems professional the responsibility of the smooth flow of data through the computer networks.

Banking and Finance- IT specialists maintain, update financial data and manage the transfer of accounts.

Office and PC- Processing storing and retrieval of data and reference information, and business communications requires IT skills. Information systems professionals oversee these tasks.

Factories- Computerisation has influenced production processes, inventory control and quality management. The operations in high tech sectors is almost completely computerised eg. The medical sector, aviation and space sciences, communications, weather labs while robotic has greatly influenced production in high precision based industries and in industries manufacturing chemical and other products which pose health hazards.

Travel Sector- E-ticketing, electronic traffic control, marketing, planning are in things in travel. The latest is digitisation for preparing travel maps.

Medical-related- Medical documentation, diagnostic procedures and electronically controlled therapy have been used in medical practice. The backend support professional are new on the scene particularly in India. These are medical transcriptionists.

Architecture planning and Design- CAD has been in use for a long time and is used for designers and architects. The specification and data is fed into the computer and visual modifications, designs and models are created through graphical images.

Scientific Research- Storing, computing, analysis and interpretation of data for scientific work as well as its use in exploration, remote sensing and managing electronically operated equipments, Computer technology and IT skills are required. In exploration on land and water computers are used for locating minerals, studying effects of natural phenomena, studying weather phenomena.

Education- Huge data bases accessible over the net, online education are facts of today. The virtual classroom is a reality.

Defence-Equipments for communication, combat and signals are today electronically operated. Infect the warfare today is a test of a nations hitch electronic capabilities.

Data Analysis and Interpretation- Artificial Intelligence has made possible logical deductions, interpretations and judgements on computerised systems.

Robotics-This field has emerged from that of artificial intelligence and it is geared to bring tremendous advancements in the industrial, health, services sectors and the domestic front.

Music-Analysation of notes to the sound effect in concert halls is controlled by the computer. The electronic keyboard, programmable devices, sound production hardware, amplification device, computer system with a display and keyboard, storage device are today revolutionising the concept of music composition and production.

Call Centres-A call centre is a place that has adequate telecom facilities, trained consultants, access to wide database, internet and other on-line support infrastructure in order to provide information and support to customers on real time basis.

Multimedia-Multimedia involves computing and audiovisual technologies to fuse video, audio, text, graphics, animation etc. in a meaningful way. All these are used to create a real life experience. Web designing and content has a lot to do with multimedia. There are animators, sound technicians, graphic artists, video technicians are multimedia professionals.

Internet-Internet connects computers across the globe through modem which is used for communicating using the telephone line. When many networks are connected across the globe millions of computers can be accessed from any single computer. Internet facility is being used by most Pc users. By 2005 it is expected that there will be 10 million households using this facility.

CAREER OPENINGS RELATED TO THE INTERNET

Dot com careers- You could do your professional job in a dotcom, design webpages, or take up a technical job on the server side. Websites of education, businesses, services, institutions, organisations, agencies provide ready options for work. They operate for the consumer on one end (B2C) and business (B2B) on the other.

Internet Service Providers- Internet connection is provided by ISPs. Internet servers require very high uptime to provide user satisfaction. Hardware specialists are hired to maintain uptime. In addition, matters relating to system administration, fine tuning performance and net security is looked after by software professionals. Large ISPs employ even telecom specialists to keep the network healthy.

Internet and Telecommunication- Telecom and IT experts world over are working overtime to ensure that union between the two great trends of our times is a great success- Mobile phones and the Internet. People will be able to browse the net on the move, carry out business transactions, make reservation, carry out search for locations, look for a little video clip without the need of the heavy use of the keyboard. IT and telecom companies have sunk in hundreds of millions of dollars to develop platforms, applications, hardware and network systems to enable internet access to mobile phone with ease and speed which will radically change the way people shop do business and entertain themselves. Teleconferencing, Voice on Internet Protocol are other areas where the internet and telecommunications technology merge.

Education- The virtual class room is a reality. Online education is very much an established phenomena.

ENTRY ROUTES

Computer engineers are post graduates in microelectronics, computers, production engineering or graduate engineers in electronics, computers.

Research and Development engineers are M.Techs/Ph.Ds.

Servicing Engineers have experience in repair and maintenance of electronic circuits and microprocessors.

Software engineers must have an engineering degree with post graduate diploma in computer applications.

Systems designers and Analyst Programmer have a Masters in Computer Applications/ engineering degree. They are good at programming skills and have experience in systems design.

Systems Analyst are Engineering graduates or graduates in Maths, Business, Physical Sciences, CA with a degree in Computer Science, Information Technology, Information Science, Information Systems or Data Processing.

Application Programming requires graduates in Arts, Science, Commerce, Statistics. They move up to become Analyst, Programmers with experience.

Operating jobs require Senior Secondary qualification, typing skills and training in various software packages as well as English regional language skill.

Sales and Marketing professionals are graduates and Degree/ Diploma holders in Sales and Marketing. They require good communication skills and may have knowledge of computers.

(j) LIGHTING

Remember Dimple Kapadia and how her elegantly designed, fragrant candles became the talk of the town? Well, with Diwali round the corner you can also be the next P3P, provided of course you have oodles of creativity. And, perhaps that is what you need the most because the business requires very little cash investment.

The primary reason for this is that the basic raw material- wax- is cheap. Learning the basic skills is also simple enough. There are dozens of candle-making styles that one can adopt.

The Internet has made it possible for candle-markers to sell their products on a global scale. You could also become a regular supplier for a crafts outlet. Says candle-maker Poonam Burman, "There is a plenty of scope for candle-makers. While individuals use candles as decorative elements, hotels/ retail outlets use them as props. The variety is so diverse that one can get candles made of glass, pebbles, flowers and even kundan work. The demand has suddenly shot up and that has created a spurt in the business".

The lure of cash is so great that even college students or people in related professions are becoming budding candle-makers! Says beautician, Bharti Taneja, who recently launched her range of aromatherapy candles, "I attended a candle-making workshop in Canada and I got so interested in it that I decided to diversify my business to include this craft. Not only is it a lucrative profession, but you are also able to give jobs to the unemployed."

Adds Khushboo Sahni, a third-year student of LSR College, Delhi University, "I took to candle making right after school. I found it interesting and eventually took it up as a profession. One thing led to another and today I take part in lots of exhibitions and get orders from a number of upmarket interior/gift shops. Further, the demand for candles is no longer restricted to just the festival season. Hence, a candle maker need not run out of orders after the festivities are over.

There are a very few courses run by established institutes, however, established candle-makers do conduct courses in the craft. The Alps Academy in Lajpat Nagar, Delhi is the only institute to have recently started a course in candle-making.

Says Taneja, "The process of making candles can be easily passed on but the aspirant must have an inborn talent". And what's more you can jump onto the bandwagon even if you are not well educated. It is, however, imperative that you learn the tricks of the trade from the right professional".

Agrees Sahni, "Ascertain the credentials of the person organising the workshop and insist on seeing his designs. For only then will you be able to make out if he/she can teach you the right method. You should also take care to see that you don't get scalded while making the candles".

The best way to sell your products is to take part in exhibitions and Diwali melas. You just have to be aware of which are the popular ones in your city and book space. If that sounds like a lot of work, then the other way to market your candles is either through word of mouth (which obviously will take some time to materialise) or approach an interior or gift shop (which are the best places to showcase your products). However, you must be skilled in the art of negotiating if you opt for the latter.

Be innovative because if you don't bring out a new range every few months, then you will not be able to make it in this profession for very long. After all, not only is there huge competition but the customer is also aware of the latest market trends, says Sahni Innovation is hence the best policy. Happy candle making.

(k) PLASTIC PROCESSING

The Central Institute of Plastics Engineering and Technology (CIPET) is an autonomous body under the department of chemicals and petro-chemicals, Ministry of Chemicals and Fertilisers of the Indian Government.CIPET was established in Chennai in 1968 with UNDP assistance. Today, the institute has 12 branches all over the country and offers more than half a dozen long and short-term courses.

CIPET caters to the needs of the industry through manpower training, processing, design and CAD/CAM/CAE, testing, consultancy, advisory and developmental services.

The centre in Chennai has been awarded the ISO 9001:2000 QMS for its training and technical services. Other centres are located at Ahmedabad, Amritsar, Bhopal, Bhubaneshwar, Hyderabad, Haldia, Imphal, Lucknow, Mysore, Hajipur and Guwahati.

CIPET is also recognised by the Madras University and the Department of Science and Technology for its Ph.D. programmes. Courses available at CIPET include a one year PGD-PE (postgraduate diploma in Plastics Engineering), B.E./B.Tech. B.Sc.Engg.(four years) in Mechanical, Chemical, Production, Polymer and Tool Engineering. The institute also offers a postgraduate diploma in plastics processing and testing; a one year postgraduate diploma in plastics mould design and a three year diploma in mechanical/ plastic technology/ tool engineering/ plastics and production engineering. Students have to qualify for a written test and an interview to get into the institute.

According to experts at CIPET, the growth of the plastics processing industry will depend on the availability of skilled manpower. With the use of modern machines, there has been an increased demand for manpower in the design and plastics processing segments. As the production of plastics increases, eight persons will be required for the production of every 100 tonnes per annum. CIPET also helps in development of plastics recycling and waste management technologies. The institute plans to set up centres in the SAARC, West Asian and South-East Asian countries.

The plastics industry in India has predominantly been in the small scale sector employing mostly unskilled and untrained manpower. However, the situation is expected to change with the globalisation of the Indian economy. Now, there is a need for trained manpower who can churn out products on par with international standards. CIPET also offers training to students, technical personnel and executives from the SAARC countries and developing nations of Africa and the Middle East.

For admission and other details, visit www.cipetindia.com

(I) RETAILING

India is still undecided when it comes to opening up the retail sector to the foreign investor.

But, the indications given by the Prime Minister at the joint concluded ASEAN summit are indications considered positive from the industry's view point. Services sector has already been marked as the numerouno when it comes to employability and contribution towards the GDP of the country. The industry which is at the nascent stage is already contributing a significant proportion, if one takes into consideration both the organized and the unorganised sector. Indian organized retailing players like Westside,Pantaaloon, Shoppers Stop, Food World, Music World are gearing up to face their much fancied rivals like Marks and Spencer, Carrefour, Walmart to name a few, once the flood gates are opened. The best way to gain competitive advantage by any and very player in the Indian market is to en-cash the availability of quality, competitive manpower. Add to it the straitegic advantages, of location and time zone differences, improvement in infrastructure like ports, airports, Special Economic Zones (SEZ) and then you can visualize the opportunities this sector is going to throw up. But are the prospective employees geared up to match up to the expectations of the new generation retailing players?

Gone are the days when the conventional mom and pop stores used to recruit unskilled manpower only to assist the proprietor in the operation of the more. US GAAP accounting was never followed, SCM was never part of the logistics. CRM was never considered important and neither were there a professional recruitment and training department. With so many changes can one do with the typical mom and pop set up? Absolutely, not.

There are opportunities for the takers be it an engineer, a management graduate, a logistics experts, an IT technocrat as the departmentalisation of the players needed professionally trained manpower. Although there are institutes offering post graduation diploma in retailing, a plain Master of Business graduate can also fit into the scheme of things.

(m) TOOL & DIE MAKING

The story of the human evolution through the ages has close affinity with the development and use of various tools and equipments they used at different stages spanning over a period of more than million years on earth.

Human evolution from a food gatherer to a hunter and then as farmer and finally as an entrepreneur has led to the development of various tools and implements. But it is the industrial society that brought in its wake a demand for a wide variety of specialized tools and trained technical work force to run the industries.

As the demand for Tool Makers and Designers began to grow, professional technical institutions and organizations were needed to manufacture specialized Tools, Dies, Moulds, Jigs, Fixtures, High precision components and conducts high standard training programs to fulfill the large quality technical human resource requirement for the industrial sector.

Recent Developments in Tool Room Technology

Many young technical students and technical trained personals even today do not understand the national and international employment potential of the Tool making and its closely related areas like computer aided design and manufacturing. Some people think Took Making means making nuts, spanners etc. Also to manufacture these products is not as simple as many people think. So generally TR area does not attract to the wide spectrum of the population of this country. Due to lack of information by the school teachers, many brilliant academic students are not able to come across this particular TRs Technology.

What is Tool Room (TR)

Tool Room is the industrial setup where the specialized Tools, Dies, Moulds, Jigs, Fixtures are designed and manufactured. These tools are used for mass production for all Plastic components, Aluminium or any casting parts from kitchen utensils to space components, industrial components etc. Many companies have their own captive TR or they assign to the professionally managed TRs.

What is a Tool?

It is an equipment used for mass production to get the maximum output with best quality in low cost and in optimum time. It can be specialized Press Tools, Dies Castings, Plastic Moulds, Jigs and Fixtures.

Who is a Tool Maker?

He is a Master Engineer who coordinates and monitors the process of Tool Design, Tool Planning, Die Machining, Tool Quality Controlling (Meterology & Metallurgy), Tool Assembly and Finally Try out. Any Tool is the child of the particular Tool Maker. Some times he even gives suggestion to the product designers or to Product Analysis Experts.

Modern TR and the Tool Engineer?

In recent years the development of the integrate components/ product design, to accomplish the comforts of the human kind, has imposed a great challenge to the TR Engineers. Indian TR industries and TR professionals have established modern TRs across the country to meet these growing demands, which contribute numerous, colourful and lucrative employment to trained manpower in this vibrant sector. A modern TR consists of large/ small number of highly special purpose computer integrated machines, interfaced with the finest softwares. In modern TRs many highly paid TR Trained professionals work as Tool/ Mould Designers, Tool Makers and Engineers, CNC & CAM Programmers, CAD Designers, CAE Specialist, Cutting Tool Specialist, Mould Flow Analyst, Process Planning Engineer, Die Metallurgy Specialist, CMM Specialist, CNC Machinist, Class A Metal Machinist and TR Fitters according to their area of expertise and academic background. Unlike other workshop the TR is a place where one can find a healthy atmosphere with mostly AC environment. Some TRs specially manufacture Air space components that normally have "Clean Room" called class 1000 dust free. The TR is a world-class work place for a Mechanical/ Production/ TR Trained Engineers to work with.

CAD/CAE/CAM in TR

The acronym of CAD/CAE/CAM is Computer aided Design/ Computer aided Engineering/ Computer aided Manufacturing. The workflow starts in the TR once it receive the Product Model or the Product Design drawing. Before accepting the model the TR Professionals check the manufacturing feasibility of the Tool for the Product.Once the product design is accepted then the brain storming session starts with TR Project team to freeze the tool design. Tool design is normally done in CAD systems. It is one of the exciting jobs in TR. The design of Mould/Tool architecture includes Core cavity creation, Draft analysis, Flow analysis, etc. The designer sends core/ cavity to the CAM station through LAN. At CAM work station CAM Programmer develops 3D Tool path and check by simulation if everything is right he then sends it through the DNC link to the CNC Shop for manufacturing. After machined, the part goes to inspection, and from there to Heat Treatment and finally to the EDM or Grinding/ Polishing etc. Finally assembly and Try out.

To accomplish the above work TR professionals uses the finest CAD/CAM softwares.

CAD/CAM Emerging Trend in TR

Emerging trends like Reverse Engineering, Rapid Proto typing, Virtual Reality, Product life cycle management helps enormously in the New Product design. Tool making/Design, pre-Tooling and post tooling particularly for the professionals who deals in the Design office.

INSTITUTIONS IMPARTING COURSES IN TOOL AND CAD/CAM TECHNOLOGY

The main institutions imparting these courses fall under the Department of SIDO Establishments chaired by Add.Development Commissioner, Ministry of Small Scale Industries in collaboration with GTZ (Germany), DANTOOL (Denmark) and UNDP etc. Some of the programs are offered at CIPET, Chennai and its extension centres across the country. NTTF Network of Institutes, Delhi State owned, TN-Department of Industries and Commerce owned Institutions etc. The best part of this institute is they are organized like a industry-institute. So the students passing from this institution experiencing the first-hand industrial experience while studying. It makes the job easy for them when they go to industries. The chart above gives an idea about most of the institutions offering the course in Tool and CAD/ CAM.

LIST OF PROGRAMS AND INSTITUTIONS

Sl.No.	*Institution*	*Courses Offered*	*Duration*
1.	CIHT,Jalandhar, SIDO TRD	TDM	4 Years
2.	Central Instt.of	DTDM	3 Years

(Contd.)

(Contd.)

Sl.No.	Institution	Courses Offered	Duration
	Tool Design Hyderabad (An UNDP Pro.) SIDO TR	PDTD ME/ M Tech	1 Year 2 Years
3.	Central Tool Room (Indo-Adv.DTDM German)Ludhiana, SIDO TR		4 Years
4.	CTTC(An Indo-Danish Pro.) 4 Years Bhubaneshwar,SIDO TR M Tech(proposed)	DTDM PD Course Other TR Pro.	 1 Year 1 Year 2 Years
5.	CTTC(An Indo-Danish Pro.) Kolkata	DTDM PD Course	4 Years 1 Year
6.	Indo-Danish Tool Room, SIDO TR	DTDM PD Course	4 years 1 Year
7.	Indo-German Tool Room Ahmedabad,SIDO TR	Adv.DTDM PD Course	4 Years 1 Year
8.	Indo-German Tool Room Aurangabad, SIDO TR	DTDM PD Course	4 Years 1 Year
9.	TRTC,Guwahati SIDO TR	DTDM	4 Years
10.	Indo-German Tool Room Indore SIDO TR	Adv.DTDM PD Course	4 Year 1 Year
11.	Central Instt. Of Plastic Engg.& Tech.Chennai and its Extension Centres	DPMT PDPMD M.Tech	3 Years 1 Year 2 Years
12.	GTTC(An Indo-	DTDM	4 Years

(Contd.)

Contd.)

Sl.No.	*Institution*	*Courses Offered*	*Duration*
	Danish Pro.)		
	Bangalore & Mysore	PD Course	1 Year
	and		
	Its Extension Centres	PG Course	1-2 Years
	(Karnataka State Owned Instt.)		
13.	Institute of Tool Engineering,	DTE	3 Years
	Dindigul/GTTC Chennai	PDTD	18 Months
	(TN State Owned Institute)		
14.	TRTC (An Indo-Danish)	DTDM	4 Years
	(Delhi State owned institute)	PG Course	2 Years
15.	CSIO, A CSIR Complex Chandigarh	Adv.DTDM	4 Years
16.	NTTF-A professionally	DTDM	3 Years
	Managed Premier Institution	PDTD	1 Year
	Bangalore,Katpati, Tellicherry,	Other PDs	1 Year
	Dharwad, Hyderabad etc.	PG Program	1-2 Years

Opportunity in TR AND CAD/CAM

The opening are good for TR Trained professionals. The starting salary ranges from Rs.7000/- to 20,000/- depending upon the area of the candidates expertise.

Many Tool Room Engineers/ Technicians immigrate to Canada, Australia, Singapore, Malaysia, Indonesia, Germany etc.

10

Farming

(a) AGRICULTURE

Agriculture is the backbone of our country, where 70% of its population depend on this for their livelihood. In this context, a career in Agri-profession in itself is a noble profession in which there is an immense scope to serve these farming communities, the real builders of the nation. Previously, this profession was considered to be less remunerative, devoid of glamour, status and challenges. Now in the changing scenario of rapid globalisation and rising world markets where agriculture has been given industrial status, a profession in a agriculture has become a very challenging and demanding career. A job in this sector holds lots of responsibilities, as it is directly linked with the farmers and mostly with their economic development. A large number of Central and State government departments, Public Sector Undertakings, private sector and non-governmental organisations are involved in the agricultural business and trade. Hence, it possess dynamic opportunities to serve in these different areas. Even if this profession does not bring high dividends, one gets and immense satisfaction of serving these poor farmers.

EDUCATION

The apex organisation to deal with all types of education and research activities in agriculture is the Indian Council of Agricultural Research, (ICAR), situated in New Delhi. In agriculture, the main course is B.Sc (Ag.), through different courses at graduate level in different allied subjects like Fisheries Science, Forestry, Home Science, Agricultural Engineering, Dairy Technology, Food Science and Technology etc. are also being offered. The eligibility condition for admission to these courses is 10+2 (Sc.) or equivalent.

Under the guidance of the ICAR, all the States have Agriculture Universities (SAUs). All the 30 SAUs and one Central Agricultural

University (CAU) are providing these courses. Besides, some traditional Central Universities like Banaras Hindu University (BHU), Visva Bharti University, Allahabad Agricultural Institute are giving admission in B.Sc (Ag.) through their own systems of selection.

Apart from these, in some states like U.P. and Rajasthan, intermediate and graduate level courses in agriculture are also being offered through different degree colleges. However, in our opinion degrees from the SAUs and the Central University should be preferred as these follow the common credit course system.

Out of the total number of seats in the SAUs and the CAU, 15% of seats are filled by the ICAR, through a common All India Entrance Test.

PROMINENT SAUs/CENTRAL UNIVERSITY

1. Acharya N.G.Ranga Agriculture University, Hyderabad
2. Central Agricultural University, Imphal
3. Chandrasekhar Azad University of Agriculture and Technology, Kanpur
4. Choudhary Charan Singh Haryana Agricultural University, Hissar
5. G.B. Pant University of Agriculture and Technology, (GBPAU & T) Pantnagar
6. Institute of Agricultural Sciences, BHU, Varanasi
7. Orissa University of Agriculture and Technology, Bhubaneshwar
8. Punjab Agricultural University, Ludhiana
9. Tamil Nadu Agricultural University, Coimbatore
10. University of Agricultural Sciences, Bangalore

All the Agricultural Universities and almost all degree colleges of traditional universities in the country also impart education in agriculture and allied sciences.

OPPORTUNITIES

There are huge opportunities in the Government sector particularly in State Governments for agricultural graduates who seek their jobs at block/ district level in different disciplines under the Department of Agriculture. Various positions like Junior Agriculture Officer, Plant Protection Officers, Agriculture Extension Officers, Cane Development Officer etc. are available.

The private agro-based industries like fertilizer, seed, farm machinery, pesticides, food processing etc. and recently NGO's have also started operating on a large scale in India to provide standardised jobs to a sizeable number of graduates. They generally prefer agricultural graduates with high proficiency

In the agriculture courses, some higher prominent course is Agri-Business Management(ABM). For this , after completion of B.Sc(Ag), they have to do PG Diploma in Agri-Business Management. The courses are being offered by some leading institutions like:-

1. National Institute of Agricultural Extension Management(MANAGE), Hyderabad
2. National Agricultural Universities like G.B.P.A.U. & T. are also offering this course of ABM.

Besides, any students interested in the banking sector, may join as Rural Development Officer or Agriculture Officer in public/private sector banks. Selection for this is done through an examination, conducted by concerned banks, where only agriculture and allied graduates are eligible. Besides, these opportunities, students keen in academics may opt for Post-Graduate courses like M.Sc(Ag.) or for Doctorate(Ph.D) degree, in different specialised subjects of agriculture. These are Agronomy, Soil Science, Genetics and Plant Breeding. Plant Physiology, Extension Education, Entomology, Plant Pathology, Statistics, Computer Application in Agriculture, Meteorology, Horticulture etc. After completion of these higher degrees they may opt for teaching or research jobs. There are a number of research institutes/ colleges functioning under ICAR. ICAR is one of the largest agricultural research organisation in the world with over 6,000 scientists. Those students who have a dream to become an agricultural scientists, have to get through the Agricultural Research Service (ARS) Examination conducted by the ICAR in different disciplines time to time.

SELF EMPLOYMENT

If you have the above mentioned qualifications, but are not interested to work under any organisation, try to open your own clinic i.e. Agro-Clinic. Here the Government of India (GOI) is also giving financial assistance to such interested students. The job involves being a plant doctor of the Agro-clinic, who prescribes suitable packages for a good crop, to the clients i.e. farmers. It means you have to help the farmers, test the soil, plan their crops, supply them the reliable information regarding weather, fertilizer application, irrigation management, insect-disease-weed management, post harvest operation, phytosanitary measures, value addition, safe storage etc. For this thorough subject knowledge, high practical experience and efficient communication skills are an absolute must. In the marketing sector, you can also start your own unit of business, taking Government help through loan.

Gone are the days of agriculture, where farmers were cultivating their fields with a wooden plough on their shoulders, throwing the seed and at last harvesting the crops. In the age of Information and Communication Technology(ICT), the present day agriculture has become high-tech agriculture or we can call it e-agriculture. To achieve global competitiveness, the Government plans to connect all the farm families with Telephone and Internet so that they could avail all the valuable information at a faster rate. A large number of Kisan Call Centres(KCC) are being opened up in different district levels to provide service at the doorstep in seconds through the ICT. The latest proposal of corporate faring is also under consideration. Furthermore, the Government plans to extend Krishi Vigyan Kendras (KVK) to each district to facilitate easy transfer of technologies from research organisations to the farmer's field. All these centres would need Agri-professionals or experts to provide their services. Considering the vastness of the sector and the challenges it posed opting for a career in agriculture seems a demanding but satisfying choice.

(b) AGRI-BUSINESS

Agriculture is the lifeline of the Indian economy. An agrarian country like India provides livelihood directly or indirectly to 70% of her population through agriculture and allied activities. In fact our nation is bestowed with diversified agro climatic zones and natural resources to produce a large number of commodities but the declining growth rate in agriculture production is now a matter of serious concern. Recently, the Prime Minister Dr. Manmohan Singh called upon all the stakeholders to plug the loopholes connected with low productivity. Lack of proper planning and direction at the national level coupled with state's dwindling resources have stood as barriers in harnessing the potentiality. Today 32 state agricultural universities, 28 general and deemed universities as well as central institutions and projects of ICAR offer agricultural education and generating farm technology in India. The Planning Commission of India is making a special drive to identify priority areas of intervention to make Indian agariculture globally competitive. It is estimated that in India the annual turnout of the agro graduates is around 17,000 out of which hardly 10% are absorbed in the public sector. The table below lists career opportunities for graduates:-

Career Opportunities	*Potential Employer*	*Job Profile*
Agri-Business Management		
* Agro Consultant	* Public & Private Sectors	* Managerial functions like purchasing, marketing, selling
* Agri-business Analyst	* Multinational Companies	* Study marketing Strategy

(Contd.)

(Contd.)

Career Opportunities	*Potential Employer*	*Job Profile*
* Production & Procurement Specialist	* Agro enterprises	* Agricultural Com-mondity export & import Trading
Resource Development and Management		
* Coordinator	* Public & Private Sector Companies	* Policy analysis liasoning
* Agricultural & allied experts	* Leading NGOs	* Planningj & evaluation
* Management trainee	* Cooperative	* Budgeting
	* Implementing viable agro-projects	
Food and Bevarage Industries		
* Food Technician	* Public & Private Sector Companies	* Processing, preservation & devel-Qulity
* Health Inspector	* FMCG Sector	* Value added pro-
* Quality Investigator		* Hygienic food Preparation
* Laboratory Technician		
* Marketing Executive		* Packating & Designing
* Food & Nutrition Executive		* Home Science Management
Teaching and Research		
* Lecturer	* SAUs	* Teaching & Research In agriculture & allied activities & experiment and analysis
* Assistant Professor	* ICAR Instt.	
* Associate Professor	* KVKs	
* Reader	* NRCs	
* Scientis	* Fertilizers & pesticide Companies	
* Technical Assistant/ Lab.Asstt./ Farm Technician/ Field Assistant		
* RA/ SRF/JRF/Field Investigator		* Arrangement of training & group meetings

(Contd.)

(Contd.)

Career Opportunities	*Potential Employer*	*Job Profile*
NGOs		
* Programme Officer * Coordinator * Livelihood Specialist * Agro Consultant * Field Officer/Social Worker * Fund Raising Officer	* Voluntary Orgn. * Charitable trusts * Funding agencies	* Programme evaluation of proj- * Arragement of training & meeting * Social mobility * Liasion with public & private sectors officials
Private and Public Sector Banks		
* Recovery Officer * Specialist Officer * Crop. Insurance Officer * Agriculture & Rural Development Officer	* Nationality (ADB) Banks * Cooperative Financial Institutions * Regional Development Bank	* Loan sanction for agriculture & allied activities * Recovery from farmers & entrepreneurs.
Rural Management		
* Manager * Management Trainee * Experts * Public Relation Officer	* Public & private sector * MNC * Rural entrepre--neurs	* Financial Management * Rural Manage- * Industrial & entrepreneurship mangement * Sales & market--ing management * Export/import Management
Agriculture Journalism		
* Reporter * Information Specialist * Publicity Officer * Videographer * Freelance Writer/ Editor	* Leading TV/Radio/ Journals/Newspaper Agencies etc.	* Farm reporting * Agriculture publi--cation * Talks for TV & Radio * Agro Information * Anchoring/ Supporting staff

(Contd.)

(Contd.)

Career Opportunities	*Potential Employer*	*Job Profile*
Agriculture Marketing		
* Sales Officer * Product Promotion Officer * Marketing Executives * Territory Officer * Area Sales Manager * Business Develop--ment Officer	* Food & bevarage Indus * Fertilizers, pestici-des & seed company such as Bayer, Ranbaxy, HLL, Excel, Tata Rallis * Farm machinery unit like KAMCO, Mahindra & Mahindra etc. * Cooperative Orgn. like APEDA, NAFED, MARKFEED, HPMC, NDDB, FCI, ITC	* Sale promotion of related products * Agro Consultan-cy * Study the mark--eting channels * Fixing marketing price
Agro-consultancy		
* Agri-experts * Information Specialist * Fund Development Specialist * Extension Specialist * Call Centre Executive * Landscape Designer * Eco-Tourism Consul-ant * Environmentalist	* Public & Private * Banks * NGOS * Mass Media & broadcasting	* Consultancy on technology * Diseases, pest weather forecas--ting * Marketing infor-mation * Liasion with publ--ice & private sectors officials * Exclusively to respond ot farmers call.
Self Employment		* Seed grower * Agro & allied farming * Farm-Enterpre--neurship * Agri-clinics & agriservice centres

Meaning- SAU= State Agricultural University, ICAR= Indian Coucil of Agricultural Research, KVK= Krishi Vigyan Kendra, HLL= Hindustan Liver Ltd., NRC= National Research Centre, NDDB= National Dairy Development Board, ADB= Agriculture Development Bank, NABARD= National Bank for Agriculture Rural Development, KAMCO= Kerala Agro Machineries, TAFE= Tractor and Farm Implements, APEDA= Agriculture and Processed Food Products Export Development Authority, MARKFED= Marketing Federation of India, NAFED= National Agriculture Cooperative Marketing Federation, HPMC= Horticulture Produce Marketing Commission, FMCG= Fast Moving Consumer Goods.

Academics

For a graduate course in agriculture one should possess a good academic career up to Higher Secondary Level with Science as a core subject. Leading universities and institutions related to this course conduct common entrance test before the commencement of every academic year. Leading agriculture and research institutes offering graduates and post graduates courses in innovative fields of agriculture are mentioned in the following table:-

INNOVATIVE COURSES OFFERED BY PREMIER INSTITUTES OF INDIA

Course Name	*Name of the Premier Institute*
Biotechnology(Bio-chemistry, Bio-informatics and Tissue culture)	* Indian Agriculture Research Instt.,New Delhi * Instt.of Biotechnology and Applied Science,Bangalore * Instt. Of Genomics and Integrated Biology,Delhi * University of Agricultural Science,Bangalore * International Instt.of Agro Informatics and Agro Management, Noida * Assam Agriculture University
Vocational Training	* Respective SAUs and ICAR Institutes

(Contd.)

(Contd.)

Course Name	Name of the Premier Institute
Agri-Business, Extension and Management	* National Institute of Agricultural Extension Management (MANAGE), Hyderabad * Indian Instt.of Management
Fishery	* Central Instt. of Fishery Education, Versova, Mumbai * Central Marine Fishery Instt. Mumbai
Dairy Technology & Animal Science	* National Dairy Research Instt.(NDRI), Karnal * Indian Veterinary Research Instt. (IVRI), Izzatnagar
Agri & Rural Management	* Indian Institute of Management * Indian Rural Management Institute (IRMI), Anand
Gender Studies	* Kerala Agricultural University(KAU), Trissur * CCS, Haryana Agricultu University, Hisar
Agriculture Cooperatives & Marketing	* Kerala Agricultural University(KAU), Trissur * National Instt.of Agriculture Marketing(NIAM), Jaipur
Agriculture Journalism	* Jawaharlal Nehru Krishi Viswavidyalaya, Jabalpur * National Instt. of Rural Development, Hyderabad
Agriculture Project Planning, Management, Monitoring and Evaluation	* Xaviers Instt. of Management * Institute of Management * TATA Instt. of Social Science * National Instt. of Rural Development * TATA Dhan Foundation

(Contd.)

(Contd.)

Course Name	Name of the Premier Institute
Entrepreneurship and Business Management	* Entrepreneurship Development Instt. of India, Ahmedabad
Environment and Natural Resource Management	* IGNOU * Indian Institute of Forest Management, Bhopal
Remote Sensing and GIS Technology in Agriculture	* National Academy of Agriculture Research and Management, Hyderabad * Utkal University, Bhubaneshwar
Correspondence/Distance Learing courses in Sociology, Anthropology, Environmental Study and Water Management etc.	* IGNOU
Food Technology	* Allahabad Agricultural University, Allahabad * JNTU College of Engineering Andhra Pradesh
Agriculture Meteorology	* Indira Gandhi Krishi Vishwavidyalaya, Raipur * GB Pant University of Agriculture Science,

Research Fellowship

A good future exists in the field of agricultural science. Research scholars may avail fellowship from ICSSR, UGC, CSIR, DST, DBT, DRDO, Swaminathan Research Foundation, Nehru Memorial Trust, UNDP, DFID, UNICEF, WHO and other leading NGOs and Funding agency.

(c) AGRICLINICS

The current Agriculture Extension worker and farm holding ratio in the country is around 1:833 which is quite inadequate to disseminate the first changing agriculture technologies to the farmers. Under the new economic compulsion of GATT and WTO, the agri-business has come under the strong and direct influence of international markets.

Indian farm sector has to produce farm goods of quality at the competitive unit cost for international market. The present public extension support system in the country can not meet the global challenges in the agriculture and allied fields. Existing Government functionaries are not properly equipped, nor adequately qualified and trained for rendering location specific specialized crop/ livestock-wise advice to the farmers. Also, public sector input supply agencies are unable to cope with the needs of last transforming and accelerated pace of agriculture production. At present, there is a need to supplement the efforts of Govt. extension system by the private partners to accelerate the process of technology transfer in agriculture. Specialised Agri-services (eg. Soil and input testing, Maintenance and Repairs, Seed/Agro processing, Artificial Insemination, Milk processing, Liquid Nitrogen Plant, Agricultural Insurance, Information Technology, Post Harvest Management etc.) also need supplementing, as the present infrastructure for providing these services is inadequate in the country. It is now felt that these gaps can be filled by qualified agriculture and allied graduates, if they are provided right kind of support system to start their own enterprise on various agriculture and allied activities.

The turnout of graduates in agriculture and allied subject per year is around 11,900. The intake capacity in Post Graduate programme in the universities is around 5500, leaving about 6400 graduates of which about hardly 2000 are able to find employment in the public and private sectors. Thus a reservoir of 9900 graduates every year is available for supporting agriculture production process if viable business opportunities are provided to them. To provide gainful employment opportunity to agriculture and allied graduates and to provide quality service to the farmers, the Ministry of Agriculture, Govt. of India in association with NABARD has launched a unique scheme of AGRICLINICS AND AGRIBUSINESS CENTRES in 2001-2002 to take better methods of farming to each and every farmer across the country. The programme aims to tap the expertise available in the large pool of Agriculture Graduates irrespective of whether they are fresh graduate or not, or whether they are currently employed or not, they can set up their own Agriclinic or Agribusiness Centre and offer professional extension services to the farmers. The Government is also providing start-up training to graduates in Agriculture, or any subject allied to Agriculture like Horticulture, Sericulture, Veterinary Sciences, Forestry, Dairy, Poultry Farming and Fisheries etc.

Objectives of the scheme

1. To supplement the efforts of government extension system
2. To make available supplementary sources of input supply and services to needy farmers.

3. To provide gainful employment to agriculture graduates in new emerging areas in agricultural sector.

Concept

Agriclinics

Agriclinics are envisaged to provide expert services and advice to farmers on cropping practices, technology dissemination, crop protection from pests and diseases, market trends and prices of various crops in the markets and also clinical services for animal health etc. which would enhance productivity of crops/ animals.

Agribusiness Centres

Agribusiness centres are envisaged to provide input supply, farm equipment on hire and other services. In order to enhance viability of the ventures, agriculture graduates may also take up in agriculture and allied areas along with the Agriclinics/ Agribusiness centres.

Eligibility

The scheme is open to Agriculture Graduates/ Graduates in subjects allied to agriculture like horticulture, animal husbandry, forestry, dairy, veterinary, poultry, farming, pisciculture and other allied activities.

Project activities

An illustrative list is given below:-

1. Soil and water quality cum inputs testing laboratories (with Atomic Absorption Spectrophotometers)
2. Pest surveillance, diagnostic and control services.
3. Maintenance, repairs and custom hiring or agricultural implements and machinery including micro irrigation systems (sprinkler and drip)
4. Agri Service Centres including the three activities mentioned above (Group Activity)
5. Seed Processing Units
6. Micro-propagation through Plant Tissue Culture Labs and Hardening Units
7. Setting up of Vermiculture units, production of bio-fertilisers, biopesticides, bio-control agents.
8. Setting up of Apiaries (beekeeping) and honey & bee products' processing units
9. Provision of Extension Consultancy Services
10. Hatcheries and production of fish finger lings for aquaculture
11. Provision of livestock health cover, setting up veterinary dispensaries and services including frozen semen banks and liquid nitrogen supply.

12. Setting up of Information Technology Kiosks in rural areas for access to various agriculture related portals.
13. Food Processing and testing units
14. Value Addition Centres
15. Setting up of Cool Chain for the farm level onwards (Group Activity)
16. Retail marketing outlets for processed agri-products
17. Rural marketing dealerships of farm inputs and outputs.

Any combination of two or more of the above viable activities alongwith any other economically viable activity can be selected by the Graduates which is acceptable to the Bank.

Project Cost and Schedule

The project can be taken up by Agriculture Graduates either individually or on joint/group basis. The outer ceiling for the cost of project by individual would be Rs.10 lakh and for the project by group would be Rs.50 lakh. The group may normally be of 5, of which one could be management graduate with qualification or experience in business development and management. The rate of interest to be changed by the financing bank to the ultimate beneficiary depends upon the amount of loan, types of bank as per the guidelines circulated to these banks by NABARD and RBI from time to time. The period of loan will vary between 5 years to 10 years depending on the activity. The repayment period may include a grace period (to be decided by the financing bank as per the individual scheme) of a maximum of 2 years. The selection of borrowers and location of the projects may be done by the banks in consultation with Agricultural Universities/ KVKs/ Agriculture department of the state etc. in their area of operations, if necessary. All other terms and conditions, banking procedure and lending norms which are normally applicable to project lending and schematic refinance mutates mutandis will also be applicable to financing of agriclinics and agribusiness centres.

Application Procedure

Applications are invited by SFAC (Small Farmers' Agri-business Consortium) by open advertisements in print and electronic media, giving program outline, eligibility criteria, activity areas/ profiles, funding scales and procedure for the scheme. Model Project outlines of about 20 identified projects are available by SFAC at the offices of district level Agriculture Offices, NABARD, LBO etc. Model Project outlines help facilitate the agricultural graduates who seek assistance under this scheme to identify the area in which they want to develop their venture and also enable them to prepare their own Techno Economic Feasibility (TEF) reports for projecting to the banks for availing finance.

(d) FLORICULTURE

Floriculture denotes cultivation of flowers, developing new varieties of commercial value, sale of flowers as raw commodities, processing, distribution etc. for the local and international market. Floriculture is emerging as a blooming business not only in India but in other countries as well. The major importing countries of flowers are Netherlands, Germany, France, Italy and Japan while the important exporters are Columbia, Israel, Spain and Kenya.

The Indian Scenario

Floriculture industry to India comprises flower trade, nursery plants and potted plants, seed and bulb production, micro propogation and extraction of essential oils. The annual domestic demand for the flowers is growing at a rate of over 25% and around Rs.90,000 crore internationally. India's share in international market of flowers is negligible. Though the art of growing flowers is not new to India large-scale commercial scale cultivation, protected cultivation in poly-houses is relatively new in our country. Enormous genetic, diversity, varied agro climatic conditions, versatile human resources offer India a unique scope for diversification in to new avenues which were hitherto unexplored or under-explored. India seems to have a biooming future of floriculture as there is a shift in the trend towards tropical flowers and this can be gainfully exploited by India.

Need of Institutional Support

During the last ten years, taking advantage of the incentives offered by the Government, a large number of floriculture units have been established in India for producing and exporting flowers to the developed countries.

Of the four zones identified as potential centers for flower production namely Bangalore, Hyderabad, Pune and New Delhi, the area around Bangalore and Pune have got the advantage of ideal climatic conditions where the temperature ranges between 15 to 30 degree centigrade. In view of this, the units established in these locations do not require either cooling or heating system.

The units located around New Delhi, though are near to the international airport but have the disadvantage of high as well as low temperatures resulting in additional capital investment for installation of cooling and heating system, besides incurring additional running cost for power and energy. Hyderabad has got the disadvantage of experiencing high summer temperature. Delhi and Mumbai are the most important markets for cut flowers. Himachal Pradesh, endowed with different agro-climatic conditions ranging from sub-tropical to dry temperate zones, has premium potential for growing cut flowers which are off season.

With a view to provide an undivided institutional support to this sector, the Department of Floriculture and Landscaping was carved out from Vegetable Crop and Floriculture in Nov. 1987. After its formation, the department is actively engaged in Teaching (undergraduate and graduate levels), research and extension education activities. Today, the discipline of Floriculture and Landscaping in the Dr.Y.S.Parmar University of Horticulture and Forestry, Solan has made significant progress and ICAR (Indian Council of Agricultural Research) has identified this centre as National Repository for Carnation under All India Coordinated Floriculture Improvement Project.

Employment Opportunities

One can work in different capacities such as consultants, farm/ estate managers, plantation supervisors, project coordinator. Research and teaching are some other avenues. Recently, marketing of Floriculture products for different ventures has also emerged as a potential segment of this field. One can also work as entrepreneur and offer employment to others.

Potential Employers

- Floriculture units
- Outdoor design consultancy firms
- City planners and builders
- Educational institutions offering related courses
- Industrial houses having landscaping units
- Cosmetics and perfume industry
- Pharmaceuticals
- Self employment

The task of floriculture

The job encompasses handling plantations, nurseries and other landscaping projects. These works need scientific management of soil preparation, sowing, harvesting,administration of nutrients and controlling the climate. Knowledge and skills of procurement, collection and distribution are some other requirements of the job. These skills and knowledge are imparted under the professional courses of floriculture and landscaping. A professional qualification combined with an inclination towards gardening and such other activities will produce efficient floriculturists and landscaping professionals.

Types of courses available in floriculture and landscaping

Following courses are available:

- Certificate of courses

- Graduate Level
- Post graduate and doctoral level

Reputed Institutions offering course in floriculture and and Landscaping

- Dr.Yashwant Singh Parmar University of Horiculture and Forestry, Nauni, Solan-173230 (HP) Website:www.yspuniversity.ac.in
- Jawaharlal Nehru Krishi Vishyva Vidyalaya, Jabalpur (M.P.) Website: www.jnkvv.nic.in
- Chawdhary Sarwan Kumar Himachal Pradesh Krishi Vishva Vidyalaya, Palampur(HP) website: www.hillagric.ernet.in
- Yashwantrao Chavan Maharashtra Open University, Nasik (MS)
- Punjab Agricultural University, Ludhiana website:www.pau.edu
- University of Agricultural Sciences, Gandhi Krishi Vigyan Kendra Bangalore website:www.uasbng.kar.nic.in

(e) HORTICULTURE

Horticulture is the main stream of agriculture. The term "Horticulture" is derived from the Latin 'hortus'(garden) and culture (cultivation), which means garden cultivation. Horticulture is the branch of agricultural plant sciences that deals with the production of fruits, vegetables, nuts and ornamentals. It is a major source of food and employment. Operationally, there are several divisions of horticulture:pomology, arboriculture and landscape architect etc. Modern and scientific horticulture began in 1928 when Imperial Council of Agricultural Research later named as Indian Council of Medical Research was constituted Research Centres were established through this council in every state. The research work is done at every centre. At present there are about 29 agricultural universities in our country where horticultural education and research is being carried out.

It accounts for food from three major sources: Vegetable, fruits and nuts.

Jobs in Horticulture

Horticulture provides a wide variety of jobs for many categories of people, directly or indirectly.

Direct Jobs:- A large number of jobs require knowledge and training in horticulture. The level of training could be vocational or at the college level.The work may be indoors or outdoors Many jobs in horticulture require diploma or degree in horticulture or agriculture. A college education provides more indepth knowledge of the field and offers job opportunities at supervisory or managerial levels and to conduct research. At present there are about 29 agricultural universities in our country where horticultural education and research is being carried out.

Job Opportunities

1. In Govt.Jobs:

(a) For M.Sc. Ag(Horticulture) and Ph.D in Horticulture

(i) Scientist: Examination conducted by the Agriculture Scientist Recruitment Board. ICAR New Delhi offers opportunities for scientists.

(ii) In Education: Lecturer, Reader, Assistant Professor, Associate Professor in Agriculture Universities and Colleges.

(iii) Training Organizer & Training Associate in Krishi Vigyan Kendra (KVK)

(b) For Graduate (Horticulture/Agriculture)

(i) Civil Services: Examination conducted by Union Public Service Commission (UPSC) for IAS/IFS (Civil Service & Allied).

(ii) As District Horticulture Officer/ District Agriculture Officer through Examination conducted by State Public Service Commission.

(iii) Technical Assistant/ Technical Officer in Agriculture Universities, ICAR, DRDO, IARI & CSIR.

(iv) Horticulture Inspector/Fruit & Vegetable Inspector/ Marketing Inspector

(v) Training Assistant in Krishi Vigyan Kendra (KVK)

(vi) Farm Supervisor

(vii) Section Officer(Horticulture/Landscaping). Horticulture or Supervisor (Horticulture).

(viii) Agriculture Development Officer

(ix) Village Level Worker

(x) Agriculture Inspector

2. Private Sector:

(i) As Horticulturist/Horticulture Officer or Supervisor (Landscape) in Industries, Farm Houses, Hotels, Golf Courses & Construction Companies etc.

(ii) As Horticulture Officer in processing companies of agriculture production.

(iii) Marketing job also in pesticides and insecticides companies.

Self Employment in Horticulture

(i) As Horticulture Consultant provide advice, design, evaluation, supervision of garden or orchanrd etc.

(ii) You can start the Agriculture clinic. Government provides money (upto Rs.10 lakhs) for this work.
(iii) Raise commercial nursery of fruit plants, flower and ornamental plants.
(iv) Seed producer of vegetables and flower crops.
(v) Fruit/Vegetable/Flower grower
(vi) Floral decoration/florist shop
(vii) Horticulture Services Contractor
(viii) Mushroom grower
(ix) Seed dealer/merchant
(x) Proprietor-cold storage
(xi) Processing work of Horticulture production
(xii) You can start/establish an institute for vocational education(Horticulture/Landscape).

Indirect Jobs: The ornamental industry has spawned a number of supporting or service industries:

(1) **RESEARCH**: Many scientists are engaged in developing new and improved types of vegetables, fruits and ornamentals. Apart from improving the agronomic and nutritional qualities of plants, horticultural scientists also devote considerable time to improve the aesthetics of ornamentals and the quality of products.
(2) **CHEMICAL INDUSTRY**: The horticulture industry depends on large amounts and varieties of chemicals including fertilizers, pesticides and growth homones. Many companies are involved in producing chemicals that are used to enhance plant production and the quality of produce.
(3) **MACHINERY**: The engineers design and produce tools and machinery for use in the production of horticultural plants. Machinery and implements are available for preparing, harvesting storing and packaging. These aids enable large scale production of horticultural plants to be undertaken.
(4) **DISTRIBUTION**: Horticultural products are transported from the areas of production to marketing outlets. Because of their largely perishable nature, horticulture produce and product require special handling on transportation to retain their quality for a long time.

Computer in Horticulture

Now, computers are widely used in the horticulture field. Special areas of computer application in horticulture include:- Designing plans, crop modeling, soil modeling, equipment automation, public information, record keeping and databases. Expert systems,

Communication, sensor technology and internet service etc. Computer technology has significant applications in horticulture, Green house automation and equipment calibration for automatic application of chemicals.

(f) ORGANIC FARMING

As the market expands, a career in organic farming/organic agriculture management will offer a lucrative career option for those who do not wish to take up a regular office job. After all, beginning 2004-05, there will be an annual demand for one lakh trained man power in the organic food sector.

If you are interested in a career in organic farming, the right time to start is now. The sky will definitely be the limit for you and after five to six years, the opportunities in the organic food sector; will be manifold.

UNDERSTANDING ORGANIC FARMING

Let us see what organic farming actually means. According to world renowned environmentalist, Dr.Vandana Shiva of Navdanya, an organisation that is spearheading the organic farming movement in India, "It is a production system based on the renewal and strengthening of ecological processes and functions of farm ecosystem in order to produce safe and healthy food. It largely excludes the use of synthetically compounded fertilizers, pesticides, growth regulators and livestock feed additives".

The system relies on crop rotations, crop residues, animal manure, legumes, green manure and off-farm organic wastes. It also ensures that pest control does not pollute the soil.

Navdanya recently organised an all-India organic farmers meet at its farm near Dehradun, where nearly 300 farmers practising the method met in an eco-friendly environment to deliberate on the vision document for 2020. Though the meet was mostly attended by farmers, a large number of budding entrepreneurs were also present on the occasion, displaying the growing popularity of the sector. Says Mithun Shah, who runs an organic food shop in Ahmedabad,"Organic farming is not for farmers alone. It can be a lucrative career option for entrepreneurs as well".

Adds Dr.Karan Raj Aggarwala, CEO, OakEcology, an optometrist-turned-ecological entrepreneur, "As an eye specialist, I realised that a number of disorders related to vision occur due to lack of proper nutrition. Hence, I did a lot of research in the field of nutrition, which brought me in touch with organic farming. I was completely bowled over by this method and decided to channelise my energies into this".

WHY ORGANIC FARMING?

The need arises because of the following reasons:-

1. Destruction of habitat and the agro-ecosystems due to chemical farming.
2. Mono-cultivation results in the loss of biodiversity.
3. Chemical farming results in narrowing down crop diversity.
4. Genetically engineered seeds pose a threat to farming.
5. The spate in farmer suicides can be traced back to chemical farming which pollutes the soil.

Says V.Bapna, Chief Project Coordinator; M.R.Morarka- GDC Rural Research Foundation, which has recently started a one year post-graduate diploma in Organic Agriculture Management in Udaipur, "A lot of research has been done on how chemical farming poses hazards to environment and human health. From this, it is quite clear that there are pesticides and fertilizer residues in our food. Organic farming, which replaces chemical fertilisers and pesticides with bio-fertilisers, bio-pesticides and natural soil enhancers, is a viable win-win alternative. The food is also safe for human consumption and the returns offered to farmers is much higher".

THE SCOPE

The market for certified organic food is huge. The figures are- EU: Rs. 2.16 lakh crores; USA: Rs. 2.12 lakh crores and Japan: Rs. 0.52 lakh crores. By 2005, India is projected to become the world's largest food factory at Rs. 6.58 lakh crores.

"Therefore, for graduates of agriculture and allied subjects, the organic sector offers many options. The areas which students could explore are production and sale of organic inputs (as entrepreneurs); in food processing or packaging firms as organic inspectors; in marketing organisations for the procurement and sale of organic food (this includes export firms too as 85 per cent of what is being produced as organic certified food in India is being exported); and environmental groups for the promotion of organic farming, "says Bapna.

Competent and trained professionals, even at the entry level, can easily earn Rs.15,000 to Rs.35,000, provided they love travelling and are ready to 'soil their hands'.

COURSES AVAILABLE

Though Agriculture as a subject is offered by most universities, specific courses in organic farming are offered by the Maharana Pratap University of Agriculture and Technology, Udaipur and the Bija Vidyapeeth, Dehradun. Whether it is long-term or short-term, the course curriculum includes topics like Organic Agricultural Practices, Engineering Technologies for Organic Agriculture, Organic Standards and Certification, Agribusiness Management and Biotechnology in Organic Agriculture.

TIPS FOR STUDENTS

Students wishing to make a career in Organic Farming must:-

1. Be prepared to 'soil their hands'.
2. Be willing to travel to remote rural areas.
3. Have a love for nature
4. Be creative
5. Be ready to fight the odds
6. Have a zest for learning
7. Be able to document material.

(g) SEED INDUSTRY

In the last four decades, India has made significant advances in agriculture where the role of the seed sector is substantial. In comparison to the total Global seed market (US$21 billion per annum), the Indian seed market share is around $ 900 million (Rs.4000 crores).

Dr.M.S.Swaminathan, an eminent scientist, has highlighted India's potential in this respect and estimated that India can capture one-fourth of the world's business in seed, transforming rural employment, income and poverty senario. So, students in agriculture have an unlimited prospect in this growing industry.

The Seed Industry includes:-

1. Genetics & plant breeding

Breeding is a creation of variation in strength for any seed producing organization. The qualified breeder should have a creative and selective eye towards selecting plants for breeding programmes.

2. Agronomy

Agronomy is called the "mother of agriculture". Before release of the new hybrid seeds or varieties, it is mandatory for the seed producers to test the seed for multilocation trials. Agronomists also have the opportunity to look after the seed production units.

3. Entomology

Damage to crop by insectpests is common. The entomologist designs crop-wise admissible insect levels using various crop protection techniques and crop-insect specific control measures.

4. Biotechnology

Biotechnology has paved the way for the introduction of transgenic crops. Biotechnologists can determine seed quality parameters faster through simpler molecular techniques and Genetic marker studies.

5. Seed Technology

Seed technologists monitor supply of best quality seeds, production. Quality testing for different parameters like germination, physical purity, moisture contents are assessed and maintained to certain standard prescribed on the Seed act before final packaging for marketing.

6. Plant Pathology

Disease is one of the major constraints in getting high yield. Pathologists have a role to take the challenge to find out the feasible solutions.

7. Soil Science

Students from soil science also have enough opportunity in the seed industry in studying the plant soil relation and their interactions.

EDUCATIONAL LEVEL/ DEGREE REQUIRED

- Students who have completed doctorate or masters in specialized subjects can take up research which is the key strength of any seed industry. Marketing is also another scope for masters.
- Agriculture graduates on the other hand, can opt for marketing or production.

ENTRANCE EXAMINATION

- XII students interested in agriculture subjects, have to appear in the ICAR (Indian Council of Agricultural Research) entrance test for getting admission at graduation in agro universities all over the country. Besides, universities also conduct their own entrance tests.
- Similarly, agril.graduates who are interested for masters have to appear for ICAR-led Junior Research Fellowship (JRF) examination and to get higher rank to opt for good institutions.
- Masters students can take admission in PhD in same university or can appear IARI-led all India examination.

REPUTED AGRICULTURAL INSTITUTES

1. Indian Agricultural Research Institute (IARI), New Delhi (It is a premier agriculture institute in India and has international reputation. IARI is a deemed university and has only postgraduate studies (Masters & Doctorate) with limited seats. For getting admission B.Sc. agricultural graduates need to get rank in top order in JRF-examination, IARI-PhD entrance (open for all India competition) will be conducted. Website is : www.iari.res.in

2. G.B.Pant University of Agriculture and Technology, Pantnagar, Uttaranchal (It has a good reputation. All agricultural subjects are taught here. Website is : www.gbpuattech.ac.in
3. Punjab Agriculture University, Ludhiana, Punjab (The university has outstanding achievements in agricultural research, education and extension. Website is : www.pau.edu
4. CCS Agricultural University, Hissar, Haryana (HAU has international repute for its advances in high yielding crops. Website is : www.haryanaonline.com/hau.htm
5. Acharya NG Ranga Agricultural University, Rajendranagar, Andhra Pradesh(It is a reputed university having 13 colleges in Agriculture, Veterinary, Home Science, Agricultural Engineering, Fisheries Science and Polytechnics). Website is : www.medistudies.com
6. University of Agricultural Sciences, Dharwad, Karnataka (It has multiple research centers and good infrastructure in the field of agriculture. Website is : www.uasd.edu
7. Bidhan Chandra Krishi Vidyalaya, Mohanpur, West Bengal (The University is one of the pioneer institutes of Agricultural Education, Research and Extension. Website is :www.bckv.edu.in
8. Orissa University of Agriculture &Technology, Bhubaneshwar, Orissa (It is also one of the oldest agricultural institutes in India) Website is : www.ouat.ac.in
9. Jawaharlal Nehru Krishi Vishwa Vidyalaya, Jabalpur (M.P.) (JNKV has good reputation in the agricultural research) Website is :www.jnkvv.nic.in
10. Tamilnadu Agricultural University, Coimbatore, Tamilnadu (It is one of the oldest reputed Agricultural University dealing with multidisciplinary departments, especially in Plant breeding and genetics. Website is : www.tnau.ac.in

11

Insurance

(a) INSURANCE

Insurance is a challenging field. Ever since economic liberalization in 1991, it has grown manifold. Today there are at least 12 major private insurance companies in the market compared to one life and four insurance companies.

Based on the Malhotra committee's recommendations, the government has opened up the insurance sector to private players, who have tied up with large overseas insurance companies. Some of the private life insurance companies are ING Vysya, Max New York Life Insurance Company, Om Kotak Mahindra, Tata AIG Insurance Co., Birla Sun Life Insurance, Raliance Life Insurance, HDFC Standard and ICICI Prudential etc. In non-life insurance segment, major private players are Royal sundaram, Cholamandalam, IFFCO Tokyo, Tata AIG etc.

Insurance sector provides good job potential. According to one conservative estimate, more than half a million jobs have been created in this sector in the last few years. Another estimate puts the figure of insurance agents or advisers at 11 lacs working in the Indian market for various insurance companies.

One can be an Insurance Consultant, Development Officer, Assistant Administrative Officer, Surveyor, Insurance Agent, underwriter, claims adjuster, risk manager.

Insurance Agent: They advise people on the most suitable policy. The educational qualifications required for becoming an insurance agent or advisor is 12th pass while for other positions, a graduate degree is essential. In addition, the candidates must also possess good communication skills, contacts, presence of mind, confidence and ability to persuade others, sincerity, hard work and commitment for service towards the clients. These additional qualifications decide the growth of a person in this field.

Agents get about 25 to 32 percent of the premium amount in the first year of the policy. In the second and third year they gets 7.5 percent and in fourth and fifth year they get about 5 percent of the premium. After about four years of good performance, an agent may also be entitled to office facilities, car, computer, telephone, maintenance, housing loan etc.

The entry of private sector into the insurance sector has brought intense competition. Earlier there were no formal courses designed to train an agent. The agents were trained informally on the job. But now more emphasis is laid on recruitment and providing formal training. Consequently, many institutes are offering insurance courses such as PG Diploma in Insurance Management or MBA(Insurance). The University of Delhi offers Insurance as one of the streams at the Undergraduate level through some of its colleges like College of Vocational Studies. Some Institutions having recognition from Insurance Regulatory Development Authority(IRDA) conduct PG course as well. In such institutes admission criteria is a bachelor's degree and some amount of field experience (Min 2 years). Besides, IRDA offers a 100 hours insurance agent course conducted by individual insurance companies. There are some institutes that offer short courses as well.

One can also join insurance companies as salaried employees by getting placement as development officer after fulfilling laid down procedures and qualifying tests.

Surveyors: An Insurance Surveyor is another important position which holds promise of career growth. He is a technically qualified person. General Insurance Companies generally recruit them. Generally persons having degree or diploma in any field of engineering are appointed as surveyors. One can also undertake it as a part time job. They are paid commission for each survey. The amount of insurance work is so much that these surveyors can earn even in six digits a month as their commission.

AAOs: The Insurance Companies, particularly the public sector also recruit its managerial cadre at Assistant Administrative Officer level. A graduate degree is the minimum qualification. The recruitment is done through a competitive examination. Persons thus recruited can go up to the Chairman;s Level.

Underwriters: They are the decision makers of the insurance companies. They have to decide whether to provide insurance to applicants. Their most important job is setting prices for insurance seekers.

Claim Adjuster: Their main job is unbiased and fair claim adjustment.

Risk Managers: They are appointed to protect organizations resources and income against possible losses. A risk manager must have personal traits of analytical and intuitive ability, efficient communication, organizational and presentation skills and team spirit. He must be able to prioritise, foresee, forecast and frame budgets.

Actuary: Formulations of insurance policies, management, marketing and advertisement are the four major functions of an insurance company. All the institutes offering courses in insurance cover these areas in their syllabi. When insurance policy is formulated, the calculation of the premium and duration of the policy are the most important functions. The fixation of premium and the duration must be consumer friendly as well as company friendly both. Actuary means a professional whose job is to calculate insurance risks and payments byk studying how frequently accidents, fires deaths etc. occur by applying mathematical probability theory, statistical and analytical methods. An Actuary's job profile includes product design, policy pricing, asset-liability management. He does scientific valuation in areas like retirement and benefits, investment and related field. Actuarial Society of India conducts training and hold examinations twice a year to become Actuary. A trained actuary finds placement in Insurance companies, actuarial firms, IRDA, Reinsurance, Tariff Advisory Committee Pension Funds, Insurance Intermediaries and Software development companies etc.

Insurance Brokers, Insurance Consultants and Reinsurance Brokers are few other insurance intermediaries who work gainfully in the insurance system.

The insurance companies offer handsome salary. At the entry level, it is always commission which forms the main source of income. The earnings are directly related to the achievement of targets. It is just possible that in the beginning targets may be little difficult to achieve. LIC is alive to this situation and therefore they provide initially three year financial and other support to its agents. Good performance is required to reach the higher level like Group leader, Claim Settlement Officer, Area Manager, Regional Manager, Zonal Manager, General Manager, Director (Insurance) etc.

HISTORY

The history of insurance sector is a fascinating one. The first insurance company was established in the year 1870 in Bombay. Insurance industry is broadly classified into two viz. Life Insurance and Non Life Insurance (General Insurance). In 1956 when the life insurance was nationalized and LIC was formed there were about 245 private insurance companies including foreign companies operating in India. Similarly, in 1972 when general insurance companies were nationalised and GIC was formed there were about 107 such companies including foreign companies. In 1973 the erstwhile national and foreign general insurance companies were grouped into four viz national insurance company, Kolkata; The New India Assurance Company, Mumbai, Oriental Insurance Company, New Delhi and United India Insurance Company, Chennai. These four subsidiaries of GIC operate all over India. They compete with each other and underwrite various classes of general insurance business. Administratively Finance Ministry is responsible for their activities in India.

Life Insurance Corporation of India: It was established in 1956. The objective was to spread insurance and mobilize people's savings. It has central office in Mumbai and seven zonal offices in Mumbai, Kolkata, Chennai, Hyderabad, Kanpur and Bhopal.The LIC has offices in Fiji, Mauritius and UK. LIC has insurance joint ventures abroad in Nairobi, Kualalumpur and Bahrain.

General Insurance Company of India: GIC alongwith its four subsidiaries operate a number of schemes. They also participate in financing of industrial projects through term and direct subscription to shares and debentures of new and existing enterprises.

The National Insurance Company Limited, Kolkata: It is the oldest insurance company in India. It was incorporated in 1906. It has its headquarters in Kolkata. It was nationalised in 1972 and made a subsidiary of GIC. The company offers about 200 policies. It covers insurance in fire, marine, banking, telecom, aviation, power, oil and energy, agronomy, plantation, foreign trade, healthcare, tea, automobile, environment, space research etc.

The New India Assurance Company Ltd: It was established in 1949. It has hqs. In Mumbai. It is the largest non-life insurance company in whole Asia-Pacific region. It provided insurance cover to the first satellite in 1980.

The Oriental Insurance Company Ltd: Established in 1947, it has its headquarters in Delhi.

The shape of General Insurance is changing very fast. All General Insurance Companies now offer All Risks Covered Policies. The emerging risks apprehensions in insurance sector is being addressed by General Insurance Companies through products like Credit Risks, Liquidated Damages, Force Majeure, Performance Guarnatees etc.

(b) INSURANCE POLICY PROCESSING CLERKS

Description

Process applications for, changes to, reinstatement of, and cancellation of insurance policies. Duties include reviewing insurance applications to ensure that all questions have been answered, compiling data on insurance policy changes, changing policy records to conform to insured party's specifications, compiling data on lapsed insurance policies to determine automatic reinstatement according to company policies, canceling insurance policies as requested by agents, and verifying the accuracy of insurance company records.

Experience

Some previous work-related skill, knowledge, or experience may be helpful in these occupations, but usually is not needed.

Education

These occupations usually require a high school/ higher secondary /diploma and may require some vocational training or job-related course work. In some cases, an associate's or bachelor's degree could be needed.

Training

Employees in these occupations need anywhere from a few months to one year of working with experienced employees.

Tasks

1. Reviews and verifies data, such as age, name, address, and principal sum and value of property, on insurance applications and policies.
2. Transcribes data to worksheets and enters data into computer for use in preparing documents and adjusting accounts.
3. Calculates premiums, refunds, commissions, adjustments, and new reserve requirements, using insurance rate standards.
4. Notifies insurance agent and accounting department of policy cancellation.
5. Compares information from application to criteria for policy reinstatement and approves reinstatement when criteria are met.
6. Collects initial premiums, issues receipts, and compiles periodic reports for management.
7. Examines letters from policyholders or agents, original insurance applications, and other company documents to determine if changes are needed and effects of changes.
8. Corresponds with insured or agent to obtain information or inform them of status or changes to application of account.
9. Receives computer printout of policy cancellations or obtains cancellation card from file.
10. Checks computations of interest accrued, premiums due, and settlement surrender on loan values.

12

Legal View

(a) LAW

Career in engineering and medicine are so popular amongst Indian students that they rarely look beyond these options if they get the right grades and if their parents have sufficient money to finance their education in these courses. Believers in destiny that we Indians are, we just "hope for the best" and presume that a degree in engineering or medicine will open up an "All Baba's cave" (profitable opportunity) for our children! Other career options are either not researched enough or are looked upon as "last resorts"- to be pursued with the disappointment of having "missed the bus". Nothing could be farther from the truth. Let us learn about an excellent career option that is not only challenging and profitable but prestigious enough for everyone to get "aboard".

Social change has necessitated a change in the form and content of educational system. This has fostered an era of academic restructuring and realignment of curriculum, syllabus and courses. Gradual realization of the importance of law in safeguarding the rights and privileges of citizens particularly of marginalized sections has certainly been a force to provide such a reckoning to law. Similarly, the perception of law as a facilitator of development along with the popularisation of the phenomena called "public interest litigation" too has contributed significantly in elevating the status of law as a favoured discipline. Through public interest litigation justice has been made accessible to millions of destitutes and civil society has received much-needed recipe. In order to achieve the desired result the principle of rule of law and supremacy of law has been invoked. Finally, its ability to transform itself from the morass of fact-twisting skulduggery and money-spinning chicanery to the watchdog of Constitution and a powerful instrument of civil society has lead to its metamorphosis.

In the context of India, law has evolved itself as an integral part of civil- political system facilitated in the process by parliamentary democracy, Constitutionalism, independent and impartial judiciary, decentralization of power, and on the enormous faith of public on judicial system. It is from this perspective that one has to look at law and legal education. The evolution and enlargement of law schools in India as a corollary to supply quality legal human resources into three-tier legal system is an offshoot of such a vision. The quality and standards of legal profession are directly related to the quality and contents of the legal education. Emphasizing this direct relationship between the profession and the legal education, justice Muthuswami Iyer as way back as in the year 1885 spoke ***""A college, therefore, where legal education is to be imparted on a scientific basis, will be of great value to the country, and exercise a very beneficial influence on the practice of law as an art"".***

There are six "National law schools" (known by different names but popularly called as law schools) in India which offer a five years composite law course after HSSC (XII) that leads to a Bachelors' in Law (L.L.B.) together with (and this is interesting) a Bachelors' in Arts/ Science (B.A. or B.Sc.) or sometimes even a Bachelors' in Business Administration (B.B.A.). So your child can be a B.Sc.L.L.B. or B.B.A.L.L.B. or B.A.L.L.B. within just five years or his/her matriculation.

Now when I was young, studying for a L.L.B. used to be really considered down-market and a sure confirmation that the Johnny couldn't get admission anywhere else. L.L.B. used to be also considered as an option which could be pursued when you had "time" (while waiting for the supplementary examination of the university since you flunked the main one and did not know what else there was to do). Since all those young persons have now become parents, they understandably twitch their nose in disapproval at LAW as a career option for their children. But the world has moved on! Law graduates passing out of these law schools do not generally practise law (which of course they can do by getting a "sanad" from any court in India); instead, they aspire to join the corporate world as assistant managers in the legal departments of big companies. Salaries are fairly decent (ranging from Rs.1.2 to 1.8 lakh per annum) and many of the employers are MNCs. Big corporations are so allergic of being sued by customers or other stakeholders that most of them have an in-house legal department that takes care of routine (and there are many) legal issues. With everyone getting "drag-them-to-court" minded, demand for internal legal managers is burgeoning.

Where are these law schools located?

All of them are either deemed universities or autonomous institutions. Most of them offer the five years composite course on a fully residential basis. The seven prominent ones are:-

(a) National University of Juridical Sciences (NUJS), Kolkata
(b) NALSAR University, Hyderabad
(c) National Law School of India University (NLSIU), Bangalore
(d) National Law Institute University (NLIU), Bhopal
(e) National Law University(NLU), Jodhpur
(f) National Law College, Mumbai
(g) Symbiosis Society's Law College (SSLC), Pune

How does one get into these law schools?

An all India entrance test decides the admissions (except NLC, Mumbai). Except for NUJS, Kolkata, which holds its entrance test sometime in February, others hold their tests in the month of May. National Law College Mumbai does not conduct any test and admits students' based on the students' HSSC scores. Presently, all the institutes have separate entrance tests; this sometimes leads to two tests being scheduled on the same day. Whenever the number of students appearing for these tests increases and the law schools realize their common good, holding a common entrance test will probably become a reality.

Students can appear for these tests while they are in XII grade. They have to be below 20 years of age and are required to secure at least 50% marks in HSSC. Selling of admission forms is announced vide newspapers and students also have an option of buying the forms through the institute's website. Many institutes also sell (at a reasonable price), actual question papers of the entrance examinations conducted in the previous years. The attached table gives important comparative information.

What do they ask in these entrance tests?

Generally the entrance tests are of two hours duration and carry negative marks for wrong answers. Most of the questions are "multiple choices-objective type" but there are also some descriptive questions and some of the institutes ask students to write a small analytical essay on a given issue. Typically, the test consists of the following sections:-

Quantitative Ability: "Tenth class" arithmetic, algebra, geometry is included in this syllabus. You do not have to know anything about calculus.

Verbal Ability: Analogies, sentence sequencing, sentence completion, identifying grammatical errors, filling in the blanks, short reading and comprehension passages, synonyms and antonyms are included in this section.

Analytical Ability: Puzzles, coding, critical reasoning, syllogisms and problems that test your power of reasoning are included in this section.

Legal Reasoning: This includes preliminary knowledge of legal definitions and situations. This is the only section that students have to prepare carefully since they have never done it before.

General Knowledge

Essay

Let me give you a typical example of a problem that tests ones reasoning ability.

There are six people W,H,M,C,G,F who are murderer, victim, judge, police, witness, hangman not necessarily in that order. There was no eye-witness, only circumstantial evidence. The murderer was sentenced to death. Read the following and determine who is who?

M knew both murderer and victim.

Judge asked C to describe the murder incident.

W was last to see F alive.

Police found G at the murder site.

H and W have never met.

With proper training, many students can therefore aspire to tread this exciting path.

"LAW IS NEITHER FORMAL LOGIC NOR THE EMBODIMENT OF INEXORABLE SCIENTIFIC LAWS. IT IS A HUMAN INSTITUTION, CREATED BY HUMAN AGENTS TO SERVE HUMAN ENDS"....

H.F. Stone

(b) LEGAL SECRETARIES

Description

Perform secretarial duties utilizing legal terminology, procedures, and documents. Prepare legal papers and correspondence, such as summonses, complaints, motions, and subpoenas. May also assist with legal research.

Experience

Previous work-related skill, knowledge, or experience is required for these occupations.

Education

Most occupations in this zone require training in vocational schools, related on-the-job experience, or an associate's degree. Some may require a bachelor's degree.

Training

Employees in these occupations usually need one or two years of training involving both on-the-job experience and informal training with experienced workers.

Tasks

1. Makes photocopies of correspondence, document, and other printed matter.
2. Schedules and makes appointments.
3. Drafts and types office memos.
4. Reviews legal publications and performs database searches to identify laws and court decisions relevant to pending cases.
5. Attends legal meetings, such as client interviews, hearings, or depositions, and takes notes.
6. Mails, faxes, or arranges for delivery of legal correspondence to clients, witnesses, and court officials.
7. Organizes and maintains law libraries and document and case files.
8. Prepares and processes legal documents and papers, such as summonses, subpoenas, complaints, appeals, motions, and pretrial agreements.
9. Receives and places telephone calls.
10. Completes various forms, such as accident reports, trial and courtroom requests, and applications for clients.
11 Submits articles and information from searches to attorneys for review and approval for use.
12 Assists attorneys in collecting information such as employment, medical, and other records.

13

Library

(a) INFORMATION SCIENCE

Modern society is characterised by abundance of information. Management of information can no longer be tackled by a layman neither can information be kept intact in libraries or archives, never to be brought out for circulation and the attention of the users. Information is power only when it is exploited to the advantage or disadvantage of the mankind. The range of information varies from a monograph to a concept, or a figure or even a small fact. In broad terms everybody needs information which include information on housing, health care, education, social welfare, private insurance savings, banks, investments, legal matters, sports, entertainment etc. The users of information now range from common man to scientists, planners and policy makers, managers decision makers, lawyers and all professional groups, businessmen, one and all.

This ever increasing importance of information has led to the growth of "Information Science" as a discipline. According to Borko, an authority on the subject, Information Science is an interdisciplinary science that investigate the properties and behaviour of information, the forces that govern the flow and use of information, and the techniques, both manual and mechanical, of processing information for optional storage, retrieve and dissemination. This interdisciplinary science is derived from and related to such fields as mathematics, logic, linguistics, psychology, computer technology, operations research, graphic arts, communications, library science, management and other smaller fields. "Borko" further stated that Information Science has both, a Pure Science Component, which enquires into the subjects without regard to its application, and an applied science component, which develops services and products. Librarianship and documentation are applied aspects of Information Science.

Current Scenario

Recent advancement in the field of library and information science has diversified the role of information professionals in developed countries. In America, Europe and Australia, people trained as librarians are now working as integral members of work groups and teams in marketing as well as research and development. In big American companies that continue to maintain a central library, these people may still be organizationally assccciated to the library career structures. But in smaller organizations that do not have the formal library, these people are appointed as information analysts. Work orientation and career structures of these information analysts is the group within which they work. Several small and medium enterprises in Western Australia have appointed information analysts who report to the chief executive officer and who are seen by their managers as potential general managers rather than as career information specialists. This trend is not limited to business organizations. Leading academic libraries are also diversifying their services.

Quite a few developing countries particularly India are gradually making headway in adopting Information Technology (IT) to their libraries and information centres. Though not enough is as yet being done in this area, still, changes are visible in the overall scenario of information centres as well as their services. Hence, there is an acknowledged need for library professionals who can serve the needs of users taking the benefits of information technology. In fact, with the information explosion and with access to information spelling power, qualified librarians can be appointed as information scientists, information manager, database manager, resource manager, knowledge worker, database administrator and even manager information systems. Primarily these all designations assume some of the other responsibilities related to computers.

Institution

Against this backdrop the information professionals capable of catering the needs of modern society are required to serve the libraries/ information centres. Therefore, curricula of some of the universities have been revised giving thrust on IT components. Department of Library and Information Science, Aligarh Muslim University (AMU) had taken a lead in incorporating the IT components in syllabi of BLISc and MLISc courses. Gradually, one hopes, syllabi of all the Universities offering library and information science course will be revised. These universities exceeding one hundred, produce more than two thousands graduates and post graduates in library and information science every year. Names of some of the institutes that teaches library & information science subject are given below:-

1. AMU, Aligarh
2. BHU, Banaras
3. Bundelkhand University, Jhansi
4. Bombay University, Mumbai
5. Calcutta University, Kolkata
6. Delhi University, Delhi
7. Deen Dayal Upadhyaya University, Gorakhpur
8. GNDU, Amritsar
9. Jiwaji University, Gwalior
10. IGNOU,New Delhi
11. Jamia Millia Islamia, New Delhi
12. Lucknow University, Lucknow
13. Madras University, Chennai
14. Mysore University, Mysore
15. Panjab University, Chandigarh
16. Panjab University, Patiala
17. Pune University, Pune
18. Rajasthan University, Jaipur

Specific Courses

Majority of these Universities run B.Lib.Sc/ BLISc as well as M.Lib.Sc/ MLISc courses while some of them are offering only B.Lib.Sc/BLISc courses. Quite a few universities also enrol students for Ph.D.Programme. Documentation Research and training centre (DRTC), Bangalore and the National Institute of Science Communication and Information Resources (NISCAIR), New Delhi which is formally known as Indian National Scientific Documentation Centre (INSDOC) offer specialized post-graduate courses in Documentation and Information Science leading to associate ship of the respective institutions. The products of DRTC and NISCAIR are most sought after particularly by the institutes and companies having IT orientation.

Central University of Hyderabad and IGNOU runs a specialized course on networking which is known as PG Diploma in LAN. Medical Library Association of India, AIIMS, New Delhi offers a diploma course in Medical Librarianship.

Eligibility

A bachelor degree in Library and Information Science (B.Lib.Sc./ BLISc) is offered as a one year programme after any stream of graduation. Postgraduate course (M.Lib.Sc./ MLISc) is offered to candidates who are having a degree in library & information science. Majority of the above mentioned institutes and universities hold entrance examinations for graduate as well as the post graduate courses. DRTC and NISCAIR conducts interview once the candidates qualify the entrance test. Their programme, Associateship in Documentation and Information Science (ADIS) which is considered equivalent to M.Lib.Sc./ MLISc is of two years duration. PGDLAN of Central University of Hyderabad and IGNOU is one year course after B.Lib.Sc./BLISc.

Library and Information Science is also offered as a subject at the B.A. level in a few universities. Certificate and diploma courses are generally run by professional association. Furthermore, there are a couple of universities such as Annamalai, Alagappa, IGNOU, Madurai etc. imparts correspondence courses for graduate as well as post graduate in library and information sciences. However, most popular and prestigious among these universities is IGNOU, MLISc syllabus of IGNOU is turned with the syllabus of NET exam conducted by UGC.

Careers

The job prospects are open for library & information professionals in academic libraries (schools, colleges, universities and other academic institutions) besides public and government libraries. However, today, the most potential market for these professionals is in Library Automation Software Companies such as Libsys, Soft link, VTLS, OPAC-Infosys, Soft-Aid Computers and a host of others. Library Automation Software vendors recruits a large number of information professionals in their marketing and support teams. The job responsibilities of these professionals are selling the products, imparting training to the users, trouble-shooting etc. These library and information professional also give useful feedbacks to the developers of the software. Software companies offer very handsome salaries to their employees and some of them are getting as high as thirty five thousands rupees per month. Companies viz. VTLS and Softlink are the US and Australian companies respectively having branch offices in India. These companies also send their employees to their headquarters in order to receive advance training in library automation.

Moreover, many newspapers, magazines and news agency organizations recruit library & information professionals. The job profile of these nicely paid professional is indexing record of their printed stories and articles. Embassies have their own information centres. Qualified library & information professionals having knowledge of the foreign language stand very good chances of getting employment in embassy. Needless to say remuneration is quite high for the employees of Embassies. Furthermore, there are more than one hundred laboratories of Council of Scientific and Industrial Research (CSIR) and Indian Council of Agricultural Research (ICAR) in India. Each lab has a large library for which it requires the services of many library and informational professionals. Professionals with Science background are preferred in the appointment in these CSIR and ICAR labs.

There are archives, generally set up by government organizations which contain public records and documents of historical importance. Library professionals having history background are recruited in these archives. NGO's are also recruiting information professionals for various works. Finally, private collections of individuals, family also very often requires the services of a qualified librarian. However, in the current scenario, library and information professionals who have understanding in the field of library automation are having very good chances of being recruited in many organizations. On the contrary, those having knowledge only in cataloguing and classification of the documents have a limited scope in their careers.

(b) LIBRARY AND INFORMATION SCIENCE

ORIGIN OF LIBRARY

The term 'Library' is derived from the Latin word *liber,* meaning book. The history of the library is linked with the story of the system of writing; in the forms of books and documents; methods and systems of preserving these and most importantly, making these available and easily accessible for use.

Earlier forms of books were day-tablets and papyrus, leather and parchments rolls. The advent of printing technology and use of papers during the sixteenth century accelerated the rate of book production. Since the beginning of the nineteenth century and more so during the twentieth century, there has been a phenomenal rise in production of books and documents. And the present time is virtually an era of literature-boom of all kinds- macro and micro, generated in varied forms and contents. Since life's needs and problems are now addressed through a variety of ways, scientifically, philosophically and spiritually, the frontiers of knowledge too are increasingly changing and extending along with. Today in the perspective of the competitive role, each country has to play in the fields of science technology and social development.

NEED FOR LIBRARIES

Marching with this phenomenon, there has been simultaneous augmentation in reading activities; the clientale (readers) are becoming more demanding and putting greater pressure upon libraries. Further, democracy makes the library serve one and all. Every citizen, high or low rich or poor, whatever his field of interest be, are able to draw upon this institution. This presupposes strengthening of libraries. Any country, not served by adequate and proper chain of libraries at national state and district levels; at educational levels- in schools, colleges, universities and research institutes and those set up especially for children, is bound to be sadly handicapped in matters of progress and prosperity. This fact has been well received in India, with greater attention to setting up and making the libraries more efficient.

NEED FOR TRAINED STAFF

A library puts other book into action. A Librarian is mediator between man and the graphic records that present and past generations have created. The very essence of library service is "to foster idealism and to strengthen the struggling aspirations of human spirits". Librarian needs to maximise the social utility of the records for the betterment of humanity. To this end, his success depends on his understanding the process of optimising the use of the recorded information.

So the earlier notion, as is usual with any new service initially, that any body even of too low an ability to make a living elsewhere, can carry on in a library is proved wrong. And the tradition, where the librarians who were themselves self-taught used to instruct their assistants in the basic skills, found unequal to the task. With the changing perception and role of a library, a librarian and his staff has to be academically and vocationally prudent. That the job requires full quota of qualified trained professionals, has been realised.

LIBRARY SCIENCE COURSES

Training of Library staff started with informal apprenticeship. The first library school was opened in USA in 1887 and a full time British library School was set up in 1919 at University College, London. In India, the Madras Library Association established a library school in 1929, which was transferred to the university in 1931. The job in a library today consists of book ordering and acquisition; journal work; classification and cataloguing of documents; budgeting and account-maintenance and, above all, providing reference service to readers. Modern library science courses have been designed, keeping in view these requirements, and the need for training meant for the different levels of staff. Following courses are being offered on the subject currently.

(a) ***Certificate Course in Library Science***: Minimum qualification for this course is Higher Secondary examination passed and duration is three to six months. This course is conducted either by Library Associations or the State Governments, or both, to prepare students to work as semi-professional or as librarians in small libraries.

The Bengal Library Association, Kolkata; Delhi Library Association, Delhi; State Central Library (Under Directorate of Education), West Bengal; Uttar Pradesh Library Association conduct such undergraduate course.

Besides, some universities like Annamalai University, Tamil Nadu, Kota Open University, Rajasthan; Madras University, Chennai; Punjab University, Patiala and University of Rajasthan, Jaipur also offer such a course of tour to twelve months duration.

(b) Diploma/Bachelor of Library and Information Science: Universities started with one year full time Diploma course in Library Science equivalent to BLib.Sc. degree for graduate students. Subsequently, this course was re-christened as BlibSc and is now conducted by almost all universities in the country. Admission to this course is through entrance test.

(c) ***Master of Library and Information Science***: This is a one year course, beyond BLibSc., started first by the University of Delhi in 1948, to prepare for senior professionals and for higher positions in libraries and Information and Documentation Centres, as also to work as teachers of library and information science. Currently, there are nearly 30 universities conducting BLISc and 60 universities offering MLISc courses in India. Further, eight universities are providing MPhill and 35 universities for PhD programmes on the subject also. Besides, Documentation Research and Training Centre (DRTC), Bangalore and Indian National Scientific Documentation Centre (INSDOC), Delhi are offering one year Associateship course in Library and Information Science and Documentation. BLISc and MLISc course are also offered under distance education programme by the Indira Gandhi National Open University, Delhi and certain other state's Open Universities.

Some foreign universities offering such courses, provide fellowship for the study, information about which can be had from British Council and USIS in India, as also from the advertisement published in the Employment News and national dailies(career page).

JOB MARKET

Efficient functioning of a library require qualified manpower in adequate number. Hence, in the recent years, demand for trained professionals has been increasing. There is much shortage of competent teachers of library science. Supply of even nominally trained library manpower is far short of demand. Automation and digitalisation in the field of library science and services has revolutionized the functioning of libraries; readers look at this institution with grater dependability for their studies and investigations. Job opportunities for librarians are available also in publishing houses, book-selling and software companies, and commercial corporate offices.

SALARY AND STATUS

Of late, library profession has emerged as a service providing good remuneration inviting young entrants in India. Revision of pay scales, especially for the academic and special libraries where qualified professionals have been placed at par with the teachers in colleges, universities and research institutes and with that of scientists in scientific research as development organisations in respect of pay and status, has made this profession all the more alluring. Salary grade in the public library systems, however, still needs attention for improvement.

Women they say made better librarians. And persons with an intrinsic love for books are likely to deliver better and gain ground in this profession. The profession of librarianship is second to none in the country today, thanks to Dr. S.R. Ranganathan, father of Library Science in India

14

Linguistic View

(a) FOREIGN LANGUAGE

A Language is a short cut to understanding a nation's history, geography and soul. Speaking it well inspires confidence, builds faster, firmer friendship and frankly speaking, impresses.

Why do people learn a foreign language? There are some people who are artists, teachers, etc, who want to get in touch with people in other countries, to learn about their art and culture. This can be done if they speak the language of the country concerned. Some do it purely for the love of a particular foreign language. Due to rapid globalisation, learning foreign languages is gaining worldwide importance for prospects of securing gainful employment.

Today, apart from English, other languages such as German, French, Spanish, Japanese, Russian, Chinese, Korean etc are in great demand due to rapidly growing BPOs in India. BPOs today require around 16 lakh personnel having good command of foreign languages but the number of people knowing these languages is barely 40,000.

Indian firms working in collaboration with foreign companies, hotels, airlines, travel and tourism industry, embassies and consulates and a host of private institutions today prefer people who know a foreign language. With the world becoming smaller, languages have become a necessity for these industries to project themselves in the best light. At present, a number of jobs are available for translators. Translation is mainly desk and library work that requires time and concentration. Chambers of Commerce maintain a list of translators who can be employed by large firms on full time basis. There is also a huge demand for people who can do secretarial work in English and one or two foreign languages. Such jobs are available in shipping firms, banks with overseas branches and hotels.

In addition to language skills, it is essential to acquire skills of public speaking. In some schools and colleges, foreign language is a part of the curriculum but for those who do not have this facility, big universities or private tutors are the best option.

(b) LINGUISTICS

What is Linguistics? Who is a linguist? What do linguists do? What is the scope of linguistics? How does linguistics differ from literature studies? How does linguistics relate to other disciplines like Sociology, psychology, philosophy, literary theory and such other disciplines? These are some of the questions, which come into our mind when we get a glimpse of this word.

The word Linguistics has been derived from Latin fingua (tongue) and istics (knowledge or science). Etymologically, therefore, linguistics is the scientific study of language. Linguistics deals with the structure and development of particular language and its relationship to other languages. It is the study not of one particular language but of human language in general. Broadly, linguistics is the study of human language, its sound, structure, meaning and function. It studies language as a universal and recognizable part of human behaviour. It attempts to describe and analyse language.

A linguist is a person who engages in such studies. Linguists are interested in all aspects of language, and in all languages of the world, but he/she is not a polyglot necessarily.

They are concerned with language variation according to social setting (socio-linguistics), geographical regions (dialectology), time periods(historical linguistics), relationship between language and mind (psycholinguistics) and many such issues. The study of linguistics can be conceived as occurring along three major axes. The endpoints of which are:-

* ***Synchronic and diachronic***- Synchronic study of a language is concerned only with the language as it is at the given time; diachronic study is of linguistic theory to something but it has a philosophy of its own and is a discipline in its own right.
* ***Contextual and independent***- These terms are used here only for convenience, as terms for this dichotomy are not well established. Contextual linguistics is concerned with how language fits into the world: its social function, how it is acquired and also how it is produced and perceived. In contrary, independent linguistics considers languages for its own sake and without externalities related to a language.

THEORETICAL LINGUISTICS

1. Theoretical linguistics is often divided into a number of separate areas, to be studied more or less independently. The following divisions are currently widely acknowledged.

2. Phonetics, the study of different sounds that are employed across all human languages.
3. Phonology, the study of patterns of a language's basic sounds.
4. Morphology, the study of the internal structure of words.
5. Syntax, the study of how words combine to form grammatical sentences.
6. Semantics, the study of the meaning of words and how these words combine to form grammatical sentences.
7. Stylistics, the study of style in language.
8. Pragmatics, the study of how utterances are used (figuratively), literally or otherwise) in communicative acts.

DIACHRONIC LINGUISTICS

Whereas the core of theoretical linguistics is concerned with studying languages at particular point of time (usually the present), diachronic linguistics examines how language changes through time, sometimes over centuries. Historical linguistics enjoys both a rich history and a strong theoretical foundation for the study of language change. Explicitly historical perspectives include historical-comparative linguistics and etymology.

APPLIED LINGUISTICS

Whereas theoretical linguistics is concerned with finding and describing generalities both within languages and among all languages, as a group, applied linguistics takes the results of those findings and applies them to other areas. It not only covers the area of language teaching but the areas of speech synthesis, speech recognition and speech/ language pathology as well. This area, not only helps to use linguistic knowledge to provide voice interfaces to computers but also provides a helping hand to the clinicians/ speech pathologists to assess and provide therapeutic measures as per the requirements of their patients.

CONTEXTUAL LINGUISTICS

Contextual linguistics is that realm where the linguistics interacts with other academic disciplines. Whereas, core linguistics studies languages for their own sake, the inter-disciplinary areas of linguistics consider how language interacts with the rest of the world. Some of these are:-

1. Socio-linguistics and anthropological linguistics, where social scientists interact with linguistics.
2. Discourse analysis where rhetoric and philosophy interact with linguistics.
3. Psycholinguistics and neuro-linguistics where medical sciences meet linguistics.

4. Other cross-disciplinary areas of linguistics include language acquisition, evolutionary linguistics, stratificational linguistics and cognitive science.

REPRESENTATIVE JOB TITLES AND AREAS OF SPECIALIZATION

1. Audiologist
2. Bilingual Education
3. Broadcaster/News Reader
4. Communication Disorders Specialist
5. Copywriter
6. Editor
7. Grant/Proposal writer
8. Interpreter
9. Language Planner
10. Lexicographer
11. Professor/Instructor/Teacher
12. Psycholinguist
13. Public Relations
14. Publishing
15. Researcher
16. Technical Writer
17. Translator and many more

A degree in linguistics can be of great value in the pursuit of careers in education, publishing, media, social services, communication, computer languages, voice analysis research, communicative disorders and other language related fields. In recent years, there has been a surge of demand from various industries for competent linguists. This is due to developments in artificial intelligence, communication sciences and computer application in natural language processing and understanding , information sciences and other high-technology activities. There are also developing fields in bilingualism, literacy, linguistic problems of ethnic minorities and other topics in applied linguistics.

Teaching is one of the best options which is provided by linguistics studies. There are openings in schools, colleges and other institutions that carry out foreign language training teaching programmes.

Several government agencies hire linguists to supervise language-training programme. Others have linguists to carry out research on various languages, or to work in specialized field such as , the determination of geographical names for mapping and other purposes.

Lexicorgraphers are involved in the publishing of dictionaries (electronic as well). They are concerned with such matters as pronunciation, the definition of grammatical terms, various languages', dialectical variation and etymology. Other areas of publishing in which linguists are involved include foreign language textbooks, editing, counselling and planning elementary and secondary programmes in reading, writing and spelling (curriculum designing).

The role of linguists in speech pathology and audio logy is varied. Through research efforts, they have improved ways of analysing and evaluating the language disintegration associated with various disorders such as aphasia, dyslexia etc. Linguistic researches have also provided valuable information about the stages normal children go through after the first word appears, enabling the evaluation of child language disorders and the design of intervention programmes based o the normal sequence of development. This is a major area, which will demand the contribution of more and more linguists in coming days.

Linguists play a major role in solving certain criminal cases. Even CBI has to take the help of a linguist in cases which involve speaker identification. As acoustic phonetics is one of the significant courses of linguistics study, a linguist proves to be a technically trained manpower for such investigations.

Today, there is a boom for call centre jobs. Linguistics caters their needs directly. These centres not only utilize the services of linguists to prepare training modules but to get their trainees trained professionally. This industry poses an everlasting demand for linguists.

Technical writing involves putting scientific and technical information into readily understandable language in the preparation of manuals, instructional materials and engineering reports. These technical writers are none other than linguists who are usually part of the team, working closely with scientists, engineers, accountants and others.

Translation studies are part and parcel of linguistics programme. A linguist is trained in translation techniques which makes him/her eligible for translator's posts both in public and private sectors.

Other than these areas, there is a new upcoming field for linguists where his/her contribution will be playing a major role. This field is our banking and financial service sector which offers managerial posts to linguists making him/her responsible for providing effective phonetics, language, input, culture and customer service training to delegates and monitor consistency of training.

In addition to above mentioned job oriented fields, if one wants to excel in research, linguistics offers comprehensive options not only in India but in other parts of the world as well. If you are willing to travel extensively, knowing various culture and civilizations around the globe, linguistics is one of the best options. Almost all major and minor funding agencies (both national and international) provide fellowship/scholarship assistance for conducting linguistic researches depending upon their area of interest.

PLACES OF EMPLOYMENT

1. Consulting firms
1. Elementary and secondary schools
2. Government service
3. Central Bureau of Investigation
4. Department of Defence etc.
5. International Organizations
6. Language Institutions
7. Media Houses
8. Publishing Companies
9. Research Institutions
10. Speech/language rehabilitation centres
11. Sign language cell
12. United Nations
13. Universities and Colleges

WHERE TO STUDY AND WHAT IS THE ELIGIBILITY

Almost all central universities in India offer research programme (M.Phil/PhD) in linguistics. Most of them run Master programme in linguistics as well. The eligibility for taking up the entrance test in these universities in Graduation in any stream. If interested to join the course in other parts of the world, linguistics is offered in almost all universities and colleges of repute beginning from the Graduation level. Detailed information regarding overseas programme may be sought from concerned colleges/ universities.

15
Medical Courses and Profession

(a) AROMATHERAPY

The word "aroma" is derived from Greek meaning "spice". However, today it is more broadly recognised as fragrance. The word therapy, as the name suggests, is treatment. Therefore, Aromatherapy literally means curative treatment by means of fragrance. It refers to a particular branch of herbal medicine that uses concentrated plant oils called essential oils to improve physical and emotional health, and to restore balance to the whole system.

Aromatherapy as a beauty therapy

Essential oils can be used to treat many skin conditioners (which after all are a result of an organic deficiency) such as acne, diffused redness and even eczema with the doctors' consent. They act as regulators in aging skins, tired tissues, very dry and dehydrated.

Aromatherapy: The world's favourite new age therapy

Aromatherapy, after gaining popularity in Europe and the U.K. is reaching Australia, the USA and Japan as well. There seems to be a long association of aromatic oils and perfumery with the Indian civilization. Aromatic Ayurvedic, massages, attar, incense stic, dhoop; all are deeply rooted in the Indian culture- be it the place of worship, religious ceremonies or thek social gatherings.

Aromatherapy and Employment Opportunities

Apart from treating the sick people and rejuvenating the fading beauties; it has the potential of offering immense employment opportunities. A course in Aromatics from a reputed institute makes one eligible for working as an Aroma therapist, aroma chemist, consultant and even as an entrepreneur and trader.

One can find suitable employment in this field as per one's mettle and interest. By working as an entrepreneur, one can reach the heights of the unfading glory and fame because the Indian scenario of this field is calling upon the entrepreneus to explore the latent.

Potential Employers

* Hospitals (having aromatherapy as a part of alternative medicine)
* Research and development organisations (working on aromatics, perfumery etc.)
* Essentials oils manufacturing companies
* Spas
* Five Star Hotels
* Perfume Industry
* Food Industry
* Pharmaceuticals & Nutraceuticals
* Cosmetic Industry

The Indian Scenario

The Indian scenario of Aromatherapy and allied activities is encouraging with the emergence of the awareness for natural products. Credit for facilitating the emergence of the concept of "retreat to nature" in India goes to the advocates of nature like Shathnaz Husain, Blossom Kochchar and Vinita Jain. By advocating the goodness of nature they not only rejuvenated the love for natural substances among Indians but also established India in the International market of natural products. Its potentiality proved by research findings succeeded in getting a nod from the medical science as well as the policy makers this awareness coupled with sanction from the medical community has paved ways for the growth of this art cum therapy in India. More and more people especially in the developed cities can be seen nowadays taking shelter with Aromatherapy for getting rid of their physical and emotional problems. Aromatherapy, as a beauty therapy is also gaining popularity. These trends hint towards a very bright future of Aromatherapy in our country as an alternative health care and rejuvenation approach.

Challenges and Opportunities

In this background, India must be prepared to take up the challenge of carving a niche for itself in the field of natural products. The demand for herbal medicine may be transitory but the role that India can play in the production of essential oils coupled with modified perfumery compounds from the available sources is going to be long lasting. But the industry has to use the modern technological process and value addition in essential oils for minimising the wastage and getting maximum output for establishing itself on the international platform. In order to cater to the technological need of the essential oils, perfumery and roma chemical industry, Fragrance and Flavour Development Centre (FFDC) has been set up by Government of India under Ministry of Small Scale Industries with UNDP/ UNIDO assistance.

The main objectives of FFDC are to function as an interface between essential oil Industries and research and development institutions in the field of agro technology and chemical technology. Since 1991 FFDC is continuously engaged in providing services to all the sectors and divisions related to fragrance development units, farming, testing, processing and other related fields. From time to time FFDC has also been organising short term training programmes aiming at cosmetologists, scientists, doctors, aroma therapists, students and entrepreneurs.

There are various research and development institutions that are continuously striving towards bringing out the hidden potentiality and discovering other dimensions of the essential oils and such other natural substances.

Institutions Offering Courses in Aromatherapy

At present, the number of institutions offering courses in Aromatherapy and Perfumery is very limited. The responsibility of catapulting this art to the soaring heights of an industry lies with the educational institutions offering related courses. Thankfully, several institutions have come up with different types of course having a professional outlook in this field. The number o such institutions is expected to increase alongwith the further flourishment of the art and its expected conversion into an industry.

* FFDC, Ministry of SSI, Govt. of India, Markand Nagar, Kannauj-209726 (UP)
  PH-05694-237491, 234465 FAX-05694-235242, WEB-www.ffdcindia.org
  (Different types of training courses are available for different functionaries of this field. Fee, minimum eligibility and other requirement for the courses are as per the nature of course)
* Keller Education Trust, VG Vaze College, Mulund East, Mumbai-400081, PH- 022-25682979,25671422/23, FAX-25914262 WEB-www.vazecollege.net
  (The institute offers two years fultime Post graduate Diploma in Perfumery and Cosmetic Management (PGDPCM) covering different dimensions of aromatic art and perfumery. Minimum eligibility for the courses are Graduates with Chemistry as the main or subsidiary subject or graduates in any subject with two years experience in the related field)

Certificate Courses

1. Pivot Point India, Delhi. WEB-www.pivotpointindia.com
2. Delhi School of Management Service, A3, Akashdeep, New Delhi
3. New Lifestyle Clinic Academy, 259, 2nd Floor, Abhishek Complex, 17th Cross, Sampige Road, Malleswaram
4. Shahnaz Hussain Women's World International School of Beauty, M 106, Greater Kailash, New Delhi

FOREIGN INSTITUTES

1. Regent Academy, 6 John Street, London
   College of the Botanical Healing Arts, 1821-17th Ave, (Near Capitola), Santa Cruz CA Post Box 3621, Santa Cruz CA WEB- www.cobha@cruzio.com

(b)AYURVEDA

Ayurveda is one of the oldest medical systems in India and finds its origin in Vedic times. The age of Ayurveda is fixed by various Scholars somewhere around 2500 to 600 B.C. Charaka Samhita and Susruta Samhita (written in Sanskrit between 1st to 4th Century A.D.) are considered as the most important works in Ayurveda.

Concept

According to Ayurveda, health is conditioned by the balance of three essential humours or tridoshas (doshas, literally mean defects) in the body viz. vata(wind), pitta(bile) and kapha (mucous or phlegm). When these humours/ doshas are in balance, that is, in a state of equilibrium, one remains healthy. The disruption of the equilibrium or imbalance of these three humours/doshas in the body causes diseases/ disorders.

Ayurvedic physicians mainly diagnose the diseases with the help of pulse, urine, faeces(stool), tongue, eyes and skin. In Ayurvedic system of medicine, mainly herbals/ plant parts are used as curative agents in the form of powders, tablets, medicated oils etc. to reestablish a balanced humoural constitution in the body.

Academics

In order to become an Ayurvedic medical practitioner, a formal medical education is mandatory. There are hundreds of medical colleges in India which offer an undergraduate degree course in Ayurveda viz.Bachelor of Ayurvedic Medicine and Surgery (B.A.M.S.), a 5 ½ years course inclusive of a 6 months/one year compulsory internship period. After completion of this course, one can opt for a Postgraduate degree i.e. Doctor of Medicine in Ayurveda (M.D(Ay.), a 3 years course.

Those who have completed Higher Secondary Course (10+2) with Physics, Chemistry and Biology can opt for B.A.M.S. course, which is equivalent to an MBBS degree. Generally, admission/selection for this course is made based on a Common Entrance Test/Exam conducted at University/State/National Level. Knowledge of Sanskrit or Hindi is essential to study any course in Ayurveda.

Some of the Medical Colleges that offer both Undergraduate course (B.A.M.S.) and Postgraduate course (M.D.(Ay.) in Ayurveda are:-

- Ayurved & Unani Tibbia College, Ajmal Khan Road, Karol Babh, New Delhi-110 005
- Dr.BRKR Ayurved College, SR Nagar, Hyderabad-500038 (AP)
- Gopabandhu Ayurved Mahavidyalaya, V.I.P. Road, Puri-752002(Orissa)
- Govt.Akhandanand Ayurved Mahavidyalaya, Ahmedabad-380001(Guj.)
- Govt.Ayurved College, Raipur-492001(CG)
- Govt.Ayurved College, MG Road, Thiruvananthapuram-695001(Kerala)
- Govt.Ayurved College, Jalukbari, Guwahati-781004(Assam)
- Govt.Ayurved College & Hospital, Vishweshwariah Circle, Sayal Rao Road,Mysore-570021(Karnataka)
- Govt.Ayurved Medical College, Dhanwantri Road, Bangalore-560009 (KA)
- Govt.Dhanwantri Ayurved College, Mangalnath Road, Ujjain-465001 (M.P.)
- Govt.Taranath Ayurved College, Anantapur Road,Ballary-583101(KA)
- Govt.Rishikul Ayurved College, Haridwar-249401 (Uttaranchal)
- National Institute of Ayurveda, Madhav Vilas Palace, Amer Road, Jaipur-302002 (Raj.)
- State Ayurved College, Tulsidas Marg, Lucknow-226004 (UP)

This list is not exhaustive. One can log on to **www.ccimindia.org** (an official website of Central Council of Indian Medicine) or www.indianmedicine.nic.in (an official website of department of AYUSH, Ministry of Health and Family Welfare, Govt. of India) for a detailed list of Medical Colleges in India which offer undergraduate and postgraduate courses in Ayurbedic Medicine.

Job Opportunities

There are various avenues of job opportunities for those who opt for Ayurvedic system of medicine as a career. Depending upon one's qualification and experience, one can find a job in Hospitals (both government and private), Dispensaries, Clinics, Nursing Homes, Health Departments and Pharmaceutical Industries, among others. Also one can practice privately as Ayurvedic Physician/ Consultant by opening an Ayurvedic clinic from his/her residence or from an easily accessible and well-populated neighbourhood.

Further, one can choose a career in teaching and research in this field. One can work as Lecturers, Readers, Professors etc. in Ayurvedic Medical Colleges and as Research Officer, Project Officer etc. in Central Research Institutes, Regional Research Institutes and other research institutions of CCRAS(Central Council for Research in Ayurveda and Siddha) that are located through India.

Ayurvedic medicine is gaining popularity both within the country and abroad due to its holistic approach and lesser side effects when compared to Allopathic medicine. Hence, there is a growing demand and bright future for Ayurvedic professionals.

(c) DENTISTRY

The dental profession has come a long way since its origin, claimed to be somewhere around 2000 BC in Egypt. From ivory stumps to precisely crafted porcelain crowns, from extractions that sent shudders of pain through each cell of the body, to painless surgical procedures and from caves to modern clinics; every aspect of Dental Sciences has been tried to be modelled to perfection. One of the most sought after fields of expertise. Dentistry presents a vast scope for clinical and research based experience. The very fact that it is a specialization to begin with makes it a course, rather a journey worth all the attention it's getting nowadays.

CAREER OVERVIEW

The Dental profession has been in great demand ever since the concepts of Oral Hygiene and Beauty came of age. The Dentist assumes such an important position in the health-care system because he can diagnose, intercept, treat, cure or prevent any disease or abnormality of the Oral cavity. As a Dentist, one of your primary jobs will also be educating the patients about maintenance of Oral Hygiene. That is when you get time off from Root Canals, Fillings, Orthodontic treatment, extractions, surgeries etc.

You can specialise in the following fields:-

ORTHODONTICS

A specialized branch of dentistry that corrects ma[illegible]ion and restores the teeth to proper alignment and function. [illegible]here are several different types of appliances used in orthodontics, one of which is commonly referred to as braces.

PERIODONTICS

The branch of dentistry that deals with diseases of the supporting structures of the teeth, including the gums, tissues and bones.

PAEDIATRIC DENSITSTS OR PEDODONTISTS are concerned with dentistry related to children. Preventive measures for dental anomalies, diseases and prevention, intervention and correction of various problems fall under this category.

PROSTHODONTICS

A speciality of dentistry involves diagnosis, treatment planning, and fabrication of artificial parts to replace missing teeth and their associated structures.

ENDODONTICS

The dental speciality that deals with injuries or diseases of the pulp or nerve of the tooth.

ORAL AND MAXILLOFACIAL SURGEONS

It is concerned with the surgery of the oral cavity and associated structures. They also treat diseases, injuries and deformities of the teeth, jaws and associated structures with the help of surgery.

COSMETIC DENTISTS are involved with the cosmetic aspects of the teeth and gums. They work to enhance the beauty of these by correcting anomalies if any.

ORAL PATHOLOGISTS are involved with the pathology of the oral cavity. They analyse the oral tissue samples, gum secretions and other related materials to identify causes of oral diseases.

FORENSIC ODONTOLOGISTS work with the forensic department of an investigating agency or in a university department. They analyse samples of teeth from mysterious death or homicide cases.

Dentist could also be involved in research like finding out the correlation between oral diseases and heart problems, oral diseases and diabetes, oral diseases and respiratory ailments, causes of oral cancer etc. Another area of research could be the synthesis and analysis of new polymers, composites and ceramics for oral applications or electrical stimulation of the muscles of mastication.

REQUIREMENTS

To be a Dentist, the first thing you need to have is average scientific and logical reasoning skills. The ability to memorise and recall scientific facts and a questioning attitude supplement this profession well. But above all, you need lots of patience and a cool temperament.

Once you get your BDS (Bachelor of Dental Surgery) degree from a DCI (Dental Council of India) recognized college, you may go in for a Master's degree i.e. MDS. This obviously improves your career prospects manifolds.

Whichever the case, you can either practice Denstistry or teach in one of the 183 Dental Colleges in India.

One of the most important requirements of the Dental profession is, that as a Dentist, you keep yourself constantly updated with the latest technologies, treatment methods and materials. It will be a must for you to read the latest journals, books, scientific updates etc. and attend CDE (Continuing Dental Education) Programmes throughout your life. If you can effectively keep a track of the latest in your field, you will make it to and stay at the top.

JOB OPPORTUNITIES

1. You can set up a private practice.

2. Work in a Government-Hospital or a Private Institute.
3. Work as a full or part time lecturer in any reputed dental college. Work in the research and advisory departments of a pharmaceutical or any other company producing oral care products and medicines like toothpaste, mouth wash, gum care products etc.
4. Solve great mysteries by entering the realm of Forensic Dentistry
5. Work as Dental Consultant to Models, Film Artists and Actors etc.
6. For the academically inclined ones, you can carry out research on subjects like Oral Cancer.
7. As visiting specialists to the General Practitioners.

CAREER MAP

In the Entrance Examinations (common for Medicine and Dentistry) four subjects i.e. Physics, Chemistry, Botany and Zoology are tested. Securing a seat in a reputed college is no child's play and takes a lot from you un terms of hard work and perseverance. However, there are many colleges that offer seats for a capitation fees of something between Rs. 8-14 lakhs.

Anyways, once you do secure a seat, you'll undergo four years of Pre-Clinical (theoretical) and Clinical (working in Clinics) training followed by one year of Rotating Internship. Rotating Internship means you will be posted for 2-3 months in each of the Specialization's (refer to career overview)Departments so that makes BDS a 5 years course.

After BDS you can either directly start working or prepare for PG Entrance Examination. There are about 350 PG seats in India contested by thousands of candidates each year. MDS (Masters of Dental Surgery) is a 3 years Course.

MONEY AND OTHER CONCERNS

If you think that you will start earning big bucks right away, you are wrong. Dentistry is one of those fields in which experience matters both to your employer as well as your patients. As a dentist fresh out of college, you'll be able to earn Rs.5,000/- - Rs.8,000/- only. You'll be held a trainee and will get the basic or easy cases to handle. Now, it all depends on you how far and how fast you go from being an apprentice to a master. An experienced dentist can earn anything between Rs.20,000/- - Rs.1,00,000/- per month. But if you have the instinct, the skill and motivation then sky is the limit.

DENTISTRY ABROAD

Dentistry is a highly respected profession in all countries of the world. In many developed countries, Dentists are one of the most sought after and richest professions. In some places, patients wait up to 2-3 months for a Dental appointment and pay as much as ten times the cost of the same treatment in India. However, most nations do not recognize the Indian Degree i.e. BDS. To practice in such countries, for example the USA, one has to give a few basic exams and then do another two years of Undergraduate course.

In some countries, for example Australia and New Zealand, all you have to do is give a Licensiating Exam, on passing that; you can practice in the respective country.

The great awareness comes slowly, piece by piece. The path of spiritual growth is a path of lifelong learning. The experience of spiritual power is basically a joyful one.

(d) HEALTH SANITARY INSPECTOR

Health Sanitary Inspector is personnel involved in the a inspection and promotion of health and sanitation measures in a community. He takes into account the quality of health and sanitation and uses his insight and judgements to implement public health activities. He conducts routine inspections and promotes and provides conditions necessary for health and hygiene.

The Health Sanitary Inspector can also be referred to as 'health assistant'. They are usually attached to various health organisations and functionaries in rural primary health care set ups viz. Block Extension Educator, Health Assistants and Health Worker.

NATURE OF WORK

A Health Sanitary Inspector is trained and responsible for:-

1. Routine inspection of food services.
2. Authorizing issuance of licenses and permits for food
3. Inspecting premises for animals
4. Inspecting recreational areas
5. Conducting routine housing inspections to ensure adequate safe and healthy housing for all people
6. Inspect dwellings to be rented for code compliance
7. Conducting percolation tests of soil
8. Authorizing and issuing permits for installation of well
9. Assuring safe drinking water to all people in the community
10. Investigating nuisance complaints and conducting inspections to assure compliance
11. Health education
12. Disease control measures

ELIGIBILITY AND ESSENTIAL QUALITIES REQUIRED

The candidates applying for the job should have a minimum qualification of 10+2 under 10+2 pattern of education with upper age limit is forty years. The age criterion is relaxed in the government and government approved institution as per the norms of the government.

The eligible candidates can apply to the various institutions according to their selection criteria. Few essential attributes which will enable a person to become a successful Health sanitary Inspector are:-

1. He should be a keen leaner and observer and able to appreciate the nature and surroundings.
2. He should understand health and sanitation as a science and discipline.
3. He should be a responsible citizen and have a genuine concern in the welfare of the people.
4. He should be a initiator and promoter of new ideas and technologies in the field.
5. He should be able to think globally and act locally in public health and sanitation.
6. He should have good communication and convincing skills.

TRAINING AND CERTIFICATES

There is one year course of Diploma in Health Sanitary Inspector. The eligible candidates can apply at various institutions. After getting into an institution they are trained academically and practically in the various concepts of health and sanitation, familiarization of environment and its components. Some states also conduct competitive exams for Health and Sanitary Inspector. Eligibility for these exams is graduation. They are trained and have to visit various government organisations and departments like Jal Boards, Water treatment plants, Sewage treatment plants, hotels, hospitals, cremation grounds etc. They are trained in such a manner that they can easily recognize health and sanitation aspects and promote the same for betterment of all. Live demonstrations of all running procedures and departments give them a much precise view and layout of their role and duties.

JOB OPPORTUNITIES

Health Inspector/ Sanitary Inspector is definite post in the government departments at the state and the central level. Government departments include Municipal Corporations, Nagar Palikas, Railways, Hospitals, Cantonment area, Government Institutes, Oil Refineries, factories etc. In the private organisations that work with hospitals, hotel, metal industry, chemical industry, textile industry, food industry, travel and entertainment industry, electrical industry etc.

Recently, National Council of Vocational Training (NCVT) an apex body for conducting vocational courses in India, under Ministry of Labour and Employment, Govt of India, has combined the two trades

Health Inspector and Sanitary Inspector into one calling it 'Health Sanitary Inspector' and affiliated it thus giving this trade more recognition in India and worldwide. The course via NCVT is running at its various ITI's. The students possessing NCVT trade certificates can also avail opportunities outside the country.

INSTITUTIONS

The few institutions offering this course are:-

1. ITI, Kichripur, New Delhi
2. ITI, Jail Road, New Delhi
3. ITI, Nand Nagar, New Delhi
4. National Industrial Training Centre, Sewak Park, New Delhi

It is time for us to stand and cheer for the doer the achiever, the one who recognizes the challenge and does something about it.

(e) HEALTH EDUCATORS

Description

Promote, maintain, and improve individual and community health by assisting individuals and communities to adopt healthy behaviors. Collect and analyze data to identify community needs prior to planning, implementing, monitoring, and evaluating programs designed to encourage healthy lifestyles, policies, and environments. May also serve as a resource to assist individuals, other professionals, or the community, and may administer fiscal resources for health education programs.

Experience

Extensive skill, knowledge, and experience are needed for these occupations. Many require more than five years of experience.

Education

A bachelor's degree is the minimum formal education required for these occupations. However, many also require graduate school.

Training

Employees may need some on-the-job training, but most of these occupations assume that the person will already have the required skills, knowledge, work-related experience, and/or training.

Tasks

1. Plans and provides educational opportunities for health personnel.
2. Collaborates with health specialists and civic groups to ascertain community health needs, determine availability of services, and to develop goals.

3. Promotes health discussions in schools, industry, and community agencies.
4. Prepares and disseminates educational and informational materials.
5. Develops and maintains cooperation between public, civic, professional, and voluntary agencies.
6. Conducts community surveys to ascertain health needs, develop desirable health goals, and determine availability of professional health services.

Correction does much, but encouragement does more. Encouragement after censure is as the sun after a shower.

(f) HEALTHCARE

There is an apprehension that in a hospital, only doctors and para-medical staffs are required. But with organised players entering the field, a number of options have opened up.

1. IT and Systems: When the world is changing to adopt the concept of wire-free working environment, the hospital industry can't stay back and observe. To optimise the resources, even the healthcare sector has to rope in experts of IT. Solutions like CRM (Customer Relationship Management), SCM (Supply Chain Management), ERP (Enterprise Resource Planning) and other latest softwares are being used even by this industry. Moreover, there is need for networking and hardware professionals to man the overall LAN and system infrastructure. Students possessing MBA in IT and Systems or even having degrees in computer applications, computer science and computer technology are preferred for such openings.

2. Finance: With so much to manage in a new hospital set up, the funds which are being processed on daily, weekly; monthly and annual basis is huge. Allocating funds as per the need and budgeting the future spending, calls for finance experts. Recruiting CAs, MBA-Finance or even cost accounts is a practice, although the edge is with MBA Finance for their ability to offer value additions in terms of general management skills. Tracking the cash flow, fund flow and budgeting for all the departments are the main jobs performed by a finance expert.

3. Clinical researchers: Most of the new generation hospitals are also performing the role of a research centre. They tie up with leading hospitals of the West like the Harvard Medical School and work on cutting edge topics pertaining to medical research. Indian patients consisting of people with varied physiologies and make up, along with the readily available manpower, are acting as a hotbed for researching the latest inventions and the ones in the pipeline on a diverse set of patients. It serves dual purpose. Companies are able to discover drugs customised to patients of a specific geography and secondly, leveraging the clinical experience in the institute to contribute towards the invention of newer molecules. MBBS, MD, PhD in subjects like microbiology, biochemistry, physiology, anatomy and biotechnology are the ones who can join the clinical research department. It is not the age old hospital where only medical and paramedical staff used to man all the departments. In a competitive world, you need horses for courses and the best way to man age such a show is to allocate responsibilities to the domain experts. After all, India is touted to be the leader in healthcare, tourism after software. The cost advantage should be used to the hilt so as to make this dream into a reality.

Human beings have a body; they live with it, they look after it, they feed it and even make it up! But do they ever bother to decipher what it wants to convey with its organs? The Body functions properly because the spirit animates the body, teaching a lesson: how God and Nature envisioned things by placing the body under authority of the spirit.

(g) HOMOEOPATHY

Homoeopathy today is one of the most accepted branch of medical profession, for patients as well as students.

Way back in the 80's and 90's an average of students were seeking admission in Homoeopathy just for prefixing a doctor's tag to their names. But in the last decade, the scenario has altogether changed. It is now largely preferred as a medical career. A student having inclination for human sciences with humanitarian and philosophical bent of mind will prefer this profession. Homoeopathy is a divine and wonder science discovered by a German Allopathic physician Dr.Christian Friedrich Samuel Hahnemann in 1796, due to his discontent of then prevailing modes of treatment.

The term Homoeopathy is derived from two Greek words, "homoios" which means like or of the same kind and "pathos" means suffering. Homoeopathy is an alternative system of medicine, based on the nature's Law of Cure, namely "Like kcures Like". The truth of this law was discovered by a German Scientist Dr. Samuel Hahnemann in 1796.

Homoeopathy differs considerably from other systems of medicine in diagnostic and treatment procedures. It goes into the details of patient's history before starting the treatment. The procedure of Homoeopathy treatment is slow, but it is claimed to remove the disease/ disorders from its roots.

Formal Medical Education

In order to become a Homoeopathic medical practitioner, a formal medical education is mandatory. There are many Homoeopathic medical colleges in India, which offer Degree Course in Homoeopathy viz. Bachelor of Homoeopathic Medicine and Surgery (B.H.M.S.), a 5 ½ year course including a compulsory internship of 1 year duration and also Postgraduate course i.e. Doctor of Medicine in Homoeopathy (M.D. (Hom.), a 3 year course including 1 year house job or equivalent thereof.

Those who have passed Higher Secondary Course (10 + 2) with Physics, Chemistry and Biology or equivalent subjects are eligible to apply for Degree course of Homoeopathy (B.H.M.S.). Generally, admission/selection for this course is made on the basis of an entrance exam./ test conducted at state/ national level. Those who have passed the Degree course in Homoeopathy (B.H.M.S.) are eligible to apply for the Postgraduate course in Homoeopathy.

In addition to the above mentioned courses, Diploma course (D.H.M.S. – Diploma in Homoeopathic Medicine and Surgery, a 4 year course including a compulsory internship of 6 months) and Graded degree course (B.H.M.S.- Bachelor of Homoeopathic Medicine and Surgery, a 2 year course including a compulsory internship of 6 months) are also available in some of the colleges. Those who have completed Diploma course in Homoeopathy (D.H.M.S.) are eligible to study Graded degree course is considered as a bridge or link short term course for the benefit of Diploma holders to raise their educational level to that of a Degree.

Some of the medical colleges that offer both Undergraduate and Postgraduate courses in Homoeopathy are given below in alphabetical order.

1. A.M.Shaikh Homoeopathic Medical College, Nehru Nagar, Belgaum –590010 (Karnataka).
2. Bhartesh Homoeopathic Medical College, Belgaum-590016 (Karnataka)
3. Dhondumama Sathe Homoeopathic Medical College, Pune – 411004 (MS)
4. Dr.Abhin Chandra Homoeopathic Medical College and Hospital, Kharvela Nagar, Bhubaneshwar (Orissa)
5. Dr.Madan Pratap Khuteta Rajasthan Homoeopathic Medical College, Jaipur-302006 (Raj.)
6. Dr.V.H.Dave Homoeopathic Medical College & Smt.S.I.Patel (Ipcowala) Homoeopathic Hospital, Anand-388001 (Guj.)
7. Father Muller Homoeopathic Medical College, Kankady, Mangalore-575002(Karnataka)
8. Govt.Homoeopathic Medical College, Iranimuttam, Thuruvananthapuram (Kerala)
9. Govt. Homoeopathic Medical College, Karaparamba, Calicut-673010 (Kerala)
10. Gujarat Homoeopathic Medical College, At & PO.-Savli-391770, District- Vadodara (Guj.)
11. I.S.P.S. Govt. Homoeopathic Medical College, Ramanathapur, Hyderabad-500013(AP)

12. Kaka Saheb Mhaske Homoeopathic Medical College, Nagapur, Ahmednagar-414111(MS)
13. National Institute of Homoeopathy, Salt Lake, Kolkata-700101 (WB)
14. Nehru Homoeopathic Medical College & Hospital, New Delhi-110 024

The above mentioned list is not exhaustive. Aspirants can log on to www.cchindia.com (an Council of Homoeopathy) or www.indianmedicine.nic.in (an official website of department of AYUSH) for a detailed list of recognized Homoeopathic medical colleges in Indian and courses offered by them.

Job Opportunities

For those who have opted for a career in Homoeopathic medicine, a wide range of employment opportunities are available in hospitals, pharmaceutical industries, teaching and research institutions etc. depending upon their qualifications and experience. One can practice privately as Homoeopathic physician by opening a Homoeopathic clinic from his/her residence or from a suitable place. One can serve in Health departments, Hospitals (government or private) Homoeopathic dispensaries, clinics, nursing homes and so on. Also one can choose a career in teaching in Homoeopathic medical colleges as Lecturers, Readers, Professors etc. and also as Reserch Officer, Project Officer etc. in research institutions.

(h) MEDICAL PROFESSION

For ages medical science has fascinated mankind and physicians have enjoyed a privileged position in society. Today also it continues to be a noble profession if practised by dedicated people with right attitude. This article gives a brief overview of career options in medical field.

The right person to become a doctor should be one who is laborious and dedicated. People looking for quick money will be disappointed in this field. But if you want to be thrilled by the pleasure of brining smile to ailing people by your healing touch, go ahead.

MBBS DEGREE

The basic degree for medical practice in Allopathic is MBBS – Bachelor of Medicine and Bachelor of Surgery. There are 229 medical colleges in India, which are presently recognized by the Medical Council of India.

Pre-medical entrance examinations are conducted by various states for their domicile students who have completed intermediate with science. Many institutes such as AIIMS, New Delhi, Post Graduate Institute (PGI), Chandigarh and CMC, Vellore conduct their own entrance tests. All India Pre-medical tests conducted by CBSE is the main national level exam. CBSE has seat reservation in all the medical colleges across Indian which are funded by the Government of India, except in Andhra Pradesh and Jammu & Kashmir (AP and J&K candidates are not allowed to attempt the exam.). The forms are available in November and the exam is conducted by the last week of April. The exam consists of objective type multiple choice questions covering Physics, Chemistry and Biology (Botany & Zoology).

MBBS Course is of 4 and ½ years duration. It is divided into three parts and includes a long list of subjects like Anatomy, Physiology, Bio-chemistry, Pathology, Microbiology, Pharmacology, Forensic Medicine, Social and Preventive Medicine, General Medicine, Paediatrics, General Surgery, Obstetrics, Gynaecology, Ophthalmology, Otorhinolaryngology etc. After successfully completing theory and practical examination in each professional part, Medical Council issues a temporary registration. After this, one year supervised practical training is given in a recognized hospital in various subjects as internship. This is followed by a permanent registration with various state medical councils or the Medical Council of India-MCI. This authorizes the new doctor for medical practice in India. A doctor has to practice within the prescribed professional and ethical norms, otherwise his license may be withdrawn.

Non MBBS science graduates may also join medical field such as biophysics, nuclear medicine and microbiology after graduation.

OPTION AFTER MBBS

After getting an MBBS degree a doctor can go for:-

1. Private practice- A comprehensive training has been given so that the doctor is competent for general practice at this level. Needless to say, further voluntary training in any hospital will add to his skill.
2. UPSC conducts combined medical service examination for vacancies in Indian railways, Delhi Municipal Corporation hospitals etc. This is a class I service with facilities and perks comparable with any other UPSC job.
3. State level job- various State Public Service Commissions recruit for their state medical services. Vacancies differ from state to state but a doctor from one state is usually eligible for other states.
4. Various other government, autonomous and private bodies such as Armed Forces, ESI, NTPC, Coal India etc. have time to time vacancies.

1. *Non Medical streams*- UPSC has included medical science as one of the subjects for Civil Service. There are some allied fields such as biotechnology and management.
2. *Going abroad*- to practice in a foreign country one needs to be registered with medical council of the country. Usually one has

to qualify a licensing examination before that. United States conducts USMLE and United Kingdom conducts PLAB for the purpose. This also gives opportunity for specialization in many fields.

3. *Further studies*- Medical Science offers a vast scope for further specialization and research. Training in India is well regulated, transparent, advanced and widely recognized.

POSTGRADUATE COURSES AFTER MBBS

Postgraduate 2 years diploma courses are available in 31 sujects and Postgraduate 3 year degree courses (M.D. for medical field and MS for surgical field) are available in 38 subjects. For admission in various courses Entrance Examination are conducted according to a pattern similar to premedical test, some institution based tests such as that conducted by AIIMS, New Delhi, PGI Chandigarh, CMC Vellore and SGPGIMS, Lucknow and finally All India Post Graduate Entrance Tests conducted by AIIMS, New Delhi.

While pursuing these courses, doctors are supposed to work in a hospital. They are also paid reasonable money as stipend. Successful completion of these courses requires practical training, theoretical knowledge and at least one research thesis. This authorizes a doctor for specialist practice.

SUPER SPECIALIZATION

After post graduation, further super specialization is available in 23 subjects awarding DM degree in medical field and MCh in surgical field. Seats are limited. For example, there are only 23 DM seats in nephrology and only 45 MCh seats in cardiac surgery in the entire country. This is a 3 years course and requires several research papers of international standard and an exit examination.

NATIONAL BOARD OF EXAMINATIONS

This provides another way of specialist training. There are more than 176 recognized medical colleges in the country and abroad in addition to over 191 accredited institutions imparting medical education in various levels and in various broad and super specialities. It ensures uniform elevated level of standard of education and after completion of training awards certificate of DNB (Diplomat of National Board) in various subjects. Diplomat word should not be confused with diploma. It value is similar to MD/MS or DM/MCh.

THE RIGHT APTITUDE AND CLARITY

It is easy to understand that medical education requires enormous patience and labour. For a lucky person who is able to clear three national entrance examinations in first attempt and who does not have any failure in exit examinations. It will take a minimum of

4.5 + 1+3+3= 11.5 years of continuous study after 12th. So one should be very clear before opting medicine as a profession.

But if you have the right aptitude to combine the science of medicine with the art of patient care, welcome to the fascinating world of healers.

(i) MEDICAL TRANSCRIPTION

Medical Transcription (MT) is a prominent area of the IT- enabled services (ITES)- one of the fastest growing sectors in the country today, both in terms of revenue and vacancies available. Estimates claim that another 50,000 jobs will be added in the MT sector by 2008.

The MT work in India comes entirely from the United States because it is one of the very few countries where the law demands that doctors/hospitals maintain detailed and accurate medical records of all patients. These are essential since they form the basis of retrieving payment after processing medical insurance claims. Data and medical procedures during research also need to be recorded. Doctors and hospitals in the US have had to pay huge amounts as compensation after courts found them liable because they did not maintain detailed, clear and accurate medical records. Medical transcription, then, is a hugely important area for them.

Material requiring transcription can include everything from patient history, consultation notes and discharge summaries to X-ray, pathology, blood and laboratory reports and even surgical reports and psychiatric evaluations. Naturally, if doctors sat down to this on their own, it would take up a lot of their time in doing what is essentially an administrative task. Consequently, a simple solution was found: medical transcription.

This is how it works: doctors now record their data/ findings in voice form. These audio files are then transmitted via satellite or (other means) to an MT company where a transcriptionist downloads the file. These files are then heard and correctly typed into a word processing system. The transcribed record is then edited, proofread and sent back to the source, again via satellite.

One reason India has become a preferred destination for this work is the time difference between the two countries. Material recorded and sent by doctors during the day in the USA is transcribed, edited and sent back to them in less than 24 hours. The other reasons are, of course, cheaper labour and a ready pool of people with a good knowledge of English.

If you think all that sounds simple, read on. The first couple of requirements are easy, a good typing speed and a willingness to work night shifts (though this is not a must). Next, while MT work may not require excellent spoken English, it does require a high degree of competence in written English-sentence structure, punctuation, everything. Since the work is highly technical, you also need to have very good listening and comprehension skills.

You will also need to be able to understand the American accent (and this varies a lot across the USA). But most of all, you need to be familiar with medical terminology and grammar, which can be very different from everyday language. A doctor dictating notes may not speak complete sentence and a transcriptionist will have to improve on this. A slight error- either in understanding or in something simple, like a comma or a full-stop- can create serious problems. Remember people's lives are at stake.

Naturally, the average graduate- even with a science background- does not possess all of these skills. So many companies take up the job of training fresh recruits. MT in India is about five years old and many of the people who started out as transcriptionists have now moved up the leader to become editors. And while there another 50,000 jobs are out there for the taking, only 5% of fresher interviewed are found suitable to go directly on the floor. A big chunk is found 'trainable' so they are often recruited as trainees to develop their skills, especially in the area of medical terminology.

Some companies provide free training and others give trainees a stipend in the range of Rs.2000-5000 per month. Most big companies assign transcriptionists to one of the specialities- oncology, internal medicine, cardiology etc. or to one particular doctor. Once you become a full fledged medical transcriptionist, the starting salaries range anywhere between Rs.5,000 to Rs.8,000 pm.

Fortunately, this is one job that is completely ability-driven. If you're good, you can even finish your training ahead of time. And promotion to editor (starting salary Rs.10,000 pm) can also come in less than two years. The next step up the ladder is to Quality Controller and there can be multiple levels of Quality Control in a mid-sized company.

HOME-BASED OPTION

Once you prove your abilities, there's also the very attractive option of working from home. You need a PC with an internet connection and the company you work for will load the relevant software for you. This includes the editing software- which may be proprietary- as well as an assortment of dictionaries and glossaries to help ensure high accuracy. In fact, some companies employ only home-based transcriptionists.

Payment is based on both your speed and accuracy and ranges between 60 paise to Rs.1.50 per line. Depending on the number of lines you transcribe- many MTs do 500-800 lines a day- you can earn between Rs.15,000 to over Rs.20,000 by putting in 8 hours a day and taking Sundays off. The accuracy rate demanded is over 95%. If you experience occasional power problems, the company is likely to let you to do your day's work from their office.

Some companies also hire home-based editors- the job is less tedious and higher-paying. In either case, there is a team of in-house editors/QCs checking your output. Sticking to deadlines is an absolute must, as is maintaining a very high level of accuracy, which means one has to be very alert. There is simply no room for slack performance.

As of now, Bangalore, New Delhi, Mumbai and Kolkata are home to most of the MT firms in the country, closely followed by Chennai and Pune. Vadodara, Rajjot, Chandigarh and Kochi are also fast catching up. And keeping in line with the ITES sector's recent decision to reach out to smaller towns. MT firms are set to open in smaller cities as well.

MT CAPSULE

Education:-Graduation, preferably with science backgrounds. Some firms even hire fresh doctors at the editor-level.

Skills:-Good typing speed, excellent listening comprehension, ability to understand Americanisms and knowledge of medical terminology. Some companies have night shifts as well.

Salaries:-Rs.5,000pm upwards for people who've completed training. Editors usually get over Rs.10,000 pm.

MT hotspots:- Banagalore, Mumbai, New Delhi, Chennai, Kolkata, Pune, Chandigarh, Vadodara, Rajkot and Kochi among others. Smaller cities to follow soon.

(j) MICROBIOLOGY

Microbiology is the study of organisms that are usually too small to be seen by the naked eye (unaided). Microbiology is a large discipline, which has a great impact on other areas of biology and general human welfare.

One can't over emphasize the importance of microbiology. Society benefits from Micro-organisms (M.Os) in many ways. They are necessary for the production of bread, cheese, beer, antibiotics, vaccines, vitamins, enzymes and many other important products. Indeed, modern biotechnology rests upon a microbiological foundation. M.Os are indispensable components of our ecosystem. They make possible the cycles of carbon, oxygen, nitrogen and sulphur that takes place in terrestrial and aquatic systems. They are also source of nutrients at the base of all ecological food chains and webs.

OCCUPATION OF PROFESSIONAL MICROBIOLOGISTS

Medical microbiologists identify the agent causing an infectious disease and plan to eliminate it. Frequently they are involved in tracking down new, unidentified pathogens such as the bacterium that cause plague, legionnaire's disease and the virus responsible for AIDS, SARS (Severe Acute Respiratory Syndrome) and Avian flu. These microbiologists also study the ways in which M.Os cause disease.

Public health microbiology is clearly related to medical microbiology. Public health microbiologist tries to control the spread of communicable diseases. They often monitor community food establishments and water supplies in an attempt to keep them safe and free from infectious disease agents.

Many important areas of microbiology do not deal directly with human health and disease but certainly contribute to human welfare. Agricultural microbiology is concerned with the impact of M.Os on agriculture.

Agriculture microbiologists try to combat plant disease that attacks important food crops, work on methods to increase soil fertility and crop yields. Currently, there is interest in using bacterial (Bacillus thuringenesis) and viral insect (Baculovirus, NPV- Nuclear Polyhedrosis Virus) pathogens as substitutes for chemical pesticides/ insecticides.

The field of microbial ecology is closely related tof agricultural microbiology. Microbial ecologists study the relationship between M.Os and their habits. They are concerned with the contribution of M.Os to the carbon, nitrogen and sulfur cycles in soil and in fresh water. The study of pollution effects on M.Os also is important because of the impact these M.Os have on the environment. Microbial ecologists are employing M.Os in bioremediation to reduce pollution effects.

Scientists working in food and dairy microbiology try to prevent microbial spoilage of food and the transmission of food borne diseases such as botulism and salmonellosis. They also use M.Os to make foods such as cheese, yoghurts, Single Cell Protein (SCP), pickles, wine and beer. In the future M.Os may become a more important nutrient source for livestock and humans.

In industrial microbiology M.Os are used to make products such as antibiotics, vaccines, steroids, alcohols and other solvents, vitamins, aminoacids and enzymes. M.Os can even leach minerals from low grade ones.

CAREER PROSPECTS

In addition to areas covered under Microbiology. Microbiologists can be employed as :-

Medical Representatives

Job profile consists of apprising the doctors with their company's products for promoting sales.

Higher Studies

After B.Sc. Microbiology graduates can pursue higher studies like M.Sc., Applied Microbiology, Medical Microbiology, M.Sc., Food Micro-biology, M.Sc., Industrial Micribiology, M.Sc., Genetics, M.Sc.,Biotechnology, M.Sc.Industrial Biotechnology, M.Sc.Bio-informatics, M.Sc.,Microbial Technology, M.Sc.,Clinical Research, M.Sc.,Molecular Biology, M.Sc.,Biochemistry, M.Sc.,Forensic Science, M.Sc.,Hospital Management. In addition PG Diploma in Hospital Administration run by Indian Institute of Hospital Managemen and Research, Jaipur.

Global Opportunities

A large number of microbiology graduates are going to western countries for higher studies for which they are required to qualify GRE and TOFEL. In addition postgraduate and Ph.D candidates go abroad to pursue Ph.D and Post Doctoral Research Fellow (PDF) in foreign Universities and R & D Centres respectively, which is highly paid and respected profession in Western world.

Research and Development Scientists

With India shifting from process patent to product patent, large pharmaceutical companies are investing in R&D. As a result, there is an employment opportunity in the area of formulation research, analytical development, clinical research and in new drug discovery.

Academician

Microbiologists become faculty in Universities, Colleges or teachers in Schools etc. For college teaching, a master's degree may be acceptable alongwith qualification of CSIR- NET, but a doctorate opens more door. Teaching and research at the university level and high level employment with good promotion prospects in non-academic research institutes, private industry and government agencies usually require a Ph.D.

Self Employment

Self employed microbiologist by setting up microbiological laboratories of their own can help in diagnosing the disease and researchers direct their own research. There are large, private research institutes that conduct Microbiological/ epidemiological studies for government agencies where there is a sudden outbreak of any epidemic disease. These studies focus on a wide variety of urban and metropolitan problems such as a sudden outbreak of any disease.

Eg.- SARS in China – 2003 Avian flu (Bird flu) in Thailand- 2004
Plague in Surat (Gujarat)
Cholera in Tamil Nadu (2004)

Acting as a consultant for finding the Total Dissolved Solids (TDS), Biologically Oxygen Demand (BOD), Chemically Oxygen Demand (COD), effluent treatment, purification of water, Biomedical wastes treatment.

Microbiologist in Diagnostic Laboratories

Job profile consists of diagnosis of disease, identifying the pathogen, testing the efficiency of antibiotic which may help the physician to prescribe the antibiotic to the patient.

Quality control

A Microbiologist can help to assess the quality of milk in dairy farms, water in Mineral Water Company, soft drink industries, pharmaceutical companies, spices industries etc.

Research

Post graduate microbiology students after completion of III Semester with 55% percentile marks are eligible to appear in CSIR-NET exam. After qualifying the exam they are can get appointed as Junior Research Fellow (JRF) with stipends at various CSIR laboratories located throughout the nation and are allowed to register their Ph.D. Other positions include Senior Research Fellow (SRF), Research Assistant (RA) and Research Associate (RA) in various government and private research institutes after completion of Ph.D.

(k) PHARMACOGNOSY

The word pharmacognosy is derived from two Greek words "pharmakon" meaning "drug" and "gnosis" meaning "knowledge". So pharmacognosy literally means knowledge of drugs. Pharmacognosy is one of the important branches of pharmacy. It deals with "the study of structural, physical, chemical and sensory characters of crude drugs of animal, vegetable and mineral origin and includes their history, cultivation, collection, storage and use". From a layman's point of view pharmacognosy is nothing but medicinal botany.

The chief functions of a pharmacognosists are to ascertain the identity/ authenticity of crude drug samples and to check adulteration/ substitution; to study the active constituents of the drug plants/ crude drugs and to investigate their chemical/ reactions; to devise methods for cultivation of suitable plants for commercial exploitation and so on.

Origin & Developments

Though the term pharmacognosy is a modern one, the knowledge of medicinal plants and their uses are as old as mankind. It has developed from ancient civilizations, where plants or plant parts have been used to cure human diseases/ disorders. The healing power of certain herbs and plant parts such as leaves, barks, roots etc. were undoubtedly discovered by accident, but once discovered, knowledge of drugs was passed on from generation to generation.

Now-d-days, people are increasingly turnig to indigenous systems of medicine which are holistic and not only treat diseases but also prevent them. Further, they are free from side effects. With the rising popularity of traditional systems of medicine, there is a growing demand for professionals in this field. In order to become a medical practitioner in Indian system of medicine, a formal education is mandatory. Further, some of the Indian systems of medicine offer specialization in pharmacognosy at postgradute level e.g. M.D. Ayurveda in Dravyaguna (pharmacognosy) and also offer research programmes in pharmacognosy. One can take up pharmacognosy as a career also in Indian systems of medicine. Aspirants can log on to : www.indiamedicine.nic.in for more information on Indian systems of medicine.

Academics

To have a good career in pharmacognosy, an aspirant should hold a doctorate degree (Ph.D) in Pharmacognosy or at least a Master's in Pharmacy (M.Pharm.) with specialization in pharmacognosy. A Bachelor's degree in Pharmacy (B.Pharm.) is the minimum qualification for a career in pharmacognosy. Further, one can enter this field by first studying a Diploma in Pharmacy (D.Pharm.), which is a basic course in Pharmacy. After completing D.Pharm lateral entry into B.Pharm. course is also available.

There are about 150 institutions across the country that offer pharmacy courses, especially undergraduate courses. Some of these institutions also offer Postgraduate courses. Those who have passed 10 + 2 with Physics, Chemistry and Biology or Mathematics subjects are eligible to study pharmacy courses, either D.Pharm (a 2 year course) or B.Pharm(a 4 year course). Admissions to these courses are done through an entrance examination conducted by State or Central Government or Universities.

Though pharmacognosy is taught in D.Pharm. and B.Pharm. as one of the subjects, one can get specialized in pharmacognosy only in the postgraduate level. M.Pharm.(a 2 year course) and thereafter in doctoral/ post-doctoral studies. About eight specializations are offered in M.Pharm. of which pharmacognosy is one. Many of the pharmacy/ pharmaceutical related institutions in India have a separate department for pharmacognosy with laboratory facilities.

Some of the universities and institutes imparting Pharmacy / Pharmacognosy courses are:- Al-Ameen College of Pharmacy, Bangalore; Birla Institute of Technology, Ranchi; Bombay College of Pharmacy, Mumbai; B.V. Patel Pharmaceutical Education & Research Development Centre, Ahmedabad; Chennai Medical College, Chennai; Cheran College of Pharmacy, Coimbatore; Department of

Pharmaceutical Sciences, Dr. H.S.Gaur Vishvidyalaya, Sagar(M.P.); Department of Pharmaceutical Technology, Jadavpur University, Kolkata; government College of Pharmacy, Bangalore; Hemchandracharya North Gujarat University, Patan, Gujarat; Faculty of Pharmacy, Jamia Hamdard, New Delhi; K.L.E. Society's College of Pharmacy, Hubli; MAEER's Maharashtra Institute of Pharmacy, Pune; Mahatma Gandhi College of Pharmaceutical Sciences, Jaipur ; National Institute of Pharmaceutical Education and Research (NIPER), Mohali, Punjab; Poona College of Pharmacy, Pune; Sinhgad College of Pharmacy, Pune; University Institute of Pharmaceutical Technology, Annamalai University, Annamalainagar; University Institute of Pharmaceutical Sciences, Panjab University, Chandigarh; University Institute of Pharmaceutical Sciences, Mumbai; Visveswarapura Institute of Pharmaceutical Sciences, Bangalore and so on. The list is not exhaustive. One can log on to : www.medicoinfoline.com for a detailed list of institutions and courses/ specializations offered.

Career

With undergraduate qualification (B.Pharm.), one can easily enter into pharmacy or pharmaceutical related jobs. However, one can take up teaching/ research as a career only with postgraduate (M.Pharm.) and/ or doctorate (Ph.D) qualification. A wide range of employment opportunities are available for pharmacy/ pharmacognosy professionals in Hospitals, Pharmaceutical Industries, Teaching/ Research Institutions depending upon their qualifications and experience.

Some of the common job profiles are as pharmacists in hospitals and medican stores, as sales/ medical representatives in pharmaceutical companies, as technicians in biochemical and pathological laboratories as analysts in chemical/ drug analysis laboratories, as drug inspectors, instructors, demonstrators, lecturers, readers or professors in teaching institutions, as scientists in research institutions and so on. Career opportunities in pharmacognosy are plentiful in developed countries like United States, United Kingdom etc.

Research Institutions

Ever since the popularisation of pharmaceutical education, in addition to students of pharmacy, students of botany are also increasingly interested in pharmacognostic research programs leading to doctoral and postdoctoral degrees.

(I) PHARMACEUTICAL SECTOR

After IT, the Pharmaceutical sector is the new sunrise industry of India. The Indian pharmaceutical sector is one, whose real potential has not been understood by the employees.

Reverse engineering had been the backbone of this industry till now. Even the global giants like GlaxoSmithKline, Pfizer, Novartis to name a few, had to bite the dust, when it came to the launching of their global brands in the Indian market. The Indian behemoths like Cipla, Ranbaxy, Cadila soon used to come out with their Indian copy-cats at a throw-away price, which the fund stricken consumer lapped up with both hands.

Gone are those days, India being a signatory to the WTO (World Trade Organisation) had to convert itself from the earlier product patent era into a process patent era. In such a scenario, the environment is a win-win one for the employers and the employees. Employers in the form of multinationals can launch their international brands in the country, without the fear of the predatory pricing adopted by their Indian counterparts.

Moreover, the sheer presence of the product patent era will compel many Indian companies to do a rethinking on the part of their strategic decisions. With this phase of consolidation, one thing is for sure, come what may, none of the existing players or the prospective ones can ever think of withdrawing or launching their offerings in the highly lucrative Indian market.

Differentiating on the basis of manpower: For knowledge based sectors, the only competitive advantage is their manpower. Pharmaceutical sector needs professionally equipped manpower, in order to cater to the huge pool of consumers. The following opportunities/ openings are available in this industry.

Sales department: An aspirant having a postgraduate diploma or MBA in marketing can opt for a career in sales. He might have to start off in the frontline cadre, but gradually as he starts performing and gains experience, he is more into sales management.

Companies generally prefer graduates having a background in pharmaceutical sciences or life sciences preferable with MBA for such openings. Job profile entails calling the consumers (read doctors), the middlemen (read the retailers and the whole sellers) with an ultimate objective of convincing everyone to purchase their offerings.

Marketing department: The marketing department or the PMT (Product Management Team) as it is referred in the industry circle, are the ones who are involved in the behind the scene activities.

They are mainly involved in making promotional strategies for the existing and prospective products, designing promotional literatures, conducting survey in the company of the sales staff so as to know about the competitor's strategies. Such openings are filled up by candidates specialising in MBA marketing with a basic degree in life sciences and pharmaceutical sciences.

These days, companies recruit people even without a basic degree in life sciences or pharmacy provided the candidate has good product knowledge and is interested in chalking out a career in marketing.

Clinical services department: This is one department where the Indian companies didn't focus much, prior to the product patent era. The reason was the availability of the readily available chemists with formal qualification in M.Sc. in Organic Chemistry, Pharmaceutical Chemistry or the Industrial Chemistry as there was no need of doctors with the basics of management. The need of the hour called for bulk processing expertise only.

But with the change in the business environment, it called for more than mere process chemistry, and thereby the need of doctors with a management background. For such positions, MBBS or MD/ MS graduates preferably with management qualifications are preferred. The job profile entails interacting with the consumers (doctors and end-user, patients), tracking the performance of various products and their technical details and subsequently, passing it off to the research and development department and the marketing department.

Human Resources (HR) and Finance: Like any other organisation, a pharmaceutical company needs HR and finance experts to manage the financial and manpower resources optimally.

Candidates with post graduation or MBA in Human Resources Management (HRM) and Financial Management are preferred for such positions.

(m) PHYSIOTHERAPY

Physiotherapy means physiotherapeutic system of medicine which includes examination, treatment advice and instructions to any person in connection with movement, dysfunction, bodily malfunction, physical disorder, disability, healing and pain from trauma and disease.

The physiotherapists skill are required by the health care team in most disciplines of medicine including surgery, neurology, orthopaedics, gynaecology, obstetrics, dermatology, ENT, cardiothoracic, vascular surgery, burns, plastic surgery, paediatrics, rehabilitation and sports medicine etc.

Purpose of Physiotherapy

The purpose of physiotherapy is to decrease body dysfunctions, reduce pain caused either by trauma, inflammation, degeneration and surgery. The various conditions in which physiotherapy is useful are as follows:-

(1) Management of a fracture and return to normal function is possible with simple methods of physiotherapy. It allows for regain of full joint movements and muscles power after healing of a fracture.

(2) In joints and soft tissue injury rapid repair of damaged tissue occurs with quick reduction of pain and swelling.

(3) Restoration of full joint movements with reduction of pain and deformity is possible in various kinds of joint diseases like osteoarthritis, rheumatoid arthritis juvenile arthritis etc.

(4) In degenerative disease of spine, physiotherapy arrests the progress of disease as in cervical spondylosis ankylosing spondylosis. Suitable arthroses are also provided for giving support to spine. It also has a major role to play congenital disease of spine like spina-bifida.

(5) Chest physiotherapy has a vital role to play in medical and surgical conditions like bronchial asthma, chronic obstructive lungs disease, pneumothorax but also surgical procedures involving spine, pelvis, extremities and abdomen.

(6) In hemiplegia or paralegia physiotherapy greatly helps the patient to gradually increase his mobility.

(7) In children physiotherapy is assuming real importance in; children with cerebral palsy, spina-bifida, clubfoot, muscular dystrophy etc.

(8) It easies labour and return to normal after delivery. It is also useful in gynaecological problems like incontinence, prolepses of uterus, pelvis inflammatory disease.

(9) Sports medicine- A physiotherapist is mandatory for any sport event. He maintains the fitness of sports person and provide first aid in case of various sports injuries.

The aims of Physiotherpy Education

1. To produce the Physiotherapists with basic knowledge and skill.
2. To enable them to recognize the disease, traumatic physical and mental conditions affecting health.
3. Take steps to prevent such disease
4. To treat such diseases scientifically.
5. To be able to recognize and referred patients for the timely intervention of other health care professional specialized in the area of investigation and skilled treatment.
6. Must be capable of undertaking further study and advancing the knowledge and be able with further training to undertake teaching, reaching and practice.

Scope of Physiotherapy

Physical therapists practice in :-

- Hospitals
- Nursing homes
- Residential homes/Rehabilitation centers
- Private Offices/Private practices/Private clinics
- Out-patient clinics

- Community health care centers/Primary health care centers
- Fitness centers/Health clubs
- Occupational Health Centres
- Special schools
- Senior Citizen centers
- Sports centers
- Teaching
- Foreign countries
- Companies
- N.G.O.
- Public settings (e.g. shopping malls)

Courses

(1) Bachelor of Physiotherapy/ B.Sc (Hons.) physical therapy, Duration:- 4 and ½ year (including Internship) Eligibility for Admission- Inter Science with Biology with 50% marks. Process of admission:- Through entrance test. Entrance test will be held in April or May. Age: not less than 17 years.

(2) Master in Physiotherapy (M.P.T.), Duration:- 2 years, Eligibility:- B.P.T. (4 and ½ year) Speciality:- Neurology, Orthopaedic/ Musculoskeletal, Sports, Cardiothoracic and Rehabilitation.

(n) PROSTHETIC AND ORTHOTICS

The Prosthetic and Orthotics Science is an allied Health and Technical Process Industry that addresses the segment of disability due to deformity, genetic mutation, spinalcord injury etc. Today improved materials and recent technologies like CAD/CAM, CNC Carving, Reverse Engineering, Laser scanning are enabling many individuals with disabilities to return to activities they previously enjoyed.

What is P&O Engineering?

- **What is Prosthetic** :

Prosthesis is an artificial replacement or extension of a missing part of the body.

- **What is Orthotics:**

Orthotics is the medical field concerned with the application and manufacture of orthoses devices which support or correct the function of a limb, improve function or relieve symptoms of disease. The word is derived from the Greek "ortho" to straighten.

- Orthotics & Prosthetic Technologists and Technicians are specialists who design, fabricate and fit the orthopaedic braces (Orthoses) and artificial limbs (prostheses) necessary for rehabilitation. Providing Orthotics and prosthetic care involves the application of clinical and technical processes to meet patient rehabilitation objectives. The professionals are experts in polymer processes, strength of materials, material science and applied biomechanical principles to develop and totally customize an Orthoses (brace) or prosthesis (artificial limb).

- **Recent Technology in P&O**: CAD/CAM (Computer –Aided Design/ Computer-Aided Manufacturing) technology is increasingly being used to help design and fabricate models from which Orthoses and prosthetic sockets are produced.

Training & Courses

The courses include classroom and practical sessions in laboratories, where students learn the fundamentals of Manufacturing, Materials, Measuring, CAD/CAM, Medical subjects and fitting of appliances. The range of options available today require the *Prosthetist/ Orthotist* to be well trained and educated to analyse the individual needs of each patient and to develop appropriate recommendations. The courses are aimed at enabling qualified Prosthetists/ Orthotists to work with physicians, therapists and other professionals involved in rehabilitation in a clinical environment. The major Training and Research centre falls under Ministry of Social Justice and Empowerment, State owned and aided rehabilitation institute. After training student may choose to Practice in the Orthotics and/or Prosthetic track. Few National Institutes offering Diploma, Degree, PG and Workshop related for P&O specific program etc. are given in the chart below.

Opportunity

O & P is an profession with a variety of exciting employment opportunities available including O&P practitioners. Technicians and Technologist, Consultants, Assistants and Fitters based on their Educational and experience background. There are numerous NGO's offering lucrative employment and also there are ample of opportunities to work for Companies who manufacture Orthoses or Prosthesis fitting and accessories. Now-a-day's many multinational companies coming up in India to open their modern plants could give good placements. According to experts, a moderate ranked fresher may get salary around 10000 INR.

Few Institutes of National Importance in P&O Engineering

Sl.No.	*Institute*	*Course*
1.	SV NIRTR,Ministry of Social Justice Olatpur, P.O.Bairoi, Cuttack-754010	Dip.in P&O, B.P.&O Engineering
2.	National Institute for Orthopaedically Handicapped, BT Road,Boon Hoogly, Kolkata-700090	B.P.& O Engineering
3.	The Institute for the Physically	B.Sc.(Hon.)-P&O

	Handicapped, Vishnu Digamber Marg, New Delhi-110 002	
4.	The Government Institute of Rehabilitation Medicine, K.K.Nagar, Chennai	Dip.in P&O Engineering
5.	The Department of Rehabilitation Safdarjung Hospital, Ansari Nagar, New Delhi	Dip.in P&O Engineering
6.	The All India Institute of Physical Medicine and Rehabilitation, Hazi Ali Park, Mumbai-400034	B.P. & O Engineering
7.	Central Polytechnic,Taramani, Chennai-600013 Engineering	Dip. In P&O
8.	CTTC (An Indo-Danish) Bhubaneshwar Department of SIDO,Ministry of SSI	Tailor Made Workshop related Course for P&O Specific Program.

(o) SPEECH-LANGUAGE PATHOLOGY AND AUDIOLOGY

SPEECH LANGUAGE PATHOLOGY

Speech language pathology is the study of disorders of speech and language. The field was referred to as "Speech and Hearing" in earlier literature. Speech-language pathologists, sometimes also called speech therapists, assess, diagnose, treat and help prevent speech, language cognitive, communication, voice, swallowing, fluency and other related disorders. They provide a range of services including prevention, identification, evaluation, diagnosis, treatment, teaching, counselling and consultation. They also engage themselves in basic and applied research activities related to human communication and its disorders. They help individuals to prevent and overcome communication problems in language, speech, voice and fluency. They work with people who can not make speech sounds or can not make them clearly; those with speech rhythm and fluency problems, such as stuttering. They also work with people who have swallowing difficulties.

AUDIOLOGY

Audiology is the study of hearing and its problems. An Audiologist measures a person's hearing, diagnosis hearing loss and prescribes a suitable hearing aid whenever necessary. He/she may also be involved in auditory rehabilitation of hearing impaired children and adults. Hearing screening, noise measurement may also be part of an Audiologist's job requirement. Audiologists assess the extent of hearing loss, balance and related disorders and recommend appropriate treatment. These services are provided to people who are deal or hard of hearing and persons at risk of hearing loss due to noise exposure, genetic causes or middle ear infections. Audiologists also work with children and adults who need aural rehabilitation, such as auditory training and speech reading, and educate parents and professionals on the prevention of hearing loss. They provide information and training on all aspects of hearing and balance to other professions including psychology, counselling, rehabilitation and education.

Speech-language pathologists use written and oral tests, as well as special instruments, to diagnose the nature and extent of impairment and to record and analyze speech, language and swallowing irregularities. They develop an individualized plan of care, tailored to each patient's needs. Speech language pathologists help patients develop, or recover, reliable communication skills so that the patients can fulfil their educational, vocational and social roles.

Job Opportunities

There are ample opportunities of getting a good job for a speech language pathologist or an audiologist. They can look for it in educational services, including preschools, elementary and secondary schools and colleges and universities. Others can be absorbed in different hospitals; offices of other health practitioners, including speech language pathologists; nursing care facilities; home healthcare services; individual and family services; outpatient care centres; child day care services; or other such facilities. They are highly paid. A few speech-language pathologists/audiologists can be self-employed in private practice. They can contract to provide services in schools, offices of physicians, hospitals or nursing care facilities or work as consultants to industry.

Most speech-language pathologists provide direct clinical services to individuals with communication or swallowing disorders. In speech and language clinics, they may independently develop and carry out treatment programs. In medical facilities, they may work with physicians, social workers, psychologists and other therapists. In schools, they can develop individual or group programs, counsel parents and may assist teachers with classroom activities. They also work with family members to recognize and change behaviour patterns that impede communication and treatment and show them communication enhancing techniques to use at home. Some speech-language pathologists conduct research on how people communicate. Others design and develop equipment or techniques for diagnosing and treating speech problems.

The number of speech-language pathologists and audiologists in private practice is rising due to the increasing use of contract services by hospitals, schools and nursing care facilities.

Where these professionals can work

- Hospitals
- Public and private schools
- Rehabilitation Centres
- Nursing care facilities
- Community clinics
- Colleges and universities
- Private practice officer
- State and local health departments
- Horne health agencies (home care)
- Long-term care facilities
- Adult day care centres
- Centres for persons with developmental disabilities
- Research laboratories

How to become a speech language pathologist and audiologist

Many colleges and universities offer graduate and post graduate programme in speech-language pathology not in India but also in other parts of the globe. Courses offer ENT, anatomy and physiology of the areas of the body involved in speech, language, swallowing and hearing the development of normal speech, and hearing; the nature of disorders, acoustics and electronics, linguistics and psychological aspects of communication. The course also includes subjects like Community oriented professional practices in speech language pathology and audiology and Basic statistics and research methods. Graduate students learn to evaluate and treat speech, language, swallowing and hearing disorders and at the same time, they also receive supervised clinical training in communication disorders.

Science combination at the Intermediate level is an essential qualification to enter into the graduation course. Most Institutes require a minimum of 50 percent marks in aggregate. The duation of the course is four years for B.Sc (Three years for course work and one year for internship). It comprises both theoretical and practical (clinical) orientation. After completion, they can pursue a M.Sc/M.A. programme in the same field or other associated field such as Linguistics, from whee they can give direction to their career to the field of Academics and research. Others can open up their own clinics or join different hospitals/ clinics and other rehabilitation units. They also become eligible to apply for various job/education in all over the world.

Some Indian Institutes that offer this course (RCI recognized)

- All India Institute of Speech and Hearing Manasagangotri, Mysore
- Ali Yavar Jung National Institute of Hearing Handicapped (AYJNIHH), Bandra Reclamation, Bandra, West, Mumbai
- AYJNIHH, NRC, Kasturba Niketan, Lajpat Nagar-II, New Delhi
- AYJNIHH, SRC, Manovikas Nagar, Secunderabad

- AYJNIHH, CRC, Kolkata
- Post Graduate Institute of Medical Education & Research, Sector-12, Chandigarh
- Nair Charitable Hospital, Dr.A.L.Nair Road, Mumbai
- JSS Medical College, Mysore
- Helen Keller's Institute of Audiology and Speech Language Pathology, Bark Colony, Secunderabad
- Dr.M.V.Shetty Institute of Speech and Hearing, AB Sheth circle, Hampanakatta, Mangalore
- Dr.SRC Institute of Speech and Hearing, Kariyana Palya, Lingarajpuram, Bangalore

(p) UNANI SYSTEM OF MEDICINE

The term Unani is derived from the word "UNAN" which means Greece in Arabic. It was the work of Greek Philosopher-Physician HIPPOCRATES (BUQRAT) (460-377 BC) who freed medicine from the realm of superstition and magic and gave it the status of Science. The theroretical framework of Unani Medicine is based on the teachings of Hippocrates. After Hippocrates, a number of other Greek Scholars enriched the system considerably, of them GALEN (JALINOOS) (131-210AD) stands out as the one who stablilized its foundation, on which Arab Physicians like RHAZES (ALRAZI) (850-925 AD) and AVICENNA (IBN-E-SENA) (980-1037 AD) constructed an imposing edifice.

Unani Medicine got enriched by imbibing what was best in the Contemporary systems of traditional medicine in Egypt, Syria, Iraq, Persia, India, China and other middle East and Far East countries. It also benefitted from the native medical systems in vogue at the time in various parts of Central Asia. That is why this system is known, in different part of the world, with different names such as Graeco-Arab Medicine, Indian Medicine, Arab Medicine, Islamic Medicine, Traditional Medicine and Oriental medicine etc.

Unani system of Medicine was introduced to India by the Arabs. The Delhi Sultans, the Khiljis, the Tughlaqs and the Moghul emperors provided state patronage to the scholars and even enrolled some as state employees and court physicians.

In 1995, the Government set up a full fledged department of Indian Systems of Medicine and Homeopathy (ISM & H) in the Union Ministry of Health & Family Welfare to boost the development of Unani Medicine and other Indian Systems of Medicine. The Department of (ISM and H) has recently been renamed as Department of Ayurveda, Yoga and Naturopathy, Unani, Siddha and Homoepathy (AYUSH). At present Unani System of Medicine, with its own recognized practitioners, hospitals educationalf and research institutions form an integral part of the national health care delivery system.

The Humors

The humoral theory presuposes the presence of four humors – Dam (Blood), Balgham(Phlegm), Safra(Yellow Bile) and Sauda (Black Bile) in the body. The temperaments of persons are expressed by the words, Sanguine, Phlegmatic, choleric and melancholic according to the preponderance in them of the respective hyumors-blood, phlegm, yellow bile and black bile, respectively. The humors themselves are assigned temperaments; blood is hot and moist, phlegm is cold and moist , yellow bile hot and dry and black bile cold and dry.

Every person is supposed to have a unique humoral constitution, which represents his healthy state. And to maintain the correct humoral balance there is a power of self preservation or adjustment called *Quwwat-e-Mudabbira* (Medicatrix Naturae) in the body. If this power weakens, imbalance in the humoral composition is bound to occur and this causes disease. In Unani Medicine, great reliance is place on this power. The Medicines used in this system, in fact, help the body regain this power to an optimum level and thereby restore humoral balance, thus retaining health. Also correct diet and digestion are considered to maintain humoral balance.

Diagnosis

Another distinctive feature of the Unani System of Medicine is its emphasis on diagnosing a disease through *nabz* (Pulse), a rhythmic expansion of Arteries, which is felt by fingers. Other methods of diagnosis include examination of *baul* (Urine) and *baraj* (Stool) etc.

Therapeutics

In Unani System of Medicine, various types of treatment are employed such as *Ilaj-bit-Tadbeer* (Regimental Therapy), *Ilaj-Bil—Ghiza* (Dietotherapy), *Ilaj-Bid-Dawa*(Pharmacotherapy) and *Jarahat* Surgery).

Regimental therapy includes Venesection, Cupping, Diaphoresis, Diuresis, Turkish bath, Massage, Cauterization, Purging, Emesis, Exercise and leeching etc. Dietotherapy aims at treating certain ailments by administration of specific diets or by regulating the quantity and quality of food.

Pharmacotherapy deals with the use of naturally occuring drugs, mostly herbal, though drugs of animal and mineral origin are also used in Unani Medicine. Similarly surgery has also been in use in this system for quite long. Infact the ancient physicians of Unani Medicine were pioneers in this field and has developed their own insteruments and techniques.

Infrastructre

There are 39 undergraduate colleges imparting education in Unani System and five Postgraduate college imparting training in nine postgraduate disciplines/departments. These colleges have a total admission capacity of about 1,505 students per year for undergraduate courses. They are either Government Institutions or set up by voluntary organisations. All these educational institutes are affiliated to different Universities.

Post Graduate Education and research facilities are available in the subjects of *iimal Advia* (Pharmacology), *Moalijat* (Medicine), *Kulliyat* (Basic Principles),*Hifzan-e-Sehat* (Hygiene), *Tashreeh* (Anatomy), *Jarahiyat* (Surgery), *Qabala-Wo-Amarz-E-Niswan* (Obstetrics & Gynaecology), *Amraz-e-Atfal* (Paediatrics). The National Institute of Unani Medicine (NIUM) Bangalore, was set up by Government of India in collaboration of the Government of Karnataka. A principal institution of Unani Medicine in the Country, the NIUM is being developed as a demonstrable model of Graduate, Post-Graduate teaching, training and research in the system.

Indian Medicines Pharmaceutical Corporation Limited (IMPCL) MOHAN UP a Government of India undertaking is engaged in the manufacture of Unani drugs.

Education

Medical Education in Unani System is recognized by the Government of India. Five and a half year course is conducted for the award of Bachelor of Unani Medicine and Surgery (BUMS), Post Graduate Course in Unani Medicine is of Three (MD) years duration. Facilities for research are also available in Unani Colleges. The education and training facilities in Unani System of Medicines are presently being monitored by the Central Council of India Medicine(CCIM) which is a statutory body.

The Centre Council for Research in Unani Medicine (CCRUM) was established in the year 1978 and started functioning independently as an autonomous organization of the Ministry of Health and Family Welfare, Govt. of India from Jan. 1979 with the objective of undertaking Multiface-ted research activities in Unani Medicine.

Those who have qualified Higher Secondary Certificate Course (10 + 2) with Science group can get admission in BUMS Course through common medical entrance test which is conducted by State and National level and BUMS qualification is must to get admission in PG Course by P.G. Entrance Test (MD).

Job Opportunities

There are so many job opportunities for those who have obtained degree in Unani System of Medicine which depends upon their qualification, experience and marks. They can get jobs in Unani Hospitals, State and Central Govt. Dispensaries., Pvt.Nursing Homes, Health Departments, Unani Pharmacies, Research Centres as a Research Officers, Medical Officers, Unani Hakeems, Pharmacists and teaching lines like Lecturers, Readers and Professors. Also can practice Unani Medicine as a Hakeem, Tabeeb (Unani Physician) or Consultant.

Following are the some academic institutions and colleges that conduct both undergraduate and post graduate courses in Unani System of Medicine in India:-

(1) Government Nizamia Tibbia(Unani Medical) College and General Hospital, Charminar, Hyderabad-500 002(AP)

(2) Hakeem Ajmal Khan Tibbia (Unani Medical) College, Aligarh Muslim University, Aligarh-202 002 (UP)

(3) National Institute of Unani Medicine (NIUM) Kottigepalya, Magadi Main Road, Bangalore-921 (KA)

(4) Ayurvedic and Unani Tibbia College, Ajmal Khan Road, Karol Bagh, New Delhi

(5) Unani Medical College, Faculty of Medicine, Jamia Hamdard, hamdard Nagar, New Delhi-110 062

(6) MIJ Unani Medical College & H.R.R.K. Hospital, Yarid Road, Versowa, Andheri(W), Mumbai-61

(7) Z.V.M. Unani Medical College and Hospital, K.B. Hidayatullah Road, New Modikhana, Camp, Pune-411 001

Despite the dramatic advances of conventional medicine, it is clear that herbal medicine has much to offer. Today, herbal medicines are coming back in to prominence. Unani medicine often compliments conventional treatments, providing safe, well tolerated remedies for chronic illness.

16

Operating

(a) CALL CENTRES

The fastest growing sector in the Indian IT Industry-both in terms of the number of people being hired and revenues generated- is the IT-enabled services segment comprising call centres and Business Process Outsourcing (ITES-BPO) sector. This sector added 70,000 jobs in the last financial year, according to NASSCOM, the industry body of software and service companies in India. IT-enabled services are support functions and services for customers provided either through the telephone or through web-based channels. BPOs are companies which provide similar functions and services but not from the country where the products have been sold. NASSCOM also estimates that by 2008, there will be 2,70,000 jobs in the customer interaction services sector. According to the US consultant Mckinsey & Co., the bulk of these BPO jobs are going to be generated by MNCs like IBM (which owns Daksh), Convergys, Accenture, GE, Citibank and HSBC. Other big players I this industry include Wipro Spectramind, ICICI One Source, 24/7 Customer.com. So what is a call centre job all about and why is it becoming a dram job for thousands of young people- many of whom are not even graduates?

There are various types of call centres. A company can set up its own call centre to deal with its own customers (i.e. a captive call centre) or it can hire a professional firm (i.e. a third party call centre) to do the job for it. Function-wise too, they are divided into inbound and outbound call centres. Outbound call centres are places from where operators- or customer service associates, as they are called- make calls to existing or prospective customers. Take, for example, a cell phone company. Part of its outbound call centre operations could be involved in locating and convincing prospective customers to take a new connection. This is also called telemarketing and is a widespread method used to sell everything from insurance policies, bank loans, credit cards and mutual funds to special offers on pizzas! Some outbound call centres also do market research to create and update databases of customers for other companies. Yet another function is to make reminder calls (e.g. Follow up on overdue payments, or to update information about the customer). At an inbound call centre, the process is reversed and a associates take calls from existing or prospective customers. Nowadays companies advertise toll free numbers that you can call for a variety of reasons. For example, a person can call to find out about a certain product- say, a printer. The person answering the call has access to all the relevant information on a computer. So the call centre associate will be able to tell the caller everything from the listed price of the printer, the showroom nearest the caller's home or office where it can be purchased, the cost of the cartridge, the number of pages it can print per minute, etc. Another toll-free number could be a technical helpline. The owner of a similar printer can call to say he has a problem with his printer. The associate taking th call will then guide the customer through various methods to fix the problem, failing which, he will advise the customer to take it to the nearest service centre and offer him details of the same.

Call centres can also be classified into domestic and international. In the former, you work for an India-based company and deal with its customers alone. The work done would depend on whether it was an inbound or an outbound call centre. An international call centre deals with foreign customers of a foreign company. That's when the associate may have to pretend to be somebody with a foreign name and pretend to live in the country where the customers are based! The caller may phone from a local number in the USA or the UK but his call will be instantaneously routed to a call centre in India. He won't know this has happened since his call will be answered by someone with a Western name and an appropriate accent and who is familiar with his culture and geography. In every case, maintaining a cordial relationship with the customer at all times is the key to success in this job. Employees are also expected to maintain the highest levels of quality and compliance.

The selection process for the job of a call centre associate, therefore, is fairly stringent. Since the bulk of growth is happening in the BPO category, fluency in English is an absolute must. It doesn't matter that you're aiming for a technical support job, if you are going to talk to a customer, your English has to be flawless. And it's not just the grammar, the way you talk should be devoid of any regional accent or MTI- mother tongue influence. This, in turn, has let to a rash of English training institutes springing up across the country. These institutes offer courses that will improve not only your grammar but also help you acquire an accent that doesn't advertise your linguistic background!! Some companies train employees to talk with an American or British accent but the focus has shifted to a neutral accent, i.e. no accent at all. This is because people everywhere now know that such services are being outsourced and Indian call centres have acquired a significant degree of respectability. The final thing on the must-have list is the willingness to work night shifts and on Sundays since most call centres work 24 X 7. Provided you satisfy the above criteria, and are called for an inteview, remember that there are several elimination rounds. The next step is to answer a written test. This could be anything- from a simple English test with analytical reasoning thrown in, or a complex technical aptitude test, or both. Some firms also administer psychometric tests. The next stages include a group discussion (where applicants are judged for their ability to talk clearly and with noise) and a listening comprehension test (to judge listening skills). If you pass, you will have at least two rounds of personal interviews. Once you're hired, you will receive training before you go live.

As with every industry, there are some down sides to working in call centres. Some people face health problems because of the rotational cycle of day and night shifts. Others face psychological problems because they're pretending to be somebody else. The most common complaint is the effect on family and social life since a call centre employee is often working when the rest of his family is eating dinner or socialising. These problems, however, don't seem to be deterring the increasing numbers of young people making a beeline for English courses so that they can become part of the 425 call centres in India, growing at an amazing rate of 40% this year. With smaller cities and town being targeted in the next phase of growth, the industry is set to make a presence all across India.

CALL CENTRE HOTSPOTS- Bangalore, Gurgaon, New Delhi, Mumbai, Pune, Hyderabad, Chennai(Smaller town to be added soon)

ESSENTIAL QUALIFICATIONS

Minimum Class XII, graduates preferred BCA,BSc(Comp.Sc) can apply for technical support jobs. Some firms take BE or Btech graduates too.

ESSENTIAL SKILLS

Excellent English, spoken with a neutral accent.

JOB REQUIREMENTS

Most call centres offer 24/7 support and function round the clock. Willingness to work night shifts is a must.

STARTING SALARY

In Metros- the salary for fresher is anywhere between Rs.8,000 to 10,000 pm plus benefits. People in marketing get sales-based incentives.

GROWTH PROSPECTS

With six months' experience you can get another job and a hike of Rs.1,000-3,000.

MOVING UP THE LADDER

With two years' experience, you can become Team Leader, Voice Coach or Quality Analyst etc. with a salary of above Rs.15,000 pm. Managerial positions are also available after a few more years.

MOVING SIDEWAYS

You can also apply for vacancies in other departments.

(b) CAMERA OPERATORS

Description

Operate process camera and related darkroom equipment to photograph and develop negatives of material to be printed.

Experience

A minimum of two to four years of work-related skill, knowledge, or experience is needed for these occupations.

Education

Most of these occupations require a bachelor's degree, but some do not.

Training

Employees in these occupations usually need several years of work-related experience, on-the-job training, and/or vocational training.

Tasks

1. Immerses film in series of chemical baths to develop images and hangs film on rack to dry.
2. Feeds film into automatic film processor that develops, fixes, washes, and dries film.
3. Exposes high-contrast film for predetermined exposure time.
4. Adjusts camera settings, lights, and lens.
5. Selects and installs screens and filters in camera to produce desired effects.
6. Measures density of continuous tone images to be photographed to set exposure time for halftone images.
7. Mounts material to be photographed on copyboard of camera.

8. Performs exposure tests to determine line, halftone, and color reproduction exposure lengths for various photographic factors.
9. Measures original layouts and determines proportions needed to make reduced or enlarged photographic prints for pasteup.

(c) COMPUTER OPERATOR

Description

Monitor and control electronic computer and peripheral electronic data processing equipment to process business, scientific, engineering, and other data according to operating instructions. May enter commands at a computer terminal and set controls on computer and peripheral devices. Monitor and respond to operating and error messages.

Experience

Previous work-related skill, knowledge, or experience is required for these occupations.

Education

Most occupations in this zone require training in vocational schools, related on-the-job experience, or an associate's degree. Some may require a bachelor's degree.

Training

Employees in these occupations usually need one or two years of training involving both on-the-job experience and informal training with experienced workers.

Tasks

1. Enters commands to clear computer system and start operation, using keyboard of computer terminal.
2. Loads peripheral equipment with selected materials for operating runs or oversees loading of peripheral equipment by peripheral equipment operators.
3. Observes peripheral equipment operation and error messages displayed on terminal monitor to detect faulty output or machine stoppage.
4. Reads job set-up instructions to determine equipment to be used and order of use.
5. Notifies supervisor of errors or equipment stoppage.
6. Answers telephone calls to assist computer users encountering problems.
7. Enters commands, using computer terminal, and activates controls on computer and peripheral equipment to integrate and operate equipment.
8. Assists workers in classifying, cataloging, and maintaining tapes.

9. Clears equipment at end of operating run and reviews schedule to determine next assignment.
10. Diagnoses reasons for equipment malfunction and enters commands to correct error or stoppage and resume operations.
11. Separates output, when needed, and sends data to specified users.

Records information, such as computer operating time and problems that occurred, such as downtime, and actions taken.

(d) DUPLICATING MACHINE OPERATORS

Description

Operate one of a variety of office machines such as photocopying, photographic, mimeograph, and duplicating machines to make copies.

Experience

No Previous work-related skill, knowledge, or experience is needed for these occupations. For example, a person can become a general office clerk even if he/she has worked in an office before.

Education

These occupations may require a high school/diploma certificate. Some may require a formal training course to obtain a license.

Training

Employees in these occupations need anywhere from a few days to a few months of training. Usually, an experienced worker could show you how to do the job.

Tasks

1. Cuts copies apart and writes identifying information on copies.
2. Loads machine with blank paper or film and places paper roll in holding tray or rack of machine.
3. Cleans and oils machine and printing plate.
4. Adjusts machine to regulate ink flow, speed, paper size, focus, exposure, and camera distance from document.
5. Places original copy in feed tray, feeds originals into feed rolls, or positions originals on table beneath camera lens.
6. Selects type, embossed plate, or paper stock according to size, color, thickness, and quantity specified.
7. Sets controls for number of copies and presses buttons to start machine.
8. Records number of copies made.

Moves heat unit and clamping frame over screen bed to form Braille impression on page.

17

Publishing

(a) DESKTOP PUBLISHERS

Description

Format typescript and graphic elements using computer software to produce publication-ready material.

Experience

A minimum of two to four years of work-related skill, knowledge, or experience is needed for these occupations.

Education

Most of these occupations require a bachelor's degree, but some do not.

Training

Employees in these occupations usually need several years of work-related experience, on-the-job training, and/or vocational training.

Tasks

1. Loads floppy disks or tapes containing information into system.
2. Activates options, such as masking or text processing.
3. Enters data, such as coordinates of images and color specifications, into system to retouch and make color corrections.
4. Activates options, such as masking, pixel (picture element) editing, airbrushing, or image retouching.
5. Studies layout or other instructions to determine work to be done and sequence of operations.

6. Enters digitized data into electronic prepress system computer memory, using scanner, camera, keyboard, or mouse.
7. Saves completed work on floppy disks or magnetic tape.
8. Views monitors for visual representation of work in progress and for instructions and feedback throughout process.
9. Enters data, such as background color, shapes, and coordinates of images; and retrieves data from system memory.
10. Creates special effects, such as vignettes, mosaics, and image combining.

(b) ELECTRONIC MEDIA

A career in electronic media offers unlimited exciting opportunities. From broadcasting production, to animation, to video game design, to digital and film editing, there are numerous ways to make your electronic media career creative and exciting.

With video games one of the top entertainment sources for youth and adults, there is an increasing opportunity for the video game savvy and creative types to enter the field of video game design and production. The job market for these positions is competitive, so it's worth the time to invest in a solid degree program to give you the skills you need to be considered for employment. Today, a number of universities and media institutions are offering degree and diploma programs in Electronic Media having specialization in Camera, Editing, Anchoring, Production and Design. A formal education in electronic media will teach you the software programs that the industry uses and will also give you the opportunity to start experimenting with creation.

A Degree in Computer graphics can help you enter the electronic media field in a number of ways. You may become a graphic designer and specialize in web design and online marketing or by having a major in digital art you may use your talents to develop CD-ROMs, video games, and web sites. As a digital artist, one can develop his/her skills with software programs and may also learn illustration and graphic design techniques.

There are also digital and editing opportunities in the film industry. There are also editing and production opportunities in the television industry. Broadcast news, television sitcoms and animated commercials or shows all require editing.

Your education will give you hands-on experience in design, editing and animation techniques while also providing you with the opportunity to test your skills and find the electronic media career that suits you best.

Creativity

People with creativity excellent communication skills and a zest to do something different, can build a satisfying and rewarding career for them in the electronic media. Besides, the well known TV journalists, news analysts and TV artists, the advent of –FM radio took radio jockeying and production to new heights. These are, few of the front line popular jobs which the media offers.

In addition, there is a range of behind-the-scene jobs such as handling cameras, sound recording, script writing editing, production etc. These are equally interesting and lucrative.With so many players in the field there is a dearth of manpower. So what one needs to have apart from an innate aptitude for these jobs is sound knowledge and training.

Many universities like Bangalore University, Guru Jambheswar University, Hissar, Devi Ahilya Bai University, Indore, Makhanlal Chaturvedi National University of Journalism, Bhopal and media institutions like Indian Institute of Mass Communication, New Delhi, Symbiosis Institute of Mass Communication, Pune and others are offering both degree and diploma program in electronic media. Most of these media departments of universities and institutes have their own studios having studio cameras, field cameras, digital VCD/DVD players, recorders, edit controllers, special effect switchers, studio monitors for post-production, channel audio mixers, preview monitors and non linear editing systems.

Eligibility

Graduates from any stream can join the courses in electronic media offered by universities and media institutions. Mostly, an entrance examination is held to select the candidates. In most entrance examinations, there is a Written Test based on current affairs and language followed by Group Discussion and Personal Interview. Courses in electronic media are job-oriented, self financed courses thus having limited seats. Since, media has a huge responsibility as an instrument of social change and public awareness, most media institutions strictly emphasizes on the academic background, communication skill, creativity, command over the language and talent while considering them for admission.

(c) E-PUBLISHING

With a qualification in publishing, you can get into print publishing or epublishing. Most courses in publishing are offered at the post-graduate level for which you require a basic degree in any discipline. An aspirant can also train on the job. You don't need any special qualifications to enter this field but must have knowledge of publishing software. If you're looking for a job in print, Quark Express/ Pagemaker will come in handy. As for a job in the Internet media, knowledge of Macro media/ Fireworks will make your prospects brighter.

You can also consider a career in desktop publishing, which involves editing, designing, laying out and typesetting manuscripts or work in the multimedia department of a publishing house. Shankar's Institute of Book Publishing and the Federation of Publishers and Book Sellers run short courses in publishing in Delhi.

(d) WORD PROCESSORS AND TYPISTS

Description

Use word processor/computer or typewriter to type letters, reports, forms, or other material from rough draft, corrected copy, or voice recording. May perform other clerical duties as assigned.

Experience

Some previous work-related skill, knowledge, or experience may be helpful in these occupations, but usually is not needed.

Education

These occupations usually require a high school diploma and may require some vocational training or job-related course work. In some cases, an associate's or bachelor's degree could be needed.

Training

Employees in these occupations need anywhere from a few months to one year of working with experienced employees.

Tasks

1. Keeps records of work performed.
2. Sorts and distributes mail.
3. Gathers and arranges material to be typed, following instructions.
4. Addresses envelopes or prepares envelope labels, using typewriter or computer.
5. Collates pages of reports and other documents prepared.
6. Adjusts settings for format, page layout, line spacing, and other style requirements.
7. Checks completed work for spelling, grammar, punctuation, and format.
8. Answers telephone.
9. Operates duplicating machine.
10. Computes and verifies totals on report forms, requisitions, or bills, using adding machine or calculator.
11. Types from recorded dictation.
12. Uses data-entry device, such as optical scanner, to input data into computer for revision or editing.

13. Types from rough draft, corrected copy, or previous version displayed on screen, using computer or typewriter.
14. Stores completed documents on computer hard drive or data storage medium, such as disk.
14. Transcribes stenotyped notes of court proceedings.
15. Transmits work electronically to other locations.
16. Files and stores completed documents.
17. Prints and makes copy of work.

18

Secretarial Profession

(a) COMPANY SECRETARY

Career as a Company Secretary is not only prestigious and financially rewarding but also carries with it a high degree of job satisfaction.

The Institute of Company Secretaries of India develops and regulates the profession of Company Secretaries in India.

There are three stages to be pursued to qualify as a Company Secretary.

FOUNDATION COURSE	5 PAPERS
INTERMEDIATE COURSE	8 PAPERS
FINAL COURSE	9 PAPERS

The Company Secretary Course is by Correspondence with provision for Optional Oral Coaching classes.

- For Foundation Course the minimum qualification is 10+2 or equivalent in any stream except Fine Arts.
- For Intermediate Course the minimum qualification is CS Foundation Pass or Graduation in any discipline, Arts/Science/ Commerce except Fine Arts.
- The Final Examination is after passing the Intermediate Course.
- 16 month Management Training is to be undergone after passing the Inter/Final examination or Practical experience.
- The ICSI and its Regional Councils and Chapters offer Placement Services to Members and Students. A qualified Company Secretary has openings both in Employment and in Practice.

Functions of a Company Secretary

A Company Secretary is:

- An expert in Company, Corporate and Securities Laws

- A Vital link between the company and its:
  - Board of Directors
  - Shareholders
  - Government and Regulatory Authorities
- A conscience seeker of the company
- A compliance officer of the company
- Corporate Planner and Strategic Manager

Employment Prospects

- A qualified company secretary has openings in Employment and as a Practising Independent Professional

Company Secretary in Employment

- Companies with a paid up share are compulsorily required to appoint a whole-time Company Secretary.
- All companies seeking listing on Stock Exchange are required to appoint a whole-time company secretary.
- Membership of the Institute is recognized for appointment to superior posts and services under Central Government.
- Membership of the Institute is an essential qualification for recruitment from Grade I to Grade IV in the Accounts branch of the Indian Company Law Service.

Prospects for a CS with the boom in IT Industry

A Company Secretary is a knowledge professional with a research bent of mind acquired through rigorous training in corporate laws and corporate management. The syllabus for the course also grills him in Information Systems and Systems Audit. As such, Company Secretaries are well versed in Information Technology as well as ITES. With his procedure orientation and mastery, Company Secretary is able to set up the EOU shop for IT and BPO industries cost efficiently. He is also well versed in foreign collaboration and joint venture agreements as well as intellectual property rights. This enables him to add value to IT or BPO subsidiaries of foreign companies in India as well as the takeover activities by Indian corporates in foreign countries in IT and ITES sectors.

As knowledge professional well versed in Indian Laws, judicial decisions as well as laws of countries with which Indian IT and ITES industry deals. Knowledge Process Outsourcing is the industry of the future with a business volumes expected by India alone from US of the order of USD 12 billion over the next five years.

Company Secretaries willing to establish themselves in the IT sector should acquire knowledge and skills in intellectual property management for the IT companies who would move up the value chain.

Technical skills in IT industry become outdated very fast. In this situation, Company Secretaries should also acquire continuous upgradation in their knowledge and skills particularly in the skill-sets required for corss cultural negotiations between India and the country of the collaborator or the customer of the IT company, both for vertical cross border integration as well as customer delight.

Opportunities abroad for CS

Many Company Secretaries are already working in various countries like the US, Canada, UK, Singapore, Malaysia, Thailand, Australia, New Zealand, Middle-east, Africa etc. With their research and legal bent of mind, their employers have recognized their professional skill sets. They also possess managerial capabilities and analytical skills.

After the globalization of services the field is opening in various countries for practicing Company Secretaries as well. India is entering into bilateral Comprehensive Economic Cooperation Agreements with countries like Singapore, Malaysia, Thailand and Mauritius etc. These agreements recognize Company Secretaries for free movement of professionals across borders. ICSI has entered into an MOU with the Institute of Chartered Secretaries and Administrators, UK. This MOU recognizes Company Secretaries of both the countries on certain conditions. The process of globalization and the process of comprehensive economic cooperation that India is initiating has also set in motion mutual recognition agreements between the ICSI and Institutes governing the profession in various other countries. This is opening up the world to Company Secretaries.

CS Course going online (virtual classroom)

Today the education for Company Secretary course is through postal and oral coaching. This deprives students from semi urban and rural areas of touch with expert faculties. In the web-based e-learning module, students will be able to learn about the subject at their desk top. They can, at their convenience, send their responses for evaluation and feedback by faculties. Faculties can give online suggestions for improvement. The virtual class room module would be launched by the end of this year. In this module students can attend classes at computer centers near their locations and interact live with the faculty on screen. This will create a hi-tech yet easy learning environment for students in all nooks and corners of the country.

Placement Services

The Institute is providing placement services to the members. As a part of the service, the Institute maintains a databank of the members registered for the placement and a list of suitable candidates is provided to the employers on request. The biodata of the members are also available on the website of the Institute for surfing by the prospective employers, who can shortlist the candidates suiting their requirements from the website itself. The vacancies for the post of Company Secretaries received in the Institute are also placed on the website for reference by the members seeking placement or change in employment. A placement folder is also maintained for reference by the members visiting the institute for placement. The members can also upload their biodata directly on the website. Similar services are also provided by the Regional Councils and Chapters located in the various parts of the country.

It may also be mentioned that the members of the Institute are occupying prestigious positions such as Managing Director, Executive Director and Vice President etc. Some of the members are occupying senior positions in the Government departments and regulatory bodies. There are ample opportunities for the members to go for practice independently.

Self Employment Practice

- After obtaining a "Certificate of Practice" from the Institute, Members of the Institute can go in for Independent Practice.
- Every company having a paid up share capital of Rs. Ten Lakhs or more but less than Rs. 2 crores is required to engage the services of a Secretary in Whole-Time Practice for issue of Compliance Certificate.

Company Secretary as independent professional

- A Company Secretary practice is recognized to issue certificates and attest documents under:
  - Companies Act, 1956
  - SEBT Act, SCRA and regulations etc. made there under Depositories Act
  - Exim Policy

Company Secretaries in Practice also render the following Services:

- Legal, Secretarial and Corporate Governance
- Corporate Restructuring
- Foreign Collaborations and Joint Ventures
- Arbitration and Conciliation
- Financial Management
- Project Planning
- Capital Market and Investor Relations

- Due Diligence
- Corporate Advisory Services

Membership

- After qualifying the Final examination and on completion of training as provided under the regulations, a candidate is admitted as an Associate Member of the Institute and can use the letters "ACS" after his/her name.

Further Academic Pursuits

The CS Course is recognized by the various Universities for admission to PhD Course appointment of Lecturers utilization of services of members by various professional/educational bodies for academic activities. ICSI conducts Post Membership Qualification (PMQ) Course in Corporate Governance for its members. For further details, kindly log on www.icsi.edu

(b) SECRETARIAL WORK

A Secretary is usually attached to an Executive and relied upon to make certain minor decisions in his/her absence or while he/she is busy. The work differs from organisation to organisation depending upon the Executive (to whom a Secretary is attached), the nature of the Executive's work/job. The work environment is most comfortable and a secretary usually enjoys all the amenities and status linked to the status of the boss.

Secretaries may be referred to as Personal Assistants, Private Secretaries or Executive Secretaries. They are responsible for a variety of administrative and clerical duties necessary to run an office efficiently.

The have a general understanding of the pattern of the business and a more detailed grasp of the work of their own organisation. Secretaries are competent professionals who take pride in their work and dedicate themselves to excellence. They are an important member of the management team of an organisation, responsible for carrying out the Executive's wishes and helping to maintain a well organised and smoothly functioning office.

A good secretary is supposed to be indispensable no matter what the areas of work are. Secretaries are expected to relieve the boss of as much routine work as possible trying to anticipate the boss's wishes and actions and, in general, acting as a buffer between his/ her work and those who lay claim to his/her time. Good Secretaries are to be in the background ensuring that everything goes well, that their bosses do not forget anything. However, they should not expect to be given credit if they do their job right.

The Work

A Secretary' work could include preparing agendas for meetings, collecting documents to support the various items, and distributing them to the people concerned. Usually secretaries write some letters, memos etc on their own, draft some for the boss's approval and signature, summarize lengthy reports and incoming letters for them.

They may be required to take dictation. Their work may also involve making travel arrangements, arranging meetings for busy people, keeping an appointment diary/ directory, taking minutes during meetings. Handling telephone calls is a basic responsibility.

A variety of office equipment such as facsimile machines, photocopiers and telephone systems are aids for secretaries. Observing telephone etiquette is an important part of the work.

Today, secretaries are increasingly using personal computers to compose correspondence, manage databases and create reports and documents via desktop publishing and using digital graphics.

Specialised secretaries such as legal and medical secretaries perform highly specialised work requiring knowledge of professional terminology and procedures.

Skills Set

Good interpersonal skills are required as secretaries must be tactful in their dealing with people. Self Confidence and organizing ability coupled with willingness to take orders and responsibility are useful traits for secretarial careers. A logical and analytical mind, discretion, good judgement, a social temperament, organisational and management ability, initiative, business acumen (for those who with to progress to executive cadre) and the ability to work independently. A keen desire to be of use and indifference to blame or lack of appreciation are useful attributes for a secretary. Time management is a basic skill to be acquired and / or enhanced.

Secretaries must be good at spelling, punctuation, grammar, oral communication and proficient on the keyboard. Employers are increasingly interested in secretaries who have knowledge of software applications such as word processing, spread sheets and database management.

Proper office manner, formal clothing and good business etiquette should be the hallmark of a professional secretary.

Tool Box

Just as any craftsman has a tool box, so should an efficient secretary. A big dictionary and a handy one, directories, time tables of rail, air, bus and waterway, information on postal/ courier/ freight rates, rules etc. Have an updated visiting cards folder, note changes in telephone numbers, addresses and changes of employers of visitors for your boss.

Training

It is relatively easy to enter the secretarial profession. A high school (plus two or equivalent) education, typing, shorthand, machine transcription and filing skills and knowledge of office procedures, word processing and computer equipment and software packages offer good prospects in the profession.

Secretarial Practice courses are conducted by polytechnics (rune by government and other bodies), vocational training institutes and Institutes of Commercial Practice. Training in office automation and use of the latest software packages is currently important. If the course does not include these aspects, a trained secretary should undergo such training separately.

Professional secretarial training is usually spread over 1-2 years (full time or part time) and may be undertaken after 10+2 level of education, although some places admit students after successful completion of matriculation or equivalent examination. Training after 10+2 level of education is advisable for maturity and confidence. Those who plan on movement upto the executive cadre should aim to complete a bachelor's degree either alongside secretarial training or through distance education with a job.

Foreign language skills, legal education, graduation in science/ tourism etc. could be useful for those who wish to join the profession in a specific industry.

Institutions

1. YWCA of Delhi, Women's Training Institute, Bangla Sahib Lane, New Delhi-110 001
2. YMCA of Nizamuddin, Nizamuddin East, Delhi-110 013
3. College of Vocational Studies, Triveni(Sheikh Sarai)-II, New Delhi-110 017
4. South Delhi Polytechnic for Women, Behind Lady Shri Ram College, Lajpat Nagar IV, New Delhi-110 024
5. Polytechnic for Women, A-3 South Extension I, Ring Road, New Delhi-110 049
6. The Stenographer's Guild, No.1, Guild Street, T.Nagar, Chennai-600 017
7. Davar's College, Mumbai
8. Department of Training and Technical Education, Muni Maya Ram Marg, Pitampura, Delhi-110 088
9. National Vocational Training Institute (NVTI) for Women, Sector-I, NOIDA-201301
10. Regional Vocational Training Institute (RVTI) for Women, 5, New Katra Road, Allahabad-211 002
11. RVTI for Women, CP/16 Block, Sector V, Salt Lake City, Kolkata-700 091

12. RVTI for Women, Kashi Nath Dhuru Street, Dadar W, Mumbai-400 028
13. City & Guilds (www.city-and-guilds.co.uk) This is an indicative listing. For local information of such courses in every state/town, contact-University/College/Vocational Training Institute
14. Directorate of Vocational Education and Training for your region.
15. Private vocational training institutes, Women's Polytechnics.

Placement Prospects

Qualified secretaries can have their pick of jobs especially in cities with vibrant corporate activity. Financial centres and cities with head offices of different corporations offer more lucrative jobs.

Secretaries with foreign language skills would be invaluable in international organizations, consulate/ embassy offices, certain industries and firms/ industries translating firms etc.

In the government and public sector undertakings, the intake of secretarial staff is usually in the form of clerical/ assistant cadre recruitment. For those with shorthand and typing skills and at least Plus Two, competitive examinations conducted by the Staff Selection Commission are relevant. Opportunities for progress into junior management cadres are possible for those who apply with a bachelor's degree, but they need to try for this while they are before thirty years of age.

Office automation and machine dictation have revolutionised the type of work done by a secretary. Changes are expected to continue. Personal Computers, electronic mail, scanners and voice message systems now allow secretaries to be better time managers and they can accomplish more in the same amount of time.

The current trend of managers and professionals handling their own correspondence directly rather than through secretaries could lead to the decline in the overall number of secretaries. Office technology could lead to further decline. However, many secretarial duties and responsibilities are interactive, involving planning, coordination, transmitting staff instructions, etc. which can not be automated. As a result, secretaries would continue to be key players in most organisations into the future.

(c) SECRETARIES EXCEPT LEGAL, MEDICAL AND EXECUTIVE

Description

Perform routine clerical and administrative functions such as drafting correspondence, scheduling appointments, organizing and maintaining paper and electronic files, or providing information to callers.

Experience

Some previous work-related skill, knowledge, or experience may be helpful in these occupations, but usually is not needed.

Education

These occupations usually require a high school diploma and may require some vocational training or job-related course work. In some cases, an associate's or bachelor's degree could be needed.

Training

Employees in these occupations need anywhere from a few months to one year of working with experienced employees.

Tasks

1. Greets and welcomes visitors, determines nature of business, and conducts visitors to employer or appropriate person.
2. Locates and attaches appropriate file to incoming correspondence requiring reply.
3. Collects and disburses funds from cash account and keeps records.
4. Compiles and maintains lists and records, using typewriter or computer.
5. Provides customer services such as order placement and account information.
6. Files correspondence and other records.
7. Schedules appointments.
8. Answers telephone and gives information to callers, takes messages, or transfers calls to appropriate individuals.
9. Mails newsletters, promotional material, and other information.
10. Takes dictation in shorthand or by machine and transcribes information.
11. Compiles and types statistical reports, using typewriter or computer.
12. Answers routine correspondence.
13. Orders and dispenses supplies.
14. Composes and distributes meeting notes, correspondence, and reports.
15. Opens incoming mail and routes mail to appropriate individuals.
16. Makes copies of correspondence and other printed matter.
17. Prepares and mails checks.
18. Records and types minutes of meetings, using typewriter or computer.
19. Maintains calendar and coordinates conferences and meetings.
20. Arranges travel schedules and reservations.

(d) MEDICAL SECRETARIES

Description

Perform secretarial duties utilizing specific knowledge of medical terminology and hospital, clinic, or laboratory procedures. Duties include scheduling appointments, billing patients, and compiling and recording medical charts, reports, and correspondence.

Experience

Previous work-related skill, knowledge, or experience is required for these occupations.

Education

Most occupations in this zone require training in vocational schools, related on-the-job experience, or an associate's degree. Some may require a bachelor's degree.

Training

Employees in these occupations usually need one or two years of training involving both on-the-job experience and informal training with experienced workers.

Tasks

1. Prepares and transmits patients' bills.
2. Transmits correspondence and medical records by mail, e-mail, or fax.
3. Greets visitors, ascertains purpose of visits, and directs to appropriate staff.
4. Maintains medical records and correspondence files.
5. Routes messages and documents such as laboratory results to appropriate staff.
6. Transcribes recorded messages and practitioner's diagnosis and recommendations into patient's medical record.
7. Compiles and records medical charts, reports, and correspondence, using typewriter or personal computer.
8. Answers telephone and directs call to appropriate staff.
9. Schedules patient diagnostic appointments and medical consultations.
10. Takes dictation in shorthand.

19

Scientific View

(a) AQUACULTURE AND MARINE BIOTECHNOLOGY

Biotechnology is the use of biological organisms or their cellular constituents in a human controlled fashion for beneficial purposes. It is growing globally and contributing billions of dollars to the economy. Animal biotechnology , industrial biotechnology, seribiotechnology, plant biotechnology, environmental biotechnology, medical biotechnology, microbial biotechnology, food biotechnology and aquaculture and marine biotechnology are some of the areas of specialization in biotechnology.

Basic groundwork for entry into biotechnology would be the science stream at plus two levels. After this, the options are to go through a degree in agriculture, veterinary science and animal husbandry, medical, life sciences, genetics, pharmacy, microbiology, botany, zoology, chemistry, chemical engineering/technology, agricultural engineering, food technology, human biology and allied subjects like aquaculture and marine sciences before going for specialization in biotechnology. One can start off with biotechnology/ genetics as a subsidiary/ subject at the graduation level after a plus two in the science group. At University of Agriculture Sciences, courses are offered at College of Fisheries for B.F.Sc. and M.F.Sc. in fisheries sciences after plus two level.

Job Opportunities

There are large number of opportunities in the aquaculture and marine sector to work as a marine biologist/marine scientist, fish farm hand like hatchery/farm operator, fisheries extension officer/ technical officer, feed mill manager, processing and production manager, fish export inspector, export manager, R&D professional, aquaculture entererepreneur, consultant in management of fish farms, both in private and govt. sector, business establishments etc.

At present, there is great paucity of skilled manpower in the area of designing, construction, management of fish farms and hatcheries.

Every state government is having fisheries department in which fisheries graduate can apply for the post of Assistant Fisheries Development Officer (AFDO)/ Fisheries Extension Officer (FEO) and District Fisheries Development Officer (DFDO). One can get job in central agencies like Marine Product Export Development Authority (MPEDA), Fisheries Survey of India (FSI) etc.

In the private sector, job opportunities are available in fish processing companies, aquaculture farms, hatcheries, aquafeed plants, fishing gear industries and in pharmaceutical companies.

In academic institutes, candidates having Postgraduate degree can apply for the post of Assistant Professor in the Faculty of Fisheries. For the recruitment of scientist in various agricultural and fisheries institutions under the ICAR, ASRB conducts an All India Competitive Exam. Agricultural Research Service (ARS) followed by viva voce.

As an entrepreneur, after obtaining the professional degree in B.F.Sc., candidate can start their own enterprise. Financial support can be obtained through NABARD or through other nationalized banks. NABARD gives financial support to the candidate having B.F.Sc. degree. The main area in which fisheries enterprise can be developed are ornamental fish culture, aquaculture, hatchery and seed production, commercial pearl production, fish disease diagnostic centre, consultancy services and establishment of agriclinics.

Candidates after bachelor or master degree can apply for higher education in fisheries, aquaculture, marine sciences and biotechnology in USA, Canada, Australia, Japan, China and in European countries as well. Apart from this, there is a demand for fisheries professional in the aquaculture and processing sectors in Gulf and African countries also.

The increasing demand for sea food, sea based medicines and growth of ecofriendly industries is likely to create a huge demand for oceanographers.

Educational Institutions

The following universities/institutes are providing education and career opportunities through M.Sc., M.Tech., Ph.D and diploma courses in various disciplines of aquaculture, marine biotechnology and ocean sciences:-

1. Andhra University, Waltair-530003
2. Goa University, P.O. Santa Cruz, Teleigao Plateau,Goa-403002

3. Berhampur University,Bhanja Bihar,Berhampur-760007
4. Cochin University of Science and Technology, P.O. Kochi-682022
5. Mangalore University, University Campus, Mangala Gangothri-574199
6. CAS in marine biology,Annamalai University, Annamalai Nagar
7. National Institute of Oceanography, Dona Paula, Goa-403004
8. Indian Institute of Technology, Kharagpur, WB-721302
9. Central Marine Fisheries Research Institute,Cochin-682014
10. Central Institute of Freshwater Aquaculture, PO-Kausalyaganga, Bhubaneshwar-751002
11. Central Institute of Fisheries Education (Deemed Fisheries University), Versova, Mumbai-400061
12. Central Institute of Brackish water Aquaculture, Santhome High Road, R.A.Puram, Chennai-600028
13. Central Inland Capture Fisheries Research Institute, Barrackpore-743101
14. Central Institute of Fisheries Technology, Matsyapuri PO,Kochi-682029
15. National Research Centre for Cold Water Fisheries, Bhimtal-263136
16. National Bureau of Fish Genetic Resources, Canal Ring Road,PO-Dilkusha, Telibagh, Lucknow-226002

There are many special institutions, which offer various short term courses, training in various fields such as hatchery management, fish processing and fish farm implement manufacturing. Some of the important institutes offering special training in this field are :- Marine Products Export Development Authority (MPEDA), TASPARC and OSSPARC Prawn Hatcheries in Andhra Pradesh and Orissa, Central Institute of Fisheries Research, Nautical and Engineering Training-Cochin and Integrated Fisheries Project-Cochin.

Apart from these, fourteen fisheries colleges are offering B.F.Sc. and M.F.Sc. in inland aquaculture, freshwater aquaculture, manculture, industrial fisheries, fish processing and post harvest technology, fish nutrition, pathology, environment, ecology and extension etc.

(b) BIO-TECHNOLOGY

Stupendous praiseworthy strides have been made for the welfare of human lives on this earth which are of course praiseworthy. But development in the field of bio-technology have relegated the precarious predicaments in human life. The firmament of biotechnology is so broadened that it envelops in its fold the entire creature on this earth.

Bio-technology is one of the last growing sectors in India as well as all over the world. This emerging field of biological sciences is going to take a leap forward in the next five years with a global share of 10 percent to 15 percent. The importance of bio- technology in India was recognized after the establishment of National Biotechnological Board in 1982, in 1986 Government of India formed a full-fledged department within the Ministry of Science and Technology.

A number of academic institutions and government agencies such as CSIR, ICAR, ICMR, DAE and DBT etc. involved in research and development activities are related to it. It not only takes several policy initiatives but also endeavours to create excellent human resource base, build up the requisite infrastructure, identity and set up centres of excellence, support R & D and manufacturing activities.

Modern Science and technology along with researches and discoveries have helped man to a comfortable journeys from one revolution to the other. The fusion of conventional belief with new scientific discoveries have been creating wonders. Biotechnology is undoubtedly an emerging and sustainable area of this future. Genetic, engineering, Genomics, Bio-computing, Bio-Medical Engineering, Biosensors, Bio-Informatics etc. will be not topics for the next decades or so.

Basic needs for all citizen can be fulfilled by application of Biotechnology as imagined by the scientists. A large share of global investment in biotechnology is in the health care sector. Development of new generation crops drops their recombinant vaccines and newer diagnostic tools are some of the exciting possibilities. We are now able to handle million of gene sequence that are individually million items/ times long. There is increased interests in natural, bio-degradable / recyclable materials.

The Department of Bio-Technology has interface with a number of other government departments, academics R&D institutions and other user agencies. Today, in collaboration with the University Grants Commission, DBT supports post graduate programme with focus on bio-technology in over 60 Universitites. I.I.Ts and other premier institutions across the country. Along with doctoral postdoctoral courses they are regular short term courses or training programme for mid-career scientists. In order to encourage researchers to promote R&D towards products and processes the DBT has instituted a number of awards.

Considerable efforts have been put to ensure food and nutritional security through R&D in biotechnology. A major thrust has been given to the area of genomics. Under the food biotechnology initiatives, a technology for scale-up of our low cost nutrients and foods has been standardized. The tissue culture industry caters to horticulture and floriculture. The herbal medicine has increased the level of interests in plants with potential in therapeutic benefits and commercial demands for herbal products in global markets. Developments of vaccines for important disease afflicting livestock and diagnostic kits for farm animal health care are several activities in this sector. All the antibiotics come under biotech banner. Chemicals, we are using are being replaced by bio-chemicals or other biotech products. Biotechnology will provide new ways of influencing raw material processing. Most of the future medications will be of biotech origin. Cloning and designer babies may become usual feature. In the field of Seri- biotechnology. DBT has initiated a programme in genetic enhancement of mulberry and non-mulberry silk worm races and host plants. The programme includes development of immuno-diagnostics tools for detection of pathogens, bio-control measures for major pests and diseases of silkworm for better productivity as well as enzyme degumming of silk.

Biotechnology offers hope for solving many of the problems our world laces. Today, most drugs are chemicals that have limitations in treatment. They onlyhelp in managing the disease, except antibiotics. Understanding the pathogen and protein chemistry at the molecular level will bring in better treatment for several diseases. Understanding of the human genome will help us to predict the likelihood of diseases and improve disease diagnosis. Agriculture biotech will give us plants that have disease resistance, improved yields and stress tolerance. Environmental biotechnology will help control pollution problems. Enzyme technology is used to produce amino acids, food processing, cellulose hydrolysis in paper processing, diagnostics and bioassays-to fabric processing. A biotech process touches everything that is use in our daily life.

Biotech is essentially an interdisciplinary pursuit utilizing chemistry, microbiology, biochemistry and chemical engineering. It has various branches of application in health care, agriculture, food processing, environmental and industrial side. The demand for biotechnologist in these areas is highest. To explode the field, we need specialists in law, engineering, computer science and others to support and explore the activity.

Bio-safety guidelines are strictly followed to prevent damage to human health and environment. A single window processing cell has been created in the DBT for speedy processing of approvals for bio-safety.

Today, there are over 150 modern biotech companies in India. Some of these have pursued a product-based business model, others have adopted a service model on the lines of IT sector. India's major strengths in bio-technology are its highly trained workforce, a very good base of infrastructure through a well networked chain of laboratories and clusters of biogeneric industries. Add to these the treasure of our biological diversity the very rich traditional knowledge base dating back to thousands of years associated with our biodiversity. Put together, these are by any standard, very formidable assets. The fruits of these efforts would hopefully become visible very soon.

In terms of global industrial growth the area of biotechnology is at present referred as the sunrise sector. Virtually every Indian University is engaged in biotech research in some form or the other. There are various courses of Biotechnology is available at many centres of repute.

THE FOLLOWING POSTGRADUATE CENTRES ARE:-

1. Centres for Biotechnology, Jawaharlal University, New Delhi, Webside- www.jnu.ac.in
2. University of Allahabad, Allahabad
3. Banaras Hindu University, Varanasi
4. Calicut University, Kerala
5. Devi Ahilyavishwavidyalaya, Indore
6. G.B.Pant University of Agriculture and Technology,Pantnagar
7. Goa University, Goa
8. Gurjat University, Ahmedabad
9. Guru Nanak Dev University, Amritsar
10. Himachal Pradesh University, Shimla
11. University of Hyderabad, Hyderabad Webside- www.uohvd.ernet.in
12. University of Jammu,Jammu
13. M.S.University of Baroda, Baroda
14. Madurai Kamraj University, Madurai
15. Punjab University, Chandigarh
16. Pondicherry University, Pondicherry
17. University of Pune, Pune
18. Punjabi University, Patiala
19. Tezpur University,Tezpur (Assam)
20. Thapar Institute of Engineering and Technology, Patiala
21. Gulbarga University, Gulbarga
22. Guru Jambheshwar University, Hisar
23. Kumaun University, Nainital
24. University of Lucknow, Lucknow
25. University of Mysore, Mysore
26. University of North Bengal, Siliguri

OTHER GRADUATE CENTRES ARE

1. Anugrah Narayan College, Patna
2. B.N.College, Patna
3. College of Commerce, Patna
4. Delhi University, Delhi
5. B.H.U., Banaras
6. Anamalli University, Kerala
7. Dr. Zakir Hussain Institute of Science and Technology, Patna
8. Birsa Institute of Technology, Ranchi
9. Birla Institute of Technology, Ranchi

(c) DAIRY TECHNOLOGY

Indian dairy industry is one of the fastest growing sector in India. One of the key chain of human development and economic growth is to bestow generously for the education of people. The main aim of Dairy Education is to give proper recognition and value to HRD to sustain the growth of Dairy industry by developing suitable trained personnel. Technology is an essential part of production and processing. New technologies are price worthy until or unless technologies evolved at research institution reach to there ultimate users, otherwise these are useless. Dairy education aims at developing new technologies for the betterment of the society and dairy industry.

Indian dairy industry has made incredible evolution for the last several years. We are proud to say that India holds number one position in the world in milk production- 88 MT (2003-2004). This production brings with it enormous challenges before the dairy industry to procure, chill, pasteurise/ process, package and distribute milk across the length and breadth of country. This also imposes great responsibilities on the Indian Dairy Industry to improve the quality of milk and open new avenues/ opportunities for employment. A recent study has estimated that there are nearly 36 million unemployed people in India. New Research and Development programme in milk production, processing and export business promotion in total perspective will generate new jobs in direct and allied activities.

In spite of being the largest producer of milk, the per capita consumption and average yield per cattle remains low and India's dairy export share is less than 1%. As per the vision of our Hon'ble President Dr. A.P.J. Abdul Kalam, India should be a developed nation by 2020. With rising income levels and serious effort to improve the milch animal, it can be estimated that India would produce 175 MT and 200 MT of milk by the year 2015 and 2020 respectively, from the present production figure of 88 MT. This will require a highly efficient network of cold storage, packaging and distribution so that processed milk and milk based products can reach the vast consumer base in an efficient and cost effective manner. These operations will only be possible by well-trained dairy technologists, through proper human resource development. Dairy education and research have gained distinct momentum for the last few decades. Degree programme in Dairy Technology has drawn a major attention after school education having science background. Research scholars and scientists are also becoming more fascinated in the areas of dairy technology education and research.

The Indian Dairy Diploma started in 1924, simultaneously at Imperial Dairy Institute, Bangalore and Allahabad to cater to the needs of the industry for technically trained personnel. The NDRI, Karnal started its bachelor's degree in dairying in 1957. Thereafter, several other institutions have been established where B.Tech., M.Tech./ M.Sc.programmes are being imparted. Our Dairy Industry is growing very rapidly @4-5 % per annum. The global milk production in the year 2003 was reported at 600 million tonnes (FAO, 2003), hence it may be calculated that with the stipulated annual growth rate of 0.5-1.0 % the World milk production by 2020 is expected to rise to 650-700 million tonnes. India's share to world milk production at that time would substantially increase from the present level of 15% to about 30%. India's dairy sector is expected to triple its production in the next 10 years in view of expanding potential for export to Europe, Middle East and South East. Also, today India is the lowest cost producer of per litre of milk in the world at 27 cents, compared with the U.S.63 cents, and Japan's $2.8. In order to take the advantage of lowest cost and increasing production of milk in this country. MNC's are planning to expand their activities here.

DAIRY EDUCATION – PRESENT SCENARIO

Adequate infrastructural support is needed for the success of any dairy education programme. It includes trained manpower, various types of equipments and appropriate system for collecting information and monitoring the activities. India has made a small but a sound network of dairy education. The National Dairy Research Institute (NDRI) which is known as Mecca of Dairy and its southern and eastern regional stations. Indian Veterinary Research Institute (IVRI), State Agricultural Universities and many other polytechnic/ institutions are playing great role in turning out dairy professionals/ managers and creating a pool of technical expertise for its ultimate users. At present, 13 Dairy Science College impart specialized education in Dairying offering B.Tech., M.Tech. and Ph.D. degrees. With a total intake of 20-30 students per Dairy Science College, an average of 250-300 graduates 30-40 postgraduates and 3-5 Ph.D scholars pass out every year.

PROCEDURE OF ADMISSION

Admissions are based on merit thus encouraging competitiveness. Degree offered by these colleges are accepted and recognized at national and international levels.

All India ,Entrance/State University, starts in the month of July-August . Date of advertisement: October/ November. All India quotas fill 100% seats of NDRI, 15% seats for UG and 25% of PG seats of SAUs.

ELIGIBILITY

B.Tech(Dairy Tech): 10+2 at intermediate level with PCM.

M.Tech(Dairy Tech): B.Tech Dairy Tech./Food Tech./Chem.Eng.

CAREER OPPORTUNITIES

Dairy Technologist gets job in various organizations. It varies from government to Private and multinationals.

GOVERNMENT ORGANISATIONS

State Dairy Development Department, Milk Scheme, Banking and Insurance Sectors, Teaching and Research Organisations (SAUs), NABARD, NDDS, NDC and AGMARK.

COOPERATIVE SECTOR:- Mother Dairy, State Dairy Cooperative Federations(Amul; GCMF, Punjab Milk Feb., PRAG, COMFED, HMMFDS, MILMA etc.)

PRIVATE SECTOR:- Bikanerwala, Kwality Walls, Ved Ram & Sons, Mahaan Protein, Dynamix India Ltd. Cipham Sterling Agro India Ltd. Modern Dairy, Heins India Ltd.

MULTINATIONAL:- Pepsi, Coca-Cola, Nestle, GSK, Cadbury, Hindustan Lever, Wockhard etc.

POSTS OFFERED

ENTRY LEVEL:- Pos, Agriculture Officer, Dairy Development Officer, Supervisor, Production Executive, Quality Control Executive, Procurement Officer, Marketing Executive.

MIDDLE LEVEL:- Shift Incharge, Production Manager, Quality Control Manager, R&D Manager, Team Manager.

TOP POSITION:- General Manager, Factory Manager, Vice President and President, Scientist, Professors

PERKS/SALARY:- It varies from 6,000 to 1,25,000 Rupees/ month s per the candidate's abilities and experience. The starting salary varies from 6000 to 40,000 Rupees per month.

POTENTIAL OF INDIAN DAIRY INDUSTRY

With 198 million cattle and 86 million buffalo, India has the largest population of milch animal in the world. They constitute more than 50 percent of the cattle in the world. Unlike other milk producing countries, 54 percent of India's milk comes from buffaloes, which is endowed with unique processing qualities. Buffalo Milk as an advantage to India, because buffalo milk especially appropriate for commercially important dairy products such as Mozzarella cheese, Casein, Cream, Paneer, Khoa etc. India may emerge as the leading supplier of these products in the world market. Indian dairy industry has to derive maximum benefits of the uniqueness and positive virtues of buffalo milk to obtain the competitive edge in the global dairy market. The increasing world production of milk has made the availability of milk and milk products much easier in most countries through imports. Most of the countries in Asian and African continents are large importers of dairy products and therefore these regions are emerging as important dairy export markets. Realizing the nutritional importance of milk in the dietary regimen, the consumption of milk and milk products is increasing in these continents, which account for over 74 percent of the world human population.

PROSPECTS OF INDIAN DAIRY INDUSTRY

All the countries in South Asia, except India, are net importers of milk and milk products. Bangladesh and Sri Lanka are major importers, their imports in 2001 was 2.55 MT and 4.58 MT, respectively. In the West Asian region, countries like Iran, Iraq, Syria, Turkey, Saudi Arabia and other countries produce small quantity of milk and meet their requirements mainly through imports. This is where the opportunity lies. During the past two years, the Asian countries accounted for almost $1/4^{th}$ of world cheese imports, more than half of world whey and almost $2/3^{rd}$ of world lactose imports. India has prospect to tap the export market for these products in the mentioned countries. A major market for the Indian milk based sweets is fast developing overseas. A niche global market has strongly emerged for ethnic Indian dairy products. Large population of Indian subcontinent origin settled in Oceans, Middle East, Western Europe and North America and they represent a lucrative export market of over US$1.5 billion. There is opportunity to take advantage of this niche market by developing dairy products of Indian ethnic origin and meeting the quality and standards required for the global market. The organised dairy industry in India is estimated at Rs.145 billion (US $ 3 billion) and is expected to reach a size of Rs.240 billion ($5 billion) by the end of year 2005.

Taking into consideration, the above factual, it can be understood that there is ample scope for employment opportunities for dairy technologists from dairy institutions with intellectually stimulating environment, high quality education, outstanding research and extension programme. The dairy technology graduates are mainly employed for procurement, production, quality control, maintenance, marketing and management of dairy industry.

EPILOGUE

Due to stringent measures of population growth, European countries, Australia and Japan will have only 15% young people of the world population by 2020. India will have to channelize our hard working and talented youth to have proper training and exposure, so that it become the centre of attraction for the rest of the world as far as human resource is concerned. Now the rest of world is looking towards Indian and Indian talent for cooperation especially in the field of agriculture and dairy in particular. The augmentation and progress in Dairying aims at rural development i.e. all dairy development projects initiate at village level. This not only helps a particular project to flourish but also helps in economic development of the country as a whole. Dairy education is not only providing jobs but also boosts the economy of rural population and farmers.

(d) Djing

Are you one of those night birds who love to party all night? Does your passion for music keep you glued to the headphones at music stores? And do you also believe that people will love your remixes more than the ones being played at the disc last night? If your answer to the above question is 'Yes', then try the option of being a DJ. This will not only fetch you good money but also make you a celebrity in no time at all.

So, who do you think a DJ is? Is he an entertainer, a professional presenter; or a music connoisseur? In fact, he is a bit of every thing rolled into one. He is a juggler- selecting and playing music back to back with coherent transition between tracks; he entertains requests in between and keeps the crowd enthralled. Says DJ Jimmy Tangree, Station Head of 93.5 Red FM, Kolkata. "Djing is all about playing good music to a crowd on the dance floor that sets the party rolling and keeps the mood high till the wee hours.

Feeling hooked? Here are a few basics about this 'hot and happening' profession.

LEARN ON YOUR OWN

Says Delhi-based DJ Jazzy Joe, "Courses are yet to be institutionalised. At present, there are guidance programmes offered by various DJs (including Joe Himself). These courses give a few basic tips and then it's all about practice". Similarly, DJ Nasha, settled in Mumbai, also runs an academy that offers three programmes for beginners- a compete CD course, a CD and Vinyl course and an advance Battle Scratching course. The fee ranges from Rs.10,000 to Rs. 25,000."Those who enrol here also get an opportunity to play at live programmes. We conduct workshops at colleges and educational institutions which give youngsters an exposure to the world of Djing," explains Nasha.

IT'S MY STYLE

Brush up on your music history and learn about new and old artistes, who's in an who's out. Music changes frequently and so do peoples tastes. Advises Tangree, "Go to discotheques to a get a feel of the kind of music played, the crowd, its reactions and also observe how the DJ feels the pulse of the crowd".

Not everyday may be fond of mixing, so do not follow the trend blindly and go about re-mixing old hits. You will have to create your own style, as DJ Ivan suggests, "You must develop your own style which would eventually be your USP. Then learn to add effects to the original tune. Like DJ Aqueel plays only Bollywood songs and I love to play Western House Music, says this Bangalore based DJ who has been with Channel V, Radio City and at present with Smirnoff India.

You do not need high end DJ equipment to practice. A small investment will fetch you a CD player and a DJ mixer. This will at least familiarise you with the basics of hosting a show.

Says Joe, "If you want to do it just for the money, don't even give it a shot. Like in all other professions, the money is small in the beginning but once you are able to make a mark, things start getting better. In Delhi, an upcoming DJ can expect anything above Rs.5,000 per month from pubs/ clubs/ lounges and this keeps getting better with time and experience. Popular DJs can get paid anything above Rs.30,000 just for a night!" Adds Ivan, "In Bangalore, there are a few places that don't mind paying Rs.15,000 a month to beginners but the starting remuneration differs from one city to another".

ATTITUDE MATTERS

As Tangree puts it, a beginner should have good PR skills, be friendly and always mingle with others. A high-handed attitude will not get you anywhere. Reiterates Ivan, "There are many who misuse the opportunity to be on TV. Djing is serious business. It is not a fad. If one is looking for quick success, then no point getting in it. It may take you just 10 hours to learn how to use the equipment but it may take you 10 years to be a good DJ!" In short- if you want fun, music and money, then become a DJ!

(e) ENVIRONMENTAL SCIENCE

Recognizing the importance of environmental studies in shaping the personality of a citizen, the Supreme Court of India has directed

UGC to introduce a basic course on environment at every level in college education. UGC has prepared a model curriculum of environmental studies and introduced it as a compulsory course at graduate level. NCERT and AICTE are looking after the environmental education at school level and technical programs, respectively.

The study of environment science includes global warming, particularly if you specialise in areas like environmental planning. Environmental planners are concerned with planning, designing and developing systems and procedures to counteract all kinds of pollution, chiefly with regard to green house gases, ozone depletion, and other aspects of global warming.

Academics

Environmental science is an interdisciplinary science. Different branches of science that include earth, life, physical, chemical and social sciences interact, along with their own developmental areas like meteorology, atmospheric chemistry, chemistry, physics, hydrology, geology, geomorphology, sedimentology, hydrogeology, oceanography, management studies, economics, law geography, soil science, terrestrial ecology, aquatic ecology, population dynamics, politics, sociology, psychology and ethics interact to form environmental science.

Various Universities and Institutes imparting environmental education in India. These are offering courses for the award of B.Sc.(Environmental Sciences), B.E. (Environmental Engineering), M.Sc. (Environmental Sciences/ Environmental Botany/ Environmental Biology/ Environmental Toxicology/ Environmental Management), M.Phill.,M.Tech.(Environmental Engineering), Ph.D., Certificate program, Diploma and PG Diploma. Environmental courses vary widely in content and form. Some concentrate almost entirely in physical sciences while other deal exclusively with general environment and in topics like ecology, pollution monitoring and control, impact assessment, environmental education and law, environmental management and implementation of programs in relation with human health.

Eligibility

***B.Sc.*:-** Intermediate with Biology/Mathematics, Physics, Chemistry, Biotechnology (Science stream).

B.E./B.Tech. :- Intermediate with Physics, Chemistry and Mathematics.

***M.Sc./M.Sc.(Ag)*:-** B.Sc. with Zoology, Botany, Chemistry or Physics, Chemistry, Mathematics/ B.Sc.(Forestry)/ B.Sc.(Ag).

M.E./M.Tech. :- B.E./B.Tech./M.Sc.

Career Opportunities

Environmental scientists can work in a wide range of jobs, for instance as atmospheric chemists, ecologists, hydrologists, energy conservationists, government environment officers, oceanographers, environmental consultants, environmental planners, environmental managers, environmental engineers, environmental journalists, environmental activities, etc. One can also start his/her career in teaching and research in various universities or institutes after qualifying National Eligibility Test (NET) conducted by UGC/CSIR.

Research Fellowships

A tremendous scope and future exists in the field of environment science. Researchers may avail fellowships from UGC, ICMR, CSIR, DST, DBT, DAE, ICAR, DRDO, Jawaharlal Nehru Memorial Fund, K.S.Krishnan Research Associateship, etc. Students can also go for overseas fellowships like DAAD(German), Belgian Government Fellowships, Chinese Government Fellowships and other fellowships under bilateral programs, for pursuing doctorate and postdoctoral studies.

Job Opportunities related to Environmental Courses

(A) *Government Jobs*

(i) Faculty in IITs and Central Universities
(ii) Junior work managers in ordnance factory board through UPSC
(iii) Research/Scientists in CPCB,SPCBs, ISRO,DAE,ITRC, NEERI, CPPRI, NRSA,NIH, CSIR labs, Pollution control committees etc.
(iv) Trainee officer (environment) in NEEPCO,NHPC
(v) Irrigation and agriculture departments
(vi) Organizations such as DBT, DST,CSIR,UGC, AICTE etc.

(B) *Semi-Government Jobs*

(i) Banks like NABARD
(ii) BHEL

(C) *Autonomous Bodies*

(i) Education and research in State Universities/ Agricultural Universities or Colleges
(1) Research Institutes like ICAR through ASRB
(2) Academic officers in NIOS
(3) Assistant Director in National Productivity Council

(D) *Private Sector*

(i) Teaching in Engineering/Management Colleges

(ii) Environmental Engineers/Scientists in national/ multinational companies/industries
(iii) Environmental consultants/professionals/ experts in companies/ consultancies
(iv) Environmental Managers/ Scientists in NGOs like WWF, CSE, CEE, etc.
(v) Environmental Journalists in media houses.

List of Universities/ Institutes imparting Environmental Education in India

State	*Place*	*University/Institute*	*Course(s)*
Andhra Pradesh	Hyderabad	Osmania University	M.Sc.(Env.Sc.)
	Vishakhapatnam	Andhra University	M.E.(Env.Engg.)
Assam	Guwahati	IIT	Ph.D.(Env.Engg./ Env.Sci.)
	Silchar	Assam University	M.Sc.(Ecology & Env.Science), M.Phill.(Env.Sci.)
Tezpur		Tezpur University	M.Sc. (Env.Science)
Delhi	Delhi	Guru Gobind Singh Indraprastha Uni.	Master of Env. Mgmt.(MEM)
		IARI	M.Sc.(Ag.),Ph.D. (Env.Science)
		IGNOU	Cert.in Environ-Mental Studies, D.L.P.
		IIT	M.Tech.(Env. Sci.& Env.Engg./ Energy &Env. Mgmt.)Ph.D.
		Indian Instt. Of Ecology and Environment	M.Sc.(Ecology & Environment) DLP
		Jamia Hamdard	Uni.M.Sc. (Env.Botany)
		Jamia Millia Islamia	M.Tech.(Env. Sci.& Engg.)
		JNU	M.Sc., M.Phill.,

(Contd.)

(Cond.)

State	Place	University/Institute	Course(s)
		TERI School of Adv. Studies, Resources)	Ph.D.(Env. Science) M.Sc.(Env.Sci./ Natural
		University of Delhi	B.Sc.(Env. Sci.),B.E. (Env.Engg.) M.Sc. (Env.Biology), Ph.D.(Env.Sci.)
Goa	Goa	Goa University	M.Phill.(Env.Sci.)
Gujarat	Ahmedabad	Gujarat University	M.Sc.(Env. Science)
Haryana	Hissar	Guru Jambeshwar Uni.	M.Sc.(Env. Science) M.Tech. (Env.Engg.) Ph.D.
J & K	Jammu	University of Jammu	M.Sc.(Env. Science)
Jharkhand	Dhanbad Mines	Indian School of Sci.&	M.Tech.(Env. Engg.)
	Hazaribagh	Vinoba Bhave Univ.	M.Sc.(Env. Science)
Karnataka	Bangalore	I.I.Sc.	Ph.D.(Ecological Sci.)
	Mysore	University of Mysore	M.Sc.(Env.Sci.)
Kerala	Cochin	Cochin Univ. of Sci & Technology	M.Sc.(Env.Tech.) Ph.D.(Env. Studies)
	Kottayam	M.G.University	MEM,M.Phill .(Env. Manage ment)
	Tiruvananth puram	University of Kerala	M.Sc.(Env. Science)

(Contd.)

(Contd.)

State	Place	University/Institute	Course(s)
Madhya Pradesh	Gwalior	Jiwaji University	M.Sc. (Env.Science)
		Master of Global	Biodiversity,Ph.D.
	Rewa	APS University	M.Sc.(Env. Biology) M.Phill.(Env.Bio.) PG Dipl. Env.Impact Assessment
		D.L.P. PG	Dipl.in Pollution Mgmt.D.L.P.
	Ujjain	Vikram University	PG Dipl. Env.Mgmt. M.Sc.(Tech.)(Env. Mgmt.) M.Phil. (Env. Mgmt.)
Maha-rashtra	Aurangabad	Marathwada Uni.	M.Sc. (Env.Sci.)
	Kolhapur	Shivaji University	M.Sc.(Env.Sci.)
	Mumbai	IIT	M.Tech(Env.Sci.& Engg.),Ph.D.
		National Instt. Of Industrial Industrial Engg. Env.Mgmt.	PG Dipl.in Safety & (PGDISEM)
	Pune	Bharati Vidyapeeth	M.Sc.(Env.Sci.)
		University of Pune	M.Sc.(Env.Sci.)
Meghalaya	Shillong	North Eastern Hill Uni.	M.Tech.(Env.Sci.)
Pondicherry	Pondicherry	Pondicherry University	M.Sc. (Ecology & Env.Science) Ph.D. (Ecology& Env.Sci.)

(Contd.)

(Contd.)

State	Place	University/Institute	Course(s)
Punjab	Amritsar	Guru Nanak Dev Univ.	M.Sc.(Hons.) (Env.Science)
	Chandigarh	Punjab University	M.E.(Env.Engg.)
	Patiala	Thapar Instt. . Of Engg & Technology	M.Tech. (Env.Sci. & Technology)
Rajasthan	Ajmer	M.D.S. University	M.Sc. (Env.Science)
	Jaipur Rajasthan	University of Environment	Dipl.in
		Eco.	Dipl.in Human
	Udaipur	Mohanlal Sukhadia . Univ	B.Sc.(Env.Sci.) M.Sc.(Env.Sci.)
Tamil Nadu Nagar	Annamalai	Annamalai University Industrial	PG Dipl.in Pollution Control
	Chennai	Anna University	M.Sc. (Env.Studies)
		IIT	M.Tech. (Env.Engg.)
		University of Madras	M.Sc.(Env.Sci
	Coimbatore	Bharathiar University	M.Sc. (Env.Science)
		TamilNadu Agri.Univ.	B.Tech(Energy & Env.(Engg)
	Madurai	Madurai Kamraj Univ.	M.Sc. (Env.Science)
Uttaranchal	Dehradun	Forest Research Instt.	PG Dipl. Biodiversity Conservation
	Haridwar	Gurukula	M.Sc. (Env.Science)
		Kangri Univ.	Ph.D. (Env.Science)
	Pantnagar	G.B.Pant University Of Agri.& Tech.	M.Sc. (Env.Science)

(Contd.)

(Contd.)

State	*Place*	*University/Institute*	*Course(s)*
			Ph.D. (Env.Science)
	Roorke	IIT	M.Tech. (Env.Engg.)
	Srinagar	H.N.B.Garhwal Univ.	M.Sc. (Env.Science)
	Garhwal		
Uttar Pradesh	Agra	Dr.B.R.Ambedkar Univ.	M.Sc.(Env.Sci./ Env.Toxicology) Ph.D.(Env. Studies/Env. Toxicology)
	Allahabad	Allahabad University	M.Sc. (Env.Science)
	Bareilly	Ruhelkhand University	B.Sc. (Env.Science)
	Faizabad	Dr.R.M.L.Avadh Univ.	M.Sc. (Env.Science)
	Jhansi	Bundelkhand Univ.	M.Sc.(Env. Science/Env. Biotechnology/ Env.Planning/ Natural Resource Mgmt.), M.Tech. (Natural Resource Management), PGDipl.in Env. Law
	Kanpur	C.S.J.M.University	M.Sc. (Env.Science)
		IIT	M.Tech. (Env.Engg. & Mgmt.)
	Lucknow	B.B.R.A. University	M.Sc. (Env.Science)
		Instt. Of Environment	PG Dipl.in Env.

(Contd.)

(Contd.)

State	*Place*	*University/Institute*	*Course(s)*
			& Management Mgmt.
		Lucknow University	M.Tech. (Env.Engg.)
	Meerut	C.C.S.University	M.Sc. (Env.Science)
	Varanasi	BHU	M.Sc. (Env.Science)
West Bengal	Bardhaman	University of Burdwan	M.Sc. (Env.Science)
	Kharagpur	IIT	M.Tech. (Env.Engg. & Mgmt.)
	Kolkata	Jadavpur University	M.E.(Env.Engg.)
		University of Calcutta	M.Sc. (Env.Science)

(f) FORENSIC SCIENCE

The world "forensic" is derived from the Latin word "forensis" meaning "forum" or "court of law". Forensic Science is a technique of using scientific methods in solving crimes. It draws upon various branches of science, such as physical, chemical, medical and biological sciences. The forensic science is multi-disciplinary and includes branches such as Forensic chemistry, Forensic physics, Forensic biology, Forensic documents, Forensic fingerprints, Forensic engineering, Forensic pathology etc.

Every MBBS student is taught a bit of forensic medicine (to be able to report any unnatural death that may come to his notice or he could get hauled up under Section 39 of the CrPC for withholding evidence from the Police). At the MD level, the syllabus for the speciality course is more in-depth, covering three modules: Forensic Pathology, Clinical Forensic Medicine and Toxicology.

Forensic Pathology covers all investigation leading to death (cause, time and manner), embalming and disposal of dead bodies, identification of unclaimed bodies, viscera examination, DNA examination etc. Students are also sensitised to the time factor because evidence lost at this stage is often lost forever.

In clinical forensic medicine, students are taught how to lift trace evidences from the blood, nails, hair, clothing, semen, a vaginal swab, tissue culture, gastric lavage etc. They are also taught how to document this evidence for the court, face a lawyer's cross examination, understand court proceedings and interpret various sections and sub sections of the CrPC,. Finally, toxicology is another extensive subject covering data maintenance on all kinds of poisons, their variants, symptoms and management in case of both acute and chronic poisoning.

Most often, forensic doctors, scientist and police investigators work on a case as a team. Yet, despite all their efforts, the evidence may not be finally admissible in court. Nothing is absolute for the judiciary.

Autopsies, however, can be conducted only by an MD in Forensic Medicine; that too for deaths occurring in a particular geographical area, as mentioned in the license issued to the doctor by the State Health Department under Section 74 of the Cr.PC. For instance, the AIIMS forensic department can conduct autopsies only on cases referred to them by the South Delhi police, unless the investigators need a second or third opinion. The forensic scientists generally use following characteristics to identify the culprit.

Fingerprint: Experts use various kinds of powders, chemicals, lasers and lights to lift prints which may be hidden to the naked eye.

Blood: How blood droplets sprayed on the floor can predict from what height the blood (and thus the body) fell to the ground.

Fibres: To lift hair or clothing samples embedded in textiles.

Bullets and Cartridges: Every gun barrel leaves unique marks on bullets and cartridges. By comparing two bullets, experts can determine whether these were fired from the same weapon.

Footprints: Footprints left by an assailant can reveal where he went or where he lives.

Voice and image prints: Technology can pinpoint the authenticity of a tape-recording, as was demanded in the case of the Tehelka tapes.

Handwriting: Experts can predict personality details from a ransom note, cheque or diaries of the accused.

There is a very little glamour and a lot of toil in the profession, especially when it comes to making endless court appearances, although there is some satisfaction when a case is cracked or a criminal nabbed.

Training: The Government of India had established in 1972, the National Institute of Criminology and Forensic Science (New Delhi-110 085) to undertake research and training in criminology and forensic science. The Government also established three Central Forensic Science Laboratories at Kolkata, Hyderabad and Chandigarh. Besides, there is a Government Examiner of Questioned Documents in Hyderabad. All State Governments have also their own Forensic

Science Laboratories to assist the police in crime investigation. One of the branches of forensic science is forensic medicine which is the application of medical knowledge to the investigation of crime, particularly for establishing the causes of injury and death. Study of forensic medicine is a part of medical education, as an area of specialisation at the postgraduate levels (MD and Diploma).

Forensic science is offered by a number of Universities at the Certificate, PG Diploma and Master's Degree level often along with criminology (or criminal science). While the entry requirement for the MSc course is a degree in science, graduates from any discipline are admitted in MA courses.

Andhra University (Visakhapatnam 530 003) had introduced in 2000, a MA degree course in Criminal Justice in collaboration with the City University of New York. The course is open to graduates in any branch and also in-service candidates working in any wing of criminal justice system including forensic science and forensic medicine.

The Bureau of Police Research and Development (New Delhi – 110 003) in the Ministry of Home Affairs undertakes research in forensic science and criminology. Besides, it offers junior Research Fellowships in five areas, viz- Forensic Chemical Science, Forensic Biological Science (including DNA Finger Printing), Forensic Physical Science, and Forensic Documents Science (including computer frauds and cyber crimes). The fellowships (Rs.5,000 per month for the first two years and Rs.5600 per month for the third year) are tenable at the three Central Forensic Science Laboratories (Calcutta 700 014, Hyderabad 500 013, Chandigarh 160 036) and Government Examiner of Questioned Documents (Hyderabad 500 153).

Institutes

Anna University (Chennai 600 025)- Post –BE Diploma in Forensic Engineering, Bundelkhand University (Jhansi-284 128)- PG Diploma in Forensic Science: PG Diploma in Criminology; University of Delhi (Delhi- 110 007)- Certificate in Forensic Science; Dr.B.R.Ambedkar University (Agra-282 004)0 MSc (Forensic Science); Dr.Harisingh Gour Vishwavidyalaya (Sagar- 470 003)- MSc (Criminology), MA (Criminal and Forensic Science); Karnataka University (Dharwad-580 003)- MA (Criminology and Forensic Science); Lucknow University (Lucknow- 226 007)- PG Diploma in Forensic Anthropology; University of Madras (Chennai-600 005)- MA (Criminology), and MSc (Forensic Science); Osmania University (Hyderabad-500 007)- MSc (Forensic Science in collaboration with AP State Forensic Science Laboratory), Panjab University (Chandigarh-160 014)- PG Diploma in Forensic Science and Criminal Science; Punjabi University (Patiala- 147 002)- MSc (Forensic Science).

Life is not easy for any of us. But what of that? We must have perseverance and above all confidence in ourselves. We must believe that we are gifted for something and that this thing must be attained.

(g) LIFE SCIENCES

The term "Biology" was given by French naturalist Lamarck (1744 - 1829). It is the combination of two Greek words "bios" – life and "logos"- study. Thus it may be concluded that Biology is the branch of science which deals with the study of life i.e. plants and animals. The science of plants is called Plant Sciences or Botany. Technically, Botany is called Phytology (Gk; Phyto- plants and logos- study). While the science of animals is known as Animal Sciences or Zoology (Gk; Zoon-animal and logos-study). Now a modified term "Life Science" is being used instead of Biology or Biological Sciences, due to its close relationship with other sciences like Physics and Chemistry. Biology is a very vast subject and comprises various disciplines.

It is increasingly observed that in the recent past some applied fields of Life Sciences as Bio-technology, Biosensors, Environmental Biotechnology, Bio computing, Molecular Biology, Genetic Engineering, Bio informatics, Biochemical Engineering, Bio Medical Engineering, DNA Finger Printing, Cloning, Gene Therapy, Genomic, Physiotherapy, Cryobiology, Marine Biology, Criminology, Toxicology, Antibiotics, Microbiology, Immunology, Environmental Engineering and Pharmacology etc. have been evolved as separate disciplines. Most of the Indian Universities, leading institutions and colleges are offering these courses at graduate and post graduate levels.

1. Career in Biotechnology

During 1970 Biotechnology emerged as a new discipline as a result of marriage of Life Sciences with technology and give rise Biotechnology. Now, it is considered as the third wave in Life Sciences where gradual and subtle transformation of science into technology as gene therapy and cloning can be observed. Biotechnology is the application of scientific and engineering principles to the processing of material by biological agents to provide goods and services. In recent years Biotechnology has created unprecedented opportunities, therefore, Government of India has established at least 32 premier institutions, almost 50 Universities and IITs where a strong infrastructure for training and research in Biotechnology have been developed. National Biotechnological Board was established in 1982. Seeing the importance of Biotechnology the Government of India in 1986 formed a full fledged department under the Ministry of Science and Technology. Now a days a number of Govt. agencies and some academic institutions such as CSIR, ICAR, ICMR, DAE, DST, DBT etc. are involved in research and developmental activities related to Biotechnology. Biotechnology offers hope for solving various problems of our world like treatment for several dreaded diseases, human genome map, agriculture and environmental problems etc. M.Sc., M.Tech and post doctoral research in Biotechnology have also been started in Institutions/ Universities. At undergraduate and postgraduate levels Biotechnology have also been introduced in various Universities syllabi. One who wants to pursue his career in this field may do B.Sc.-Biotechnology, B.Sc.- Information Science, B.Sc. R.D. & I.T.-Bachelor of Science in Radio Diagnostic and Imaging Technology, M.Sc.-Biotechnology, M.Sc.-Information Science (MIS), M.Sc.I.T.- Information Technology, M.Tech, research (Ph.D) and post/doctoral research from various Universities of leading institutions. Indian Institute of Technology, Delhi and Kharagpur are also offering a five year integrated course in M.Tech. One should have qualified JEE test for admission in this integrated course in M.Tech. After completion of these courses one may start his career as a biotechnologist, molecular biologist, manager, scientific officer, technical officer, scientist, lecturer (after qualifying NET examination conducted by CSIR/UGC) and organic chemist in various pharmfaceutical companies, government and non-governmental organisations, drug institutions, Universities and its affiliated colleges. Students of Biotechnology stream may also join production and marketing department and research and development department of various industries and multinational companies.

2. *Career in Microbiology*

Microbiology continues to progress rapidly each year with the aid of new techniques, new research findings and new insights into micro organisms and their many activities. Microorganisms proved to be much more important to mankind than what could be thought of them earliest. During past few years applications of microorganisms to environment and in industries in particular enlarged tremendously. Keeping in view such developments, the students of Life Science stream who wants to pursue his career in Microbiology can do B.Sc. Microbiology and B.M.M.- Bachelor of Medical Microbiology at graduate level offered by various Universities and its affiliated colleges of India. The essential basic qualification for admission in these courses is 10+ 2 or intermediate. However, some selected Universities and leading institutions are also offering M.Sc., M.Tech, Research (Ph.D) and Postdoctoral research in Microbiology. The prime object of this subject is to identify and diagnose various diseases in man and animals, spreading through different pathogenic microorganisms and also invent drugs and vaccine for their eradication. After completion of graduate level courses one may be lab technician in different government, non-government hospitals and nursing homes. After obtaining higher education one may be appointed as a microbiologist, scientist in leading institutions, food processing, various NGOs, biotech, bioprocesses business, drug institutions and pharmaceutical companies. One may also be appointed as a lecturer in any institution, Universities and its affiliated colleges by qualifying NET examination conducted by CSIR/ UGC twice in every year.

3. Career in Environmental Science

Since the United Nations Conference on Environment and Development in Rio in June 1992, it has been felt throughout the world that the conservation of biological diversity is one of the most important challenges of the present and immediate future. Since than each country has prepared its biodiversity conservation strategy. Global warming, green-house effect, ozone-layer depletion, deforestation and acid rain some of are burning problems can be solved by the implementation of environmental laws strictly. Students of Life Sciences can pursue their career in this field as a environmentalist by obtaining higher education as M.Sc., M.Phil,M.Tech, research (Ph.D) or postdoctoral research offered by various Universities and leading institutions of India. Now Environmental Science has been included as a compulsory subject at graduate level for all streams as art, commerce and science in all Universities and its affiliated colleges throughout India by the Supreme Court order. After obtaining higher education in Environmental Science one may starts his/her career as scientist, research officer, technical officer, engineer, urban planner, architect, district forest officer (DFO), Forest Ranger, Project Coordinator, Counsellor and Manager in various governmental organisations (state and federal both), non- governmental organisations (NGOs), NTPC, NHPC, Private Foundations, Environmental Organisations, National parks, sanctuaries, nuclear power stations, municipalities, ministries, consulting companies, drug institutions, pharmaceutical companies, Universities, Laboratories and in research and development department of several industries. In near future there will be a demand of scientists, lecturers, community developers and entrepreneurs for the protection of environment and wildlife on large scale in various organisations, industries, Universities and its affiliated colleges throughout India.

4. Career in Pharmacology, Forensic Science and Toxicology

The students of Life Science stream who possess excellent communication skills and drive to motivate people can pursue their career as pharmacist, analytical chemist, sales representative, medical representative, drug inspector and dealer in various reputed pharmaceutical companies after passing B.Sc. (Life Science),

B.Pharma or f D.Pharma. 10+2 with Bio/Maths students with minimum 17 years of age can take admission in B-Pharma/ D-Pharma.

5. Career in Paramedical Sciences

There are various courses in Paramedical Sciences as B.P.T. – Bachelor of Physiotherapy, B.O.T.- Bachelor of Occupational Therapy, B.Sc. M.L.T.- B.Sc. Medical Laboratory Technology, B.Sc. R.D. and I.T.-Bachelor or Science in Radio Diagnostic and Imaging Technology, B.Sc.- Radiography, Bachelor in Speech Therapy, Diploma in Ophthalmic Technology, Diploma in X-Ray, Diploma in Radiology, Diploma in General Nursing & Mid Wifery, Diploma in Hospital Management, B.Sc. Nursing, Medical Transcription, Prosthetics and Orthotics Engineering , Rehabilitation etc. are offered through various Universities and its affiliated colleges. The essential basic qualification for admission in these courses is 10+2 (Bio/Maths) with minimum of 17 years of age. Higher education as M.P.T.- Master of Physiotherapy (after B.P.T.) and research is also available in some selected Universities and institutions of India. Paramedical Sciences possess purely professional courses and one may start his/her career as a technician, transcriptionist, Radiographer, prosthetics & orthotics engineer, nursing assistant, laboratory assistant in various government and non government hospitals, clinics, defence services, railways, nursing homes, public health organisations, NGOs, research institutions and in various drug manufacturing firms. One may also be appointed as physiotherapist in different government and non government hospitals and also may establish his/her own profession as pathology lab, hospital or clinic.

6. Career in Nutrition

It is also the best option for Life Sciences students to be a dieticianist or nutritionist. For this one must be a graduate in Life Science. Most of the Indian Universities and its affiliated colleges are offering these courses.

After passing graduation one can undergo BTC, B.Ed and can be a teacher in primary, junior Secondary level. Higher education as M.Sc.- Food Technology and research (Ph.D) may also be obtained from CFTRI Mysore and some other Universities. In present situation there is demand of dieticianist and nutritionist in various food processing companies, fitness clubs, health clinics, institute of athletics etc. on large scale. One may also be appointed in government and non government hospitals and nursing homes at handsome salary. After obtaining specialization in the field of food and nutrition one can be an Administrator, Dieteticianist, Nutritionists, Quality Controller, Consultant Hospitality Services, Supervisor, Manager in different organisations and Institutions and may also be a technologists, coordinator in welfare departments, programme officers and counsellors.

(h) OCEANOGRAPHY

Oceanography, an interdisciplinary science integrating the principles of physics, chemistry, mathematics, geology, meteorology and biology is an important area of study. Where sea water wets the solid crust, oceanography enters the domain of geology. Where marine forms of life exist or land forms migrate by way of the sea, oceanography merges with biology. Where it reflects sunlight, is distilled into the atmosphere or exerts a drag on the winds, oceanography is joined with meteorology. And where man must combat or find uses for the sea or sea water itself, oceanography is allied with engineering and technology. Oceanography is a challenging and adventurous field providing opportunity to those with an insatiable interest to explore the realm of the unknown that exist within the ocean. It also gives a lifelong learning opportunity to students and research professionals.

BRANCHES OF SPECIALIZATION

In the traditional view, oceanography is subdivided into three main branches i.e. (1) Physical Oceanography (2) Chemical Oceanography (3) Biological Oceanography. But today it is equally appropriate to include Marine Meteorology, Submarine Geology and Geophysics and certain branches of engineering and fundamental parts of science.

Physical oceanography deals with the study of the physical properties of the ocean and the relationship between the sea and the atmosphere. This includes chemical and biological information as a part of the description of the oceans and cross-checking on the validity of physical reasoning.

Chemical oceanography is the study of chemical parameters such as salinity and oxygen content etc. These parameters help the physical oceanographers to know about the origin of water masses of the ocean. Determination of essential micronutrients elements-nitrogen and phosphorus are of great value to Marine Biologists concerned with fertility of the sea.

Biological oceanography is nothing but the study of the relationship between marine organisms and their environment. Marine Geology is the study of topographical features, rocks, sediments and physical composition of the ocean floor.

Economic oceanography, however, leads beyond fishery resources to consideration of waste disposal problems, the recovery of metals and salts from the sea, the extraction of power from the waves and tides, a study of motion of ships, in a seaway and of the management of ships to take advantage of favourable currents and weather as well as the construction of well-drilling platforms which will withstand the onslaught of waves and erosion of currents.

Marine Archaeology involves the study of the systematic recovery and study of material evidence, such as shipwrecks, graves, buildings, tools and pottery remaining from past human life and culture that is now covered by the sea.

ROLE OF OCEANOGRAPHERS

Oceanographers study the motion and circulation of ocean water, its physical and chemical properties and how these properties affect the coastal waters, climate and weather and the living organisms. The work of an oceanographer involves collecting samples, conducting surveys, analysing data using sophisticated instruments in the sea for long hours. Depending upon the area of specialization, the professionals work as oceanographer in the several field such as physical oceanography, chemical oceanography, geological oceanography, marine biology. The oceanographers spend long time in sea because it is a research- oriented profession. And team work is highly essential in this field. Many government and private organizations provide many projects that integrate the separate discipline of oceanography.

WHERE TO STUDY

Indian has a long coastline spanning over 7,500 Kms and positioned in the central part of the Indian ocean. Oceans plays an important role in the social and economic life of the people in the region and hence there is a growing interest to study them. The growing importance and possible area of oceanography has led to many educational institutions offering specialized courses. Due to the practical necessity of conducting these courses in close proximity to the sea, most of these educational institutions are situated in coastal states.

The National Institute of Oceanography(NIO), Goa, NIOT, Chennai and Council of Scientific and Industrial Research (CSIR) and many organizations and institutions are working for the development of trained man power and quality research in ocean science and technology. These organizations conduct a number of training programmes for students and research professionals.

There are many educational institutions offering post-graduate courses in Oceanography, Marine Sciences and Geology etc. Some of them are:-

(1) Andhra University, Waltair offers MSc (Marine Sciences) with specialisation in Marine Biology, Marine Geology, Marine Geophysics, Marine Chemistry, Physical Oceanography, MSc Meteorology, MSc Marine Biology and Oceanography and BSc in related fields.

(2) The University of Madras offers MSc (Marine Geology), MSc(Ocean Life Science). For MSc (Marine Geology) the requisite qualification is BSc with Geology in main or equivalent exams, while for MSc(Ocean Life Sciences) it is BSc with Botany or Zoology as main subjects.

(3) Berhampur University, Orissa offers MSc (Marine Sciences) and BSc degree.

(4) Utkal University, Bhubaneshwar, Orissa offers MSc (Marine Zoology) and BSc and B.Ed(Science).

(5) Karnataka University offers MSc (Marine Zoology) and the required qualification is BSc degree.

(6) Cochin University of Science and Technology offers MSc (Marine Biology), (Oceanography), (Marine Geology), (Marine Geophysics) and the requisite qualification for gaining admission to the courses is BSc degree.

QUALIFICATION

First of all the candidates should be sea worthy, have a sense of adventure, courage and determination, be patient and possess a sharp mind. Knowledge of swimming and diving are additional qualifications that may come in very handy. A BSc. Degree holder is one of the pure sciences is eligible for gaining admission to the MSc in Oceanography. At Ph.D level, MSc in any basic science is essential for eligibility to commence marine research. The majority of courses in Oceanography are of two years duration.

OPPORTUNITIES

There are huge opportunities in the field of Oceanography. Post Graduates in this discipline can expect a starting salary between Rs.8,000/- and Rs.10,000/- and a lot of additional incentives as a junior research fellow in the field of research. They are also eligible to apply for the National Eligibility Test (NET) which is conducted by CSIR. The highest salaries at senior levels ranges from Rs.50,000/- to Rs.80,000/-. Government organizations like the Geological Survey of India, Meteorological Survey of India, National Remote Sensing Agency (NRSA), Space Application Centre(SAC), Defence Research and Development Organization(DRDO), National Institute of Oceanography(NIO) and many Ocean Science and Technology Cell etc. offer a good number of job opportunities for Oceanographers.

Public Sector Organizations such as Oil India, Oil and Natural Gas Corporation Ltd.(ONGC) and many private companies like Reliance Petrochemicals Ltd., L&T etc. engaged in searching for vast see floor deposits and evaluating natural energy production from waves, currents and tides also hire Oceanographers. Post Graduate find jobs in shipyards as port engineers, software structural designers for Computer oriented fields and Hydro Dynamics, Many shrimp farming hatcheries and processing units also hire Oceanographers for their purpose.

(i) PSYCHOLOGY

Psychology is the scientific study of living organisms, with a special attention given to human behaviour. As a science, psychology is interested in understanding more and more about the behaviour of an organism and as a profession, it is concerned with application of this knowledge to the prediction and control of behaviour. Psychologists study human behaviour and mental process to understand, explain and change people's behaviour. Psychology is no more restricted within the academic walls. It has become more practical and applied. The knowledge of psychology is being used in educating children, guiding youth, rehabilitating the handicapped, training personnel, selling products, easing group tensions and race conflicts. It has permeated almost every sphere of human endeavour.

One may specialise in any one of the following branches of psychology.

BRANCHES OF PSYCHOLOGY

***Applied Psychology*:-** concerned with the practical application of psychological principles to resolve various psychological problems.

***Experimental Psyshology*:-** involves designing, conducting and analysing experiments to develop knowledge regarding animal and human behaviour. However, it is a general term referring to the methods employed in studying behavioural process. The areas of specialisation include, comparative psychology, learning psychology and physiological psychology.

***Personnel Psychology*:-** It is mainly used in the selection of new employees and their promotion and transfer etc. It also helps in selection of suitable candidates for admission to professional and technical institutes. It is used in the defence ministry for selection of the officers and allocation of assignments in various units according to their capacities. It also helps in the evaluation of their performance.

***Educational Psychology*:-** Educational psychology develops and evaluates material and procedures in educational and training programmes. It mainly helps in studying the emotional problems of the children and teenagers. Sometimes established tests are also administered besides personal counselling to know the reasons of the emotional and personal problems.

Social Psychology:- Studies the effects of groups and individuals on the thoughts, feelings, attitudes and behaviour of the individual , e.g., the way in which our social attitudes develop and how members of families, neighbourhood, and communities influence each other.

Counelling Psychology :- Guidance and Counselling is the process of helping an individual discover and develop his educational, vocational and psychological potentials. It has emerged as one of the most important areas of practical application of psychology. The counsellor may give his client information about his own abilities and interests as determined by psychological tests or about educational opportunities and the requirements of various occupations.

Industrial Psychology:- It is mainly used in industry for increasing production and creating better human relationships among workers. It helps in providing mental relaxation in the work environment. The industrial psychologists also help in creating understanding between labour and management. It mainly focuses on issues such as motivation and morale at the work place.

Engineering Psychology:- Engineering psychologists, in collaboration with engineers, design equipments to facilitate human performance. Their job is not confined to the designing of industrial machinery but it also covers such products as kitchen gadgets, radios and telephone dials etc.

Consumer Psychology:- The use of consumer psychology has increased because of tough competition in selling products. It helps in creating effective communication from the manufacturer or distributor to the consumer. Consumer psychology may undertake market research survey to understand the buyers' motives. The findings of the survey influence decisions regarding the ways to present a product through the medium of television or print.

Clinical Psychology:- Clinical psychology study the effects of drugs on behaviour. This area is mainly meant for those who have got medical knowledge and want to treat mental disorders through psychological testing techniques.

PERSONAL CHARACTERISTICS

The psychologists work with all kind of persons to study the interest, aptitudes and temperament etc. Hence, they should possess caring aptitude to provide required confidence to their clients. Good communication skills also help them in performing their jobs efficiently.

EMPLOYMENT OPPORTUNITIES

The psychologists study mental and emotional problems of human beings. They have to study the factors that affect the conduct of human beings and growth and development of individual's personality. Sometimes psychological tests are also administered to measure mental characteristics of human beings such as intelligence, aptitude and ability etc. Some of the important positions in the field of psychology are:-

Counsellors/Vocational Guidance Officers:- Counsellors provide vocational information to the students on career building. They have to collect comprehensive information about occupations, educational and training facilities, employment opportunities etc. Group guidance programmes for disseminating occupational information are conducted by the counsellors. Sometimes they have to administer psychological tests to assess an individual's merits and demerits. In educational institutes they are known as career master/ teacher counsellor. When they work in an employment exchange they are known as vocational guidance officer.

Industrial psychologists/ personnel managers/ industrial relation officer:- The industrial psychologists are responsible for formulating and executing policy matters with regard to industrial units. Their work relates to recruitment, training, terms and conditions of employment and statutory obligations towards workers. They are responsible for effective use of the manpower available and implementation of welfare schemes. They act as a coordinator between the management and the workers' representatives for the redressal of their grievances.

Rehabilitation Officers:- They work in rehabilitation and vocational centres for the handicapped and mentally retarded. They study the weaknesses and strengths of their clients in relation to their vocational goals. They initiate correspondence with specialists and employers, social service agencies for rehabilitation of the handicapped. They also arrange for their proper placement. They assist their clients for artificial orthetics and prosthetic appliances required for near normal dependability.

Child Psyshologists:- They work in child guidance clinics. These centres mainly study psychological, social biological and environmental factors which are important in the growth of a child.

Teaching Professionals:- There are teachers, lecturers and professors who teach psychology in colleges and universities and do research work. They can also find employment in NCERT and SCERT, where they undertake research work in the field of various branches of psychology.

They may also find jobs in the Ministry of Labour as employment Officer, Vocational guidance officer, training officer etc. The Ministry of Defence also provides ample job opportunities to the psychologists in their Psychological Research Wing and Service Selection Boards.

There are psychiatrists who are basically medical professional but specialise in psychological medicines. These persons deal with diagnosis and treatment of mental diseases and disorders. They study abnormal behaviour of the patients.

EDUCATIONAL AND TRAINING FACILITIES

Psychology is offered as a subject at 10 +2 level. Many universities offer psychology as a subject at graduation/ post graduation level in both the arts and science streams. The University of Delhi; Bharathiyar University, Coimbatore; University of Madras; Rani Durgavati University,Hissar offer post graduate courses in Applied Psychology. One can also do his post graduation in Psychology through correspondence available at following Universities:- Allahabad, Andhra, Annamalai, Avadh, Devi Ahilya Vishwavidyalaya, Kurukshetra, Madras, Marathwada, Nagpur, Patna, Poona, Rajasthan, Ranchi, Ravi Shankar, Rohilkhand, Saurashtra, Shivaji, South Gujarat, Sri Venkateswara, Utkal and Vikram etc.

Certificate course for 10+2 in Guidance is available at Indira Gandhi National Open University, P.G.Diploma in Guidance and Counselling of one or two years duration is available at Himachal Pradesh University, Shimla; Punjab University, Chandigarh; Rani Durgavati University, Jabalpur; Ravi Shanker University, Raipur; MS University, Baroda; University of Bombay, Mumbai; Barkatullah University, Bhopal; Regional Institute of Education (NCERT), at Bhopal, Mysore and Ajmer and Mother Teresa Womens' University, Kodaikanal.

Various universities offer specialised courses such as MJP,Rohilkhand (MA-Clinical Psychology); National Institute for Mental Health and Neuro Sciences, Bangalore- Ph.D and M.Phil (Clinical Psychology); Ranchi Institute of Neuro Psychiatry, Ranchi- M.Phill (Medical and Social Psychology); Ph.D.(Clinical Psychology) ; and M.Phill & Ph.D. (Psychiatric Social Work); Pune University (Diploma in Child and Family Counselling), Child Guidance and Industrial Psychology; Madras University, (Diploma in Sports Psychology); Osmania University (Diploma in Child Psychology and Family Relations).

The need for selection of the right person particularly for the senior level posts is being felt greatly because of tough competition in the employment market. The recruiting agencies namely Union Public Service Commission, State Public Service Commissions, Railway Recruitment Boards etc. require the services of a psychologist for assisting the board in the selection of the right candidate. With the increasing number of the educational institutes the need for more and more guidance counsellors is being felt to provide educational and vocational guidance to the students. Many public schools employ psychologists as counsellors. The professional institutes screen the applicants for admission to the various professional courses. They require the services of a psychologist for administering the psychological tests. There are ample self employment opportunities in the field of psychology. They may start their own guidance/ counselling centres for providing educational and vocational guidance. With the rapid growth of industrialisation and educational facilities, the need for qualified psychologists is expected to increase in the near future.

(j) TRICHOLOGY

Trichology is the scientific study of hair and scalp disorders which include hair thinning, male and female pattern baldness, seborrhea dermatitis, scalp eczema & psoriasis, scalp itching, premature graying, head lice, hair breakage & damage. It is derived from the Greek word 'Tricho' meaning 'hair'. It is a disciplined area of study that began in London, England in 1902. Trichology deals with hair, its anatomy, growth and disease and thus involves in-depth study of chemistry, biology, anatomy and physiology. With the popularization of paramedical sciences, this field has gained much importance in the recent years.

Hair, as a tissue of excretion, is a perfect gauge for physical conditions and acts as a barometer for the body systems. The importance of hair in one's life can be realized by the fact that cause of death of a person can be diagnosed by the analysis of a single hair. In order to be an expert in the area of trichology, knowledge must be gained in the areas of the causes, symptoms, diagnosis and prognosis of specific hair and scalp disorders. Also, a trichologist should be able to recognize certain systemic conditions which are otherwise treated by other medical practitioners.

The International Association of Trichologists (I.A.T.), Australia, is a leading organization in the field of trichology with worldwide society of over 400 certified trichologists. In India, this field gained recognition in 1986 with the establishment of 'Richfeel Trichology Centre' founded by Dr. Apoorva Shah & Dr.Sonal Shah, India's first certified trichologists. In the words of Dr.Apoorva Shah, "Trichology offers tremendous scope for growth in India, as the application and use of trichology is much more than just cosmetic". Recently, MET-Richfeel Institute of Trichology has been launched to impart the science of Trichology and create career opportunities for a Trichologist. The Institute is a tripartitite association between Mumbai Educational Trust, Richfeel/ Trichology Centre and International Association of Trichologist (I.A.T.), Australia.

As a first step, trichologist thoroughly consult the client questioning about his health, diet, family history, hair care etc. A trichologist works in close association with dermatologists, endocrinolgosts, dentists, nutritionists, psychiatrists and cosmetologists.

Though persons working in this area at present are few, but there is an increasing potential for employment growth. After having super specialization in the field of hair and scalp, one can practice as a super specialist doctor. A trichologist can also offer consultancy to beauty saloons and multinational companies. A person with knowledge of trichology can also work as a clinical researcher for hair & scalp, or as an expert witness in the court of law. Self employment and assistance to doctors and paramedical specialists are other viable options.

Both diploma and degree courses are available in this field. Diploma in trichology is of three months duration and is open to paramedics, pharma graduates, clinical researchers, nurses, R&D professionals, science graduates, beauticians and hair stylists. A six month program leading to an international degree certification in trichology can be taken by medical doctors only. These courses can be undertaken by correspondence (distance learning) through I.A.T, Sydney and I.A.T, Adelaide. Indian residents can undertake these courses at the MET-Richfeel Institute of Trichology, Mumbai Educational Trust, Bandra West, Mumbai (http://www.met.edu). Diploma in Advanced Hair Science can be done from Institute of Cosmetic and Laser Surgery Centre, Borivali (W), Mumbai.

(k) VETERINARY SCIENCES

In India, the Veterinary education is as old as the human civilization. Yet it is not very popular among the students preparing for competitive examinations to make their career in the medical or related fields. Veterinary Sciences, encompass the courses to make its students proficient in normal structure and function, animal husbandry practices, treatment, prevention and control of animal disease and public health aspects with the ultimate aim of alleviating animal sufferings and improving socio-economic status. There are five veterinary universities (Table 1) and 35 veterinary colleges under State Agricultural Universities (Table 2) in our country. Syllabi in all the veterinary colleges are based on the recommendations of Veterinary Council of India. All the colleges offer courses for the award of Bachelor of Veterinary Sciences and Animal Husbandry (B.V.Sc. & AH), Master of Veterinary Sciences(M.V.Sc.) and Doctor of Philosophy(Ph.D.) degrees.

Admission in graduation programme is through competitive examination which is conducted by the respective colleges/universities and is mostly restricted to the students belonging to the concerned states. 15% of total seats in each college are filled by Veterinary Council of India through an All India Competition basis. The intake capacity of the most veterinary colleges ranges between 60-80.

The bachelor level degree programme (B.V.Sc.&AH.) is of 5 years duration divided in 10 semesters. In most of the veterinary colleges, the educational process is an evolving process and not merely an acquisition of knowledge. There is a multidisciplinary/ approach at the beginning and last 3 semesters are devoted mainly to self learning through problem-solving approach, group discussion, seminars, hospital practices etc. More emphasis is given on small group teaching and 50% time is devoted to practical training. Whole syllabus of Veterinary Sciences is divided into 187 credit hours and is distributed in 4 subgroups i.e. animal husbandry courses (45 credits), basic veterinary courses (43 credits), clinical and other applied courses (50 credits) and reproduction and other courses (49 credits). The total instruction days are 210 in a year and are not negotiable; this overcomes the problem of free holidays.

The entrance examination is held around May/June and application procedure starts around February to April every year. The students who have passed or are appearing in intermediate or equivalent examination with physics, chemistry and biology as subjects can apply for admission in BV.Sc.&AH. Programme.

Livestock and poultry farming in Indian has assumed greater significance as more than 6-7% of national income comes from this sector. Globally speaking India is first in milk production and 4th in egg/poultry production. The importance of animals to mankind lies in the fact that they can obtain their nourishment from grasses and other fibrous forage which people can't directly utilize. In turn animals provide human with an adequate supply and proper balance of energy, minerals, vitamins and essential proteins through milk, meat, eggs, etc. In addition to the source of food, animals (dog, cat, etc.) are good companions of man. In the light of national rural development programmes, the role of veterinarians becomes very much challenging not only in the area of livestock health but also in the area of agro based industries. The veterinary graduates just after completing their degree may get job in various government and private agencies(Table3) or else they can start their own clinic, pathological/ diagnostic laboratory or animal/poultry breeding farm. In urban areas dog breeding is one of the best option for the Veterinarians.

In government, the Veterinary Officer job starts from the scale of Rs.8000-13500 with usual allowances as per the state/central government rules. The central government and some state government are also providing non-practising allowances(NPA) to the tune of 25% of basic pay which is added to the basic salary for all practical purposes. Hence, a startup salary is around Rs.15000 for a veterinarian in government. Many private concerns provide a good pay package and lucrative perks to the Veterinarians.

It should be understood that the veterinary profession is not less than any other similar profession like medical, dentistry etc. In this area, the job opportunities are enormous in various sectors as listed in Table 3. Besides, one can become entrepreneur by way of dog breeding, diagnostic labs, animal and poultry farms etc.

Students who wish to take admission in the veterinary profession may contact the Registrar/ Controller of Examination of the Veterinary University/ State Agricultural Universities to which the Veterinary Colleges are affiliated. Secretary, Veterinary Council of India, 16/15, W.E.A. Arya Samaj Road, Karol Bag, New Delhi-110 005 may be contacted for admission against 15% seats allocated to the council.

Future of veterinary profession seems to be very bright and in near future it will flourish to provide a growth in terms of GDP. As there is reduction of cultivable land in rural areas, the focus of government is more on animal keeping and utilization of their by-products for safe and organic farming. India has also obtained an U.S. patent on indigenous cow urine for its medicinal properties which will be further exploited to develop various drugs to treat human ailments. Veterinarians will play a key role in the development of "Cow Therapy Medicines(Panchgavya)" which is considered as a future therapeutic approach to control infections in man and animals.

VETERINARY UNIVERSITIES IN INDIA

1. Pt.Deen Dayal Upadhyay Veterinary University and Go Anusandhan Sansthan, Mathura (UP)
2. West Bengal Veterinary University of Animal and Fishery Sciences, Kolkata (WB) (Email-wbuafs@ub.nic.in)
3. Maharashtra Animal Science and Fishery University, Nagpur (MS) (Email-atsherikar@hotmail.com
4. Tamilnadu Veterinary and Animal Sciences University, Chennai (TN) (Email- tanuvas@vsnl.com)
5. Karnataka Veterinary and Fishery Science University, Bidar (KA) (Email- dirahkar@hub.nic.in)

JOB OPPORTUNITIES IN VETERINARY PROFESSION

GOVT. JOBS

1. State Govt. job in Veterinary Hospital, Vaccine Institute, Slaughter House etc. as Veterinary Officer and as PCS Officers
2. Central Govt. job

a. Through UPSC in IAS/IPS
b. IB for treatment of dogs
c. Central breeding farms i.e. cattle or poultry farms
d. Armed forces like RVC, BSF, ITBP

SEMI GOVT. JOBS

1. Banks
2. Insurance Companies
3. Pradeshik Cooperative Dairy Federations (PCDF)

AUTONOMOUS BODIES

1. Research Institutes like ICAR and related Institutes through ASRB
2. Education and research in state agricultural universities/ veterinary colleges
3. National Dairy Development Board (NDDB)

PRIVATE SECTOR

1. Pharmaceuticals and vaccine institutes
2. Pharmaceutical industries
3. Livestock and poultry farms
4. Stud farms
5. Trust hospitals
6. Cattle and poultry feed processing industries

20

Teaching

(a) MONTESSORI TEACHING

The Montessori system of education was innovated by Dr.Maria Montessori (1870-1952) who was ahead of her time in recognizing the important stages of a child's learning and discovering the appropriate ways and means for the growth of a child's creativity. Born in Italy in 1870, Maria Montessori moved to Rome with her parents in 1875 at the age of five. Although her father Alessandro embraced traditional views on female education, it was the more liberal approach of her mother, Renilde Montessori that encouraged Maria Montessori to explore her natural inclination to learn, regardless of the social restrictions placed on women in the male dominated society of the day. In so doing, Renilde played an active role in her daughter's upbringing, and indeed, the whole philosophy behind what is now known as the "Montessori Method".

A quality Montessori classroom has a busy, productive atmosphere where joy and respect abound. Within such an enriched environment, freedom responsibility, and social and intellectual development spontaneously flourish. In other words, Montessori as a human nursery in which human seedlings are converted into plants and then placed in the garden of life.

The main premises of Montessori education are:

- Children are to be respected as different from adults and as individuals who differ from each other.
- The child possesses an unusual sensitivity and intellectual ability, unlike those of the adult, to absorb and learn from his environment, both in quality and quantity.

- The first six years of life are the most important years of a child's growth when unconscious learning gradually emerges to the conscious level.

The Modus operandi of Montessori Programmes:

- **The approach**:- Montessori programmes aim to help children reach their full potential in all areas of life. Specially trained teachers, guide and help the child to experience the joy of learning and ensure the development of self-esteem. The system simply provides the experiences from w[illegible]hildren create their own knowledge.
- **Materials**:- There are especially designed play- learning and material and furniture that speed up jearning by increasing the inquisitiveness and creativity of the children.
- **Positive attitude**:- Most learning activities are individualized, so that a child engages in a learning task that appeals to her and builds a positive attitude toward learning.
- **Developing self- confidence**:- Tasks are designed so that each new step is built upon what the child has already mastered. This removes the negative experience of frequent failure, contributing to the child's healthy emotional development.
- **Habit of concentration**:- The ability to listen attentively to what is said or demonstrated presupposes effective learning. Through a series of absorbing experiences, the child forms habits of extended attention, increasing her ability to concentrate.
- **An abiding curiosity**:- Opportunities are offered for the child to discover qualities, dimensions and relationships amidst a variety of stimulating learning situations thereby developing curiosity, an essential element in creative learning.

Today, parents are well aware of the benefits of an appropriate environment for the successful intellectual, social and emotional development of their children. In a way, it has become a trend to get children trained in Montessorie for formal schooling. That is why this [illegible] gradually expanding and acquiring a professional approach. [illegible] several educational institutions offering professional courses [illegible]ori teaching.

1. Infant/Toddler Diploma programme
2. Pre-school/Kindergarten Diploma Programme

Employment Scenario in India:

Trained Montessori teachers are in great demand in our country in view of the development of this field. This job is considered to be very respectable and full of creativity. With the emergence of branded play-schools like 'Kidzee', Montessori sector of our country is expected to flourish.

Potential Employers:

1. Creches
2. Play Schools
3. Pre-schools
4. Self-employment in the form of managing crèches

Educational institutions offering courses in Montessori teaching:

1. SZM Montessori Training Course, 30 NS Patkar Marg, RTI Annexe, Mumbai- 400007, PH: 223679161/2
2. Calcutta Montessori Training Centre, email: bose@cmtc.in
3. Netaji Subhash Open University (NSOU) 1, Woodburn Park, Kolkata-700020 PH-033-22835157, email-admin@wbnsou.com
4. Zee Interactive Learning Systems Ltd. Centres:
   (b) Valecha Chambers, 3rd Floor, Plot No.B-6, Andheri Link Rd, Andheri West, Mumbai-400053 PH 022-26743900, 26743901
   (b) FC-20, Sector 16-A, Film City, Noida-201301, PH-0120-5311320

(b) TEACHING

A successful teacher is one who is able to foster creative thinking, develop skills as well as instil a desire for lifelong learning among students. Teaching is a noble profession. It is considered to be a pursuit that has the potentials to make or mar the destiny of the people. The administrators, doctors, scientists, engineers and all other professionals are the proud products of a sound teaching order. Job of teaching is self-rewarding so far as experience, knowledge and emotional satisfaction is concerned. In this profession you may work, earn and remain youthful as all the time you are among the youth. The teaching community includes pre-primary and primary teachers, school teachers, subject teachers, general teachers, teacher of physical education, science, commerce, medicine, engineering and technology and language; lectures and readers in colleges and universities.

With ever increasing growth in population and awakening among the populace, there has been a substantial increase in number of school teachers, particularly female teachers. Although a large number of teachers are available in humanities, yet shortage is generally felt in finding suitable hands to take up teaching jobs in engineering, medicine, technology etc. To attract persons of right calibre to the teaching profession, a lot has already been done to improve the working conditions of the teaching community at all levels. Teachers are permitted to appear as private candidates for various university examinations to improve their qualifications. They may also add to their income by writing books, evaluate answer sheets or acting as invigilators, examiners or paper setters. Private tuition work may also be a source of their additional income particularly in big cities. The profession demands cheerful, cool and friendly temperament and immense patience and energy, since working with students- whether children or grown-up youth- can cause considerable strain. Persons with physical defects, such as impediment of speech, poor hearing, nervous disorders, etc. are likely to be handicapped in the profession. Teaching profession should be adopted by persons who regard it as a service to the society and are prepared to inspire and guide the youth by contributing to their success and building up their character. A teacher's designation depends upon the level or the type of training he has undergone.

Besides teaching, teachers may be asked to attend to various other items of work depending upon their placement. In schools, generally, teachers are asked to allot, collect and check home work of students. Science teachers conduct and demonstrate experiments in science laboratories. They also have to evaluate the performance of science students. The teachers also conduct promotion tests and prepare examination results. In schools, they have to guide students about their academic, social and personal problems in group or on individual basis. In other words, we may say the teachers have to play the role of guardians in some of the situations.

PERSONAL QUALITIES

Coherent speech, above average intelligence, liking for study and learning, self-disciplined, sense of humour and fair play, adaptability and thorough knowledge of the teaching subject etc.

PRE-PRIMARY SCHOOL TEACHERS teach children of nursery and kindergarten classes adopting Montessor or playway methods of education. They have to emphasise on developing values of obedience, cleanliness, punctuality and cooperation among their students. Generally, it is a single teacher's responsibility to keep one group of students busy during the entire school day. He has to supervise various activities performed by these students.

PRIMARY SCHOOL TEACHER- teaches students of primary classes i.e. from Ist to Vth standard in all subjects such as arithmetic, language, history, geography and general science. He is responsible for conducting tests and examinations and prepare examination results.

SENIOR SECONDARY SCHOOL TEACHER- He teaches one or more subjects to the students in regional/ national language or English. He also allots and checks home work, gives practical instructions in science subjects in laboratory with the help of laboratory demonstrators and attendants.

PHYSICAL TRAINING INSTRUCTOR/ PHYSICAL EDUCATION TEACHER

He imparts physical education to students. He is responsible for organizing group activities like games, sports, mass physical drills etc. He also sometimes organises inter institution sports competition and athletic events. In some schools he is responsible for maintaining discipline amongst students. He looks after the upkeep of the play grounds and sports equipments. There are drawing/ art teachers, music teachers, home science teachers etc. They have to acquire specialised skill/ training in their own field.

SPECIAL EDUCATORS

Teachers who have dedicated themselves to the cause of the handicapped children have perhaps outgrown the garb of nobility as their job requires much more. Dedicated to a cause teachers of the handicapped have a unique ability to empathise with these children while; helping them learn. The task is daunting but each child's experience through the learning process offers a unique reward to the specialist teachers. Disabilities among children are generally accompanied by a number of problems, both behavioural as well as related learning or cognition. The job of special educators is complex as it demands comprehensive skills for approaching the needs and requirements of each child with special needs. Special type of skill/ training is required for managing various kinds of handicaps in children.

THE SCHOOL COUNSELLOR

He guides or counsels individual students regarding various problems such as educational, vocational, personal etc. Besides providing educational and occupational information, he is also supposed to provide comprehensive counselling service in the form of interviewing, testing and group guidance etc. Allocation of students for different streams of education, may be done by the school in consultation with counsellor.

LECTURES

The college/ University teachers are designated as lecturer, reader and professor. Sometimes, they are designated as lecturers in subject concerned such as Lecturer in Mathematics or Lecturer in Commerce and so on. Senior lecturers in their respective subjects who look after a particular department are designated as head of the department in that discipline. In case of science, engineering and medical students, he also supervises demonstration and practical work in the laboratories. He refers material/ publications for further specialised study. One of his responsibilities is to conduct seminars and tutorials. Some of the lecturers are also given the responsibility of setting examination papers for university examinations, evaluation of answer books and preparation of results.

TRAINING

For becoming a primary/nursery teacher one has to undergo specialised training of one or two years duration. In Delhi, State Council of Education Research and Training, Defence Colony, New Delhi-110 024 conducts two years Diploma in Early Childhood care and Education for 10+2 pass candidates (45% marks) in the age group of 17-30 years. The admission is through a written test followed by interview. One may also go for BTC, JBT, ETC, etc. available in number of institutes.

For teaching high school classes, graduates undergo one year B.Ed course available in number of colleges/institutes. Indira Gandhi National Open University, New Delhi; H.P. University, Shimla; M.D.University, Rohtak, Punjabi University, Patiala, Kurukshetra University, Kurukshetra etc. offer B.Ed. through correspondence for teachers of recognised schools who have two years experience. One may go for M.Ed.(One year course) after doing B.Ed. Ph.D and M.Phill courses in education are also available in some universities. Those who aspire to be a physical education instructor, B.P.Ed is must. It is a 3 years course after 10+2 or one year course after graduation. Those who teach Senior Secondary classes are post graduates in their subjects plus B.Ed/ M.Ed. The school counsellor are generally post graduates in Psychology or education. P.G. Diploma in guidance and counselling of one year duration is available in various institutes.

For becoming a lecturer, one should possess excellent academic record and a Doctorate degree. Some universities recruit lecturers through press advertisement while others recruit through NET (National Education Test) conducted by University Grants Commission twice a year. For lecturers in Science subjects the NET is conducted jointly by UGC-CSIR. Most of the states conduct SLET examination for inducting lecturers in examination for inducting lecturers in the colleges located in the respective state. The advertisement for NET is issued in leading dailies.

In recent years there has been a good demand for teachers not only in the country but abroad also. UK & USA has asked for Indian teachers. Well known teachers may find suitable job opportunities in International Organisations such as WHO, UNESCO and UNICEF etc. Some may join well known research institutes or even may become visiting professors in foreign universities. Some well known professors may be appointed Chairman/Member of the Committee/ Commissions set up by the Government.

1. Institutes offering BA, B.Ed./B.Sc.,B.Ed., course; duration 4 years, eligibility 10+2
2. Regional Institutes of Education (NCERT) at Ajmer, Bhopal, Bhubaneshwar and Mysore; Barkatullah University, Bhopal; Devi Alhilya University, Indore; M.D.Saraswati University, Ajmer; Utkal University, Bhubaneshwar; Shivaji University, Kolhapur, University of Mysore, Mysore.
3. Delhi University- (Aditi Mahavidyalaya, New Delhi-110 039; Gargi College, New Delhi-110 049; Jesus and Mary College, New Delhi-110 021; Lady Sriram College, New Delhi-110 024; S.P. Mukherjee College, New Delhi-110 026 and Institute of Home Economics) Bel Ed; 4 years, 10+2 (For Girls only) Total seats-210.
4. Institute offering B.Ed/M.Ed. courses in special education:BHU, Varanasi; Kurukshetra University, Kurukshetra; MJP, Rohilkhand University, Bareilly, University of Mumbai, Mumbai, Osmania University, Hyderabad; SNDT Women's University, Mumbai.
5. Institutes offering PG Diploma in Guidance and counselling: Ravi Shanker University, Raipur; M.S.University, Baroda, University of Mumbai, Muumbai, Rani Durgavati University, Jabalpur; Punjab University, Chandigarh; Barkatullah University, Bhopal and Regional Institutes of Education (NCERT) Bhopal and Mysore etc.
6. M.Ed (through correspondence) - Karnataka State Open University, Mysore; Kota Open University, Kota; Nalanda Open University, Patna; Yashwant Rao Chavan Open University, Nasik and Andhra University, Vishakhapatnam.

(c) TEACHER ASSISTANTS

Description

Perform duties that are instructional in nature or deliver direct services to students or parents. Serve in a position for which a teacher or another professional has ultimate responsibility for the design and implementation of educational programs and services.

Experience

Previous work-related skill, knowledge, or experience is required for these occupations.

Education

Most occupations in this zone require training in vocational schools, related on-the-job experience, or an associate's degree. Some may require a bachelor's degree.

Training

Employees in these occupations usually need one or two years of training involving both on-the-job experience and informal training with experienced workers.

Tasks

1. Presents subject matter to students, using lecture, discussion, or supervised role-playing methods.
2. Helps students, individually or in groups, with lesson assignments to present or reinforce learning concepts.
3. Plans, prepares, and develops various teaching aids, such as bibliographies, charts, and graphs.
4. Prepares, administers, and grades examinations.
5. Confers with parents on progress of students.
6. Discusses assigned teaching area with classroom teacher to coordinate instructional efforts.

Prepares lesson outline and plan in assigned area and submits outline to teacher for review.

21

Technician

(a) CARTOONISTS

Description

Create original artwork using any of a wide variety of mediums and techniques, such as painting and sculpture.

Experience

A minimum of two to four years of work-related skill, knowledge, or experience is needed for these occupations.

Education

Most of these occupations require a bachelor's degree, but some do not.

Training

Employees in these occupations usually need several years of work-related experience, on-the-job training, and/or vocational training.

Tasks

1. Sketches and submits cartoon or animation for approval.
2. Labels each section with designated colors when colors are used.
3. Develops color patterns and moods and paints background layouts to dramatize action for animated cartoon scenes.
4. Discusses ideas for cartoons, comic strips, or animations with editor or publisher's representative.
5. Renders sequential drawings of characters or other subject material which when photographed and projected at specific speed becomes animated.

6. Creates and prepares sketches and model drawings of characters, providing details from memory, live models, manufactured products, or reference material.
7. Develops personal ideas for cartoons, comic strips, or animations, or reads written material to develop ideas.
8. Makes changes and corrections to cartoon, comic strip, or animation as necessary.

(b) DENTAL LABORATORY TECHNICIAN

A dental technician is a personnel who makes artificial teeth, which replaces natural teeth in the mouth. This involves making of a single tooth or multiple teeth and can be a fixed prosthesis or a removable one. A dental laboratory technical is an important and responsible member of the dental health care team. He generally works in coordination with a dentist or dentists and takes the work order as per their requirements. The technican is a skilled person who has command over the use of small hand instruments, has artistic ability and provides great accuracy and attention in producing the minutest detail in his work.

What does a Dental Technician do?

The duties and work sphere of such a technician is quite challenging as every specific prosthesis he makes has to be according to the specific needs of the patient. He follows the instructions and specifications of the dentist and also sees the patient, if necessary. He takes the impressions from the dentist and builds an artificial prosthesis, which has to reproduce similar functions and be in harmony with the oral cavity as well as to give patient satisfaction.

He create full dentures, removable partial dentures, crowns, veneers and orthodontic appliances.

Tools / Equipments

A dental lab technician works with hand instruments and operate various electronic and manual devices like induction casting machines, furnaces, manual saw or lathe and model trimmers.

Demands of the Profession

1. They should have the ability to perform fine motor skills and work for long hours.
2. Their eyesight should be 20/20 and they should not be colour blind.
3. They should be able to appreciate the shape of a tooth and should have a great colour scheme.
4. Their memory should be sharp and they should have the ability to read, write and retain.

Training/Qualification:

A dental technician is usually trained for a period of two years. The course is certified dental laboratory technician in which he learns to make all the prosthesis along with which he learns to operate all the tools and equipments, gets complete know-how of the materials used and becomes familiar with all the technical terms used in dentistry.

Where does the Dental Technician Work?

1. They work in commercial dental laboratories at various levels.
2. They can set up their own dental laboratory big or small.
3. They can work as chain side assistants to the dentists.
4. They are employed in dental colleges and hospitals.
5. Along with their regular job they can also start a lab at their home. It can be taken up as a part time profession too.
6. There is a great demand for dental technicians outside India. Given the mismatch between the demand for especially in the field of cosmetic dentistry, and their supply, job opportunities for skilled technicians are excellent.

List of Few Institution are:

1. MRA Dental College, Bangalore
2. Govt. Dental College, Loni, Maharashtra
3. Kasturba Gandhi Medical College, Lucknow
4. Armed Forces Medical College,Pune
5. RAGAS dental College and Hospital, Chennai
6. National Industrial Training Centre, New Delhi

   all that now is and all that is not.

(c) DIETICIANS AND NUTRITIONS

Description

Plan and conduct food service or nutritional programs to assist in the promotion of health and control of disease. May supervise activities of a department providing quantity food services, counsel individuals, or conduct nutritional research.

Experience

A minimum of two to four years of work-related skill, knowledge, or experience is needed for these occupations.

Education

Most of these occupations require a bachelor's degree.

Training

Employees in these occupations usually need several years of work-related experience, on-the-job training, and/or vocational training.

Tasks

1. Develops and implements dietary-care plans based on assessments of nutritional needs, diet restrictions, and other current health plans.
2. Supervises activities of workers engaged in planning, preparing, and serving meals.
3. Plans, conducts, and evaluates dietary, nutritional, and epidemiological research, and analyzes findings for practical applications.
4. Evaluates nutritional care plans and provides follow-up on continuity of care.
5. Confers with design, building, and equipment personnel to plan for construction and remodeling of food service units.
6. Plans and prepares grant proposals to request program funding.
7. Writes research reports and other publications to document and communicate research findings.
8. Develops curriculum and prepares manuals, visual aids, course outlines, and other materials used in teaching.
9. Inspects meals served for conformance to prescribed diets and standards of palatability and appearance.
10. Plans, organizes, and conducts training programs in dietetics, nutrition, and institutional management and administration for medical students and hospital personnel.
11. Consults with physicians and health care personnel to determine nutritional needs and diet restrictions of patient or client.
12. Instructs patients and their families in nutritional principles, dietary plans, and food selection and preparation.
13. Monitors food service operations and ensures conformance to nutritional and quality standards.

(d) FILM LABORATORY TECHNICIAN

Description

Evaluate motion picture film to determine characteristics, such as sensitivity to light, density, and exposure time required for printing.

Experience

A minimum of two to four years of work-related skill, knowledge, or experience is needed for these occupations.

Education

Most of these occupations require a bachelor's degree, but some do not.

Training

Employees in these occupations usually need several years of work-related experience, on-the-job training, and/or vocational training.

Tasks

1. Records test data and routes film to film developer and film printer for further processing.
2. Examines developed film strip to determine optimal exposure time and light intensity required for printing.
3. Threads film strip through densitometer and exposes film to light to determine density of film.
4. Computes amount of light intensity needed to compensate for density of film, using standardized formulas.
5. Exposes film strip to progressively timed lights to compare effects of various exposure times.
6. Reads gauges on sensitometer to determine film's sensitivity to light.
7. Threads film strip through sensitometer and exposes film to light.

(e) MEDICAL RECORDS AND HEALTH INFORMATION TECHNICIANS

Description

Compile, process, and maintain medical records of hospital and clinic patients in a manner consistent with medical, administrative, ethical, legal, and regulatory requirements of the health care system. Process, maintain, compile, and report patient information for health requirements and standards.

Experience

Previous work-related skill, knowledge, or experience is required for these occupations.

Education

Most occupations in this zone require training in vocational schools, related on-the-job experience, or an associate's degree. Some may require a bachelor's degree.

Training

Employees in these occupations usually need one or two years of training involving both on-the-job experience and informal training with experienced workers.

Tasks

1. Compiles and maintains medical records of patients to document condition and treatment and to provide data for research studies.

2. Maintains variety of health record indexes and storage and retrieval systems.
3. Enters data, such as demographic characteristics, history and extent of disease, diagnostic procedures, and treatment into computer.
4. Prepares statistical reports, narrative reports and graphic presentations of tumor registry data for use by hospital staff, researchers, and other users.
5. Contacts discharged patients, their families, and physicians to maintain registry with follow-up information, such as quality of life and length of survival of cancer patients.
6. Assists in special studies or research, as needed.
7. Reviews records for completeness and to abstract and code data, using standard classification systems, and to identify and compile patient data.

Compiles medical care and census data for statistical reports on diseases treated, surgery performed, and use of hospital beds.

(f) PHARMACY TECHNICIANS

Description

Prepare medications under the direction of a pharmacist. May measure, mix, count out, label, and record amounts and dosages of medications.

Experience

Some previous work-related skill, knowledge, or experience may be helpful in these occupations, but usually is not needed.

Education

These occupations usually require a high school diploma and may require some vocational training or job-related course work. In some cases, an associate's or bachelor's degree could be needed.

Training

Employees in these occupations need anywhere from a few months to one year of working with experienced employees.

Tasks

1. Assists pharmacist to prepare and dispense medication.
2. Prepares intravenous (IV) packs, using sterile technique, under supervision of hospital pharmacist.
3. Counts stock and enters data in computer to maintain inventory records.

4. Cleans equipment and sterilizes glassware according to prescribed methods.
5 Mixes pharmaceutical preparations, fills bottles with prescribed tablets and capsules, and types labels for bottles.
6 Receives and stores incoming supplies.
7 Processes records of medication and equipment dispensed to hospital patient, computes charges, and enters data in computer.

22

Self Employment Opportunities

(a) SERVICE INSTITUTES & PROGRAMMES

Whether you have decided to launch a new business from home or decided to work from home, certain basic aspects should be borne in mind.

Working from home takes strong discipline and concentration, if you have been working in a regular office envoronment and are not sure about working independently, then try it out experimentally before signing off from your full time job.

ORGANIZATIONS/INSTITUTIONS/PROGRAMMES/SCHEMES

In the process of surveying opportunities for self employment and working from home, budding entrepreneurs can make use of certain programmes and institutions.

Here is an indicative listing of leads to follow.

Small Industries Service Institutes (SISIs)

Small Industries Services Institutes throughout the country organize Entrepreneurship Development Programmes of 4 to 6 week duration (with normal intake of 30 participants) as a regular feature. The purpose of such programmes is to cultivate the latent traints and capabilities of the youth (both men and women).

During the programmes participants learn various aspects that are necessary and useful for setting up and managing small scale industries.

Specific programmes are targeted at particular items/ activities. Participants learn about the scope and potential of different items, which can be manufactured in a small scale industry, its technical feasibility, economic viability and commercial prospects as a self employment venture. The practical and theoretical inputs are supplemented by visits to small scale units and hand on practices on machinery/ process. This enables them to prepare or be assisted in their own project report. Project reports are duly appraised, evaluated and corrected in consultation with the experts.

- SISI, Agra
  34, Industrial Estate, Nunhal, Agra-282006
- SISI, Ahmedabad
  Harsiddh Chamber, 4th Floor, Ashram Road, Ahmedabad-380014
  (www.sisiabd.com)
- SISI, Allahabad
  E-17/18,Industrial Estate, Naini, Allahabad-211009
- SISI, Bangalore
  Rajaji Nagar, Bangalore-560044)
  (www.sisikarnataka.org)
- SISI, Chennai
  65/1,G.S.T. Road, Guindy, P.B. 3746, Chennai-600032
  (www.sisi-chennai.com)
- SISI, Cuttack
  Vikas Sadan, College Square, Cuttack-753003
  (www.sisiorissa.org)
- SISI,Gangtok
  Tadong Housing Colony, PO-Tadong,Gangtok-737102
  (www.sikkim.nic.in)
- SISI, Goa
  Opp. Konkan Railway Station (Kepem road), PO Box 334, Margao-403601
  (www.sisigoa.nic.in)
- SISI,Guwahati
  Bamuni Maidan,Guwahati-781021
  (www.sisiguwahati.com)
- SISI, Haldwani
  Kaladungi Road, Haldwani-263139
- SISI, Hubli
  Industrial Estate, Gokul Road, Hubli-580030
- SISI,Hyderabad
  Narsapur X Road, Balanagar, Hyderabad-500037
  (www.sisi-ap.com)
- SISI, Imphal
  C-17/18,Takyelpat Industrial Estate, Imphal-795001
- SISI, Indore
  10, Industrial Estate, Polo Ground, Indore-452003
  (www.sisiindore.com)
- SISI,Jaipur
  22, Godown, Industrial Estate, Jaipur-302006
  (www.sisijaipur.gov.in)

- SISI, Kanpur
  107, Industrial Estate, Kalpi Road, Kanpur-208012
  (www.sisikanpur.com)
- SISI, Karnal
  Industrial Development Colony, Near ITI, Kunjpura Road, Karnal-132001
  (www.sisiharyana.org)
- SISI, Kolkata
  111 &112, B.T. Road, Kolkata-700035
  (www.sisikolkata.org)
- SISI, Ludhiana
  Industrial Area B, Ludhiana-141003
  (www.sisidh.com)
- SISI, Mumbai
  Kurla-Andheri Road, Saki Naka, Mumbai-400072
  (www.sisimumbai.com)
- SISI, Muzaffarpur
  Goshala Road, PO-Ramna, Muzaffarpur-842002
- SISI, Nagpur
  'C' Block, C.G.O.Complex,Seminary Hill, Nagpur-440006
  (www.sisinagpur.com)
- SISI, New Delhi
  Okhla Industrial Estate, New Delhi-110020
  (www.sisinewdelhi.com)
- SISI, Patna
  Industrial Estate, Patna-800013
  (www.sisipatna.org)
- SISI, Raipur
  Small Industries Service Institute (Branch)
  Opp.Chhatisgarh Club, Civil Lines, Raipur-492 001
- SISI, Ranchi
  Kokar Industrial Estate, Ranchi-834001
  (www.sisi-ranchi.com)
- SISI, Solan
  Chambaghat, Solan-173213
  (www.sisihimachal.com)
- SISI, Srinagar
  36, B/C, Gandhi Nagar, Jammu-180004
- SISI,Trichur
  Kanjany Road, Ayyanthole,Trichur-680003
  (www.sisikerala.org)

Prime Minister's Rozgar Yojana
(www.smallindustryindia.com)

The scheme is designed to create and provide sustainable self-employment opportunities to educate (upto class VIII) unemployed youth (18-35 years of age) in the country. It covers economically viable activities including agriculture and allied activities but excluding direct agricultural operations like raising crop, purchase of manure etc. The District Industry Centres and the Directorates of Industries are mainly responsible for implementation of the scheme along with banks.

Rural Self Employment

Department of Rural Development (www.drd.nic.in) offers Swarna Jayanti Gram Swarozgar Yojana as a self employment programme for the rural poor.

Women Entrepreneurs

Special efforts are being made to encourage women entrepreneurs to come forward. The Small Industries Development Organization(SIDO) (www.laghu-udyog.com or www. smallindustryindia .com), the various State Small Industries Development Corporations (SSIDCs), the nationalised banks and even NGOs are conducting various programmes including Entrepreneurship Development Programmes (EDPs).

For potential women entrepreneurs, without adequate educational background and skills, SIDO has introduced process/ product oriented EDPs in areas like TV repairing, printed circuit boards, leather goods, screen printing etc. Enterprise Training for Women (ETW) supported by SIDBI is being offered in various cities for women with business ideas who are above 25 years of age, fluent in English and at least 12 years of schooling.

Knowledge Driven Enterprises

We have a large well educated scientific and technical manpower with the vision for entrepreneurship but not the confidence to set up independent enterprises. It is in this context that the National Science and Technology Entrepreneurship Development Board (NSTEDB), can be of great help. NSTEDB was established by Government of India in 1982 with the broad objective of promoting gainful self employment amongst the S&T manpower in the country and to setup knowledge based and innovation driven enterprises. Details/ formats and guidelines on the NSTEDB and related programmes are given on the websites www.nstedb.com and www.techno-preneur.net or contact National Science and Technology Entrepreneurship Development Board (NSTEDB), Department of Science and Technology, Technology Bhawan, New Mehrauli Road, New Delhi-110 016.

More Leads to Follow

- An Undertaking of Association of Lady Entrepreneurs of Andhra Pradesh, H.N.8-2-677/B/1, Road No.12, 3rd Right Beside Banjara Castle, Banjara Hills, Hyderabad-500034 (www.aleap.org)
- Institute of Entrepreneurship Development, IED Bihar, B.S.F.C. Building, 5th Floor, Fraser Road, PB No.114, Patna-800001, A-23, Sector 62, Industrial Area, Phase-II, Noida-201301
- Centre for Development of Entrepreneurship, Haryana Institute of Public Administration , 76, HIPA Complex, Sector 18, Gurgaon-122001 (www.hipa.nic.in)
- J&K Entrepreneurship Development Institute, Directorate of Information, Jammu & Kashmir Government, Opposite Partap Park, Abhi Guzar Lal Chowk, Srinagar
- Kerala Industrial and Technical Consultancy Organization Ltd.,PB No.1820, Ravipuram M.G. Road, Cochin-682016 (www.kitco-cochin.com)
- Centre for Entrepreneurship Development of Karnataka, Plot No.1 (A&B), Belur Industrial Area, Belgaum Road, Dharwad-580011, Karnataka (www.nitpu3.kar.nic.in)
- Maharashtra Centre for Entrepreneurship Development, A-38, MIDC Railway Station, Aurangabad-431005
- Centre for Entrepreneurship Development, Madhya Pradesh, 60, Jail Road, Jehangirabad, Bhopal-462008 (www.cedmapindia.com)
- Institute of Entrepreneurship Development, Orissa, N-1/224, IRC Village Nayapally, Bhubaneshwar-751015
- Entrepreneurship Development & Management Laboratory Building, 22 Godown, Industrial Area-1, Jaipur-302019
- Tamil Nadu Centre for Entrepreneurship Development CED-SIPO,Campus No.4, T.B.Road, Madurai-625010
- National Institute of Entrepreneurship and Small Business Development (NIESBUD), A-23, Sector-62, Industrial Area, Phase-II, Noida-201301 (www.niesbud.nic.in)
- Institute of Entrepreneurship Development(UP), A 1&2, Sarojini Nagar, Industrial Area, Kanpur Road, Lucknow-226008
- Directorate General of Employment & Training, New Delhi (www.dget.nic.in)
- Entrepreneurship Development Institute of India Ahmedabad, PO Bhat-382428, Dist.-Gandhinagar, Gujarat(India) (www.edindia.org)

Open Learning Program on Entrepreneurship which is an online course (E-Course) on Entrepreneurship, developed by Entrepreneurship Development Institute of India, Ahmedabad and supported by NSTEDB, Department of Science and Technology, Govt.

of India. This course covers all topics related to Entrepreneurship. It also helps prompt budding entrepreneurs to take right decision for the business.

1-Year Post Graduate Diploma in Business Entrepreneurship & Management (specialisation in Family Business Management or New Enterprise Creation or Agri-Entrepreneurship) open to graduates through an entrance test and personal interview.

Admission for Post Graduate Diploma in Management of NGO is meant for those who wish to join or set up a Non Governmental Organisation(NGO).

Whenever you dream about starting a business a multitude of typical start up and growth questions will plague you.

One of the most frequently asked questions is, "What kind of business is easy to start and guaranteed to be successful"?

Ambiguity

You have to accept that the world of entrepreneurship is going to be an ongoing puzzle; there will be ambiguity and if you can not handle that, avoid it altogether.

Risk

Risk is always associated with making an entrepreneurial venture successful.

Index

A

Abul Kalam, APJ, Ind.Pres., 14, 309
Academic Institutions and Colleges for Unani System of Medicine, 281
Accountants, 19
  Description, 19
  Education, 19
  Tasks, 19
  Training, 19
Accounting
  Financial Management, 60
  Principles, 22
  System, 19, 20
Acid Rain, 46
Actuaries, 35, 36
  Courses, 37
  Duties and Tasks, 39
  Employers, 37
  Examination Scheme, 37
  Institute offering Courses, 37
  Qualifications, 37
  Role in Insurance, 36
  Society of India, 37
  Trainee, 37
  Training, 39
Advertising, 137
Aeronautical
  Education and Space System, 111
  Engineering, 101
Aeronautics, 14
Aerospace System, 110
Agricultural
  Biotechnology, 307
  Engineering, 198
  Engineers, 159-161
  Career, 159, 160
  Role, 159
  Institutes, 219, 220
  Research Service, 304
  Universities, 160-163, 198, 210
Agro-Based
  Industries, 199
  Management (ABM), 199, 200
Agro-Clinics, 200, 207, 208, 304
Agro-Processing Enterprise, 159
AIIMS Forensic Departments, 323
AIIMS, Delhi, 259, 261
Air Force Academy, 96
Air Hostess,
  Education Qualifications, 109
  General Requirements, 108
  Promotional Avenues, 110
  Selection Procedure, 109
  Specific Requirements, 108
Air India, 110
Air Pollution Management, 46
Aircraft Maintenance Engineers (AME) License, 112
  Training Institutions, 115
Aircraft Manufacturing Industry, 111
Airport Authority of India (AAI), 114
Aligarh Muslim University, Aligarh, 232
All India Coordinated—Floriculture Projects, 212
Allied Teaching Culture (ATC) of Gem, 179
Alps Academy, Delhi, 190
Ambani, Dhirubhai, 51
Amity Business Scheme, Noida, 67
Amity School of Communication, 137
Anti-Smuggling Operation, 102
Arab Medicine, 278
Architect Training Facilities, 74

Areas of Specialization in Foreign
  Languages, 242
Armed Forces, 9, 94, 97, 163, 166
  Medical College (AFMC) Pune, 95
  Recruitment Procedure, 94-95
  Women in-, 95
Army Act, 1950, 165
Aromatherapy, 245, 246
  Institutions Offering Courses, 247
  Job Opportunities, 245
  Potential Employers, 246
Art Institutions in India and Abroad, 92-93
Art, Craft Technology of War, 97
ASEAN Summit, 192
Asian Disaster Preparedness
  Centre (ADPC), 43
Assessors, 21
  Duties and Tasks, 22
  Education, 21
  Jobs, 21
  Training, 21
Astronaut, 110
Atharvaveda, 90
Audiologists, 275-277
  Job Opportunity, 276
  Working Fields, 277
Audit Records, 21
Auditing Standards, 22
Auditors, 20
  Duties, 20
  Education, 20
  Training, 200
Auto CAD Training, 174
Automation, 146
Autopsies, 323
Aviation
Agencies, 113
  Industry, 112
  Sector, 111
Ayurveda, 248
  Courses, 248
  Medical Colleges, 249
  System, 249
Azim Premji, 51

B

Bangladesh and Sri Lanka, 312
Banking Sector, 31
Bhangra of Punjab, 82
Bharat Muni, 90
Bharat Natya Shastra, 79
Bhartiya Kala Kendra, 83
Bhathkhanda Sangeet Vidyalaya,
  Lucknow, 87
Bilingualism, 242
Bill Gates, 51
Bio-Computing, 306
Biocomputing, 325
Bio-Fertilizers, 209
Bio-Medical Engineering, 137, 306
  Institutions, 138
Bio-Pesticides, 209
Biophysics, 260
Bio-Safety Conditions, 307
Biosensors, 325
Biotechnology, 303-307, 325, 326
  Animal, 303
  Aquaculture, 303
  Education Centres, 308-309
  Environmental, 303, 307, 325
  Food, 303
  Industrial, 303
  Marine, 303
  Medical, 303
  Microbiological, 303
  Plantation, 303
  Seri-, 303
Border Road
  Organization, (BRO), 163, 165-167
  Task Force, (BRTF), 164
BPO Industry, 294
Brake Dance, 87
Budget Analysis, 20
Building Rules and Bylaws, 73
Business Process Outsourcing
  (BPO), 282, 283

C

Cabin Crew, 107-109, 112
CAD System (Computer Aided
  Designing), 168, 169
CAD/CAM System, 195, 273
Call Centre Hotspots, 283
  Bangalore—Chennai, 283
CAM System (Computer Aided
  Manufacturing), 168, 169
Canadian Development Agency, 58
Candle Making, 190

Career
Opportunities for Agriculture Grades, 201-204
Prospects in Theatre, 92
Types Details, 48
Carnatic Classical Music, 80, 86
Cartoonist Jobs, 349
Central Council for Research in Ayurveda and Siddha, (CCRAS), 249
Central/Regional Research Institutions, 249
Central Forensic Laboratories, 323
Central Institute of Plastic Engineering and Technology, (CIPT), 191, 192
Central Pay Commisison, 166
Centre for Disaster Management, 43
Chambers of Commerce, 239
Champaben Bhagat Education Trust, 174
Charak Samhita, 248
Chartered Accountancy, 22
Chartered Accountants Examination Tips, 23
Chawla, Kalpana, 110
Chheu Dance of Bihar, 82
Chip Design Industry, 172
Choreography (Choreographers), 82, 83, 89
CIM (Computer Integrated Manufacturing) System, 168
Citibank, 282
Civil Service Regulations, 165
Classical Dance Forms, 80
CMC Vellore, 259, 261
Coast Guards, 9
College
of Fire Technology, 174
of Fisheries, 303
of Sports and Physical Education, 147-148
Columbia—Kenya, 211
Commercial Pilot License (CPL), 112, 115
Communication and Information Technology, 60
Community Managers, 68
Company Secretary, 293, 295-297
Employers and Prospects, 294
Functions, 293
Prospects Abroad, 295
Services, 296
Company's Act, 1956, 25
Comprehensive Economic Cooperation Agreements, 295
Computer
Based Tests, 22
Graphics, 289
Operators, 285
Operators, Education and Training, 286
Operators, Tasks and Duties, 286
Computerized Reservation System, 109
Comte, August, 148
Confederation of Asian and Pacific Accountants (CAPA), 27
Construction
Industry, 72
Projects, 40
Conventional Planners, 120
Education, 120
Experience, 120
Tasks, 120, 121
Training, 120
Copywriting and Advertising, 9
Corporate Financial Management Tax Adm.—Capital Market, 30
Corporate Financing Educational Qualifications, 31
Corporate Financing, 30
Cost Accounting Records, 25
Cost Effectiveness, 40
Cost Production, 25
Costing System, 25
Cost-Saving Methods, 40
Council of Logistic Management, 62
Country Planners, 73
Crime Investigation, 324
Crimes, 322
Criminal Procedure Code, 322, 323
Criminology, 323
CSIR (Council of Scientific and Industrial Research), 306, 326, 327, 330, 337
Customers Relations, 60

D

Dairy Education, 309, 310
Dairy Industry, 309, 310, 312
Dairy Science College, 310

Administrative Procedure, 311
Career Opportunity, 311
Eligibility, 311
Dairy Technologists, 310
Dairy Technology, 198, 310
Dance Stalwarts, 79
Birju Maharaj, 79
Jay Rama Rao and Vanashri Rao, 79
Mallika Sarabhai, 79
Radha and Raja Reddy, 79
Sudha Chandran, 79
Dance Therapy (Movement), 83, 84
Danish International Development Agency, 58
DDA/GDA, 76
Defence
Air Bases, 114
Forces, 9, 112, 113
Services, 100
Services, Entry into-, 100
Delhi Sultans, 278
Dental Health Care, 350
Dental Lab
Technicians Jobs, 350
Technicians List of Institutions, 351
Technicians Training, 351
Desktop Publishing, 288
Experience, Education and Training, 288
Tasks and Duties, 288
Detective Services, 9
Die Making, 193
Dies, Tools, Jigs, Moulds, and Fixtures, 193, 194
Dieticians Jobs, 352
Disaster Management, 42, 44
Centre (USA), 43
Curriculum and Courses, 42
Institute (DMI), 43
Disaster Mitigation and Rehabilitation, 44
Dr. YS Parmar University of Horticulture and Forestry, Solan, (HP), 212
Dramaturgy, 79
DRDO (Defence Research and Dev. Org), 331
Drought Management, 42
Duplicator Machine Operators, 287

E

Eco Tourism, 48
Economic
Development, 11, 14
Fields, 126
Liberalization, 221
Sector, 30
Economics, 126
Agriculture, 126
Business, 126
Development, 126
Econometrics, 126
Financial, 126
Industrial, 126
International, 126
Labour, 126
National Resources, 126
Rural, 126
Welfare, 126
Economists, 27
Duties, 27
Education, 27
Tasks, 27
Training, 27
Economy, 30, 54, 72, 149
Ecosystem, 44, 54
Education, 11, 13, 14, 40, 41, 48, 58, 119-124, 128, 146, 149, 174, 289, 295, 299-301, 304
Aims, 14
Agriculture, 201
Education, Conventional, 10
Distance, 299
Environmental, 47
Environmental Related, 45
Legal, 299
Institution For Oceanography Studies, Opportunities, 331
Institutions, 330
National Policy on-, 10
Physical, 146, 147
Eligibility for Courses, 147
Need, 146
Objectives, 146
Education, 198
Institution for Oceanographic Studies, Administrative Requirement, 331
Institutions for Montessori Teachers, 343
Institutions for Oceanographic Studies, 330-331

Institutions in-, 304, 305
Aquaculture, 304
Biotech, 304
Marine, 304
Oceanography Sciences, 304
Electronic Media, 289
Universities offering Courses, 290
Eligibility and Places of Study of Foreign Languages, 242
Emergencies, 43
Biological, 43
Chemical, 43
Nuclear, 43
Employment
Generation, 159
Opportunities, 45
Opportunities Departments Details, 75
Opportunities for Architects, 75
Engineering, 110
Agriculture, 159-163
As a Career, 181
Biomedical, 110
Eligibility for AIEEE, 182
Genetic, 306, 325
Industrial, 110
Industries, 180, 181
Jobs, 181-182
Job Opportunity, 183
Materials, 110
Optical, 110
Science and Technology, 159
Entrepreneurship
Courses, 360-361
Development Program, 356
Institution of India, 360
Training for Women, 359
Environmental
Courses and Opportunities, 316, 317
Degradation and Pollution, 45
Education Imparting Institutions, 49
Organization, 327
Planners, 312
Planning, 312
Science, 327
Enzyme Technology, 307
E-Publishing, 290
European Forestry Research Institute (Finland), 56

F

Fashion Technology, 128
Fashion Technology, Programme in-, 128, 130
Fast Moving Consumer Goods (FMCG), 138
Federal Disaster Agency (USA), 43
Female Literacy, 11
Femina Miss India, 53
Fertility and Mortality, 11
Film
and TV Courses, 131-132
and Video Editors, 28
Industry, 289
Laboratory Technicians, 352
Education, Training, Jobs, 334-355
Filmfare Awards, 53
Financial
Markets, 32
Sector, 32
Service Sector, 30
Firemen Courses, 174
Fisheries
Science, 198
Survey of India (PSI), 30
Five Year Plan (9th), 58
Five Year Plan (10th), 42
Floriculture Courses and Institutions, 212, 213
Floriculture Industry, 211
Flying Clubs in India, 117, 118
Folk Art Form, 48
Food
and Beverages, 60
Processing Industry, 175
Science and Technology, 198
Technologies, 175, 328
Technology course Institutions, 176
Foreign Trade, 132
Forensic
Biology, 322
Chemistry, 322
Documents, 322
Engineering, 322
Finger Prints, 322
Medicines, 322
Pathology, 322
Physics, 322
Scientists, 323

Forest
    Administration, 54
    Ecosystem, 55
    Management, 55
    Research Institute (Malaysia), 56
    Research Institute, 54, 55
    Resources, 54
Forestry, 52, 55, 58, 59, 198
    Courses Eligibility, 57
    Education and Research, 56
    Research/Training Institute in India, 56
Formation Cutting Platoon, 164
Fragrance and Flower Development Centre (FFDC), 246, 246
FTII (Film and TV Institute of India), Pune, 131

G

Gandharva Sangeet Vidyalaya Bombay, 87
Gandhi, Indira, 13, 17
Garba of Gujarat, 82
GATT (General Agreement on Trade and Tariffs), 207
Gemnology, 177, 178
    Courses in-, 178-179
    Scope of-, 179
Gemnological Institute of America, 179
General Insurance Corporation (GIC), 35, 223, 224
General Reserve Engineering Force, (GREF), 163, 165, 166
Genetic and Plant Breeding—Soil Science, 218, 219
Genomics, 306
Geography Information System, 47
Geological Survey of India, 331
German—Korean (Languages), 239
Global Warming, 315, 327
Globalization, 295
Graphic and Industrial Designs, 92
Graphic Design Technologies, 289
Green House Gases, 315, 327
Green Houses Gases, 46
Gulf and Africa, 304
Gymnastics, 146

H

Health Sanitary Inspectors, 253
    Eligibility, 253
    Job Descriptions, 254
    Job Opportunity, 253
    Training and Career, 254
Herbal Products, 307
Herbs, 54
Higher Learning Institution in Economics, 127
Homoeopathy, 257
    Colleges, 258-259
    Formal Medical Education, 257
    Job Opportunity, 259
Horticulturists Job Opportunities, 214
Hotel Industries, 110
Hotel Management, 59-61
    Course and Prospects, 61
    Education Institute, 59-60
    Eligibility Criteria, 59, 61
Hydrological Cycles, 54

I

IARI (Indian Agriculture Research Institute), 219
ICAR, 198, 201, 212, 219, 235, 304, 306
ICFA (Institute of Chartered Finance Analysis of India), 32
ICMR (Indian Council of Medical Research), 235, 306, 325, 327
IITs (Kharagpur and Roorkee), 75
Importing Countries of Flowers, 211
    France, 211
    Germany, 211
    Italy and Japan, 211
    Netherlands, 211
India and China, 22
Indian
    Administrative Service (IAS), 13
    Airlines, 110
    Airspace, 114
    Army, 96-98
    Classical Dances, 79
    Cost Accountant Service (ICAS), 26
    Council for Forestry Research, 56

Council for Forestry Research, Centres, 56-57
Council of Agriculture Research, 160, 161
Dairy Industry, 309, 311, 312
Dairy Products, 312
Dance, 91
Diamond Institute, 178
Economy, 36
Farm Sector, 208
Financial System, 31
Foreign Service, (IFS), 13
Forest Service (IFS), 13
Forest Service, 54, 57
Gems Market, 179
Institute of Foreign Trade, 132
Institute of Human Management, 61
Institute of Information Technology, 101
Master Courses, 101
Institute of Mass Communication, 137
Institute of Packaging Regional Centres, 141
Military Academy, 96, 98, 99
Navy, 102
Ocean, 330
Oil Corporation (IOC), 31
Ordinance Factory Services (IOFS), 13
Police Service, (IPS), 13
Traditional Paintings, 92
Universities, 26
Veterinary Research Institute, Karnal, 310
Industrial
Automation, 172
Revolution, 146
Industries, 45, 46
Information Analysts, 232
Information Science, 231
Information Technology, (IT), 22, 44, 50, 62, 64, 97, 183-185, 189, 232
And Planning, 22
Industry, 183, 282, 284, 295
Kiosk, 210
Projects, 68
Revolution, 172
Sector, 294
Sector, (ITSECTOR), 171, 183
Information, Communication and Technology (ICT), 200, 201
Infosys Technologies, 50
Institute of Cost and Works Accountants of India, 25, 26
Eligibility, 26
Recognition, 26
Regional Centres, 25
Objectives, 25
Institute of Mass Communication, 290
Institutions Imparting Forensic Education, 324
Insurance
Agents, 221
and Pension Plans, 39
Policy Processing Clerks, 224, 225
Education, 224
Task and Duties, 224
Training, 224
Regulatory Development Authority, (IRDA), 222
Sector, 35, 37, 221, 222
Surveyors, 222
Insurance, Banks—Treasury Managers, 30
International
Agencies in Field of Forestry, 58
Association of Trichology, (IAT), 336
Aviation Organization (ICAO), 114
Federation of Accountant Committee (IFAC), 27
Foreign Trade, 132
Maritime Institute Noida, 101
Union for—Natural Resources, 58
Universities Imparting Forestry Education/Res., 56
Internet
and Telecommunication, 189
Journalism, 136
Media, 290
Investment Industry, 32
Iran—South Africa, 312
Irrigation Projects, 54
Islamic Medicine, 278
IT Enabled Service, (ITES), 282, 294
ITC—Andhra Pradesh Paper Mills, 58

J

Japan Bank for Consultants, 58
Jawahar Lal Nehru Manipur Dance Academy, 87
Jazz, 87
Jewelry Designing, 9
Job Opportunities in Field of Economics, 127-128
Journalism
- and Photography Institutions, 144-145
- Courses Details, 133

Judiciary, 323
Juvenile Delinquency, 147

K

Kalakshetra Chennai, 83
Kathak Kendra, New Delhi, 83
Khiljis, 278
King Solomon's Mines, 177
Kisan Call Centres (KCC), 201
Krishi Vigyan Kendras, 201

L

Law as a Career, 227
Law Conservation, 46
Legal Secretaries, 229
- Experience, Education, Training and Tasks, 230

Liberalization, 11, 12
Liberalization, Privatization and Globalization, 30
Library and Information Science, 232-234
Library Science as a Career, 234
Library Science Courses, 233, 236, 237
Life Insurance Corporation, (Private Sector), 35, 221, 223, 224
Life Jackets, 107
Light Music, 86
Linguists, 240-243
- Applied, 241
- Contextual, 241
- Diachronic, 241
- Theoretical, 240

Livestock Council and Poultry Farming, 338
Loans, 32
Logistic Management
- Courses and Institutions, 64, 65
- Job Categories, 65
- Jobs- Industries, 65

Logistic Management, 62-64

M

Macro Media/Fireworks, 290
Madhav Sangeet Vidyalaya Gwalior, 87
Magical Academy of India, 84
Major Classical Dance of India, 80
- Bharatnatyam, 80, 86
- Kathak, 80
- Kathakali, 80, 81
- Kuchipudi, 80, 86

Manipuri, 80
Mohiniyattam, 80
- Odissi, 80, 82, 86

Malaysia, 295
Malhotra Committee Recommendations, 221
Management Accountancy, 24, 25
Management Policies, 20
Managers,
- Packaging, 139
- Purchasing, 122
- Purchasing, Duties and Tasks, 122
- Purchasing, Education, 122
- Purchasing, Experience, 122
- Purchasing, Training, 122
- Information System, 186

Manmohan Singh, 201
Maria, Montessori, 340
- Education, 341

Methods, 341
- Program, 342

Marine Engineering, 101
Maritime Zone of India, 102
Mass Communication, 137
Media Institutions, 289
Medical
- and Engineering Courses, 23
- Council of India, 259
- Education Institutions, 261
- Education, 248
- Laboratory Technology, 328
- Transcriptions, 262

Medicinal Plants, 54

Merchant Navy, 9, 102
  Job Avenues, 104
  Physical Standards, 103
  Qualification Required, 102
  Ranks, Rating and Promotions, 105
Meteorological Survey of India, 331
Ministry of
  Agriculture, 42
  Civil Aviation, 42
  Culture and Tourism, 59
  Education, 87
  Environment and Forests, 43
  Home Affairs, 42
  Housing and Planning, 278
  Industry and Technology, 183
  Information and Broadcasting, 86
  Railways, 42
  Science and Technology, 306, 325
Modern
  Economy, 14
  Visual Art, 91
Moghul Emperors, 278
MTV Miss India, 53
Mudras, 80, 81
Multimedia, 9
Multinational Corporations, (MNCS), 67, 227, 282
Museologists, 264, 267
  Career Opportunities, 265
  In Diagnostic Laboratories, 267
Museology, 89, 260, 264
  Eligibility, 89
  Institutions offering Courses, 90
  Science of Museum, 89
  Scopes and Opportunities, 89
Music Composers, 88
Musical Instruments, 86

N

NABARD, 84, 208, 210, 304
Narsimhan Committee, 31
NASA, 110
NASSCOM, 282
National
  Council for Hotel Management and Catering Technology (NCHMLT), 59
  Awards, 87
  Biotechnology Board, 325
  Commission on Agriculture, 1976, 54
  Council of Vocational Training (NCVT), 254
  Dairy Research Institute (NDRI) Karnal, 310
  Defence Academy, 94, 96-98
  Forest Policy, 55
  Institute of Advertising, 137
  Institute of Bank Management, 32
  Institute of Criminology and Forensic Science, 323
  Institute of Fashion Technology (NIFT), 128
  Institute of Oceanography, Goa, 330, 331
  Institutions Offering CAD/CAM Courses, 169-170
  Law Schools, 227, 228
  Parks, 327
  Remote Sensing Agency, 331
  Science and Tech Entrepreneurship Development Board, 359, 360
  Thermal Power Corporation, 327
Natural Disasters Management, 42
Naval Civil Defence College, 43
Naval Defence Academy, 94, 96
NCC (National Cadet Corps), 95
NCERT (National Council of Educational Research and Training), 315
Networking and Communication, 101
New India Insurance Company, 224
NGO, 45, 57, 68
NHPC, 327
Non-Timber Forest Products, 54
Northern India Music, 86
NSD (National School of Drama), 78
Nuclear
  Medicine, 260
  Stations, 45, 327
  Tests, 48
Nursery Teachers Training Institutions, 346

O

Oberoi Centre for Learning and Development, 61
Oceanography, 110, 329, 331
    Role, 330
    Specialized Branches, 329
Officers Training Academy, Chennai, 97, 99, 100
Oil and Natural Gas Commission (ONGC), 31, 332
OIL India, 332
Olympics, (Athens), 98
On the Job Training, 21
On-Line Journalism, 134
Operational Policies, 22
Operational Reports, 39
Organized Farming Courses, 217
Oriental Insurance Company, 224
Oxford Forestry Research Institute (UK), 56
Ozone Depletion, 46, 315, 327

P

Packaging
    Certificate Courses, 141
    Course in India, 139
    Diploma Courses, 140
    Institutions, 140
Padma Bhushan, 87
Padma Shree, 87
Paintings—Decoration Arts, 91
Paramilitary Services, 10
Pay Roll Examination, 21
Perfumery and Roma Industry, 246
Pest Surveillance, 209
Pharmaceutical Sector, 269
Photojournalism, 143
Physical Education Teachers, 345
Physiotherapy, 271
    Courses, 273
    Educational Aims, 272
Purpose, 271
    Scope of-, 272
Pilot Training Institutions, 114, 115
Planning, 9, 52, 55, 72, 181, 201
Planning Commission, 201
Poetry, Sculpture—Theatre, 79
Poisoning, 323
Police Services, 9
Pollution, 45
Pollution Control Laws, 45
Pop Music, 87
Population Explosion, 126
Post Graduate Institution, Chandigarh, 259, 261
Potential States (Places) of Flower Production, 211
    Bangalore, 211
    Hyderabad, 211
Punee, and New Delhi, 211
Prayag Samiti, 87
Print and Electronic Media, 210
Printing Workers, 121
    Education, 121
    Experience, 121
    Tasks, 121-122
    Training, 121
Private
    Flying Clubs, 110
Pilot License (PPL), 112, 115
    Foreign Banks, 32
    ABN AMRO, 32
    Bank of America, 32
    Bank of Punjab, 32
    Citi Banks, 32
    HSBC, 32
    ICICI, 32
    IDBI, 32
Professional
    Management in China, 68
    Secretariat Training Institutions, 299-300
Profit Planning, 25
Project
    Management Associates Noida (UP), 67
    Management, 67, 68
    Monitoring, 25
    Reports, 357
Prominent
    Entrepreneurship Institutions, 360
    Institutes Imparting Marine Education, 103-104
Property Laws, 22
Psychology/Branches, 332-333
Public Address System, 109

R

Rain Fall Pattern, 46
Rap, 87

Rathore, Maj. Rajyavardhana, 98
Real Estate Managers, 68
 Description, 69
 Education, 69
 Tasks, 69
 Training, 69
Receptionists Jobs, 123-124
Record Examination, 21
Record Keeping Funds, 19
Regional
 Councils, 25, 26, 296
 Organization, 45
 Theatre, 78
Regulations, 22
Rehabilitation and Vocational Centres, 334
Reliance Petrochemicals, 332
Religious Festivals, 91
Remote Sensing, (RS), 47
Remote Sensing Technologies, 47
Reports, 20
Reputed Institutions of Architects, 74-75
Research and Communication, 22
Retirement Funds, 36
Rig Veda, 90
Rituals, 90
Roy, Subrata, Sahara Group, 51
Rural Entrepreneurship Development Programme, 84

S

SAARC, 192
Safety Check, 107
Sales and Marketing, 10
Samveda, 90
Sanctuaries, 327
Sangeet Natak Academy, 87
Scheme of Agro-clinic and Agribusiness Centres (NABARD), 208
Scheme of Agro-clinic, Objectives, 208, 209
School of Planning and Architecture, 75
Scientists and Technologists, 113
Sea Based Medicine, 304
Sea Food, 304
Secretaries
 Jobs, 301
 Medical, 302
Security Administration, 44
Seed Industry, 218
Selection Procedure in Journalism, 136
Service Sector, 30
Service Selection Board (SSB), 112
SFAC (Small Farms Agri-Business Consortium), 210
Shakuntala (Kalidasa), 91
Ship Building Industry, 54
SIDO (Small Industries Development Organizations), 359
Singapore, 295
SISI (Small Industries Service Institutions), 356
 Centres, 357, 358
Smoke Bombs, 52
Social Forestry, 55
Social Structure, 148
Sociology Subjects, 149
Software Engineer, 185
South Asian Federation of Accountants (SAFA), 27
South East Asian Countries, 192
Special Economic Zones, (SEZ), 192
Specialization in Agriculture, 162
Specialized Training for Nursery Teachers, 346
Sports, 146
Standard Costing System, 25
State Agricultural Universities (SAU), 55, 199, 310
State Small Scale Industries Development Corporations, (SSIDCS), 359
Steel Authority of India Limited (SAIL), 31
Student Pilot License (SPL), 112, 115
Supply Chain Management, 62-64
Sushant School of Architecture, 75
Susruta Samhita, 248
Swarna Jayanti Gram Swarozgar Yojna, (SJGSY), 359
Swedish International Development Agency, 58
System Designers, 186
System Propounders, 185

T

Taj Group, 61
Tariff Advisory Committee Pension
    Funds, 222
Tax
    Advisory Services, 30
    Reports, 22
    Strategies, 20
Teachers Training Institutions, 347
Techno-Economic
    Feasibility, (TEC), 211
    Studies of Projects, 25
Telemarketing, 283
Thailand and Mauritius, 295
Tolani Maritime Institute Pune, 101
Tool Room Technology, 193
Tools and CAD/CAM Technology
    Institutions, 195
Town Planners, 73
Town Planning, 76
Toxic Wastes Hazardous, 46
Trade and Tourism Industry, 239
Trained Montessori Teachers, 342
    Employment, 342
Training, 119
    Institutes for Actors, 78
    Institutes for Actors, Eligibility, 78
    Program, 43
    Programme (Magic), 85
Travel and Tourism, 10
Tribal Cultures, 48
Trichology, 336
Tsunami Disaster, 97
Tughluqs, 278
TV Industry, 289
TV Journalism, 290

U

UN (United Nations), 44
    Conference on Environment Development, Rio, 327
    Development Program, 42, 49, 191, 246
    Disaster Management Training Program, (UNMTP), 43
    Disaster Relief Coordinator, 43
    Member States, 43
    Peace Keeping in Congo, 100
    Peace Keeping Missions, 97
    System, 43
Unani
    Medical Education, 280
    Medicine, 278
    Medicine System of India, 278, 279, 280
UNESCO, 346
UNICEF, 346
United India Insurance Company, 224
Universities/Institutions
    Imparting Environmental Education, 315, 217, 322
    Imparting Library & Information Science Education, 233
University
    Grants Commission, 306, 315, 326, 327
    of Agricultural Societies, 303
US, 22, 236
    And Canada, 56
    And UK, 283
US—Africa, 295
US—Belgium, 179
Useful Courses after 10+2, 158
US—European Countries, 304

V

Vedas, 80
Ventilation System, 109
Veterinary
    Council of India, 338
    Profession Scope, 339
VLSI
    Architecture, 171
    Courses, 173
Vocal Music, 86
Vocational
    Courses, 10
    Training, 21, 40, 41
    Training Institutions, 299

W

Waste Disposal Organization, 45
Water-Contamination, 45
Wedding Management, 70
Welcome Groups, 61
Western
    Australia, 232
    Music, 87

Wild Life, 54
Habitats, 43
Parks and Sanctuaries, 47
WIPRO Technologies, 50
Women Entrepreneurship, 359
Working Capital Management, 30
World
Bank, 58
Health Organization, (WHO), 346
Trade Organization (WTO), 30, 207, 270
Regime, 175
War II, 24, 180
Wide Fund for Nature, 58

Y

Yajur Veda, 90
Yogic Asanas, 146